Praise for Jagdish Bhagwati's *In Defense of Globalization*

"Until further notice *In Defense of Globalization* becomes the standard general-interest reference, the intelligent layman's handbook, on global economic integration."

—*The Economist*

"Bhagwati combines the hard-nosed perspective of a liberal on trade and investment with the soft-hearted sensitivities of a social democrat on poverty and human welfare. He thus has an admirable ability to address patiently and sympathetically globalization's well-meaning but wrong-headed critics."

—Richard Cooper, *Foreign Affairs*

"What's most important about this book is its caution about globalization—namely, that it has to be managed, both in terms of how quickly it proceeds and what policies are put in place to reduce its unpleasant economic and social side effects."

—*Washington Post*

"Critics of globalization will find a few things to admire in Bhagwati's outlook. He limits his defense of globalization to trade, direct investment, and migration. The book's short chapter on capital markets echoes many of the concerns of globalization's critics. Bhagwati forcefully denounces 'the Wall Street-Treasury Complex' that cajoled developing countries into eliminating capital controls. Literary references flow from the pages, from Lady Murasaki to King Lear to Woody Allen."

—Daniel W. Drezner, *New York Times Book Review*

"A book brimming with engaging arguments and good sense. *In Defense of Globalization* will encourage the faithful who believe in economic freedom as a value worth pursuing in and of itself, but also those more pragmatic souls who see it as a necessary if less-than-lovable means to achieve poverty reduction and other worthy social goals. Of all the books defending globalization, Jagdish Bhagwati's may offer the best chance to reach those readers not fatally blinded by anti-market ideology."

—Daniel Griswold, *National Review*

"An important contribution to an often incoherent debate. As we expect of Mr. Bhagwati, it is cogently argued and well-written. It sets out a persuasive case in favor of globalization. And because of Mr. Bhagwati's impeccable credentials, there is a better chance his book will be given a fair hearing than might be the case with some other authors. Put simply, Mr. Bhagwati has 'street cred.'"

—Anne Krueger (Acting Director of the IMF), *Financial Times*

"Mr. Bhagwati slams through fact after fact, statistic after statistic, demolishing those who claim the poor are worse off because of globalization. If Mr. Bhagwhati doesn't get a much deserved Nobel Prize for economics, he should get one for literature. His writing sparkles with anecdotes and delightful verbal pictures."

—Mike Moore, *New York Sun*

"Does the international market economy worsen poverty in developing countries? Does it erode democracy? Hurt the cause of women? Trash the environment? Exacerbate the exploitation of child labor? Bhagwati's answers to all these questions make for a supremely worthy read."

—*Business 2.0 Magazine*

"If Bhagwati can't convert the unbelievers into enthusiastic globalizers, probably no one can. . . . Bhagwati demonstrates admirable fairness toward his opponents. . . . [A]n amusing, charming, and erudite debater."

—Paul Gray, *New Leader*

"This work is of major importance, as it authoritatively tackles the main intellectual charges against globalization. . . . Hopefully, this book will convince at least some of those who gullibly joined the fashionable, but dangerous anti-globalization movement that in doing so they have actually abandoned themselves to the devices of intellectual manipulators, political demagogues, and economic reactionaries. The post–Cold War era's dominant economic trend finally gets its defense sheet."

—*Jerusalem Post*

"Passionate and well-reasoned. . . . *In Defense of Globalization* probably won't dissuade ardent trade opponents from their protests. But if they expect to have a reasoned debate—or even to know what it is they're protesting against—they'll need to read it."

—Bill Day, *San Antonio Express-News*

"A splendid and highly readable tour de force; arguably the best book yet on the great issue of our time."

—Fred Pearce, *New Scientist*

"No one has crusaded more zealously on behalf of free trade than Jagdish Bhagwati. *In Defense of Globalization* sums up his case, and for free-trade advocates under siege, it arrives not a minute too soon. The book is certainly engaging."

—Mark Levinson, *American Prospect*

"No other book on globalization covers as wide a range of issues as Bhagwati's. Indeed, his book is the best one-stop shopping for readers seeking a panoramic view of all the controversies that make up the globalization debate. . . . Perhaps the best reason to pick up this book is Bhagwati's inimitable writing style. The book is laced with amusing vignettes and turns of phrase. . . . All readers can profit from his provocative insights and lively style."

—Douglas A. Irwin, *Finance and Development*

"In this elegant book, one of the world's preeminent economists distills his thinking about globalization for the lay reader. . . . Armed with a wit uncharacteristic of most writing on economics and drawing on references from history, philosophy, and literature as well as some "state of the art econometric analysis,' he sets out to prove that the anti-globalization movement has exaggerated claims that globalization has done little good for poor countries. . . . This is a substantial study that is as about as enjoyable and reassuring a work of economics as may be possible to write in this uncertain age."

—*Publishers Weekly* (starred review)

"An engaging work. . . . Bhagwati convincingly refutes misconceptions about globalization and offers sound recommendations for governing it properly."

—*Library Journal*

"The new century's major economic issue is Globalization, Yes? or Globalization, No? Columbia University's Bhagwati, regarded as a master economist by all trade experts, has prepared for the intelligent public an even-handed analysis of the pros and cons. Read and ponder."

—Paul A. Samuelson, M.I.T., Nobel laureate in Economics.

"Jagdish Bhagwati has written a brilliant book about the conflict between freedom and justice. The book is beautifully written: provoking without sermonizing. You may not always agree with him—I don't—but *In Defense of Globalization* is bound to become a classic."

—Richard Sennett, London School of Economics

"This book will make history. It will also be a blockbuster, not only because of the depth of Bhagwati's powerful argument backed by extensive research, but also because it is immensely readable and surely the most humorous piece of economics ever written."
—Hernando de Soto, author of
The Other Path and *The Mystery of Capital*

"In a profession that prizes elegance of algebra more than prose, Jagdish Bhagwati is a sparkling exception. He is a brilliant academic economist . . . who also happens to be a gifted, mischievous and passionate writer. . . . [He offers] a smorgasbord of elegant prose, superb economics and impish opinions."
Zanny Minton-Beddoes, *Times Literary Supplement*

"Mr. Bhagwati has long been a Nobel Prize contender for his contributions to the theory of international trade—contributions leavened by apt metaphors, clear examples and even poetry."
Sylvia Nasar (Author of *A Beautiful Mind*), *The New York Times*

"Jagdish Bhagwati is a leading economist of international trade—many think the world's leader in the field and also a public intellectual. . . . He writes with panache."
Charles P. Kindleberger, *The International Economy*

"One of the world's most eminent economists"
Jeffrey Frankel, *Foreign Affairs*

"Of the scholars who have engaged in the public debate on trade, none matches Jagdish Bhagwati"
Martin Wolf, *The Financial Times*

"In Bhagwati's hands, economics, the dismal science, is transformed into a delightful art. Without sacrificing rigor, and skillfully blending history, politics, economic analysis, and wit, he makes reading [him] a treat."
Paul Streeten, Former Fellow, Balliol College, Oxford

In Defense of
Globalization

With a New Afterword

JAGDISH BHAGWATI

A Council on Foreign Relations Book

OXFORD

UNIVERSITY PRESS

Oxford University Press, Inc., publishes works that
further Oxford University's objective of excellence
in research, scholarship, and education.

Oxford   New York
Auckland   Cape Town   Dar es Salaam   Hong Kong   Karachi
Kuala Lumpur   Madrid   Melbourne   Mexico City   Nairobi
New Delhi   Shanghai   Taipei   Toronto

With offices in
Argentina   Austria   Brazil   Chile   Czech Republic   France   Greece
Guatemala   Hungary   Italy   Japan   Poland   Portugal   Singapore
South Korea   Switzerland   Thailand   Turkey   Ukraine   Vietnam

Copyright © 2004, 2007 by Jagdish Bhagwati

First published in 2004 by Oxford University Press, Inc.
198 Madison Avenue, New York, NY 10016
www.oup.com

Oxford is a registered trademark of Oxford University Press

Library of Congress Cataloging-in-Publication Data:
Bhagwati, Jagdish N., 1934–
In defense of globalization / Jagdish Bhagwati.
p. cm.
"A Council on Foreign Relations Book."
Includes index.
ISBN-13: 978-0-19-533093-9 (pbk.)
ISBN-10: 0-19-533093-5 (pbk.)
1. Globalization—Economic aspects. 2. Globalization—Social aspects.
3. Anti-globalization movement. I. Title.
HF1359 .B499 2004   337—dc22 2003023641

The Council on Foreign Relations is dedicated to increasing America's understanding of the
world and contributing ideas to U.S. foreign policy. The Council accomplishes this mainly by
promoting constructive debates and discussions, clarifying world issues, and publishing *Foreign
Affairs*, the leading journal on global issues. The Council is host to the widest possible range of
views, but an advocate of none, though its research fellows and Independent Task Forces do
take policy positions. From time to time, books and reports written by members of the
Council's research staff or others are published as a "Council on Foreign Relations Book."

THE COUNCIL TAKES NO INSTITUTIONAL POSITION ON POLICY ISSUES AND HAS NO AFFILIATION WITH
THE U.S. GOVERNMENT. ALL STATEMENTS OF FACT AND EXPRESSIONS OF OPINION CONTAINED
IN ALL ITS PUBLICATIONS ARE THE SOLE RESPONSIBILITY OF THE AUTHOR OR AUTHORS.

1 3 5 7 9 8 6 4 2
Printed in the United States of America
on acid-free paper

For
Padma
&
Anuradha

for affection and indulgence

Contents

III Other Dimensions of Globalization

IV Appropriate Governance: Making Globalization Work Better

V In Conclusion

Preface

D oes the world need yet another book on globalization? Not a day goes by without impassioned authors and activists, whether anti- or pro-globalization, putting their oars into these agitated waters. Magazines and newspapers also write incessantly on the issue, and polls are taken and discussed on why there is "global rage" or why, as it happens, many support the process, especially in developing countries.[1]

But when all is said the fact is that we lack a clear, coherent, and comprehensive sense of how globalization—and I refer to economic globalization (which embraces diverse forms of international integration, including foreign trade, multinational direct foreign investment, movements of short-term portfolio funds, technological diffusion, and cross-border migration)—works and how it can do better. There are evidently many who think that globalization may be economically benign, increasing economic prosperity in the conventional economic sense of enlarging the pie, but that it is also socially malign, that it diminishes, not enhances, the war on poverty, the assault on gender discrimination, the protection of culture both indigenous and mainstream, and indeed much else. The majority of those who agitate seem to agree on one thing: the rapaciousness of multinational corporations, which they believe are the principal beneficiaries, and the main agents—the B-52s, as I call them in this book—of this socially destructive globalization.

Far too often they produce "gotcha" examples (which I describe later), with fears masquerading as evidence. But then their pro-globalization opponents who refuse to buckle under this assault also fail to produce a concerted and total defense, based on a systematic examination of these contentions and concerns that builds up to a vision of the global system that is profoundly more optimistic yet suggests ways to make this globalization even better.

So, for the most part, we have fierce opponents locked in combat, but each side without a constructive blueprint for globalization. Where we need a total war, we instead have combatants engaged in battles over fragmented fronts. Each warrior reminds us, as Dr. Johnson once said with characteristic wit, of the pedant in Hierocles who, when he offered his house for sale, carried a brick in his pocket as a specimen! In this book, I offer a view of the whole house.

I focus for intensive analysis in Part I on understanding the anti-globalization movement and defining its concerns, while analyzing the growth of non-governmental organizations that play a principal role in the anti-globalization phenomenon and can play an important role in the design of appropriate governance to improve outcomes from globalization. In Part II I consider the social implications, on different dimensions such as gender issues and poverty, of trade and direct foreign investments (by corporations), concluding that they are, generally speaking, benign—that is, that globalization has a human face. I conclude therefore that the concerns of the more thoughtful of the anti-globalization critics, that economic globalization has adverse social implications and therefore that globalization lacks a human face, are mistaken.

In Part III I consider separately other facets of economic globalization: short-term capital flows and the movements of people across borders. Short-term capital flows, which broadly consist of transactions in stocks and related financial instruments for short-term gains as distinct from direct equity investment by enterprises for long-term gains, and human movements across borders (legal and illegal, voluntary or forced by crisis and circumstance) are in fact two principal forms of economic globalization that raise a number of difficult questions, some similar to and several others different from the ones on which I concentrate. And they deserve attention in a book that is addressed to globalization on a broader scale than just trade and direct foreign investment.[2]

In Part IV I consider the design of institutional changes, both domestic and international, that are necessary to make the generally good effects of globalization even better. In this analysis also I part from the anti-globalization critics: the appropriate governance—that is, institutions and policies—that goes with a globalization that is seen as having a human face is very different from that which attends a globalization that is seen as lacking a human face.

In short, I argue that the notion that globalization needs a human face—a staple of popular rhetoric that has become a dangerous cliché—is wrong. It raises a false alarm. Globalization *has* a human face, but we can make that face yet more agreeable.

This book is the culmination of intense work over the last two years. I have written and lectured about globalization as my ideas took shape.

But this work remains the full-bodied development of my ideas and my vision concerning globalization over many years of academic reflection and policy experience. I have propagated these views in my work two years ago as special adviser to the United Nations on Globalization, where Secretary General Kofi Annan now seems to lean more toward the view that globalization is part of the solution, not part of the problem, but that we do need institutional changes and support mechanisms to smooth out its occasional rough edges.

I have developed a number of debts in writing this book. Chief among them is to the Council on Foreign Relations, where Leslie Gelb, Larry Korb, and Theo Gemelas have provided excellent support. Bowman Cutter, who chaired a study group that discussed drafts of different chapters, has been a source of ideas, and I am greatly indebted to him indeed. I have also profited from the writings, ideas, and comments of Robert Baldwin, Sheri Berman, Magnus Blomström, Judith Bruce, Steve Charnowitz, Vivek Dehejia, Arthur Dunkel, Dan Esty, Gene Grossman, Carl Hamilton, Blair Hoxby, Douglas Irwin, Pravin Krishna, Robert Lawrence, Assar Lindbeck, Robert Litan, Patrick Low, Pradeep Mehta, Sir James Murray, Arvind Panagariya, the Swedish trade minister Leif Pagrotsky, Jairam Ramesh, Dani Rodrik, Kenneth Roth, John Ruggie, André Sapir, Manmohan Singh, Bo Södersten, T. N. Srinivasan, Alan Winters, and many others. A work on this canvas cannot be written without standing on the shoulders of many.

I owe a great debt to Tim Bartlett, my editor at the Oxford University Press. His careful and searching comments and suggestions have made my writing more informed by evidence and examples even while maintaining lucidity and accessibility.

Research assistance was provided by Olivia Carballo and Tanya Finnell, successively my research associates at the Council on Foreign Relations. Olivia started the book with me until she left for the London School of Economics in the fall of 2002, leaving me nostalgic about her good humor, unflagging enthusiasm, and keen grasp of the issues I was addressing. Tanya took over a year ago and has assisted me hugely with her enormous intellectual curiosity and her amazing ingenuity in tracking down sources and providing valuable editorial and substantive suggestions as the book began to acquire final shape. I cannot thank them enough.

Niah Shepherd, Michael Punzalan, and Adam Heal undertook research on parts of the book. Bikas Joshi, Jennifer Manuel, and Rica Asuncion have also provided helpful research support on specific issues. I am indebted to all of them.

August 2003   Jagdish Bhagwati

I

Coping with
Anti-Globalization

1

Anti-Globalization: Why?

Globalization first became a buzzword. Davos and the *New York Times* columnist Thomas Friedman celebrated its virtues, its inevitability. But then came the anti-globalizers. Globalization then became a more conventional four-letter word. The Ruckus Society and the French sociologist Pierre Bourdieu proclaimed its vices, its vincibility.

As this dialectic has unfolded, it is tempting to think that there is a primeval curse on the phenomenon. After all, if you care to count, globalization is in fact a thirteen-letter word. It has become by now a phenomenon that is doomed to unending controversy, the focal point of always hostile passions and sometimes violent protests. It is surely a defining issue as we move further into the new century. The reasons this has happened cry out for comprehension. Without such understanding, and then informed refutation of the fears and follies that animate the anti-globalizers, we cannot adequately defend the globalization that many of us seek to sustain, even deepen.[1]

What *is* the globalization that is in contention? Globalization can mean many things. Here, however, I plan to focus exclusively on *economic* globalization; indeed, that is what I shall mean when I simply say "globalization" throughout this book. Economic globalization constitutes integration of national economies into the international economy through trade, direct foreign investment (by corporations and multinationals), short-term capital flows, international flows of workers and humanity generally, and flows of technology: phenomena defined and treated more fully below.

Economic globalization is the favored target of many of the critics of globalization. It is distinct from other aspects of globalization, such

3

as cultural globalization (which is affected, as I shall discuss in Chapter 9, by economic globalization) and communications (which is among the factors that cause the deepening of economic globalization).

Why are the critics of globalization agitated? What bothers them? There are two main groups that need to be distinguished, and I shall develop this distinction and build systematically on it below. First, there is a multitude of hard-core protesters who have deep-seated antipathy to globalization. They come from different intellectual and ideological directions and do not all share the same ideas and sentiments. But many buy into a linked trilogy of discontents that take the form successively of an ethos composed of an anti-capitalist, anti-globalization, and acute anti-corporation mind-set.[2] These views are interlinked because globalization is seen as the extension of capitalism throughout the world, whereas multinational corporations are seen as the B-52s of capitalism and its global reach.[3] Beyond understanding where their discontents come from, as I do presently, there is little that one can do to enter into a dialogue with them.

Second, however, there are the critics of globalization whose discontents are well within the parameters of mainstream dissent and discourse. In their essence, these discontents translate into the arguments that economic globalization is the cause of several social ills today, such as poverty in poor countries and deterioration of the environment worldwide. These critiques, which amount in my view to a gigantic non sequitur, are of a very different order from the hard-core criticisms, which reflect implacable hostility to globalization. The former are susceptible to, indeed invite, reasoned engagement. These critiques need an extended and careful response. I provide that in several chapters in Part II by demonstrating that, in fact, the various social causes that we all embrace, such as advancement of gender equality and reduction of poverty, are advanced, not set back, by globalization.

Am I leaving the prince out of *Hamlet* by not giving center stage to the critiques of international institutions such as the World Bank (which concerns itself with development), the International Monetary Fund (dealing with stabilization of economies in the grip of financial crises), the World Trade Organization (which oversees the world trading system and its progressive liberalization), bilateral aid agencies such as the U.S. Agency for International Development, and trade treaties such as the North American Free Trade Agreement (NAFTA)? These institutions have often been targeted at their annual meetings by demonstrators who object to their "conditionalities" for assistance or their ambition to liberalize trade, depending on the institution being attacked.

But these demonstrations are mainly a clever guerrilla tactic, as I argue later: with thousands of newspaper and television reporters present, violence and ingenuity in street theater make a splash around the world. The specific critiques are what need to be addressed, rather than sweeping condemnations. These I do take seriously and examine fully at different places in the book as they relate to areas of concern, such as in Chapter 7, when I consider the complaint of some women's groups that International Monetary Fund (IMF) conditionalities have harmed women.

I also consider, in appropriate places throughout the book, the charge that globalization is a result of the iron fist of conditionality (i.e., preconditions for getting aid or trade opportunities) wielded by bilateral and multilateral aid agencies. Whether the conditionalities are effective and binding (as the critics believe) or are loose and often evaded (as I argue) and whether trade liberalization is "forced" by these institutions (as is alleged) or is often embraced by nations because they believe it is good for them to abandon costly protectionism (as I contend) are matters that I deal with, particularly in Chapters 16 and 18.

As for the charges of hypocrisy, double standards, and unfair trade that are passionately leveled today at these international institutions and also at the rich nations—in particular, that they maintain protection for themselves while they force others into free trade—these charges have been made by reputable non-governmental organizations (NGOs) such as Oxfam and by the World Bank in its occasionally desperate get-them-off-our-backs mode. But, as I have written extensively elsewhere with documentation and only sketch in this book, these beliefs and allegations are often little more than rubbish.[4]

In particular, the average industrial protection in the poor countries is still significantly higher than in the rich countries; the chart in Chapter 16 shows this clearly. That chapter also considers the reasons, which have nothing to do with hypocrisy, why protection in the rich countries has not been reduced more on labor-intensive industrial products. In agriculture, there are extensive tariffs in the importing poor countries as well. Moreover, significant subsidies, often through heavily subsidized inputs such as water and electricity, can be found in agriculture even in poor countries such as India and Mexico.

Besides, only an ignoramus would coach the poor countries to talk of "unfair trade," for this is the code phrase used by the protectionists in rich countries to cut off imports from the poor countries by alleging that they obtain their competitiveness in ways that amount to unfair competition and unfair trade. Trade experts of all political persuasions have spent decades exposing the cynical use of this phrase and decrying its usage, but then in come the know-nothings, who persuade the unsuspecting poor countries to embrace it.[5] When it comes to the two sets of nations, poor and rich, battling it out as to who is the worse unfair trader, do not be surprised when the poor nations find themselves at a disadvantage.

If all this were of no relevance, I would grin and bear it. Regrettably, many of the leaders in the poor countries have now come to believe that the trading system is unfair and hypocritical, and therefore they can focus on others' protectionism and forget about their own. That their protectionism, currently at average levels higher than in the rich countries, can only hurt their own prosperity and therefore the war against poverty will be demonstrated in Chapter 5. Causing harm to the poor countries cannot have been the intention of Oxfam, yet the road to hell is paved with good intentions. Oxfam knows a little, but not enough, about trade policy, I am afraid, and I have been moved to remark, not just in this instance, that mission creep, even by non-creeps, is often not a good idea.[6] Their overreach subtracts from the great good that they have done when they concentrate on what they do best.

So much then for conditionalities, double standards, unfair trade, and hypocrisy. Let me turn instead to the central tasks that I have set out to explore in this book: the sources of anti-globalization sentiments, the concerns that globalization lacks a human face, the reality that it does have one, and the governance that must accompany globalization once one recognizes that it is generally a benign force for social agendas.

Exaggerating the Perils of Globalization

At the outset, it is necessary to recognize that the perils of globalization happen to be exaggerated because of what I like to call the fallacies of aggregation.

Different Aspects of Globalization

Recall that globalization, even in its economic aspects, has many dimensions. It embraces trade and long-term direct foreign investment by multinationals as well as flows of short-term portfolio capital whose rapidity and size have caused havoc in places ranging from Bangkok to Buenos Aires. But it also should include now-sizeable migrations, legal and often illegal, across borders. And it extends to the diffusion and transfer of technology (such as AIDS-fighting drugs) among producing and consuming nations. Such economic globalization, in turn, is distinct from globalization, say, on dimensions such as increased international accessibility of print and other media (e.g., Internet access to newspapers and magazines, and the reach of CNN and the BBC today) or growing enrollments of foreign students.

Yet the popular discourse on globalization has tended to blur the lines between these different dimensions and to speak of globalization and its merits and demerits as if it were a homogeneous, undifferentiated phenomenon. Indeed, recent years have seen many polls on attitudes toward "globalization," some of which I discuss below, and practically all of them are marred by a failure to specify which aspect of even economic globalization they are polling the respondent about. So we have no way of finding out what exactly the respondent has in mind when she says that globalization is good for herself or for the poor or for her country.

In fact, the rot goes even deeper. In particular, in the many debates that I have had with Ralph Nader and other opponents of freer trade before, during, and after the 1999 ministerial meeting of the World Trade Organization in Seattle (which broke up in mayhem as a result of violent demonstrations by anti-globalization groups), the critics have invariably strayed into the financial crisis that devastated East Asia in the latter half of the 1990s. They argue as if the case for freer trade had been exposed as illusory by this financial crisis. But openness to trade had been at the heart of the East Asian "miracle," whereas imprudent and hasty freeing of financial flows was at the heart of the brutal interruption of this miracle. To throw beneficial trade out of the window because financial flows have caused a crisis is surely illogical.[7]

The case for free trade and the argument for free capital flows have important parallels. But the differences are yet more pointed. The freeing of capital flows in haste, without putting in place monitoring and regulatory mechanisms and banking reforms, amounts to a rash, gung-ho financial capitalism. It can put nation-states at serious risk of experiencing massive, panic-fed outflows of short-term capital funds, which would drive their economies into a tailspin.

The freeing of trade can hardly do this. If I exchange some of my toothpaste for one of your toothbrushes, we will both have whiter teeth, and the risk that we will have our teeth knocked out by this exchange is negligible. By contrast, the proper analogy for capital flows is playing with fire. When Tarzan sets a fire to roast his kill, he feeds himself and has little to fear: a forest fire is hard to set off. But when he returns to England as the long-lost Earl of Greystoke, he can carelessly and easily set his ancestral home on fire.

Yet, manifest as this asymmetry is to any but the most ideological economists, it is a common affliction even among highly educated members of the public such as Ralph Nader. Indeed, they assume that if one is for free trade, one must be for free direct investment, for free capital flows, for free immigration, for free love, for free everything else! I must confess that while the case for free trade suffers from this fallacy, making our business of defending the merits of free trade more precarious, I myself have profited from it. Thus, when I wrote in 1998 of this asymmetry between free trade and free capital flows in the magazine *Foreign Affairs,* right after the East Asian financial crisis had broken out, alerting all to it, that turned out to be newsworthy. That I—widely complimented or condemned, depending on your viewpoint, as the "world's foremost free trader"—had "admitted" that unfettered capital flows could be dangerous was considered to be a heresy worthy of the greatest attention. While a few others, such as my new (Columbia) colleague Joseph Stiglitz and my old (MIT) student Paul Krugman, had also registered their reservations in their own way, I was the one who became the poster boy for many who were fearful of "globalization." And yet, in all truth, I had thought that I was saying the obvious; I had in fact never thought otherwise!

The North-South Divide: An Ironic Reversal

The debate on globalization is overlaid and overwhelmed by yet another fallacy that asserts that the disillusionment with globalization, typified by the street theater and the campus protests, is worldwide and reflects a majoritarian discontent. But this belief is not true.

In fact, anti-globalization sentiments are more prevalent in the rich countries of the North, while pluralities of policy makers and the public in the poor countries of the South see globalization instead as a positive force. This was the finding of the World Economic Forum's extensive poll on global public opinion on globalization, carried out by the Canadian polling firm Environics International, with twenty-five thousand urban respondents in twenty-five countries, and presented at the WEF's annual meeting in New York in early 2002.[8]

I call this an ironic reversal since the situation was exactly the other way around in the 1950s and 1960s. At that time the rich countries were busy liberalizing their trade, investments, and capital flows. They saw international integration as the magic bullet that would bring them prosperity, and it did produce the golden age of rising tides that lifted all boats until the OPEC-led explosion of oil prices unsettled the world economy beginning in the mid-1970s. But the poor countries were fearful of international integration.

Raúl Prebisch, the Argentinian economist, talked then of the dangers to the "periphery" from the "center" in international interactions. The sociologist Fernando Henrique Cardoso of Brazil invented the *dependencia* thesis, arguing that the poor countries would be relegated to a dependent status in the international economy. The Chilean sociologist Osvaldo Sunkel used the striking phrase "integration into the international economy leads to disintegration of the national economy." President Kwame Nkrumah of Ghana, whom the CIA helped dislodge, wrote of "neo-colonialism": the embrace by the former colonial powers of innocent-looking instruments such as aid that would intentionally create a crypto-colonialism.

I characterized these fearful attitudes at the time as "malign impact" and "malign intent" paradigms, contrasting with the economist's conventional thinking that international integration would benefit all, rich and poor, and was therefore a "benign impact" phenomenon (which need not have benign intentions motivating it), whereas aid and other assistance were "benign intent" policies (which of course might nonetheless have unintended malign outcomes).[9]

Many poor countries that bought into these fearful ideas and turned away from using international trade and investment flows as opportunities to be seized turned out to have made the wrong choice. Their failures, and the example of the success of the countries of the Far East that used international opportunities to great advantage instead, have proven salutary. The result has been a turn by the South toward more globalization. The sociologist Cardoso, who had warned of *dependencia*, became President Cardoso of Brazil, seeking to take Brazil into more, not less, globalization. The WEF poll on globalization was simply recording this swing of sentiment.[10]

By contrast, the fearful "malign impact" ideas have come to haunt several groups, among them the labor unions, in the rich nations. And this reversal, this contrast with the poor countries, is exactly what the WEF poll was picking up. The rich tapestry of reasons why this has happened is of both interest and concern, and I will address it shortly.

But before doing that, it is worth also noting that recent polls show a waning, rather than an enhancement, of the acute anti-globalization of the 1990s. The WEF poll found also that the positive views of globalization (as an omnibus and ill-defined phenomenon) had become more positive in North America and Europe, even while they remained lower than those in the countries of the South, big pluralities of whose residents continued to express high expectations of globalization. This is also the finding from polls conducted by the Center on Policy Attitudes of the University of Maryland: "Overall, Americans tend to see globalization as somewhat more positive than negative and appear to be growing familiar with the concept and more positive about it. A large majority favors moving with the process of globalization and only a small minority favors resisting it."[11] The most recent poll by the Pew Global Attitudes Project, under the guidance of President Clinton's secretary of state, Madeleine Albright, of thirty-eight thousand people interviewed in forty-four countries found that "majorities in every nation surveyed say growing business and trade ties are at least somewhat good for their country and for themselves" and that while social and economic discontent can be found everywhere, "yet for the most part they are not inclined to blame such troubles on growing interconnectedness."[12]

But it may be too optimistic to go by these polls, as they may also reflect changed circumstances in national economic performance. Good times dampen anti-globalization attitudes, while bad times deepen them. The WEF poll is revealing on this: the lowest pluralities in favor of globalization among the poorer nations are in Indonesia, Turkey, and Argentina, where economies have been through turmoil. And so the task of understanding the anti-globalization sentiments, and responding to them if globalization is to be successfully maintained and managed, remains pressing.

Globalization Today: Different from Yesterday

If globalization's perils tend to be exaggerated in the ways I just discussed, they are also understated by many who say, "Well, we have always had globalization, and it is no big deal." True, rapid integration of the world economy occurred in the late nineteenth and early twentieth centuries. We can go back to the end of the nineteenth century, for instance, and find that trade, capital flows, and migrations were no less then than they are today. If multinationals bother you, then just think of the great East India Company, which virtually paved the way for the British conquest of India, and the Dutch East Indies Company, which dominated Indonesia. Trade grew rapidly along with European outward expansion, as did settlements in the new areas opened up by exploration and conquest. Capital flowed profusely, financing the building of railways in Africa and the extraction of minerals worldwide. Many historians have noticed that the years spanning the two world wars were an interruption of the upward trends in the expansion of world trade and investment, and that it is possible to interpret the postwar liberalization of trade and investment flows as leading to a resumption of the trends set into motion prior to World War I. But all this misses the fact that there are fundamental differences that give globalization today a special, and at times sharp, edge.

First, the earlier integration of the world economy was driven more by technological developments in transportation and communications than by policy changes. It's true that British prime minister Robert Peel repealed the Corn Laws in 1846, bringing free trade unilaterally to England in the first dramatic move away from mercantilism. We also know that in various ways many European nations, notably France, followed suit with some trade liberalizations of their own, though historians have not yet decided whether their actions were induced by the example of Britain's success with free trade, as expressly predicted by Peel.

But none of these policy changes did as much to integrate the world economy in the latter half of the century as did emerging technological revolutions in transportation by railways and in the oceans. Technological advances in these sectors rapidly reduced costs of transport and communication continually through the nineteenth century. Martin Wolf, the *Financial Times* columnist, has observed: "The first transatlantic telegraph was laid in 1866. By the turn of the century, the entire world was connected by telegraph, and communication times fell from months to minutes."[13]

Of course, the rate of technological change in moving goods and services and knowledge cheaply and rapidly across nations has continued unabated, even accelerating according to some observers. Thus, Wolf writes: "The cost of a three-minute telephone call from New York to London in current prices dropped from about $250 in 1930 to a few cents today. In more recent years, the number of voice paths across the Atlantic has skyrocketed from 100,000 in 1986 to more than 2 million today. The number of Internet hosts has risen from 5,000 in 1986 to more than 30 million now."[14]

But today's most dramatic change is in the degree to which governments have intervened to reduce obstacles to the flow of trade and investments worldwide. The story of globalization today must be written in two inks: one colored by technical change and the other by state action. In fact, even the early postwar hostility toward global integration in many of the poor countries has, as already remarked upon, yielded steadily to the progressive embrace of globalization. But this fact forces upon our attention a disturbing observation: governments that can accelerate globalization can also reverse it. Herein lies a vulnerability that cannot be dismissed complacently. The earlier globalization, in the end, was interrupted for almost a half century with rising trade barriers epitomized by the infamous 1930 Smoot-Hawley Tariff of the United States and declining trade flows and investments after World War I through to the Great Crash of 1929 and World War II.

Second, the new information technologies have created a landscape where movements of services and capital are faster by several orders of magnitude. The rapidity with which huge amounts of funds moved out of East Asia within less than a week in 1998, the precipitous outflows from Mexico in November 1994, and many other instances of substantial and rapid-fire outflows of capital have created immense management problems that elude the grasp of countries that face difficult developmental weaknesses and challenges but want to embrace financial globalization or are forced to do so. Financial panics, crashes, and manias are nothing new, as the renowned economist Charles Kindleberger has reminded us; but their magnitudes and the speed at which they arrive are indeed qualitatively a different, and potentially more dangerous, phenomenon.

Third, the sense of vulnerability, or economic insecurity, is arguably greater today than in earlier periods because the growing integration of nations worldwide into the international economy has intensified competitive pressures from actual and potential rivals elsewhere. In Adam Smith's time, over two centuries ago, orange producers in the tropics had little worry about competition from Glasgow even though oranges could be grown in glass houses: the cost difference would be so high that the tropical farmers felt secure behind a solid buffer of competitive advantage. England's producers of manufactures also enjoyed easy dominance in many cases because England was ahead of all on industrialization. But today, in most commodities and activities, technology matters and has diffused greatly, both because many have access to similar pools of knowledge and because multinationals can take scarce knowledge almost everywhere if they choose, as they often do, and they do produce globally. The buffer has therefore shrunk dramatically in most activities, and international competition is fierce and feared.

The inevitable effect has been to prompt firms everywhere to worry about "fair trade." Each looks over his foreign rival's shoulder to see if any difference in domestic policy or institutions gives this competitor an "unfair" advantage. The result has been a growing demand for ironing out any such differences, including in labor and environmental standards, as firms seek "level playing fields," ignoring the fact that it is differences, whether of climate and skills or of domestic institutions and policies reflecting local conditions, that lead to beneficial trade among nations.

While these demands, familiar in the rich countries for the most part, have transformed the debate on globalization, and their many ramifications will be subjected to critical examination at different places in this book (especially in Chapters 10 and 11), the other important implication of intensified world competition is that it has exposed producers in the poor countries to increased risks as a result of shifting to world markets in search of greater prosperity. Thus farmers who shift from traditional staples to cash crops because of higher returns at current prices face the prospect that this shift will lead them into ruination if rivals elsewhere with lower prices suddenly move into the market: a phenomenon that is more likely in a world with many potential suppliers with small margins of difference in competitiveness. Since few farmers in the poor countries are likely to take these downside possibilities into account, sudden misery is a possibility that has at times resulted from the shift to global markets. The absence of institutional support to handle these downsides (an issue analyzed, with sad examples of devastation following the shift to market crops and solutions to this problem, in Chapter 16) has become a major source of worry.

Finally, fears that globalization intensifies interdependence among nation-states and increasingly constrains their ability to provide for the welfare of their citizens have a salience that did not quite obtain in the earlier period. The growth of the welfare state in the twentieth century—even though we had elements of it starting earlier, as with social security, whose origins go back to Bismarck in Germany—has created a mind-set, an ethos, where the state is expected to be responsible for the welfare of its citizens. The novel fear today is that globalization places limits on the freedom to discharge this critical responsibility.

And so the complacent view that there is nothing new about globalization is simply wrong. We do need to look at the phenomenon closely, seeking to analyze and address the fears that are novel and indeed appear to be plausible at first blush.

A Trilogy of Discontents

Anti-Capitalism

As the twentieth century ended, capitalism seemed to have vanquished its rivals. Francis Fukuyama's triumphalism in his celebrated work *The End of History and The Last Man* (1990) was like a primeval scream of joy by a warrior with a foot astride his fallen prey.[15] It was not just the collapse of communism in Europe and China's decisive turn away from it. As the energetic anti-globalization NGO Fifty Years Is Enough laments, even the Swedish model (with its enhanced Social Democratic commitment to the welfare state, backed by a markedly progressive and redistributive tax system) had lost its appeal. The much-advertised model of "alternative development" in the Indian state of Kerala, with its major emphasis on education and health and only minor attention to growth, had also run into difficulties, much as President Julius Nyerere's celebrated socialist experiment in Tanzania had run the country's economy into the ground. This vanishing of different possibilities has led to what I have called the tyranny of the missing alternative, provoking a sense of anguished anti-capitalist reactions from both the old and the young.

The old among the disenchanted are few, and so they perhaps matter less than the young, who are many. They are among the anti-capitalists of the postwar years, ranging from socialists to revolutionaries. The communists and Marxists are captive to a nostalgia for their vanished dreams.

When the World Economic Forum met in Davos, Switzerland, in February 2001, there was an anti-Davos meeting in Brazil at the same time.[16] The rhetoric in Brazil was one of revolution. I recall George Soros, who properly considers himself to be a progressive financier, going into a debate from Davos on the video monitor with some of the anti-Davos participants. I recall his frustration, indeed astonishment, when he realized that he was seen as the enemy, not a friend, much as U.S. Democrats were chagrined that Ralph Nader thought during the last presidential election that they were no different from the Republicans.

Soros, who had not previously interacted with these groups, just did not get it: as far as these anti-capitalist revolutionaries are concerned, anyone who is into stocks and bonds should be put *in* stocks and bonds. Indeed, these groups, who were memorializing Che Guevara and listening to Ben Bella, were the exact antitheses of the Arthur Koestlers of the world, who wrote of the god that failed. They were working from a script about the god that died but will come again, much like born-again Christians. They only had to keep the faith.

But we who favor globalization must also confront the young. And if you have watched the streets of Seattle, Washington, Prague, Montreal, and Genoa, where the anti-globalizers have congregated with increasing militancy, or if you see their impassioned protests on the campuses, as I have watched the Anti-Sweatshop Coalition's activities at my own university (Columbia), there can be no doubt that we have here a phenomenon that is truly important in the public space and also more potent: the nostalgia of the fading generation cannot compete with the passions of the rising generation.

So how is the discontent of the young to be explained? Of course, a rare few among them share their predecessors' revolutionary bent. Consider Global Exchange, an NGO that describes itself as a "human rights group"—this is the in term, much as "socialism" was three decades ago, and its moral resonance immediately gets you onto higher ground and gives you a free pass with the media and the public. It professes radical politics and gets endorsement from the great linguist and activist Noam Chomsky, among other left intellectuals. Its pronouncements on the World Trade Organization are dramatic and drastic: "the WTO only serves the interests of multinational corporations" and "the WTO is killing people."[17]

But Global Exchange and its radical chic are really a fringe phenomenon. There are several explanations, other than strong socialist convictions, of what animates the young in particular. Each may explain part of the reality, while collectively they provide a more complete explanation.

1.   Far too many among the young see capitalism as a system that cannot address meaningfully questions of social justice. To my generation, and that of the British left-leaning intellectuals such as George Bernard Shaw that preceded it, the Soviet model was a beguiling alternative. Indeed, my much-translated 1966 book *The Economics of Underdeveloped Countries* contains a distinct nod toward the Soviet Union: "The imagination of many . . . nations has been fired, perhaps most of all, by the remarkable way in which the Soviet Union has raised itself to the status of a Great Power by its own bootstraps and in a short span of time."[18] How appalling a misjudgment this view of the Soviet alternative seems today, and how commonplace it was then!

That capitalism may be viewed instead as a system that can paradoxically destroy privilege and open up economic opportunity to the many is a thought that is still uncommon. I often wonder, for example, how many of the young skeptics of capitalism are aware that socialist planning in countries such as India, by replacing markets systemwide with bureaucratically determined rations of goods and services, worsened rather than improved unequal access because socialism meant queues that the well-connected and the well-endowed could jump, whereas markets allowed a larger number to make it to the check-out counter. I have always been astonished at the number of well-meaning socialists, whose aspirations I admire, who continue to fall for the erroneous view that controls and direct allocations are an appropriate answer to inequality.

2.   But the anti-capitalist sentiments are particularly virulent among the young who arrive at their social awakening on campuses in fields other than economics. English, comparative literature, and sociology are fertile breeding grounds.

Thus, deconstructionism, espoused by the French philosopher Jacques Derrida, has left the typical student of literature without anchor because of its advocacy of what amounts to an endless horizon of meanings. Terry Eagleton, the sympathetic chronicler of modern literary theory, has written: "Derrida is clearly out to do more than develop new techniques of reading: deconstruction is for him an ultimately political practice, an attempt to dismantle the logic by which a particular system of thought, and behind that a whole system of political structures and social institutions, maintains its force."[19]

True, Derrida's technique will deconstruct any political ideology, including Marxism. Typically, however, it is focused on deconstructing and devaluing capitalism rather than Marxism, often with nihilistic overtones, which creates the paradox that many now turn to anarchy not from Bakunin but from Derrida.

The near-nihilist influence of the deconstructionism of Derrida in feeding anti-capitalism has been matched by the equally profound influence of Michel Foucault: these have amounted to a double whammy, courtesy of Paris. Foucault's emphasis on discourses as instruments of power and dominance has also led to what is often described as an "anti-rational" approach that challenges the legitimacy of academic disciplines, including economics, and their ability to get at the "truth." There is little doubt that the language of power, and the focus on it, feeds in turn the notion, discussed later, that corporations will dominate and exploit the workers under the liberal rules that define capitalism, and by extension, globalization.[20]

The heavy influence of Marxist texts on students of literature, on the other hand, has been beautifully captured by V. S. Naipaul in his compelling portrait in *Beyond Belief* of the Pakistani guerrilla Shabaz, who went from studying literature in England to starting a revolution in Baluchistan that failed:

> There were close Pakistani friends at the university. Many of them were doing English literature, like Shabaz; it was one of the lighter courses, possibly the lightest, and at this time it was very political and restricted. It was encouraging Marxism and revolution rather than wide reading. So Shabaz and his Pakistani friends in their Marxist study group read the standard (and short) revolutionary texts, Frantz Fanon, Che Guevara. And while they read certain approved Russian writers, they didn't read or get to know about the Turgenev novels, *Fathers and Sons* (1862) and *Virgin Soil* (1877), which dealt with conditions not unlike those in feudal Pakistan, but questioned the simplicities of revolution.[21]

Feeding the anti-globalization movement are also the post-colonial (poco) theorists, who, following Edward Said's pathbreaking writings, have a profound suspicion of Western scholarship as an objective source of interpretation and conceptualization of the colonial societies that were part of the global polity that European expansion created. That suspicion breeds hostility both to Western disciplines such as economics and to the threat that they see from them to the cultures of the communities and nations that have succeeded the colonial rule.

Thus the post-colonial theorists become natural allies of the deconstructionists, the diverse post-modernists (pomos), the Foucault cultists, and the Marxists, in their anti-globalization sentiments in the literature departments. The cauldron draws its boiling waters from many spigots.

As for sociology, many of its students are influenced equally by the new literary theory and the old Marxism. They stand in contempt of economic argumentation that would refute their rejectionist beliefs about capitalism by asserting that economics is about value whereas sociology is about values. But they are wrong today on both counts.

Economists will retort that as citizens they choose ends, but as economists they choose the (best) means. Moreover, accused of indulging the profit motive, they respond with the Cambridge economist Sir Dennis Robertson that economics is addressed heroically to showing how "man's basest instincts," not his noblest, can be harnessed through appropriate institutional design to produce public good. Adam Smith would surely have died an unsung hero if he had peddled the pedestrian argument that altruism led to public good.

The presumption that sociology is a better guide to virtue than economics is also misplaced. Certainly its related discipline, social anthropology, has traditionally leaned toward preserving cultures, whereas economics in our hands is a tool for change.[22] When I studied in England I was fascinated by social anthropology and deeply buried in the writings of the legendary A. R. Radcliffe-Brown and many others, but I still wound up preferring economics for my vocation. What other choice could really have been made by a young student from a country afflicted by economic misery? Indeed, if reducing poverty by using economic analysis to accelerate growth and therewith pull people up into gainful employment and dignified sustenance is not a compelling moral imperative, what *is*?

But I should add that many of these students are also susceptible to the bitingly critical view of economics as an apologia for capitalism that was brilliantly propounded by Rosa Luxemburg in her classic essay "What Is Economics?"—the first chapter of a proposed ten-chapter work, only six chapters of which were found in her apartment after her murder. She had argued that "the new science of economics," which had reached the status of an academic discipline in Germany, was tantamount to an attempted legitimation of the "anarchy of capitalist production" and was essentially "one of the most important ideological weapons of the bourgeoisie as it struggles with the medieval state and for a modern capitalist state." The "invisible hand," with its rationalization of markets, had a hidden agenda, hence it lacked plausibility. This analysis attracts many.

3.   But I also think that an altogether new factor on the scene that propels the young into anti-capitalist attitudes comes from a different, technological source in a rather curious fashion. This is the dissonance that now exists between empathy for others elsewhere for their misery and the inadequate intellectual grasp of what can be done to ameliorate that distress. The resulting tension spills over into unhappiness with the capitalist system (in varying forms) within which they live and hence anger at it for its apparent callousness.

Today, thanks to television, we have what I call the paradox of inversion of the philosopher David Hume's concentric circles of reducing loyalty and empathy. Each of us feels diminishing empathy as we go from our nuclear family to the extended family, to our local community, to our state or county (say, Lancashire or Louisiana), to our nation, to our geographical region (say, Europe or the Americas), and then to the world. This idea of concentric circles of empathy can be traced back to the Stoics' doctrine of *oikeiosis*—that human affection radiates outward from oneself, diminishing as distance grows from oneself and increasing as proximity increases to oneself. In the same vein, Hume famously argued that "it is not contrary to reason to prefer the destruction of the whole world to the scratching of my finger" and that "sympathy with persons remote from us is much fainter than with persons near and contiguous."[23]

Similarly, his contemporary Adam Smith wrote in 1760 in *The Theory of Moral Sentiments,* which is as celebrated among moral philosophers as *The Wealth of Nations* is among economists:

> Let us suppose that the great empire of China, with all its myriads of inhabitants, was suddenly swallowed up by an earthquake and let us consider how a man of humanity in Europe, who had no sort of connexion with that part of the world, would be affected upon receiving intelligence of this dreadful calamity. He would, I imagine, first of all express very strongly his sorrow for the misfortune of that unhappy people, he would make many melancholy reflections upon the precariousness of human life and the vanity of all the labors of man which could thus be annihilated in a moment. He would too, perhaps, if he was a man of speculation, enter into many reasonings concerning the effects which this disaster might produce upon the commerce of Europe and the trade and business of the world in general. And when all this fine philosophy was over, when all these humane sentiments had been once fairly expressed, he would pursue his business or pleasure, take his repose or

his diversion, with the same ease and tranquility as if no such accident had occurred.

The most frivolous disaster which could befall himself would occasion a more real disturbance. If he was to lose his little finger to-morrow, he would not sleep to-night; but, provided he never saw them, he would snore with the most profound security over the ruin of a hundred million of his brethren. The destruction of that immense multitude seems plainly an object less interesting to him than this paltry misfortune of his own. To prevent, therefore, this paltry misfortune to himself would a man of humanity be willing to sacrifice the lives of a hundred million of his brethren, provided he had never seen them?[24]

What the Internet and CNN have done is to take Hume's outermost circle and turn it into the innermost. No longer can we snore while the other half of humanity suffers plague and pestilence and the continuing misery of extreme poverty. Television has disturbed our sleep, perhaps short of a fitful fever but certainly arousing our finest instincts.[25] Indeed, this is what the Stoics, chiefly Hierocles, having observed the concentric circles of vanishing empathy, had urged by way of morality: that "it is the task of a well tempered man, in his proper treatment of each group, to draw circles together somehow towards the centre, and to keep zealously transferring those from the enclosing circles into the enclosed ones."[26]

At the same time, the technology of the Internet and CNN, as Robert Putnam has told us, has accelerated our move to "bowling alone," gluing us to our TV sets and shifting us steadily out of civic participation, so that the innermost circle has become the outermost one.

So the young see and are anguished by the poverty and the civil wars and the famines in remote areas of the world but often have no intellectual training to cope with their anguish and follow it through rationally in terms of appropriate action. Thus, as I watched the kids dressed as turtles at Seattle, during the riotous 1999 WTO ministerial meeting, protesting against the WTO and the Appellate Body's decision in the shrimp-turtle case (discussed in Chapter 11), I wondered how many knew that the environmentalists had really won that decision, not lost it. The ability to unilaterally impose requirements on foreign shrimpers on the high oceans to use turtle-excluding devices (nets with narrow necks), failing which imports of shrimp would be disallowed, was upheld, not denied. When I asked, of course, no one knew the facts, and so they did not really understand what they were protesting. When I mischievously asked some if they had read Roald Dahl's famous story "The Boy Who Talked with Animals," about a boy who freed a giant turtle and sailed away on it into the far ocean, they shook their turtle heads.[27] It has become fashionable to assert that the demonstrating youth know much about the policies they protest; but that is only a sentiment of solidarity with little basis in fact. True, there are several serious NGOs with real knowledge and serious policy critiques, such as the World Wildlife Fund, and I shall presently consider their phenomenal growth and the opportunity they present for making economic and social well-being a shared success between the agents of economic globalization and the civil society—the two great phenomena as we enter the twenty-first century. But they are not the tumultuous many who are agitating in the streets.

4.   Overlaying the entire scene, of course, is the general presumption that defines many recent assertions by intellectuals that somehow the proponents of capitalism, and of its recent manifestations in regard to economic reforms such as the moves to privatization and to market liberalization (including trade liberalization), are engaged, as Edward Said claims, in a "dominant discourse [whose goal] is to fashion the merciless logic of corporate profit-making and political power into a normal state of affairs." Following Pierre Bourdieu, Said endorses the view that "Clinton-Blair neoliberalism, which built on the conservative dismantling of the great social achievements in health, education, labor and security of the welfare state during the Thatcher-Reagan period, has constructed a paradoxical *doxa*, a symbolic counterrevolution."[28] In Bourdieu's own words, this is "conservative but presents itself as progressive; it seeks the restoration of the past order in some of its most archaic aspects (especially as regards economic relations), yet it passes off regressions, reversals, surrenders, as forward-looking reforms or revolutions leading to a whole new age of abundance and liberty)."[29]

But, frankly, this view stands reality on its head. Of course, we have known since Orwell that words do matter, and the smart duelists in the controversies over public policy will often seize the high ground by appropriating to themselves and their own causes, before their adversaries do, beguiling words such as *progressive*. Thus, believe it or not, protectionists in trade have been known to ask for "tariff reform"; today, they ask for "fair trade," which no one can deny except for the informed few who see that it is used to justify unfair trade practices. Phrases such as "corporate profit making" and "trickle-down" do the same for the friends of Bourdieu, creating and fostering a pejorative perception of the market-using policy changes that they reject.

It is therefore not surprising that today's critics turn to the same linguistic weapons as the anti-capitalist forces of yesterday. But let us ask: is it "conservative" or "radical" to seek to correct, in light of decades of experience and in the teeth of entrenched forces, the mistakes and the excesses of past policies, no matter how well motivated? In fact, as reformers know only too well, it takes courage and élan to challenge orthodoxies, especially those that are conventionally associated with "progressive" forces.

As for the policies themselves, the fierce binary contrast drawn by Bourdieu is an abstraction that misses the central issues today. The debate is really not about conservative counterrevolution and the enlightened past order. It is rather about shifting the center of gravity in public action more toward the use of markets and less toward dirigisme. It is not about "whether markets"; it is about where the "limits to markets" must be drawn. This is a question that, as will be discussed, provokes spirited complaints from the recent communitarians who wish the limits to markets to be drawn more tightly.

The present-day turn toward reforms in the developing countries is also prompted by excessive and knee-jerk dirigisme. As I often say, the problem with many of these countries was that Adam Smith's invisible hand was nowhere to be seen. Their turn to economic reforms is to be attributed not to the rise of "conservatism" but to a pragmatic reaction of many to the failure of what a number of us once considered to be "progressive" policies that would lift us out of poverty, illiteracy, and many other ills. As John Kenneth Galbraith once said about Milton Friedman—and here I take only the witticism and not sides—"Milton's misfortune is that his policies have been tried."

Anti-Globalization

Anti-capitalism has turned into anti-globalization among left-wing students for reasons that are easy to see. After all, Lenin wrote extensively about imperialism and its essential links to capitalism, and present-day writers such as Immanuel Wallerstein have seen the growing integration of the world economy in related ways as the organic extension of national capitalism.[30]

Lenin's views on imperialism provide an insight into a principal reason why anti-globalization is seen by those on the left so readily as following from anti-capitalism. In his famous work *Imperialism: The Highest Stage of Capitalism*, Lenin stated that the distinctive characteristics of capitalism in the form of monopolies, oligarchy, and the exploitation of the weak by the strong nations compel us to define it as "parasitic, decaying capitalism."[31] Nikolai Bukharin, for whose work *Imperialism and the World Economy* Lenin wrote a preface, considered that imperialism with its attendant globalization of the world economy is little more than capitalism's "[attempt] to tame the working class and to subdue social contradictions by decreasing the steam pressure through the aid of a colonial valve"; that "having eliminated [through monopolies] competition within the state, [capitalism has] let loose all the devils of a world scuffle."[32]

The notion that globalization is merely an external attenuation of the internal struggles that doom capitalism, and that globalization is also in essence capitalist exploitation of the weak nations, provides not only an inherent link between capitalism and globalization but also makes globalization an instrument for the exploitation of the weak nations. And this certainly has resonance again among the idealist young on the left. Capitalism seeks globalization to benefit itself but harms others abroad. The Lenin-Bukharin argument then leads, as certainly as a heat-seeking missile reaching its target, to anti-capitalist sentiments.

Anti-Corporation Attitudes

But central to that perspective is the notion, of course, that it is the "monopolies" (for that is indeed how the multinationals are often described even today in much of the anti-globalization literature) that are at the heart of the problem: they do not benefit the people abroad; they exploit them instead. Indeed, this notion of globalization as an exploitative force that delays the doomsday for capitalism at home and harms those abroad has captured some of the more militant among the naive youth today.

The anti-corporation attitudes come to many others who are not aficionados of left-wing literature, also from the obvious sense that multinationals are the principal agents and beneficiaries of capitalism and of globalization.[33] Yet others find it plausible that multinationals must necessarily be bad in a global economy because global integration without globally shared regulations must surely amount to an advantageous playing field for multinationals. These corporations would then be able to seek profits by searching for the most likely locations to exploit workers and nations, thereby putting intolerable pressure on their home states to abandon their gains in social legislation. This is what is known as a race to the bottom. Indeed, this view is so credible that even a shrewd and perceptive intellectual such as Alan Wolfe, who sees through cant better than most, has recently written disapprovingly and casually of the "policies of increasingly rapacious global corporations."[34]

These anti-corporation arguments are not supported by the facts; Chapter 12 shows why. But many believe them. And they zero in with a "gotcha" mentality, seizing on every venal misdeed of a multinational they can find, seeking to validate through these specific examples their general anti-corporation biases. This surely accounts for the return of

Ralph Nader, the great scourge of manifest misdeeds by corporations. It has also magically transformed Julia Roberts, whose triumph in *Pretty Woman* reflected chiefly her marvelous good looks, into an acclaimed actress in *Erin Brockovich* and introduced the gifted actor Russell Crowe to celebrity on the screen in *The Insider,* both movies where a David takes on the Goliath in shape of a truly venal corporation.

The anti-corporation militancy that is on the rise among the young anti-globalizers is also strategic. We have witnessed the brilliant way in which the anti-globalizers managed to use the meetings of the international agencies such as the World Bank, the IMF, and particularly the WTO (originally the GATT), the pride of progressive architectural design regarding the management of the world economy and the permanent legacy of legendary men of vision, to protest and to profess their anti-globalization sentiments. After all, these meetings were where the world's media gathered. What better place to create mayhem and get attention from the vast multitude of reporters looking for a story? So while the old guerrillas struck where you least expected them, these new guerrillas have struck where you most expected them: at these meetings.

The same strategic sense has been displayed in going after the corporations as well. Nike and Gap, two fine multinationals, now have a permanent set of critics, with newsletters and websites worldwide. With Nike and Gap having overseas operations in numerous locations, it is not possible to avoid lapses altogether from whatever is defined as good behavior: the host governments often force the hiring of domestic managers who are regrettably part of cultures that are not as egalitarian and mindful of the dignity of others working below them as the West would like them to be. When lapses occur, these firms become obvious targets in a propaganda war that is stacked against them. Naomi Klein, the Canadian writer, admits frankly that, faced with the amorphous but overwhelming phenomenon of globalization, the only way to get at it is to latch on to something concrete and targetable.[35]

The same strategic thought recurs in the writings of other anti-capitalist activists. Thus the Nicaragua Solidarity Network of Greater New York reported that in Brazil "[o]n Mar. 8 [2001], International Women's Day, women linked to landless rural worker movements in Rio Grande do Sul state gathered in front of a McDonald's restaurant in Porto Alegre, the state capital, to protest. . . . Nina Tonin, a member of the National Board of Directors of the Movement of Landless Rural Workers (MST), said the group chose McDonald's because it is '*a symbol of the intervention politics of the big monopolies operating in Brazil.*'"[36]

So they go after the corporations that spread and constitute the globalization that is reprehensible. We then also see teenagers carrying placards outside Staples, the office products chain that has succeeded immensely throughout the United States, and demonstrating in front of Starbucks while their more militant adult friends threw stones through the coffee chain's windows in Seattle. I talk with them at every opportunity; I find enthusiasm, even idealism, but never any ability to engage concretely on the issues they take a stand on. But then the Kleins of the anti-globalization movement are not fazed; it is all strategic, it is in a good cause.

Indeed, it is hard to understand the deep and unyielding hostility to multinational corporations, manifest on the streets and on campuses, except by analogy to earlier times. Perhaps the classic parallel is with the stigma attached to usury in medieval times: interest and moneylenders then, as profits and corporations now, invited implacable hostility. The exaction of interest was forbidden by ecclesiastical and civil laws, its practice turned into a crime. Even as trade and globalization increased with mercantile expansion and laws began to change (with occasional relapses), usury remained beyond the pale, contrary to conventional and persistent norms.

> By 37 *Henry VIII, cap. ix,* the old laws against usury are, indeed, abolished, and a rate of ten percent is indirectly legalized by the fixing of severe penalties for any rate higher; but the practice is condemned, and classed with corrupt bargains. . . . In 1552, however, by 6 *Edward VI, cap. xx,* the act of Henry VIII is annulled . . . and severe penalties are enacted against any usury whatever, "forasmuch as Usurie is by the word of God utterly prohibited, as a vyce most odious and detestable . . ." In 1570, by 13 *Elizabeth, cap. viii,* 6 *Edward VI* is annulled and 37 *Henry VIII re-enacted, but* "forasmuch as all Usurie, being forbidden by the Law of God is synne and detestable . . ." It is expressly provided that all offenders shall "also be punished and corrected according to the ecclesiastical laws heretofore made against usury."[37]

Other Ideological and Intellectual Sources of Anti-Globalization

While the sources of anti-globalization rooted in anti-capitalism in the diverse ways set out so far are dominant in the current discourse, there are others, not quite so influential, that cannot be ignored.

The Right

In this variegated landscape, complementing those who lean on the left are forces on the right. Thus for every Ralph Nader there is a Pat

Buchanan. But the Buchanans are instead knee-deep in xenophobia and crude assertions of national identity and sovereignty. These beliefs lead directly to proposals to isolate America from commerce by building tariff walls. Thus in the 1990s Buchanan called for tariffs against the Japanese, asking for a 10 percent tariff on every Japanese import, and has argued recently against letting Chinese imports freely into the United States.[38] Interestingly, the right-wing extremists in India's ruling Bharatiya Janata Party are also fanatically for self-reliance in trade and incoming foreign investment.

The anti-globalization sentiments on the right extend easily to anti-immigration attitudes, whereas the left's fascination with anti-globalization rarely extends to a fortress mentality on immigration. While some liberal environmental groups slide into anti-immigration rhetoric when they argue that immigration adds to environmental problems, the general posture of the liberal anti-globalization groups is one of benign neglect. Surprisingly, however, there are a rare few progressive segments of the anti-globalization movement that are for free immigration. The anthropologist David Graeber has drawn attention to the Italian group Ya Basta!, whose platform includes guaranteed free movement of people across borders: an objective that has simply no political salience or social resonance, to be brutally frank.

Communitarianism and Limits to Markets

The "liberal international economic order," as the spread of capitalism and markets worldwide is sometimes described, has also been challenged by political philosophers of influence, these coming from the Anglo-Saxon campuses rather than from the banks of the Seine. Thus, communitarians in the United States such as Michael Sandel of Harvard and Michael Walzer of Princeton's Institute for Advanced Study have tried to define limits on the use of markets.

To illustrate, Sandel has objected to the use of global-efficiency-enhancing international trade in permits for carbon dioxide emissions among members of the Kyoto treaty on global warming. With such trade, Brazil would be able to reduce its emissions but effectively sell the reduction achieved as a tradable permit to the United States, which would then credit it as a contribution toward the fulfillment of its own target of emission reductions, thus reducing by the traded amount the emission reduction it had to achieve. This trade would mean that a country where the real cost of reducing carbon dioxide emissions is higher would be able to buy the tradable permits from one where the real cost was lower: the world cost of reducing emissions would obviously fall with such trade. But Sandel once argued in a *New York Times* op-ed article why it was "immoral" to buy the rights to pollute: we expect everyone in a community to make a shared effort toward such goals.[39] A good example would be that our community would be offended if the rich boys could buy their way out of fighting a war (though one must admit that the substitution of a professional army for conscription is precisely a case where that communitarian sense has given way to the notion of efficiency). Sandel himself produces the example of parking spaces for handicapped people. The community would be offended if the rich could buy permits to use such spaces. But here again, the rich can always park their BMWs in these spaces and pay the fines if caught. To my knowledge, no one threatens that the luxury cars illegally parked in these spaces will be destroyed and the violators will be incarcerated, thus raising the effective price paid for such spaces by the rich to levels that really do amount to prohibition. In short, while communitarian principles do intrude frequently to place limits on markets, and hence on the principle of efficiency that markets help to implement, the communitarian spirit itself is subject to limits in practice.

It is likely that the extent of communitarian limits on markets will erode with capitalism taking hold. This is what Marx had in mind as he observed what he called the "commodification" process—what economists call increased commercialization. Thus, the balance between altruism, love, duty, and the other virtues, on one hand, and pursuit of self-interest, on the other hand, may shift away from those virtues as capitalism progresses. For instance, love may become sex, with reverence and mystique yielding to gratification. It is hard to see this in one's own culture, but during O. J. Simpson's trial I was struck by the fact that when newspapers described how he had been looking through the window as Nicole made love to her boyfriend, they all said that she and her friend had had dinner, come home, had coffee, and then "had sex." Mind you, none said they had "made love." So making love was reduced to having sex, the way they had dinner and then coffee. And, just as you might remark that the coffee was an espresso, the reports added that the sex was oral!

But the communitarians surely exaggerate the commodification that markets wreak. There is movement the other way too, and often it comes about because of the rapid pace of technical change, which has accelerated both the pace of economic globalization and that of globalized civil society. The cloning debate shows how societies will seek to place limits on what will be left to markets.

In the world as we know it, therefore, both communitarian and liberal principles coexist in varying forms. The important question is not whether we should have one or the other but whether capitalism and globalization are such an inexorable force that they propel society into a headlong rush away from traditional communitarian values and ways. The evidence for such an alarmist conclusion is not compelling.

Anti-Americanism

Yet another source of anti-globalization sentiments is the resentment that comes from the rise of the United States to a military and economic hegemony so unprecedented that the French call America, with which they have a notorious love-hate relationship, a hyperpower, as if being called a superpower is no longer the highest accolade.

Since this hegemony is exercised in the global context, the resentment of the United States follows worldwide. The loss of the Soviet Union as a countervailing superpower is mourned, even as the collapse of the scourge of communism is celebrated. The anti-Americanism that American power and its exercise—no matter how benign and invited—creates is then an important source of anti-globalization sentiment. Throwing sand into the gears of globalization is seen as a way to spit on American hegemony, if not to limit the exercise of it in the political, cultural, and economic domains.

So we then face a motley crew, a mélange of anti-globalizers animated by different ideas and passions and yet appearing to be an undifferentiated mass. Nonetheless, those of us who favor globalization cannot retreat from the task of meeting their concerns head-on. In the end, despite the chaotic nature of the anti-globalization movement, we can impose some commonalities and order before we offer a response. That is just what I propose now to do.

2

Globalization: Socially, Not Just Economically, Benign

Many of the early anti-globalizers, even when differentially animated by one or more of the concerns and intellectual arguments I have outlined, typically described themselves in unison as seeking recognition as "stakeholders" who sought a voice, even a vote, and at times a veto, in the globalization process.

But, as became fairly clear fairly soon, there were two kinds of stakeholders: those to be seen in the streets and heard at times in strident voices, who wished to drive a stake through the global system, and those who wished to exercise their stake so as to participate in and influence the system. The former are "stake-wielding" groups, the latter "stake-asserting" groups.

Indeed, the street-theater stake-wielding NGOs see themselves as the "people's pitchforks," to be used in the war against globalization. It is a sad reality that politicians such as the affable President Bill Clinton, who could feel your pain before you did, indulged the stake-wielding groups even when they broke into violence, while politicians with firmer backbones chided them instead.[1] Prime Minister Tony Blair, with admirable forthrightness, called the violent among them "louts," that archaic but evocative epithet that has unfortunately vanished from American parlance, when they trashed Trafalgar Square and much else on May Day some years ago.

By contrast, the stake-asserting NGOs—such as the Center for Science and Environment in India and the International Forum on Globalization in the United States—prefer to be in the corridors rather than out in the streets, urging reasoned discourse as a way to advance their agendas, and using the sedate methods of glossy, researched pamphlets and policy briefs to put their oars into the policy waters.[2] They worked quietly at seminars and debates at the Madison Hotel during the WTO meeting in Seattle while the demonstrators and their militant friends took to the streets. And they plotted with the assembled conclave of the heads of leading U.S. foundations to get on the gravy train of grants for research and participation at meetings that were hitherto confined to more conventional scholars on campuses.

The tension between the stake-wielding and stake-asserting NGOs has now become manifest: I was witness to the heads of some leading NGOs, with serious preoccupations and matching research, at the 2001 Davos meetings urging that we not mix them up with these noisy pro-testers either.

If the stake-wielding proponents of hard-core anti-globalization attitudes were all we had to contend with, our prospects would be pretty dim. We would be talking to them across a chasm that they would not cross. If they extend their hand across the divide, it is not to shake your hand but to wrestle brutally with it. Fortunately, however, they are no longer the most compelling players on the stage.

The center of gravity among the anti-globalization movements has actually been shifting toward the stake-asserting groups, which are im-passioned but have a definable set of concerns that can be met by en-gagement and dialogue. These are the vast numbers of fairly serious civil society organizations that have emerged worldwide. As explored and explained in Chapter 4, some powerful ones have turned away from the traditional preoccupations with advancing domestic social agendas, such as the elimination of dowry payments and implementation of land re-forms to assist the landless, to an external preoccupation with the effects of economic globalization.[3] Yet others, created deliberately to address worldwide concerns, have also emerged.

So as we sit down with these groups, alongside or across from them at the table, we must ask: what worries them? I would argue that it is the broadly social effects of economic globalization that they are concerned with. They have profound questions, and often alarming certainties, about globalization's ill effects on many social fronts, such as the effect on poverty and on child labor. These dramatic concerns have dominated the globalization debate so much that people commonly assume that economic globalization harms, not advances, social agendas—that glo-balization *needs* a human face.

Indeed, we now confront the ready assumption (that is endemic by now even in some international institutions) that if capitalism has pros-pered and economic globalization has increased while some social ill has worsened, then the first two phenomena must have caused the third! It has gotten to an almost farcical level where if your girlfriend walks out on you, it must be due to globalization—after all, she may have left for Buenos Aires. These critics need to be asked, with a nod to Tina Turner's famous song "What's Love Got to Do with It?": what's globalization got to do with it?

The chief task before those who consider globalization favorably, then, is to confront the fears that while globalization may be economically benign (in the sense of increasing the pie), it is socially malign.[4] These fears relate to several areas, among them accentuation of poverty in both rich and poor countries, erosion of unionization and other labor rights, creation of a democratic deficit, harming of women, imperiling of local mainstream and indigenous cultures, and damage to the environment.

It is perhaps interesting to recall that (admittedly different) social effects were not entirely ignored by the earliest economist proponents of trade in nineteenth-century England. They argued, however, that these effects beyond the economic realm were benign, not malign. Just one quote from John Stuart Mill should illustrate:

> [T]he economical advantages of commerce are surpassed in importance by those of its effects, which are intellectual and moral. It is hardly possible to overrate the value, in the present low state of human improvement, of placing human beings in contact with persons dissimilar to themselves, and with modes of thought and action unlike those with which they are familiar. Commerce is now, what war once was, the principal source of this contact. . . . There is no nation which does not need to borrow from others, not merely particular arts or practices, but essential points of character in which its own type is inferior.[5]

But today's alarmist anti-globalization critics of the social effects of economic globalization would consider yesterday's pro-globalization writers to be complacent by contrast with themselves. And at first blush, which is what many are happy to settle for, their fears do appear often to be plausible. But the key task before us today is to consider whether, on closer analytical and empirical examination, these fears turn out to be well founded. We must also ask where the balance of arguments seems to lie. This is precisely the analysis that I undertake in Part II.

If I conclude, as I do after the close examination in Part II, that economic globalization is on balance socially benign, then the proponents of the view that globalization *needs* a human face are raising a false alarm. This is not an idle conclusion. It has important implications for appropriate governance to oversee and manage the phenomenon.

If you believe that globalization needs a human face, that it is largely a malevolent social force, you will want to inhibit, constrain, reshape, and challenge it; you will want perhaps to throw sand into the gears, and in extremis to throw it into the tank and bring the engine to a halt, much as the stake-wielding anti-globalization groups wish to do. But instead, as I hope to convince the readers of this book, if you believe that globalization has a human face, you will think of a very different set of policies and institutions to accompany it. Among them, you will want to think of policies to enhance, supplement, complement, and accentuate its good outcomes.

To illustrate: if you believe that globalization creates more, rather than less, child labor, you will want to draw back from globalization. But if you conclude that globalization reduces child labor, you will want to know what added policies will reduce it yet more.

Given that Part II concludes that globalization has a human face, Chapter 3 sketches how the question of appropriate governance must be addressed in that event. Chapter 15 specifically and Part IV generally do this in depth.

3

Globalization Is Good but Not Good Enough

What, then, are the principal dimensions of an approach to making the beneficial globalization process work even better? I will sketch here the three principal prescriptions that need to be kept in view:

The beneficial outcomes are only what economists call a "central tendency," which is to say that they hold for the most part but not always. They leave room for downsides, and we must have institutional mechanisms to cope with such adverse outcomes if and when they materialize.

Also, we will want to go faster in achieving social agendas than globalization permits and facilitates. The question then is: what choice of policy and institutions will achieve that acceleration?

Finally, we can never forget also that a transition to more rewarding globalization requires careful steering and optimal speed of policy changes, not maximal speed à la the "shock therapy" of excessively rapid reforms that devastated Russia.

Handling Possible Downsides

Occasionally globalization will do harm that requires attention. We must create institutions and policies that either reduce the probability of such downsides or can be triggered so as to cope with them, preferably doing both. Let me illustrate.

Consider the recent concerns raised by some NGOs about the rapidly proliferating shrimp farms along the coasts of India, Vietnam, Thailand, and many other countries, including some in Latin America. I first came across these concerns in my work for Human Rights Watch.[1] It seemed a trifle odd that shrimp should be considered a human rights issue instead of being eaten and enjoyed! Besides, shrimp farming in India had led to substantial exports and had contributed to enhancing India's growth and its fight against poverty, the eradication of which could be legitimately regarded as a human rights concern. On examination, however, it was clear that this was precisely the sort of occasional downside of globalization of trade and direct investment that needed to be addressed. What was the problem?

Coastal shrimp farming was damaging the surrounding mangroves because of discharge of chemicals and backup of uneaten feed, disrupting the livelihood of fishermen and others subsisting traditionally in the surrounding areas.[2] Evidently a twofold institutional response was necessary: there should be a way to compensate and assist those who had already been damaged; more important, there must be the introduction of a "polluter pay" tax on the discharges and effluents in current farming.

Take yet one more example, extensively developed in Chapter 16, that illustrates how there should also be institutional international change to mitigate globalization's occasional dark side. Recall that with greater openness in trade there often comes a sense of economic insecurity from the fear that more openness will create greater volatility of prices and hence of jobs. Even though the objective evidence for this fear is not compelling—recent empirical analyses suggest that labor turnover has not particularly increased in the United States and United Kingdom despite ongoing globalization—the fear is palpable and prompts antiglobalization sentiments.[3] It therefore suggests that a way to support globalization politically may well be to provide additional adjustment assistance for those laid off in a way that can be linked to such volatility from import competition. I and several others have therefore long suggested that such assistance be provided as the economy is opened up to greater trade.[4]

Accelerating the Pace of Social Change

Then again, the pace at which globalization advances social agendas need not be accepted as satisfactory. After all, the sustained 2 percent growth rate annually during the Meiji era in Japan is no longer considered the "miracle" it was once regarded as. Today, if a developing country registers growth below 6 percent annually, it is regarded as a failure. We have addressed much analysis and effort to securing such an accelerated growth rate. Why not the same with the speed at which we achieve social agendas?

So we need to consider the ways in which we can reinforce the benign social effects of globalization. Thus, child labor is known to decline as economic growth occurs. But what can we do to accelerate its removal? This is where the question of appropriate choice of policy instruments, and international agencies to oversee them, becomes pertinent.

The current conflict is between federations of unions such as the International Confederation of Free Trade Unions (ICFTU) and the American Federation of Labor–Congress of Industrial Organizations (AFL-CIO), on one hand, and those such as the Indian trade unions (whose membership exceeds eight million—not a great deal below that of the AFL-CIO, and a figure that is more striking when one remembers that agricultural labor has not been unionized in India) and key developing-country NGOs such as the Third World Network of Malaysia and the Consumer Unity and Trust Society of India, on the other. The former group wants trade sanctions under WTO auspices through the adoption of the WTO Social Clause, which would make export market access conditional on implementation of labor standards by the member countries to reduce child labor and to achieve other "core" labor rights (defined under the International Labor Organization's Declaration of Fundamental Principles and Rights to Work, and spelled out in Chapter 12). The latter group would rather see non-sanctions-based approaches and the location of the issue at the ILO instead. My own sympathies lie with the latter position, for reasons that are explained in Chapters 10 and 17.[5]

Optimal, Rather Than Maximal, Speed of Globalization

Again, the question of appropriate management of globalization requires attention to the speed at which globalization must be pursued. The difficulties that Russia got into under shock therapy, which was a program of very rapid stabilization and reform measures, are a reminder that the best speed is not necessarily the fastest speed. Or take the prescription to dismantle tariffs. Maximal speed would mean that they are eliminated forthwith. But this may mean that the government falls and the tariffs are reimposed; gradual reduction over a few years would then have been preferable. To use an analogy, if you kick a door open, it may rebound and close instead, whereas gentle pressure on it would ensure that it remains open.

A dramatic example of mismanagement of globalization, which is the focus of Chapter 13, is the imprudent and hasty freeing of capital flows that surely helped to precipitate the Asian financial and economic crisis starting in 1997. Again, if one thinks of immigration, discussed in Chapter 14, it is clear that a rapid and substantial influx of immigrants can precipitate a reaction that may make it extremely difficult to keep the door open. There is clearly prudence in proceeding with caution, even if one considers, as I do, that international migration is an economically and socially benign form of globalization.

And so, in these different ways, globalization must be managed so that its fundamentally benign effects are ensured and reinforced. Without this wise management, it is imperiled. I shall also argue that this management will be better and more effective if the governments, international institutions, corporations, and intellectuals who celebrate and reinforce globalization joined hands with the non-governmental organizations that generally discount and oppose it, creating what UN Secretary General Kofi Annan calls a partnership, achieving what I call a shared success. So before I get on with my principal themes of globalization with a human face and how to make it work better, I turn now to a close look at these NGOs.

4

Non-Governmental Organizations

The questions about globalization today owe their salience, shape, and content to non-governmental organizations, often described as "civil society" groups. What are they? Why have their numbers increased to a level that none had anticipated a quarter century ago? How may their energies and passions be harnessed to produce a yet better globalization?

The Profusion of NGOs

Lester Salamon of Johns Hopkins University has called the spread of NGOs in recent years the global "association revolution":

> The upshot [of this "striking upsurge" in "organized voluntary activity and the creation of private, nonprofit, non-governmental organizations"] is a global third sector: a massive array of self-governing private organizations, not dedicated to distributing profits to shareholders or directors, pursuing public purposes outside the formal apparatus of the state.[1]

Writing in 1994, Salamon estimated the NGOs at levels as high as 275,000 in the United Kingdom alone and roughly 20,000 in the poor countries. Besides, the numbers were growing rapidly: in France, 54,000 "private associations" had been formed just in 1987, whereas 11,000 had been formed during the 1960s.

As it happens, this growth has been sustained and perhaps has even accelerated. Writing in the aftermath of the Seattle riots that disrupted the WTO's ministerial meeting in November and December 1999, *The Economist* reported an estimate of the NGOs in India at a million and of NGOs worldwide at two million: a proportion that could not have been guessed at by the layman from the virtual monopoly of Western-dominated NGOs on the streets and in the corridors of the Seattle meetings.

In fact, the definition of NGOs is both nebulous and shifting. They are commonly defined as any non-profit organization that is independent from the government.[2] Is the sheer fact of organization beyond one person necessary? Should we refuse to admit a lone activist as an NGO? (In fact, I called myself a "single-person NGO" when I was on the platform at a gigantic, bomb-threat-marred Seattle meeting with NGOs on the day prior to the negotiating sessions of the 1999 WTO meeting.) To refuse to do so would militate against the poor countries where organization and finance are in short supply and many NGOs are shoestring operations. I was amused to see at the 1999 WTO meeting the spokesmen for Japan's Chamber of Commerce, the Keidanren, and other business groups introduce their organizations as NGOs, denying implausibly the common view that you had to be a non-profit or representing non-profits to qualify as an NGO.

Given the high visibility of the anti-globalization NGOs today, it is easy to forget that these NGOs represent only a small fraction of the groups that have emerged worldwide. Indeed, the NGOs range over issues and objectives as diverse as outlawing bigamy, changing inheritance laws to enable women to inherit, or eliminating female circumcision as a barbaric relic of the past. Only a few are focused narrowly on the global economy and global issues.

Among globalization-focused NGOs are the Washington-based Economic Policy Institute, which addresses American and European labor unions' fears that trade with poor countries is creating poverty in the rich countries by depressing unskilled workers' wages; the vastly successful Sierra Club, which worries about globalization's effects on the environment; Ralph Nader's group, Public Citizen, which has ceaselessly agitated against globalization and denounced the WTO; and the International Forum on Globalization in the United States. Few but growing in public presence are the poor-country NGOs, the most prominent of which are the Third World Network, whose articulate head is the Malaysian intellectual Martin Khor; the Consumer Unity and Trust Society, the leading NGO in India on trade and globalization issues, run by Pradeep Mehta;[3] and the Center for Science and Environment, in New Delhi, which focuses on environmental issues and has achieved legendary status for the insights and programs that it has put on the world environmental agenda from a poor-country Southern perspective.[4] There are also many lesser groups that have turned up whenever an opportunity presents itself to engage and confront the globalizers.

Why This Meteoric Rise?

This rise of non-profit groups of varying sizes, ranging from low-key, empty-till mom-and-pop outfits to media-savvy, cash-plush, lawyer-infested razzle-dazzle juggernauts, for all kinds of public-interest causes reflects an accentuation of the altruistic activism directed at charitable and social reform causes that is hardly new in many societies.

The Poor Countries

The million NGOs in India as of a few years ago are the inheritors of activism that included individuals and groups that sought reforms in archaic religious traditions. They also benefit from a civic conscious-ness that was aroused by the non-violent movement for India's freedom that led to large numbers of dedicated Indians marching in the streets, some braving the *lathi* charges (the attacks with stinging batons that you see in the opening scenes set in South Africa in the remarkable film *Gandhi*), others going underground, and many turning to working in the villages for rural uplift once independence arrived in 1947.

Notable among those who devoted themselves to social progress were the members of the Servants of India Society, founded almost a century ago in 1905. Having returned from exceptional academic success at En-glish universities such as Oxford and Cambridge, they accepted educa-tional positions at a pittance over a lifetime to further the cause of higher education.[5]

Yet another striking example of altruism comes from the state of Gujarat, from which Gandhi came and whose altruistic traditions he inherited and exploited. A great controversy erupted over the plans to dam the Narmada River in Gujarat (and two other states), a project that involved the construction of thirty major dams and three thousand smaller ones. Many activists objected to the dam project and to the dam-age it would inflict on the communities living on the lands to be sub-merged. Although it was not correct for the activists to argue that resettlement was being ignored, the agitation served to focus extra at-tention on this important aspect of the construction of these dams. In October 2000 the supreme court of India, after six years of agitation and delays, declared itself satisfied with the final resettlement plans and gave the green light to the dam project.[6]

Interestingly, however, modern activism in India, and indeed else-where, reflects two other defining and decisive factors, one technologi-cal, the other educational. The chroniclers of globalization, chief among them the *New York Times* columnist Thomas Friedman, have noted how modern communications technology such as the Internet has enabled NGOs to coalesce quickly into effective movements within and across nations. But this still does not answer the question of why NGOs seeking public good should be springing up in the first place.[7] Surely one answer has to be the unprecedented growth of female education.

I recall sitting down to lunch in the early 1960s with the planner Pitambar Pant on the lawn of his home, in the mild sun of the vanishing Indian winter in the month of January, when the flowering shrubs that are the pride of the bureaucratic bungalows are pregnant with signs of new life. I had started teaching in Delhi University, having just left Pant's planning office, and noticed that women students seemed to outweigh the men in my classes. This was symptomatic of the growing numbers of women going for higher education. Pant and I wondered where they would all go. We thought they would be doctors, bureaucrats, politicians, lawyers, scientists, and much else. But we did not think that, animated by altruism while also informed and equipped to pursue it by their education, they would become both leaders and followers in the immense tide of NGOs now seeking to change Indian society in progressive directions.

So we find that the mantle of social activism in India, long worn mostly by men, has now fallen on the shoulders mostly of women. The ecofeminist Vandana Shiva is the most prominent in the Western media, but she is just one of a multitude. Indeed, doing good has become so much the thing to do in India that where the parents of a young man once might have bid for a bride by offering riches or a green card for immigration into the United States through marriage, the joke today on the Indian subcontinent is that they must offer the bride her own NGO![8]

This fits in with the pattern I observe in the United States. Interact here with the environmental, human rights, and other NGOs, as I often do, and mostly you run into dedicated and impassioned women. Alice Tepper Marlin of Social Accountability International, Sidney Jones of Human Rights Watch, and Lori Wallach of Public Citizen are only the more visible among the many women who now, if I may mix metaphors, man the barricades in these battles.

Civil Society, Anti-Politics and Parallel Politics

The factor that has driven the growth of civil society in the East European countries, on the other hand, is the anti-politics that intellectuals such as Václav Havel of the former Czechoslovakia and György Konrád of Hungary defined and cultivated as the most effective weapon for democratic progress in regimes governed by communists.

Their writings reflected recognition of the impossibility of forming a meaningful democratic opposition within the Communist Party. New strategies were necessary. The dissident intellectuals opted for parallel politics at the level of individual morality and action, outside the framework of (corrupted) politics. As Havel wrote in his classic essay "The Power of the Powerless," which became the great samizdat document of the Czech and Polish dissidents:

> In societies under the post-totalitarian [i.e., communist as contrasted with a conventional totalitarian dictatorial] system, all political life in the traditional sense has been eliminated. People have no opportunity to express themselves politically in public, let alone to organize politically. The gap that results is filled by ideological ritual. In such a situation, people's interest in political matters naturally dwindles and independent political thought, in so far as it exists at all, is seen by the majority as unrealistic, far-fetched, a kind of self-indulgent game, hopelessly distant from their everyday concerns . . . because it is on the one hand entirely utopian and on the other hand extraordinarily dangerous, in view of the unusual vigor with which any move in that direction is persecuted by the regime.
>
> Yet even in such societies, individuals and groups of people exist who do not abandon politics as a vocation and who, in one way or another, strive to think independently, to express themselves and in some cases even to organize politically, because that is a part of their attempt to live within the truth.
>
> The fact that these people exist and work is itself immensely important and worthwhile. Even in the worst of times, they maintain the continuity of political thought.[9]

This visualization of the power of parallel politics, brilliantly conceived in the totalitarian context and reminiscent of the great Indian leader Mahatma Gandhi's similar emphasis on morality, truth, and conscience as weapons to be deployed under foreign rule, was evidently successful in pitting values against tanks. But it ran into an obvious problem once communism had collapsed. How could anti-politics work when the politics had become democratic and, for the freed countries of Eastern Europe, now was "ours"?

As the new regimes began to struggle with democratic governance, the politics of values was no longer effective. It was replaced by politics defined by democratic processes such as elections and parliaments. In turn, politics was now dominated by ideas and interests that dictated the realities of choices on issues such as the policies and institutions to be devised to guide economic transition. These were precisely the areas where the anti-politics of the inherited civil society dissidents was at a loss. Toppling governments is different from running them, especially when the dislodged government has left gigantic tasks at the new government's doorstep.

Konrád (through his writings), like Gandhi (through his public actions), stayed out of conventional politics and the high office that it could have brought, content with defining the moral ethos within which the new politics might operate. On the other hand, Václav Havel accepted the presidency of Czechoslovakia. But he would lose out to Václav Klaus, who led the group of politicians whose hands were at the helm and who had specific blueprints to offer regarding the economic reforms that had to be the bedrock of the new regime's success. Klaus might well have said, "Talk comes cheap; it's the policies, stupid!"

But if the dissident intellectuals were wrong to think that the politics of values could displace and replace the politics of democratic processes and interests, was it possible instead that the civil society they advocated, founded on apolitical action and a parallel politics (as distinct from anti-politics), could now have a valuable role to play? This indeed turned out to be the case.

Thus while the anti-politics of Havel and Konrád, as the affirmation of values by autonomous individuals in antithesis to the state, had yielded to the new reality of democratic regimes, the notion that a parallel politics should complement rather than substitute for the electoral democratic political process took its place.

Civil society, in the form of associations of citizens organized to articulate and advance progressive societal agendas, gradually became the focal point of the dissident intellectuals' attention. In debate with Václav Klaus on the role of NGOs in the new Czechoslovakia on May 25, 1994, Václav Havel argued that the post-communist society would be one

> with a large measure of self-government, where citizens assume their role in public affairs. Citizens must shoulder their share of responsibility for social development. Civil society is a social space that fosters the feeling of solidarity between people and love for one's community. There are various minority needs that a representative democracy cannot, in its present form, safeguard. Civil society encourages ordinary people to participate in government, thereby strengthening relations between citizens and their state.[10]

And György Konrád argued in the same vein that, "given the rise of the state . . . the voice of civil society is needed more than ever"[11] and that

> the survival of humanity, government by law, respect for individuals and minorities, freedom of thought, and moderation of state power remain the most important tasks of civil society.[12]

Slow to take off, because four decades of communist rule have discouraged citizens from high-risk associational activity, groups such as Hungary's Democratic Charter that constitute the parallel politics of civil society have grown steadily in Eastern Europe. Thus Salamon has written:

> [The growth of civil society networks] has only accelerated since the overthrow of the communist governments. As of 1992, several thousand foundations were registered with governmental authorities in Poland. In Hungary, 6,000 foundations and 11,000 associations had been registered by mid-1992.[13]

This explosion can be documented also for Russia, Bulgaria, and other former socialist countries.

Given Václav Havel's own intellectual history and political preference for parallel politics, it is not surprising that he would look kindly on the NGOs that converged on Prague for the IMF–World Bank annual meetings in September 1999. He arranged for the heads of these institutions to meet with prominent NGOs such as Jubilee 2000 even as his riot police clashed with the demonstrators on the streets.

Transition to Global NGOs

The transition from national to global or "transnational" NGOs is a phenomenon with complex causes, of course.[14] The sense, as also the reality, that the world economy has been steadily integrating has led to a twofold phenomenon: the older domestically oriented NGOs have felt, in some instances, that their efficacy requires international coordination and hence networking with others sharing these beliefs; and new NGOs with a global focus have sprung up for similar reasons.

In both cases, the fact that communication today via e-mail and the Internet makes organization and coordinated civil action so much easier than when Mahatma Gandhi, for instance, organized the civil disobedience movement in India in the 1930s and 1940s surely has played its part. But the technology has only been an enabling instrument; the energizing impulses, it has often been argued, are informed by "principled ideas or values."[15]

In fact, this self-description and flagging of virtue lie at the heart of the reason why these groups have flourished despite the free-rider problem that the economist Mancur Olson discovered as a barrier to organization by a diverse and diffused set of actors. According to Olson, "concentrated" producers (who tend to be few in number) would be able to band together to pursue their common interests, and hence push for trade protection. But the "diffused" consumers (who tend to be many in number) would not, because each would think that her vote did not matter and that it would be frustrated by the free riders, the consumers who expect to profit from her vote while making no commitment of their own. In the case of the NGO movement, where organization has flourished, this free-rider problem is transcended by the glue that the values orientation provides, by the sense of solidarity and commitment that follows from the shared presumption that the strength of numbers and activism alone can guarantee success in their cause. Thus while diffused consumers may succumb to the free-rider problem, and seem traditionally to have done so where their own economic welfare is involved, this does not happen when citizens are motivated by focused altruism instead.[16]

Making Globalization Work

I have only sketched what seem to be the principal reasons why NGOs have become immensely important today. Their views that economic globalization constitutes a threat to our social well-being need therefore to be examined with care, as I will do in Part II, starting with the next chapter. But, since they represent a phenomenon that is as demanding of our attention today as the continuing economic globalization, and since their objectives will be shown in this book to be advanced (rather than diminished, as they fear) by such globalization, it should be possible to join hands to advance the same objectives more deeply through the design of appropriate governance, which I will turn to in Part IV.

But, in joining hands, I must caution that the functioning of the NGOs has raised certain questions that need to be addressed.

Halos Should Not Be Shields

Just as we insist on transparency and regulation for other agents and actors in society, it is important to see that these demands cannot be evaded by NGOs, especially if we are to work with them in the public domain. The tendency on the part of some of them to turn their halos into shields is unwise and unacceptable.

The NGOs that claim the moral high ground because they profess a moral commitment need not be taken at their word.[17] Just recall Charles Dickens' compelling portrait of Mr. Pecksniff in *Martin Chuzzlewit*. Comfortable in his professed empathy for humanity, and even christening his daughters Mercy and Charity, Pecksniff turns out to be a scoundrel in truth. But if Dickens portrays the hypocrisy of this "humanitarian philosopher" in garish colors, the verse of W. H. Auden alerts us to the need for critical scrutiny in a gentler tone:

> Base words are uttered only by the base
> And can for such at once be understood,
> But noble platitudes: —ah, there's a case
> Where the most careful scrutiny is needed
> To tell a voice that's genuinely good
> From one that's base but merely has succeeded.[18]

Many independent observers, including those who are NGO-friendly, have therefore argued that the transparency many of the NGOs ask from others needs to be extended to them as well. The *New Republic* published a scathing criticism of Lori Wallach, the head of Global Trade Watch for Ralph Nader's Public Citizen, alleging that she would not let Mike Dolan, a staff member who was active in Seattle, talk to its reporter, Ryan Lizza, about the financing of Public Citizen's anti-trade activities by the infamous protectionist Roger Milliken.[19] Milliken is the textile magnate from South Carolina who has over the years financed several of the most rabid conservatives.[20] When I met Wallach at Davos in 2001, I asked her why Public Citizen would not reveal the names of its contributors. She responded with arcane legalisms such as the right to make anonymous donations, none of them insurmountable in my view if Public Citizen wished to put principles such as transparency before the pursuit of profits. I use the word deliberately, as profits are not all that different from contributions insofar as they both imply the acquisition of cold cash.

If transparency is not routinely practiced by NGOs, it would be nothing short of a miracle if NGOs did not produce their own counterparts of the occasional corruptions of some multinationals such as Enron. Lest anyone thinks that NGOs are exempt from the laws of human nature, recall the lapses by one of the most venerated non-profit organizations, the Vatican—consider its historical record on anti-Semitism or its collaborations, first with the conquistadors in South America and next with the oppressive dictatorial regimes that afflicted the region until very recently—and by charities such as the United Way (whose CEO turned out to be not quite a moral example to the rest of us) and the American Red Cross (whose practice of secretly reassigning funds gathered in a disaster to its general war chest, practicing a deceptiveness that amounts to fraud, came to light after the outpouring of charitable contributions following September 11).

Nor are the NGOs and their rank and file beyond practicing the occasional lie, much like the corporations, politicians, and bureaucrats they excoriate. Consider the attempt by anti-whaling groups at demonizing Norway and its prime minister Gro Brundtland, a great environmentalist and later head of the World Health Organization, over Norway's carefully limited expansion of whale fishing; the deliberately misleading attacks on conservationists who had the temerity to suggest a rational way of culling and managing elephants; and IKEA's discovery that a German film about the use of exploitative child labor by its suppliers was simply faked. These are only among the most disturbing of such activities, all presumably in the name of a good cause.

Another recent example is even more striking because it was perhaps based not on outright fraud but rather on the desire to inflate numbers to motivate remedial action. Let me quote extensively from reporter Norimitsu Onishi's story in the *New York Times* on "miscounting child deaths and slaves for programs and politics." Onishi was writing about the charges that child workers were forced to work in Ivory Coast's cocoa plantations:

> Many accounts in British and American news media last year spoke breathlessly of 15,000 child slaves . . . producing the chocolate you eat.
>
> The number first appeared in Malian newspapers, citing the Unicef office in Mali. But Unicef's Mali office had never researched the issue of forced child laborers in Ivory Coast. The Unicef office in Ivory Coast, which had, concluded that it was impossible to determine the number.
>
> Still, reported often enough, the number was gladly accepted by some private organizations, globalization opponents seeking a fight with Nestlé and Hershey, and some journalists. . . .
>
> This month, the results of the first extensive survey of child labor in cocoa plantations in Ivory Coast and three other African nations were released by the International Institute of Tropical Agriculture, a nonprofit, multinational organization that works in Africa. The survey . . . found that almost all children working in cocoa fields were children of the plantation owners, not forced laborers.
>
> As for child workers [most of them ages fifteen to seventeen] unrelated to the plantation owners. . . . Ninety percent of the children, the study says, knew the intermediary or broker who hired them for the plantation work. . . .
>
> "None reported being forced against their will to leave their home abode . . ." Jim Gockwoski, who is based in Cameroon and has worked in African agriculture for a decade, added: "Anyone that's lived in Africa knows kids help out on the farms, probably more in developing countries than developed ones. But even in the United States—my own background is a farming background—we grew up helping on the farm. Everyone was surprised when all the wild figures—15,000 trafficked children—were being thrown around.[21]

Onishi's observation, perhaps a trifle too cynical, is that "politics is sometimes more influential than precision. . . . Since they were released early this month, the institute's findings have received little attention—perhaps only 1 percent of what the 15,000 figure received."

So we must confront the unpleasant reality that NGOs are not exempt from the human failings that characterize the corporate CEOs that they often militate against. It is therefore hard not to agree with the recent conclusion by a United Nations report, prepared by the consultancy Sustainability, that international NGOs "must become more accountable if they are to retain their influence and position of trust."[22]

Cultural and Political Context

It is also necessary to recognize that NGOs, no matter what universalism they profess, are grounded in national political and cultural contexts. This constrains their universalism when it comes to choice of causes and campaigns. Let me take just two examples.

The uproar that followed in Europe over the ruling by the WTO's Dispute Settlement Mechanism in favor of the United States against the European Union's prohibitions on production and imports of hormone-fed beef (discussed in Chapters 9 and 11) led to little sympathetic protest by the otherwise articulate U.S.-based NGOs.[23] To my knowledge, there were none of the usual full-page $50,000 advertisements denouncing the WTO in the nation's leading newspapers. It is hard to believe that the U.S.-based anti-WTO NGOs were not mindful of the fact that it was an issue that affected the U.S. economy; rather, it seems plausible that they had decided, perhaps unconsciously, to avoid getting into a bruising campaign that would cost them some goodwill within the United States, where they are based.

Then again, when the WTO found, correctly again as it happens, against the United States for providing subsidies to exporters operating through offshore subsidiaries, the U.S.-based NGOs should have rejoiced. After all, Ralph Nader, the great scourge of the corporations, has long railed against "corporate welfare." Alas, one did not hear a squeak of protest, not even a squeal of delight, from him or other anti-trade, anti-WTO activists! Or did the deafening and nationalistic protests of the U.S. media drown out the sound of champagne bottles being opened by him and other activists?

Rich- and Poor-Country NGOs

The problem of the cultural context is acute also for another reason. Globalization involves issues of the balance of power, and hence also of democratic governance, between groups and between nations. The NGOs-multinationals divide is therefore crisscrossed by a within-NGOs divide that reflects a poor-rich country divide. The divide between NGOs does not get any media or political attention in the rich countries. But it needs to be recognized if the institutional changes we contemplate to improve globalization are not going to be those devised (in what many in the poor countries are inclined to denounce as the "new neo-imperialism") by the powerful groups, including the NGOs of the rich nations, which have their own cultural and political biases.[24]

In fact, while the rich-country NGOs think of themselves as providing "countervailing power" against the far richer corporations in their midst, it is ironic that some of the truly small NGOs in the rich countries themselves have voiced their fears over "unequal" competition from the far bigger and richer NGOs. A hilarious spoof is found in the caricatured report in mid-2001 of "calls today for multinational pro-anarchy pressure groups to be investigated for monopolistic practices after the NW3 branch of the Radical Left Movement for Socialist Revolution was disbanded due to lack of interest."[25] The report goes on to say that the group's spokesperson, Nigel Wilkinson, "believes that global anarchy movements such as the ones responsible for the G7 riots in Seattle . . . are to blame for forcing out smaller, independent operations like his. . . . These large American anti-capitalist movements have effectively taken over the militant scene in this country." As if this were not amusing enough, the report goes on to say: "Wilkinson has seen his group's membership dwindle by almost 70 percent over the last year from a peak of three members to just one—himself."

More seriously, however, anyone who visits the poor countries cannot fail to see the contrasts in funding and organization that divide the poor- and rich-country NGOs. The contrast in the offices and budgets of the Sierra Club in the United States and the Center for Science and Technology in India is a vivid example. The poor-country NGOs, with their shoestring budgets, feel overwhelmed by the hugely more prosperous NGOs of the rich countries. In fact, even the limited funding that the poor country NGOs receive is rarely from their own countries' governments, and mostly from the foundations that are themselves located in the rich countries, whereas the rich-country NGOs occasionally get funded by the rich-country governments, while appearing to many in the public domain as independent agents incorruptible and uncorrupted by the moneys they seek and receive.

The contrast between the rich- and poor-country NGOs was brought home to me also by the work I did for this book on different unions' attitudes toward the inclusion of the Social Clause in the WTO. Recall that the Social Clause is a persistent political demand of the AFL-CIO but one that is passionately opposed by the Indian unions. I visited the leaders of nearly all the labor unions in India. Their offices were straight out of the nineteenth century, if not earlier: modest, sparsely furnished, run by leaders who had no ostentation and limited budgets reflecting the small membership dues in a poor country. But then take the AFL-CIO building, across from the celebrated Hay-Adams Hotel, which faces the White House across a lawn and Pennsylvania Avenue. When I was attending a conference at the U.S. Chamber of Commerce building, I was told that it was near the Hay-Adams. So I walked across the street to this imposing and sumptuous structure, only to find that it was the AFL-CIO building!

The salience of this rich-poor divide is evident also when the poor countries object to what seem like obviously good proposals, such as the acceptance of amicus curiae briefs (which in the United States can be filed by qualified organizations and individuals who are not direct parties to a case). Such briefs by NGOs are seen by the poor countries as giving the rich countries two oars to put in the disputed waters. When these NGOs back U.S. legislation that is opposed by the poor countries (as in the earlier-cited shrimp-turtle case at the WTO), their actions are seen as reflective of their own countries' positions, and their substantial resources, financial and legal, are seen as making this threat even more palpable. We cannot ignore, without sowing seeds of discord, the relative size and resources of NGOs in rich and poor countries, and the inference of the bias it builds into defining the globalization agendas and priorities in favor of rich-country definitions of public interest.

Recognizing a problem often prompts its resolution. NGOs are increasingly aware of these shortcomings, and signs of change are already visible. Their role as partners in creating and sustaining appropriate governance is therefore a task that can be pursued with confidence.

II

Globalization's Human Face:
Trade and Corporations

5

Poverty: Enhanced or Diminished?

In Act III, Scene 4 of *King Lear*, the proud old king, transported profoundly by the tragedy that relentlessly unfolds and engulfs him, kneels to pray as a storm rages around him, to regret his neglect of the wretched of the earth:

> Poor naked wretches, whereso'er you are,
> That bide the pelting of this pitiless storm,
> How shall your houseless heads and unfed sides,
> Your looped and windowed raggedness, defend you
> From seasons such as these? O, I have ta'en
> Too little care of this!

and then to cry for empathy and justice:

> Take physic, pomp;
> Expose thyself to feel what wretches feel,
> That thou mayst shake the superflux to them,
> And show the heavens more just.

How well Shakespeare's Lear seems to capture our present situation! Echoing Lear's sentiments half a millennium later, nearly 150 prime ministers and presidents of the world's nations converged in September 2000 for the UN's Millennium Summit, embracing poverty removal as their goal. They resolved to "halve, by the year 2015, the proportion of the world's people whose income is less than one dollar a day and the proportion of people who suffer from hunger."[1]

They were joined at the time by countless NGOs that had congregated for parallel events, by the bureaucrats that head the international institutions (such as the World Bank and the UN Development Programme) charged with developmental objectives, and by the liberal media.

Of course, the acute sensitivity to poverty and the moral commitment to reduce it are nothing new. It would be strange indeed if the many enlightened leaders and intellectuals of these nations had not already resolved to wage a war on poverty half a century ago. That, in fact, was the very focus of the leaders in the many independence movements that resulted in extensive decolonization at the end of the Second World War. Let me just cite India's first prime minister, Pandit Jawaharlal Nehru, a Fabian by temperament and training from his student days in Cambridge. Writing in 1946, he recalled the resolve of the prewar National Planning Committee of Mahatma Gandhi's Indian National Congress to

> insure an adequate standard of living for the masses; in other words, to get rid of the appalling poverty of the people . . . [to] insure an irreducible minimum standard for everybody.[2]

Writing some decades earlier, even the conservative Winston Churchill, who had observed acutely a shift in public opinion in the decade of the 1880s, had remarked:

> The great victories had been won. All sorts of lumbering tyrannies had been toppled over. Authority was everywhere broken. Slaves were free. Conscience was free. Trade was free. But hunger and squalor were also free and the people demanded something more than liberty.[3]

Indeed, few in the twentieth century have not had poverty on their minds and a passion to remove it in their hearts.

It's the Policy, Stupid

So, the compelling question is altogether different as we consider the issue of poverty as the new century, and even the new millennium, begins: what do we know now, after five decades of experimentation, that will make our efforts even more effective? In short, drawing on former President Clinton's words, we must assert: "It's the policy, stupid." But then, which policy?

And that returns us to the central question: does globalization, in the specific form of freer trade (and inward direct foreign investment, addressed directly in Chapter 12), imply a closer integration into the world economy, part of that poverty-reducing policy, or are wisdom and knowledge on the side of those who claim the contrary? As it happens, the proponents of globalization have it right.

Two types of supporting argumentation can be produced: shrewd observation and scientific evidence. A brilliant observer such as the Swedish journalist Tomas Larsson in his new book, *The Race to the Top: The*

Real Story of Globalization, has written from his firsthand experiences in Asia and described with telling stories and portraits from the ground how poverty has been licked by globalization. Let me cite one example that stayed with me long after I had read the book:

> [B]etting on poultry [in cockfighting] wasn't what I had in mind when I came to Navanakorn, an industrial area in the northern outskirts of Bangkok. I'd taken the afternoon off from the UNCTAD conference to find out for myself what globalization looks like up close. The combined chicken farm and gambling den is right next door to a Lucent factory that manufactures microelectronics components—the factory floor of the broadband revolution and the knowledge economy.
>
> The work is done in large square buildings that look like giant sugar cubes. At the entrance stands a shrine honoring Brahma with yellow garlands and small wooden elephants. . . . Inside are thousands of Thai laborers.
>
> "When they started, the workers came on foot. Then they got motorbikes. Now they drive cars," says the rooster guardian. "Everyone wants to work there, but it is hard to get in."
>
> . . . On my way back into town I amble through the industrial estate in search of a ride. A shift is ending. Thousands of women (for it is mostly women who work in the foreign-owned electronics factories) pour through the factory gates. I pass restaurants, drugstores, supermarkets, jewelers, tailors, film shops, vendors of automatic washing machines.[4]

The scientific analysis of the effect of trade on poverty is even more compelling. It has centered on a two-step argument: that trade enhances growth, and that growth reduces poverty.

These propositions have been supported by many economists and policy makers of very different persuasions over the years. Thus as long ago as 1940 the famous Cambridge economist Sir Dennis Robertson characterized trade as an "engine of growth," a colorful phrase that has caught on in the scholarly literature on trade and growth.

But the argument that growth would reduce poverty can be found in Adam Smith himself, as when he wrote that when society is "advancing to further acquisition . . . the condition of the laboring poor, of the great body of the people, seems to be the happiest."[5] And in modern times, Jawaharlal Nehru wrote just as India was about to become independent and all minds were turning to the enormous task of reducing India's massive poverty through planning:

> [To] insure an irreducible minimum standard for everybody, the national income had to be greatly increased. . . . We calculated that a really progressive standard of living would necessitate the increase of wealth by 500 or 600 per cent. That was however too big a jump for us, and we aimed at a 200 or 300 per cent increase within ten years.[6]

Indeed, this connection between growth and poverty reduction was built into the earliest five-year plans, starting from 1951: they tried to accelerate the growth of the Indian economy while remaining focused on poverty reduction as a general target. But it was made yet sharper by the leading Indian planners in the early 1960s when they zeroed in on the target of raising the income of the bottom 30 percent of India's population to a minimum level within a specified period.

It fell to me to work on this problem since I had just returned from Oxford and was the economist assigned to assist the proponents in the Indian Planning Commission of this plan to raise the minimum incomes of the poor. I assembled the income distribution data that were available at the time; their quality was pretty awful because of inadequate statistical expertise in most countries, nor were they standardized for international comparability. But a quick scan seemed to suggest that there was no magic bullet: countries seemed to have somewhat similar income distributions regardless of their political and economic cast. So the primary inference I made was that if there was no way to significantly affect the share of the pie going to the bottom 30 percent, the most important thing was to grow the pie. In short, my advice—what I might call with some immodesty the Bhagwati hypothesis and prescription—was that growth had to be the *principal* (but, as I argue below, not the only) strategy for raising the incomes, and hence consumption and living standards, of the poor.

In this view, growth was not a passive, trickle-down strategy for helping the poor. It was an active, pull-up strategy instead. It required a government that would energetically take steps to accelerate growth, through a variety of policies, including building infrastructure such as roads and ports and attracting foreign funds. By supplementing meager domestic savings, the foreign funds would increase capital formation and hence jobs. Those of us who were present at the creation therefore dismiss as nothing but ignorance and self-serving nonsense the popular and populist propositions that, first, growth was regarded as an end in itself and poverty removal was forgotten until a new, socially conscious generation of economists who worried about poverty arrived on the scene, and second, that the strategy of growth in order to reduce poverty was a laissez-faire, hands-off, passive strategy.

Growth and Poverty

We were also aware that growth had to be differentiated. Some types of growth would help the poor more than others. For instance, as argued more fully below, an outward trade orientation helped the Far Eastern economies in the postwar years to export labor-intensive goods; this added to employment and reduced poverty rapidly. In India, the emphasis on autarky and on capital-intensive projects reduced both growth rates and increase in the demand for labor, so the impact on poverty was minimal.

Then again, growth can paradoxically immiserize a country and hence its poor as well (unless corrective policies are undertaken simultaneously). In 1958, I published a paper on what I called "immiserizing growth," where I demonstrated that an economy could become worse off even though it had grown through accumulating capital or improving productivity.[7] The argument was straightforward. Consider Bangladesh, which exports a lot of jute. Growth in the shape of more jute production, resulting in greater exports, would depress the international price of jute. Suppose then that one hundred additional bales of jute have been produced. If the world price of jute remains the same at $50 a bale, Bangladesh's export earnings go up by $5,000. But if the world price falls such that Bangladesh's total export earnings fall drastically as the additional hundred bales are exported, the total earnings of Bangladeshi jute exports could fall by as much as $6,000. This loss of $6,000 (from what economists call, in jargon, the fall in the Bangladeshi terms of trade) then outweighs the $5,000 gain from growth. Immiseration is the result.

This paradox earned me a lot of attention, partly because economists love paradoxes; whoever got attention for saying the obvious?[8] But partly it was also because many developing countries feared that international markets were tight in exactly the way I had hypothesized in arriving at the paradox of immiserizing growth. This was either because of economic reasons such as market saturation or because of protectionism that would choke off markets as soon as more exports materialized. My theory of immiserizing growth showed exactly how crippling that could be to a developing country's growth prospects.[9] The way to avoid this adverse outcome, of course, is to diversify away from jute production and exports.[10] So when you can depress your export prices by selling more because you are a major supplier, restrain yourself; push in other directions. A suitable policy can always nip the immiserizing growth paradox in the bud, ensuring that growth does amount to an increase in the size of the pie.

But then consider simpler and more obvious, but no less compelling, examples of immiseration that follows from *others'*, as against one's own, growth. Think of the green revolution, the evocative phrase used to describe the arrival and use of new and vastly more productive varieties of wheat and rice that had been invented with support from the Ford and Rockefeller Foundations and for which Dr. Norman Borlaug got the Nobel prize for peace in 1970.[11] When the new seeds arrived, the farmers who benefited were naturally either those who had access to credit because they had assets and hence adequate collateral, or those who could afford to be risk takers with new technology because they had a cushion of wealth to fall back on in case things did not work out. So there you have the divide that attends every transition to a major new technology: rarely do all march in step like a Roman legion. But then imagine what happens when some innovate and increase their production so that the price falls, while others have not innovated and their stagnant output now is sold at a lower price. Those who lag behind do not merely fall behind; they fall by the wayside, struck by a blow not of their making. Thus many feared that the green revolution would usher in the red revolution! But this did not come to pass. Why?

For one thing, policies were devised to ensure that immiseration of the laggards generally did not occur. Agricultural prices did not fall because of increasing demand, which resulted from investments that added new jobs and incomes. The government in India also actively used price support schemes, providing a floor to possible declines in prices. And as for the different fear that landless labor would be replaced by the higher yields, the reality turned out to be far more agreeable. The joint use of new seeds and irrigation led to multiple cropping; this resulted in an increased demand for labor on farms, prompting improvement in wages. Yet another possible source of immiseration with new seeds is the emergence of new pests and diseases that can be destructive of yields and of farming more generally. In the Indian case again, the government was careful to establish a substantial scientific support system that contained these dangerous possibilities.

So appropriate policies will always enable us to profit from growth and to moderate, even prevent, unpleasant outcomes for the poor. While some governments have not been careful (as discussed in Chapter 16 on coping with the potential downsides of globalization), other governments have not been blind to these problems. Other interesting issues, however, must be addressed.

First, recall that different types of growth (e.g., growth paths resulting from reliance on heavy industry as against light industry, or those favoring capital-intensive as against labor-intensive investments) affect the poor differentially. Many economists in the early years of development planning favored a growth strategy that relied on massive import substitution in heavy industry (such as steel and electrical machinery) rather than on the exports of light manufactures (such as toys and garments), on the choice of high capital intensity in production techniques, and on the proliferation of public enterprises (beyond utilities) that turned out to be white elephants making gargantuan losses. Such a development strategy undermined the cause of the poor by reducing growth and by delinking it from increased demand for the low-grade labor that constitutes the bulk of the poor.[12] If growth had been outward-oriented, with labor-intensive goods and light manufactures being exported in far greater quantities, it would have increased the demand for labor and helped the poor far more.[13] So freer trade would have promoted growth that was even more effective in reducing poverty through the salutary effects of increased demand for unskilled labor.

Second, what can we do to improve the access of the poor to expanding opportunities in a growing economy? It is not always true that growth will pull up the poor into gainful employment. Even though growth opens the doors, the traction in the legs of the poor may not be enough to carry them through these doors. For example, tribal areas in India where poverty is acute may not be connected sufficiently to the mainstream economy where growth occurs. And we know from inner-city problems in the United States that the supply response of its youth to jobs downtown may be minimal unless we also address structural problems such as the allure of drugs, transportation bottlenecks, and the lack of role models in broken and single-parent families struggling against terrible odds. I should add that those who grow up in the inner city also need to acquire the carriage and demeanor that are critical for service sector jobs downtown—though you need them less in the kitchen, where you flip hamburgers, than in the front, where you face the customers. This reminds me of the economist Alan Blinder's sophisticated spoof of the tendency by us economists to reduce everything to economic terms: he produced an economic analysis of why chefs have bad teeth and waiters have good teeth!

But if you know the history of developmental economics, then you also know that the earliest development-policy makers tried hard to improve the access of the poor to growing incomes by making it easier for them to borrow to invest. This was done in India by forcing banks to open branches in rural areas and by asking them to lower collateral requirements. The problem with this policy was that it often resulted in bad debts. A breakthrough, however, came with the invention of microcredit programs, which go down to the very poor. The problem was solved by lending very small sums to a number of poor clients for tiny investments that improved their ability to earn a livelihood, and by letting each borrower (or "agent," as economists call her) effectively monitor other borrowers. This, as against the lender (or "principal") trying to monitor the borrower, works wonders: it reduces bad debts dramatically.[14]

But an alternative innovative idea for improving the poor's access to investment has come from the economist Hernando de Soto in his book *The Mystery of Capital*.[15] Essentially, de Soto argues not that we ought to forgo collateral from the poor, but that we must recognize that they often have a huge amount of capital in the form of land and other property. The problem, de Soto says, is that these assets do not enjoy property rights and the associated rule of law that protects and enforces those rights. This prevents the poor from being able to collateralize these assets in order to borrow and invest. De Soto has made this case beautifully and convincingly, citing the nineteenth-century American experience. There is no doubt that his prescription must be tried.

We must also improve the poor's access to investment by making sure that bureaucrats are replaced by markets wherever possible. As I remarked earlier, the anti-market protesters do not adequately appreciate that, as has been documented by numerous development economists who have studied both the working of controls and the rise of corruption in developing countries, far too many bureaucrats impose senseless restrictions just to collect bribes or to exercise power.[16] Letting markets function is therefore often an egalitarian allocation mechanism. I can do no better if I am to persuade skeptics than to tell here the bon mot that Sir Arthur Lewis, the Nobel laureate in development economics from St. Lucia (which has the distinction of having produced two Nobel laureates, the other being the poet Walcott) shared with me.[17] Lewis was adviser to the centrist, intellectually inclined Hugh Gaitskell in the British Labor Party. When he met Thomas Balogh, a radical economic adviser to British prime minister Harold Wilson, he told him: "Tommy, the difference between your socialism and mine is that when you think of yourself as a socialist, you think of yourself as behind the counter; when I think of myself as a socialist, I think of myself as being in front of it."[18]

But the ability of the poor to access the growth process and to share in the prosperity depends at least as much on their ability to get their voices heard in the political process. Without a voice, it is highly unlikely that they will get appropriate and effective legislation.[19] Democracy gives the poor precisely that voice, but it obviously works well only when there are political alternatives instead of a single-party state. NGOs provide yet another support mechanism for the poor; and the Indian supreme court took great strides in the 1980s and 1990s by giving legal standing to social action groups (as the Indian NGOs are called) to bring action before the courts on behalf of the poor.[20]

Let me add that growth is also a powerful mechanism that brings to life social legislation aimed at helping the poor and peripheral groups. Thus, rights and benefits for women may be guaranteed by legislation that prohibits dowry, proscribes polygamy, mandates primary school enrollment for all children (including girls), and much else. But it will often amount to a hill of beans unless a growing economy gives women the economic independence to walk out and even to sue at the risk of being discarded. A battered wife who cannot find a new job is less likely to take advantage of legislation that says a husband cannot beat his wife. An impoverished parent is unlikely, no matter what the legislation says, to send a child to school if the prospect of finding a job is dismal because of a stagnant economy. In short, empowerment, as it is called today—a fancy word for what we development economists have long understood and written about—proceeds from both political democracy and economic prosperity, and it is a powerful tool for aiding the poor.

Finally, we need to go beyond just having incomes of the poor grow. Growing incomes would do little good if frittered away, for instance. So, drawing on a 1987 lecture I gave on poverty and public policy, let me say that we have a final set of problems that need to be addressed once income has been provided:

> First, as sociologists of poverty have long known, the poor may spend their incomes on frills rather than on food. As the Japanese proverb goes, to each according to his taste; some prefer nettles. Perhaps you have heard of the seamen's folklore that recounts the story of the sailor who inherited a fortune, spent a third on women, a third on gin, and "frittered away" the rest.
>
> In fact, there is now considerable econometric evidence . . . that supports the commonsense view that increases in income do not automatically result in nutritional improvement even for very poor and malnourished populations.[21] Their high income elasticities of expenditure on food reflect a strong demand for the nonnutritive attributes of food (such as taste, aroma, status and variety), suggesting strongly that income generation will not automatically translate into better nutrition.
>
> . . . Should we actively intervene so that the poor are seduced into better fulfillment of what we regard as their basic needs? I do [think so]. In fact, I see great virtue in quasi-paternalistic moves to induce, by supply and taste-shifting policy measures, more nutrient food intake, greater use of clean water, among other things, by the poor. In thus compromising the principle of unimpeded and uninfluenced choice, for the poor and not for the others, evidently I adopt the moral-philosophical position that I do not care if the rich are malnourished from feeding on too many cakes but do if the poor are malnourished from buying too little bread, when their incomes can buy them both proper nourishment if only they were to choose to do so. In this, I am in the ethical company of Sofya (Sonia) Marmeladova in Dostoevsky's *Crime and Punishment* who, in turning to prostitution to support her destitute mother, sacrifices virtue for a greater good.[22]

Of course, the question then also arises as to the distribution of the consumption, even when adequate and desirable, *within the household*. This obviously takes us right into the question of gender discrimination, a question whose relationship to globalization is discussed in Chapter 6. This is, of course, an active issue today, with the rise of feminism.[23]

Trade and Growth

But then, was our earlier optimism about the benign relationship between trade and growth also justified despite the fact that one could readily imagine circumstances where, instead of helping growth, trade could harm or even bypass growth? Indeed, economists can, and do, readily build formal models to derive these unpleasant possibilities.[24] We need, however, to know *empirically* what happens in practice. And empirical evidence supports the optimism.

First, consider the late nineteenth century. Historians of this period have often thought that protection, not free trade, was associated with high growth. Paul Bairoch, in the *Cambridge Economic History of Europe*, has argued that "protectionism [went with] economic growth and expansion of trade; liberalism [went with] stagnation in both."[25] Recently, the economic historians Kevin O'Rourke and Jeff Williamson have reinforced this impression by deriving a statistical association, through running what statisticians call regressions, between economic growth and import tariffs from 1875 to 1914.[26]

But the later work of Douglas Irwin has refuted that proposition.[27] By adding to the regression analysis several countries that were on the periphery of the world economy but integrating into it, as one should, Irwin manages to break the positive association between tariffs and growth. Equally important, he shows that the rapidly growing countries, Canada and Argentina, had high tariffs but that these tariffs were for revenue and had few protective side effects. The two countries were in fact splendid examples of outward-oriented countries that built prosperity on their pro-trade orientation.

Second, we can also turn to analyses that take into account complexities that the many-country regressions necessarily ignore. These typically involve deeper examination of specific episodes that speak to the issue at hand or consist of sophisticated country studies in depth.

Two examples of such analyses, both supportive of the merits of freer trade, can be found in the empirical literature. Just because specific tariffs led an industry to grow, we cannot conclude that the strategy contributed to economic prosperity and hence growth. Recognizing this, Irwin has produced a fascinating case study of whether a classic "infant industry" tariff levied in the late nineteenth century in the United States on the tinplate industry really promoted that industry *and* whether that promotion was cost-effective.[28] Irwin's careful answer is that the McKinley tariff protection accelerated the establishment of the industry by a mere ten years, since the U.S. prices of iron and steel inputs were already converging with those in Britain and therefore making U.S. production of tinplate profitable in any event, but that this acceleration was economically expensive because it does not pass a cost-benefit test.

At the same time, the modern evidence against an inward-looking or import substitution trade strategy is really quite overwhelming. In the 1960s and 1970s, several full-length studies of the trade and industrialization strategies of over a dozen major developing countries, including India, Ghana, Egypt, South Korea, the Philippines, Chile, Brazil, and Mexico, were undertaken at the Organization for Economic Cooperation and Development (OECD) and the National Bureau of Economic Research, the leading research institution in the United States.[29] These studies were very substantial and examined several complexities that would be ignored in a simplistic regression analysis across a multitude of nations. Thus, for instance, in examining whether the 1966 trade liberalization in India worked, T. N. Srinivasan and I wrote a whole chapter assessing whether, after making allowance for a severe drought that blighted exports, the liberalization could be considered to have been beneficial compared to a decision to avoid it. Only after systematic examination of the actual details of these countries' experience could we judge whether trade liberalization had truly occurred and when; only then we could shift meaningfully to a limited regression analysis that stood on the shoulders of this sophisticated analysis. The result was to overturn decisively the prevailing wisdom in favor of autarkic policies.[30] Indeed, many of us had started with the presumption that inward-looking policies would be seen to be welfare-enhancing, but the results were strikingly in the opposite direction, supportive of outward orientation in trade and direct foreign investment instead. Why?[31]

- The outward-oriented economies were better able to gain from trade. The layman finds it hard to appreciate this because, as the Nobel laureate Paul Samuelson has remarked, perhaps the most counterintuitive but true proposition in economics has to be that one can specialize and do better.
- Economists today also appreciate that there are scale economies in production that can be exploited when trade expands markets. This is particularly the case for small countries. For this reason, Tanzania, Uganda, and Kenya, which had protected themselves with high tariffs against imports in the 1960s, found that the cost of their protection was excessively high, with each

country producing a few units of several items. They decided in the 1970s therefore to have an East African Common Market so that they could specialize among themselves and each could produce at lower cost for the larger combined market.

- Then there are the gains from increased competition. Restriction of trade often is the chief cause of domestic monopolies. Freer trade produces enhanced competition and gains therefrom. India provides an amusing illustration. Sheltered from import competition, Indian car manufacturers produced such shoddy cars that, when they went up to India's Tariff Commission for renewal of their protection, the commissioners wryly remarked that in Indian cars, everything made a noise except the horn!

- In order to maintain outward orientation, countries must create macroeconomic stability (chiefly, low inflation). Inflation-prone economies with fixed exchange rate regimes, where countries only reluctantly adjust their exchange rates in response to inflation, would soon find that their currency had become overvalued. This overvaluation would make exporting less profitable and importing more rewarding, thus undermining the outward-oriented trade strategy. Hence countries committed to export-promoting trade strategy had to have macroeconomic stability, and they therefore earned the economic advantages that follow from good management of the economy.

  Today, some critics of the advantages of outward-oriented trade strategy argue that we proponents of such a trade strategy fail to appreciate that the gains come not from the trade strategy but from "fundamentals" such as macroeconomic stability. They are wrong. Aside from the fact that we did think of this almost a quarter of a century ago, it is wrong to suggest that macroeconomic stability—for example, an economy not plagued by high inflation—will necessarily lead to an export-promoting trade strategy. India and the Soviet-bloc countries enjoyed splendid macroeconomic stability, to the point where a wit observed that Karl Marx and Milton Friedman were strange bedfellows. But the economies were autarkic in trade: trade policy itself nullified the advantages that macroeconomic stability would bring.

- Finally, as discussed in Chapter 12, direct foreign investment would also be lower in the presence of trade restrictions. It would also be less productive. Trade barriers would mean that such investment would have to be primarily for the domestic market, which was generally limited, whereas in outward-oriented economies it would be for world markets, which were not. Then again,

just as trade barriers reduce the efficiency of domestic investments and incur the loss from protection, so do they reduce the
efficiency of foreign investments.

Third, consider the contrasting experience of India and the Far East.
From the 1960s to the 1980s, India remained locked in relatively autarkic
trade policies; the Far Eastern countries—Singapore, Hong Kong, South
Korea, and Taiwan, the four Little Tigers—shifted to outward orientation dramatically. The results speak for themselves: exports and income
grew at abysmal rates in India, at dramatic rates in the Far East. India
missed the bus. No, it missed the Concorde!

Of course, the trade strategy has to be put into the full context of
other policies that enabled it to translate into gigantic growth-enhancing
outcomes for the Far East and into tragic shortfalls for India. To see this,
consider the East Asian "miracle," as economists christened it: it is not
surprising that the practitioners of the dismal science call a splendid
economic performance a miracle! This spectacular performance was, it
is widely recognized now, due to very high rates of productive investment almost unparalleled elsewhere. Sure enough, the Soviet-bloc countries had experienced similar rates of investment, but it had all turned
out to be unproductive investment. The "blood, sweat, and tears" strategy of getting Soviet citizens to forgo consumption in the interest of
investment and growth of income had proven to be a failure.

The high rates of investment reflected, in turn, the fact that the East
Asian countries turned outward beginning in the 1960s and therefore
had world markets to work with when planning their investments. By
contrast, India turned inward, so its investment was constrained by the
growth of the domestic market. Growth in that market in a largely agricultural country meant the growth of agricultural output and incomes.
But nowhere in the world has agriculture grown, on a sustained basis, at
more than 4 percent annually, making it a weak basis for a strong investment performance!

The Far East's phenomenally high investment rates also were excep-
tionally productive. They were based on export earnings, which therefore enabled the investment to occur with imported capital equipment
embodying advanced and productive technology.[32] Besides, these countries had inherited tremendously high literacy rates that ensured the
productive use of new technologies. Accommodating, even ahead-of-
the-curve expansion of higher education also helped to increase the productivity of the investment. So the Far East generally was characterized
by a virtuous interaction among beneficial policies: outward orientation, high literacy, and emphasis on higher education.

But the primary role must be assigned to the outward orientation that set up the system for high and productive investments.[33] Education by itself, especially higher education, is unlikely to help. Unemployed educated youth will likely burn tram cars rather than lead to greater growth. The Kevin Costner movie *Field of Dreams,* in which this gifted actor's character builds a baseball field and dreams that the superstars of baseball have come there to play (but do not in fact when the reality check is in) is probably the best corrective to those who think that education by itself was the magic bullet that created the East Asian miracle.

Fourth, what do the many multi-country cross-sectional studies of this question show today? Not all show a positive relationship between trade and growth. What one can say, however, is that such statistical evidence, by and large, is consonant with the views of the free trade proponents.

The latest set of such studies, by David Dollar and Aart Kraay of the World Bank, show that if one focuses on post-1980 globalizers such as Vietnam and Mexico, which were in the top third of developing countries in terms of the increase in the share of trade in GDP during 1977–1997, they show better growth performance. Since trade will generally grow even if trade barriers are not reduced, it is important to note that this group also cut import tariffs by three times as much as the non-globalizing two-thirds.[34] These authors also observe that while growth rates in the non-globalizing developing countries have generally slowed down in the past two decades, globalizers have shown exactly the opposite pattern, with their growth rates accelerating from the level of the 1960s and 1970s.[35] This is certainly true for China, and to a lesser but certain degree for India, two countries that together have nearly 2.5 billion people within their borders.

India, China, and Elsewhere

So, with the usual caveat that in the social sciences one can rarely establish the degree of credibility for one's argument that one can aspire to in the physical sciences, one can conclude that freer trade is associated with higher growth and that higher growth is associated with reduced poverty. Hence, growth reduces poverty.

The best way to see that is to focus on the two countries, India and China, that have the largest pool of world poverty. Both shifted to outward orientation roughly two decades ago, and this contributed to their higher growth in the 1980s and 1990s. China adopted aggressively outward-oriented economic policies in 1978. India also began opening its insular economy in a limited fashion in the 1980s and more systematically and boldly in the 1990s. According to World Bank estimates, real income (gross domestic product) grew at an annual average rate of 10 percent in China and 6 percent in India during the two decades ending in 2000. No country in the world had growth as rapid as China's, and fewer than ten countries (and, except for China, none with poverty rates and population size comparable to India's) had a growth rate exceeding India's during these years. What happened to their poverty? Just what common sense suggests: it declined.

Thus, according to the Asian Development Bank, poverty declined from an estimated 28 percent in 1978 to 9 percent in 1998 in China. Official Indian estimates report that poverty fell from 51 percent in 1977–78 to 26 percent in 1999–2000. Contrast what happened in India during the quarter of a century prior to the economic reforms and the abysmally low annual growth rate of 3.5 percent. During that period, the poverty rate remained stagnant, fluctuating around 55 percent. China's track record on poverty reduction in the pre-reform period is dismal as well, but there were also major adverse effects from the huge famine during the Great Leap Forward of Chairman Mao and from the disruptive Cultural Revolution. This experience, showing how growth will in fact reduce poverty, just as I had predicted and prescribed at the Indian Planning Commission in the early 1960s, has been shown to be valid in other countries where Dollar and Kraay have examined the experience carefully, among them Vietnam and Uganda.

More recent estimates by my Columbia colleague Xavier Sala-i-Martin have underlined the same conclusion dramatically. He has estimated poverty rates worldwide, using data for ninety-seven countries between 1970 and 1998. His conclusion on the relationship of growth to poverty reduction is as strong a corroboration as I can find of my 1960s conjecture that growth must be reckoned to be the principal force in alleviating poverty:

> [T]he last three decades saw a reversal of roles between Africa and Asia: in the 1970s, 11% of the world's poor were in Africa and 76% in Asia. By 1998, Africa hosted 66% of the poor and Asia's share had declined to 15%. Clearly, this reversal was caused by the very different aggregate growth performances. Poverty reduced remarkably in Asia because Asian countries grew. Poverty increased dramatically in Africa because African countries did not grow. As a result, perhaps the most important lesson to be learned . . . is that a central question economists interested in human welfare should ask, therefore, is how to make Africa grow.[36]

So when we have moved away from the anti-globalization rhetoric and looked at the fears, even convictions, dispassionately with the available empirical evidence, we can conclude that globalization (in shape of trade and, I will argue later in Chapter 12, direct equity investment as well) helps, not harms, the cause of poverty reduction in the poor countries.

What about Inequality?

Poverty, of course, is different from inequality. True, as many sociologists have reminded us, I may feel poorer if the rich consume commodities in a way that makes me feel more deprived. Equally, the same degree of inequality will often appear more intolerable if it is in the presence of acute poverty. Thus in a country such as India, where poverty is still immense, affluence and its display are particularly galling. So are they in Russia today, where the nouveaux riches, a few of whom have fortunes similar to those of Western tycoons such as George Soros and Ted Turner, and their offspring, who spend holidays in St. Moritz and drive through Moscow in BMWs and Mercedes-Benzes, coexist with substantial numbers of people immiserized during a mismanaged transition.

Whether increased inequality matters, and if so, how, depends therefore very much on the society in question. In contrast to modern Russia, a society where income and wealth are unequal may nonetheless be stable if that income is not spent ostentatiously but instead devoted to social uplift. The Jains of India and the Dutch burghers who suffered the "embarrassment of riches" referred to in the title of Simon Schama's book about them accumulated capital and amassed wealth but spent it not on self-indulgence but on doing social good.[37] That made capitalism's unequal outcomes inoffensive, softening capitalism and its inequalities. Yet another way in which inequality becomes acceptable is if those who are at the bottom of the scale feel that they can also make it: inequality is accepted because it excites not envy but aspiration and hope. Capitalism's inequalities then become tolerable, not because the rich deny themselves self-indulgence but because they make the poor fancy that these prizes may come to them someday too. Evidently this part of the American dream frustrates the inequality-conscious Americans, who see the poor not voting the way they "should."

Indeed, the consequences of increased inequality, in any event, might be paradoxically benign, rather than malign. If a thousand people become millionaires, the inequality is less than if Bill Gates gets to make a billion all by himself. But the thousand millionaires, with only a million each, will likely buy expensive vacations, BMWs, houses in the Hamptons, and toys at FAO Schwarz. In contrast, Gates will not be able to spend his billion even if he were to buy a European castle a day, and the unconscionable wealth would likely propel him, as in fact it has, to spend the bulk of the money on social good. So extreme inequality will have turned out to be better than less acute inequality!

In short, the preoccupation with inequality measures—and there are several—is somewhat ludicrous unless the economist has bothered to put them into social and political context. Cross-country comparisons, no matter what measure is deployed, are just so much irrelevant data mongering, it must be confessed, since societies are diverse on relevant dimensions and therefore inequality cannot be judged outside particular contexts.

And this lunacy—how else can one describe it?—extends to what the World Bank, with its abundance of economists and funds, has been doing in recent years, which is to put all the households of the world onto one chart to measure worldwide inequality of incomes.[38] But what sense does it make to put a household in Mongolia alongside a household in Chile, one in Bangladesh, another in the United States, and still another in Congo? These households do not belong to a "society" in which they compare themselves with the others, and so a measure that includes all of them is practically a meaningless construct.

But since some play this particular global inequality game, others must follow suit. Since the World Bank found, in a 2001 study, that a small increase in inequality had occurred between the late 1980s and the early 1990s—an astonishingly small period to work with since the measured changes are likely then to be transient, just a blip—the question has been posed in just this way by others. Thus, in the thorough study cited earlier on poverty, Sala-i-Martin calculates also the inequality à la World Bank, using nine alternative measures thereof. He concludes that according to all these measures, global inequality declined substantially during the last two decades. These findings are supported also by the recent work of Surjit Bhalla.[39] Between them, they raise a massive discordant note in the chorus singing from a libretto lamenting increasing inequality in the age of globalization.

And so globalization cannot be plausibly argued to have increased poverty in the poor nations or to have widened world inequality. The evidence points in just the opposite direction.

6

Child Labor: Increased or Reduced?

C hild labor is a continuing scourge in poor countries, and has sadly not disappeared from the rich countries altogether (even a country as rich as the United States still has children at work, not just selling lemonade and cookies on the roadside or hosing down your car for a buck, but in the poor counties in the South where migrant labor works under exploitative conditions). The International Labor Organization (ILO), the international agency charged with overseeing the world's labor issues, has estimated that 100 million to 200 million children under fifteen are at work. Of these, ILO estimates that almost 95 percent are in poor countries, and half of these are in Asia. An estimated 100 million of these children often do not go to primary school.[1]

The problem has been long-standing and is historically inherited. It is extremely improbable, therefore, that it has much to do with today's—or even yesterday's, rather than yesteryear's—globalization. Its principal causes are altogether different and lie rooted in poverty instead. Yet some anti-globalization and anti-child-labor activists tend to merge into a symbiotic relationship. Globalization is regarded by them, if not as a cause of child labor in the workforce, at least as a phenomenon that increases the incentive to use it and hence as a cause of its perpetuation and even enlargement. Yet there is little evidence of this perverse and malevolent relationship. The truth is that globalization—wherever it translates into greater general prosperity and reduced poverty—only accelerates the reduction of child labor and enhances primary school enrollment and hence literacy. And as I argued from my analysis of the East Asian miracle, literacy in turn enables rapid growth. So we have here a virtuous circle.

The Blame Game

Often the word *globalization* is smuggled into a galling description of exploitative child labor, creating the impression that globalization somehow has something to do with the wicked situation. Many examples could be cited. One might suffice.

In a disturbing pamphlet on the exploitation of children as domestic servants—indeed, their occasional subjection to near-slavery and even physically abusive treatment—the South Asian Coalition on Child Servitude (SACCS) writes, in a pamphlet titled *Invisible Slaves*, about a child, Ashraf, who was beaten and badly burned by his employer, Hamid Hussain, a senior civil servant in New Delhi, for the crime of drinking the remnants of milk left over by the employer's children:

> Now Ashraf [after being rescued] is staying at Mukti Ashram, one of the rehabilitation centers of SACCS. . . . SACCS after observing the *growing cases of torture on domestic child laborers in different levels of society in post-globalization India* . . . vowed to focus on this sector. [Italics added][7]

Of course, SACCS has not documented that there are "growing cases" of such reprehensible torture. And even were its increasing incidence true, the organization certainly has not linked the phenomenon to globalization. Yet the admirable activists who lead SACCS have fallen into the trap, so assiduously set by some of their civil society counterparts abroad, that lays all the ills of the world at the door of globalization. Indeed, as you read and are shaken by the story of what happened to Ashraf, it needs a wild imagination to think that Hussain's actions had anything to do with India's globalization, halting and limited as it has been in the half century after independence in 1947.

What Does Economic Analysis Tell Us?

But forget what SACCS and other activists believe and let us look at what economic analysis suggests and what careful studies show.

Now, it is easy enough to construct models of family household behavior where improved incomes—as a result of increased trade opportunity, for instance—prompt greedy parents to put children to work. Yet the evidence seems to suggest exactly the opposite, for a variety of reasons. Poor parents, no less than rich parents, generally want the best for their children. Poverty is what drives many to put children to work rather than into school. Parents will choose to feed their children instead of schooling them if forced to make a choice. When incomes improve, poor parents can generally be expected to respond by putting children back in school. This is what economists call the "income effect": education of one's children is a superior good, the consumption of which rises as incomes rise.

Besides, even if one thinks of children's education as an investment good, one might well expect the parents to react to increasing income by sending children to schools—often it means that the third or fourth child, or the female child, who was at work, is now put into school—for two reasons. First, the incentive to invest in children's education should rise because a stagnant economy offers fewer job prospects than a growing one. This incentive will not always translate into effective response if there are serious structural constraints (for example, inner-city children cannot access jobs that are in areas they cannot get to because of lack of transportation), but these inadequacies themselves may change as the demand to ease these constraints rises with available opportunities that people want to exploit.

More importantly, increased income can also enable poor parents who have been previously constrained from sending children to school by lack of access to credit to do so now. In fact, there is substantial evidence that the credit-constraint argument has relevance in many poor countries.

The economists Priya Ranjan, Jean-Marie Baland, and James Robinson have argued that the returns to primary education have been estimated as being so attractive in many poor countries with a great deal of child labor that the most likely hypothesis for children not being sent to school is that poor parents are unable to borrow money to send their children to school and then repay their loans later.[3] In short, the credit markets are imperfect. So the growth of parental income and hence the easing of this credit constraint (which can certainly follow from improved incomes following globalization) should lead to greater school enrollment and reduced child labor.

The economists Rajeev Dehejia and Roberta Gatti have empirically explored this theory, with data for 163 countries. They argue that development in the form of improvements in the financial sector, which in turn is correlated in other studies with the ability of small borrowers to access credit, is associated with a reduction in the use of child labor.[4] These authors and Kathleen Beegle use household-level data in Tanzania to demonstrate more convincingly the role of credit constraints in the phenomenon of child labor. They examined how agricultural households responded to temporary declines in income. Since the fall in income is temporary, one would expect households to borrow, if they could, rather than take children from schools and put them to work in order to earn. They found that in response to such income shocks, the credit-constrained households increased the use of child labor, whereas households with access to credit in fact borrowed and were able in consequence to offset over half of the increase in child labor.[5]

This implies, of course, that simply proscribing the use of child labor is unlikely to eliminate it; it will only drive poor parents to send their children to work by stealth and often into even worse "occupations" such as prostitution.[6] This happened in Bangladesh, with some young girls falling into prostitution when garment employers who feared the passage of the U.S. Child Labor Deterrence Act (1993)—known as the Harkin Bill because of its sponsor, the well-known liberal senator Tom Harkin—which would have banned imports of textiles using child labor, dismissed an estimated fifty thousand children from factories.[7]

More Evidence

As it happens, we do have some additional, compelling evidence, based on state-of-the-art econometric analysis using extensive data on Vietnamese households, that supports the view that globalization actually reduces child labor. The economists Eric Edmonds and Nina Pavcnik of Dartmouth College essentially use change in the domestic price of Vietnam's primary staple and export product, rice, to examine the link between globalization and the use of child labor. From 1993 to 1998, they find that the average price of rice in Vietnam increased 29 percent, partly because a rice export quota self-imposed on Vietnamese exports had been relaxed.[8] "Since [1989], the government had gradually liberalized its export regime, allowing rice exports to more than double (to about 3 million tons in 1996). By 1997, Vietnam's export quota was no longer binding, and Vietnam was fully exposed to the international price of rice."

Vietnam happens to be a country where 26 percent of children ages six through fifteen work in agriculture and about 7 percent work elsewhere, providing therefore an opportunity to study how globalization might affect the use of child labor. It turned out that households that earned extra income from higher rice prices substituted these extra earnings for the earnings from their children's work. Interestingly, anticipating my focus in the next chapter on the gender implications of globalization, the extra income appeared to benefit older girls, who experienced "the largest declines in child labor and the largest increases in school enrollment."[9]

And so economic argumentation and the empirical evidence do not lend support to the feared adverse link between child labor and globalization in the shape of trade.

A Caveat

Nonetheless, one caveat must be entered. I have considered the effect on child labor within the poor countries when globalization proceeds. But what about globalization and trade in children across borders? Here there is some reason for concern and action.

The increased demand for labor in some of the labor-scarce Middle Eastern nations without modern protections and rights, especially Saudi Arabia, has led to the cross-border movements of women and their children, employed as domestic labor, often in poor conditions. Child prostitution has also intensified, with female children being transported across borders and sold into brothels. These are products of globalization only in the sense that there are profits to be had in movements across borders. And all are agreed that these developments call for corrective action.

7

Women: Harmed or Helped?

Japan comes at us like images in a kaleidoscope. Less than two decades ago we were panicked by its economic prowess into declaring the end of the American century and the arrival of the Pacific century. Its economic might and its uniquely different and impenetrable ways also fed our paranoia: many thought of the Japanese as Superman and Lex Luthor rolled together, omnipotence and evil genius, into the formidable Godzilla of Japanese monster movies. But today the country is almost an economic wasteland, mired in recession and paralyzed into inaction. Today Japan is seen as a threat not because of its strength but because of its weakness.[1]

Japan's paradoxes continue when we think of Japanese women. Japan has the unique distinction of having produced the first female novelist of gravitas, Lady Murasaki, in the eleventh century. Her novel *The Tale of Genji* is widely considered to be the greatest work of Japanese literature; in its nostalgia for the passing society, it recalls Marcel Proust's *Remembrance of Things Past* and Junichiro Tanizaki's *In Praise of Shadows*. And no student of Japanese literature can ignore her contemporary, ten years her senior, Sei Shonagon: a talented writer, her major opus, *Makura no Soshi*, is a classic read even now. Yet when one sees Japan today, the state of its women is almost tragic, closer to that in traditional societies than in the West; indeed, it offends our modern sensibilities.

This was brought home to me when, several years ago, I was at a conference in Tokyo. My Oxford tutor, Sir Donald MacDougall, who had been a wartime adviser to Winston Churchill and was now in London, was there along with his economist wife, Lady Margaret Hall, an Oxford don at the time. As we were boarding the bus, the respectful bureaucrat from Japan's Economic Planning Agency shepherding us announced the MacDougalls as "Professor MacDougall and Mrs. MacDougall." So I interrupted him to say: "Excuse me, they are Mr. MacDougall and Professor Mrs. MacDougall." My reward came not in heaven but in this world, and it was immediate: Margaret came over and gave me a warm kiss on my cheek, with a glowing "Thanks, Jagdish." It made my day.

Globalization Helps Women: Two Examples

One can go around the world and find discrimination against women. It arises at several levels and in different ways. Gender studies has brought this pervasive phenomenon to center stage. But again, my focus here is not on the documentation of this phenomenon or its explanation. Rather, it is on the central question: has globalization accentuated, or has it been corrosive of, the discriminations against women that many of us deplore and wish to destroy?

Japanese Multinationals Going Abroad

That globalization can help rather than harm women emerges dramatically when one examines how globalization has affected the women of Japan. In the aftermath of the great outward expansion of Japan's multinationals in the 1980s and early 1990s, Japanese men executives were sent to the United States, England, France, and other Western nations (Japanese women then rarely made it through a very low glass ceiling). These men brought with them their Japanese wives and children. In New York, they lived in Scarsdale, Riverdale, and Manhattan. And the wives saw at first hand that Western women, though they have some way to go, were treated better. So did the young children become not docile Japanese who are taught the value of social conformity and harmony but rambunctious little Americans who value instead the individualism that every immigrant parent confronts when the children return home from school and say, "That is the way *I* want to do it." Schools are where cultural conditioning occurs subliminally, even explicitly. The women and children who then returned to Japan became agents for change. They would never be the same again.

Feminism, women's rights, other human rights, due process for citizens and immigrants, and a host of other attributes of a modern society began slowly to replace the traditional ways of Japanese culture, and globalization in the shape of Japanese corporations' expansion abroad had played a critical role.

That influence has also come, of course, from other (non-economic) forms of globalization such as the vast increase in Japanese students in Western universities in recent years. Just a decade ago at Columbia, where I teach, the largest nationality in an entering class of over four hundred in the School of International and Public Affairs was Japanese. Many of these students steadily adapted themselves to American ways. Instead of bowing low to the "revered teacher," the *sensei,* they learned to put their feet on the table, even crudely blow bubble gum, in class. And as they returned to Japan (though now a few began to stay on, like students from most other countries) they brought American responses to the increasing trade feuds with the United States. Thus, when the Hosokawa-Clinton summit in Washington failed in 1993, the Japanese prime minister's staff essentially said, "If you object to our trade practices, see you in court!" But President Clinton's staff thought we could still deal with the Japanese in the old ways, through bilateral confrontations and deals. As I explained in an article in *Foreign Affairs* at the time, we thought we were fighting the samurai, but we were fighting GIs.[2]

Price and Prejudice: Trade and the Wage Gender Gap

But the favorable effect on women's issues in Japan because of globalization in the form of extensive outward flow of Japanese multinationals to the West is not the only example one can find. My favorite example is the study of globalization in trade on the gender wage gap between 1976 and 1993 in the United States by the economists Sandra Black and Elizabeth Brainerd.[3]

Such wage discrimination can be explained in alternative ways. One persuasive theory, due to the Nobel laureate Gary Becker, is that men are paid more than women by employers, even though they have no greater merit and productivity within the firm, simply because of prejudice.[4] But this prejudice has its price: any firm that indulges it is going to be at a competitive disadvantage vis-à-vis firms that hire without this prejudice and pay men no more than they pay women.

Now, if we have a closed economy and all domestic firms share this prejudice, it will not make any one firm less competitive: all firms will be equally handicapped. But when we introduce foreign competition, the foreign firms that do not share this prejudice will be able to gain in competitiveness over domestic firms that indulge the prejudice. Liberalized trade, which enables foreign firms to compete with the domestic firms in open markets, therefore puts pressure on domestic firms to shed their prejudice. The gender wage gap will then narrow in the industries that must compete with imports produced by unprejudiced firms elsewhere.

But consider a related but different and more potent argument. If markets open to trade, competition will intensify, whatever the reason that enables foreign firms to compete with our firms in our domestic and international markets. Faced with increased competition, firms that were happy to indulge their prejudice will now find that survival requires that any and all fat be removed from the firm; cost cutting will mean that the price paid for prejudice will become unaffordable. Again, the gender wage gap will narrow.

The remarkable thing is that Black and Brainerd find that this did actually happen, confirming the predictive power of sophisticated economic reasoning. Firms in the United States that had been subject to relatively less competitive pressure but which then experienced competitive pressure due to openness to trade showed a more rapid reduction in their gender wage gap.

Women's Fears

Yet some influential women's groups and prominent feminist scholars have expressed fears concerning the impact of globalization on their agendas and interests, among them the following.

Global Care Chains

Consider the recent argument, which has gained some currency, by the sociologist Arlie Russell Hochschild regarding the so-called global care chains and their deleterious effect on women.[5] These refer to the phenomenon where women migrants from poor countries have children who are being looked after by girl siblings, grandmothers, or other female relatives while the migrants, as maids and nannies, look after the children of women in the cities of the rich countries. Hochschild argues that this global care chain puts all women at every point in the chain at a disadvantage.

Why? For the migrant women: "Studies suggest that migrants . . . remain attached to the homes and people they leave. . . . Indeed, most of the migrant workers . . . interviewed talked of going back but, in the end, it was their wages that went home while they themselves stayed on in the USA and Italy. Many of the migrants . . . seemed to develop a 'hypothetical self'—the idea of the person they would be if only they were back home. About their own motherhood they seemed to feel two ways: on one hand, being a 'good mother' was earning money for the family, and they were used to a culture of shared mothering with kith and kin at home; at the same time, they felt that being a good mother required them to be with their children and not away from them." Being in a care chain, the author concludes, is "a brave odyssey . . . with deep costs."⁶

Regarding the children back home, the phenomenon was also considered distressing, with the migrants' affections "diverted to their young charges" away from "their own young." Hochschild quotes Sauling Wong as lamenting that "mothers are diverted from those who, by kinship or communal ties, are their more rightful recipients." Moreover, in sociological and psychological terms, the care chain raised added questions: "Can attention, solicitude and love be 'displaced' from, say, [the migrant] Vicky Diaz's son Alfredo, onto, say, Tommy, the son of her employers in Los Angeles? And is the direction of displacement upwards in privilege and power?"⁷

But even if these sentiments had emerged from a proper sample rather than from interviews of not necessarily representative migrants, they would have to confront the fact that as long as the choice to migrate had been made voluntarily, the psychic costs—and possibly gains, as in the case of our own maid of many years from Haiti, who escaped from an abusive husband—were outweighed by the psychic and economic gains. It is important to emphasize also the fact of psychic gains that can accrue because the migrating woman enjoys the liberating environment, both economic and social, that working away from her family, in a feudal and male-dominated environment back home, will imply. I have seen it with our maid, who has grown over the years in self-respect and dignity.

Besides, Hochschild seems to transfer to the migrant workers the values of her own culture: the great emphasis on the nuclear family is often alien to the culture of the poor countries with their extended families, as is well known to students of economic development. Children are often close to, and get looked after by, siblings, aunts, and grandmothers; migration or no migration, that is utterly normal even if it is a phenomenon that will pass as economic development takes off. As the nuclear family has become dominant in the rich countries, the men and women who constitute it are thrown back on one another for virtually all tasks, including child rearing, adding to the stress that an extended family can relieve.⁸

Thus, even if attention was paid naively only to psychological consequences, it is more likely that many women in the global care chain are better off rather than suffering from emotional "deficit" and distress. The migrant female worker is better off in the new world of attachments and autonomy; the migrants' children are happy being looked after by their grandmothers, who are also happy to be looking after the children; and the employer mothers, when they find good nannies, are also happy that they can work without the emotionally wrenching sense that they are neglecting their children. In short, the idea of the global care chain as a chain that binds rather than liberates is almost certainly a wrongheaded one. It fits into the preconception that Hochschild seems to be afflicted with regarding economic globalization as well, as when she says:

> The declining value of child-care anywhere in the world can be compared with the declining value of basic food crops, relative to manufactured goods on the international market. Though clearly more necessary to life, crops such as wheat, rice, or cocoa fetch low and declining prices while the prices of manufactured goods (relative to primary goods) continue to soar on the world market. Just as the market price of primary produce keeps the Third World low in the community of nations, so the low market value of care keeps the status of the women who do it—and, by association, all women—low.[9]

I am afraid this is nothing short of gibberish. The assertions about the declining prices of primary products are familiar decades-old assertions that are untrue but keep recurring in uninformed circles. But even concerning child care, on what evidence does she arrive at the notion that it has a declining value? In truth, as women have gone into the workplace, the demand for child care, whether at home or in centers outside the home, has only grown, and the price of such child care has risen. In fact, one sees a shortage of high-quality child care facilities everywhere as women struggle to find them so they can be freed from all-too-explicit and facile charges of child neglect and the guilt that follows from them.

But it is not just the (economic) *price* of child care that has risen, creating a demand in turn for subsidy to child care. The (social) *value* of child care also becomes more manifest as mothers seek it from others instead of providing it themselves freely at home because of their traditional role.

In fact, there is another important consequence to ponder as women have entered the workforce in great numbers. This has meant that the subsidy they were implicitly providing to child care at home is no longer available. So, from a social viewpoint, one can argue that this traditional subsidy now must be replaced by an explicit subsidy to child care if children, who need nurture and care, are to turn into good adults and citizens. This also means that child care's importance, its social value, is now visible, not hidden by the submerged and subsidized provision of it by women confined to the home.

Unpaid Household Work

Women's Edge, which is a leading NGO promoting gender agendas, has registered several complaints, among them: "The economic theories the WTO espouses and the macro-economic policies that the WTO oversees fail to take into account women's unpaid household work (maintaining the household, growing food for the family, caring for children and relatives). . . . The United Nations estimates that if monetized, the value of unpaid women's household work would equal $11 trillion . . . per year."[10]

National income statisticians have long recognized this neglect, and it is not the only non-market activity that has been considered: volunteer work outside the family, whether by women or men, is yet another example. What is unclear, however, is why we should get the WTO to worry about getting national income accounts adjusted for this and other deficiencies!

Does the fact that women often do unpaid work affect the efficiency of resource allocation in an economy? Surely it does. It implies that the true cost of the output, chiefly child rearing, from that unpaid work is being underestimated. Therefore, this output will be overproduced relative to the case where the women were being paid at market wages. But then there is also an offsetting argument suggesting that the output will be underproduced instead. This is because child care and child rearing have socially desirable spillover effects for which the market does not reward women as it should. If the latter argument is weightier than the former, this would provide an argument for subsidizing child care.

Of course, since the participation of women in the workforce is both good in itself, as it provides women with a choice to work in the home or outside, and is also good for us, since it has several economic payoffs such as bringing into play the talents and contributions of a hitherto neglected half of the workforce, there is a further argument for a subsidy to women in the form of child care support.

But these and other implications of women's unpaid work are matters of domestic policy. It defies common sense to attack either the WTO or the freeing of trade for the absence of such policy initiatives by nation-states that are members of the WTO or that are seeking gains from trade by freeing trade. Yet Women's Edge and other groups do make that illogical leap, and others, when they make assertions such as "Trade agreements need to recognize women's competing demands and ensure that women benefit from trade to the same extent that men do."[11] The "same extent"? Can we manage to achieve such parity of results from trade liberalization for any group, whether women, Dalits (India's untouchables), or

African-Americans or Hispanics in the United States? Can we manage such equality of outcomes for *any* policy reform? And yet these are assertions by serious groups: Women's Edge *is* at the cutting edge of the women's NGOs.

Other Aspects of Women's Work

Yet another issue these groups raise is that in some traditional societies, women produce crops for home consumption and men produce cash crops. If cash crops expand due to trade liberalization and access to world markets, their argument goes, men will benefit but not women; the women might even be harmed. Consider also the claim that "in sub-Saharan Africa . . . a switch to export-promotion crops . . . has often diverted resources from domestic consumption. Men have controlled the extra cash earned from this strategy and the nutritional status of women and children declined."[12]

But what the author is saying is that intra-family decision making can lead to increased incomes being spent on frills rather than on food. Indeed, it can. But then (as I discussed in Chapter 5, on poverty) there is a case here not for bypassing the opportunity to bring increased incomes but for social policy to accompany the increased prosperity such that the untoward effects on nutrition and the health of women and children are avoided. A situation where incomes are stagnant, or even undermined by the imposition of costly trade protection and other harmful economic policies, can also put pressure on men to indulge their taste for frills at the expense of the nutritional status and health of their families; I would submit that it is equally likely to do so. It is smarter to have income-enhancing policies go hand in hand with progressive social ones (which will be more likely to emerge and take hold if we empower women by providing them with the economic opportunities that a growing and prosperous economy will create) instead of reducing incomes so that they are divided and spent better for women.

Trade Agreements and the WTO Pursue Trade and Profits, Not Development and Women's Welfare

The National Organization for Women (NOW) and Feminist Majority, the former an important organization that has done notable work to advance women's rights in the domestic sphere in the United States, have argued:

Current international trade agreements, liker NAFTA, violate the rights of women workers. Women workers in many factories, located in Export Processing Zones (EPZs [zones set aside to attract export-oriented firms]), have reported physical abuse, sexual harassment, and violence, and mandatory pregnancy testing as a condition for employment. Women workers in EPZs are forced to work long hours for extraordinarily low wages in poor working conditions. In Ciudad Juarez, Mexico, over 200 women have been murdered, many of them on their way to and from their work in the EPZs.[13]

But these groups fail to ask: what are the conditions of work in Mexico outside the EPZs? Are not the Mexican unskilled workers suffering yet worse conditions in local, trade-unrelated industries and occupations? Do women enjoy shorter hours of work as they, and men, struggle to survive on the farms and in rural occupations? If two hundred women have been murdered on their way to and from work, is the blame to be assigned to the foreign firms that provide the employment or to the Mexican state that, not just here but through much of Mexico, is unable to provide security to women as they move to and from work? Or one may well ask how many women have been raped or murdered in American cities, often as they go to and from work; do we blame American businesses for this atrocious state of affairs, or do we ask politicians to improve and augment police patrols? In short, what has freer trade got to do with it?

This problem does not exist in a vast majority of EPZs because the young female workers live on campus instead of commuting back to their families at night (and perhaps having to walk through unguarded fields since the buses do not carry them all the way). But where it does, a socially responsible policy toward their employees would be for the larger firms in the EPZs, when the state fails to provide such security to women workers, to take steps, in concert with other large firms, to impress on the host government that the firms' continuing presence in the EPZs will be imperiled if such security is not immediately provided for their workers. Indeed, since the basic safety of its workers has to be part of what a firm must accept as an obligation at the factory level, it must also be regarded as a firm's obligation to ensure their safety in getting to and from work, even if that provision must be made by the host government rather than the firm itself.

Again, Oxfam has argued in its earlier-cited 2002 report on the world trading system that unregulated multinationals are "producing poverty-level wages and severe forms of exploitation, with female workers suffering the worst excesses."[14] Fortunately, the notion that multinationals are the cause of low wages rather than an antidote to them by increasing the demand for labor in the poor countries, or that they exploit workers, male or female, when they actually pay higher wages than the average in alternative occupations, will not stand scrutiny, as discussed fully in

Chapter 12.[15] So the proposition that female workers "suffer the worst excesses" makes little sense when the excesses themselves are illusory and the bulk of the evidence is to the contrary.

Yet another influential women's group, the International Gender and Trade Network (IGTN) agrees that "trade serves as one of the instruments for achieving the goals that we seek: prosperity, stability, freedom, and gender equality." But then it claims that "there is no guarantee that free trade is the best policy for women" and that "[t]he current WTO trade process is predatory, mercenary and destructive to livelihoods."[16]

In reaching such hard-line conclusions, IGTN makes the standard mistake of assuming that the WTO, and presumably free-traders, subscribe to the doctrine that trade is a goal rather than an instrument. Thus they assert: "The current world trade regime poses the wrong questions. Instead of asking what kind of multilateral system maximizes foreign trade and investment opportunities, it should ask what kind of multilateral system best enable[s] the people of our nations to pursue their own social priorities and developmental objectives."[17] But this ignores massive evidence that freeing of trade is pursued because it is argued, on both theoretical and empirical grounds, that it produces prosperity and, as firmly argued in Chapter 5, has a favorable impact on poverty as well. As an economist normally accused of being "the world's foremost free trader," I have always argued for freer trade, not as an objective but rather (in the context of the poor nations such as India, from where I come) as an often powerful weapon in the arsenal of policies that we can deploy to fight poverty. Perhaps the misunderstanding on the part of critics such as IGTN comes from the fact that every time we push for free trade, we do not restate its value as an instrument: we just fight for free trade. As my famous Cambridge teacher the radical Joan Robinson used to say, it is only humorless economists who spell everything out. And certainly only the dreary ones do that every time. But now that we must contend with strong voices and weak ears, perhaps we cannot afford not to be explicit and to reiterate endlessly why we want what we want!

I must add, in all fairness, that IGTN also makes the valid, and important, criticism that the WTO has been corrupted by various lobbies (in the rich countries) into being no longer a pure trade institution: "the WTO does not fundamentally pursue free trade. . . . We believe that it has taken on board non-trade issues. The role of the WTO should be reduced to enable it to deal solely with trade."[18] Indeed, as Chapter 12 makes clear, the multinationals, chiefly the pharmaceutical and software firms, lobbied successfully to get the United States, and then other rich-country governments, to back the WTO's Agreement on Trade-related Aspects of Intellectual Property Rights, turning the WTO into a royalty collection agency. And now the labor lobbies want to introduce labor standards into the WTO as well, emulating the corporate lobbies. The fact of the matter is that every lobby in the rich world—there are far too few in the poor countries—now wants to capture the WTO and turn it into an institution that advances its own agenda, using the WTO's ability to implement trade sanctions. Ironically, one could view the attempts of women's groups to include the gender agenda and gender-impact preconditions in the WTO as yet one more instance of such an ambition, whose result would be to further cripple with overload the efficiency and objectives of an essentially trade-related institution.

Obsession with Export Processing Zones

A number of women's groups are obsessed with EPZs, seeing them as the brutal face of globalization and, in ways discussed below, as the source of much of the devastation that globalization wreaks on women in the poor countries.

But note first that the EPZs, while they have played a part in the outward-oriented strategy of several countries, are rarely as dominant as critics imagine. Besides, their relative importance in overall exports often diminishes over time because the advantages offered by EPZs gradually become available nationwide. Thus, Taiwan's exports from its three EPZs—at Nantze, at Kaohsiung Harbor, and near Taichung—were no more than 10 percent of her overall exports in the 1960s; by the early 1980s, their share had fallen yet further, to 6 percent. As James Shapiro reported for Taiwan in 1981, focusing on better infrastructure facilities and reduced bureaucratic hassles: "The zones are no longer as attractive to investors as they were in the 1960s because the conditions have changed. Many of the original attractions of the zones are now available everywhere in Taiwan."[19]

In the case of inward-looking countries, as they begin to gradually shift to an export orientation, the EPZs represent attempts at introducing a set of reformist policies, such as zero tariffs, that cannot be introduced widely because of political obstacles in the country at large. This initial step leads to a steady loosening of the rest of the country through demonstration in the EPZs of the advantages of such a policy reform. The success of the EPZs leads to acceleration of reforms in the rest of the country, which then leads to better performance by the entire country. This is the story of China, where the coastal province of Guangdong turned into a gigantic export platform and then the rest of the country followed, however haltingly.

Next, the preference for young women workers in the EPZs is deplored as a tactic by which employers get pliable, docile, and uncomplaining workers who are unwilling to unionize to improve their wages and working conditions. Besides, the fact that many are let go and are replaced by other young women cripples their *ability* to unionize as well. Typically, Spike Peterson and Anne Runyon argue, "In many countries, women's proportion of formal-sector employment has significantly increased—with women sometimes displacing men—as employers seek the cheapest, most reliable workers. In this case, women are gaining employment, but typically under *conditions that exacerbate worker vulnerabilities and exploitation*" (italics added).[20]

But this critique is not the slam dunk that it seems. For example, the decline in unionization in the United States over nearly a half century is principally due to several trade-unrelated factors.[21] Improvements in minimum wages, the general rise in wages, and governmentally enacted legislation for workplace safety—the OSHA regulations—have reduced the value of unions for many workers. If workers in the EPZs feel that while they may not be doing as well as they would like, these jobs are still better than others they might obtain, their interest in unionizing may be less than compelling. That, rather than the lack of bargaining power because workers are female or temporary or both, could well be the decisive factor.

In some cases, workers who stay longer with firms will be less likely to want to join unions than less permanent workers: the former may have a more cooperative and conciliatory attitude toward their employers than the latter. Moreover, sociological studies of female workers in Central America, for instance, report interviews with women such as "Maria, who has worked for the plant for seventeen years"; "the company for which she works is known for maintaining and rewarding its better and stable workers."[22] It is therefore perhaps an exaggeration to argue that firms in EPZs necessarily see more profit in keeping workers on a short leash. Besides, as Nicholas Kristof and Sheryl WuDunn, whose work on Asian sweatshops is cited more fully in Chapter 12, have noted, the young women they interviewed wanted to accumulate money, worked hard and long hours by choice, and returned home by choice.[23]

Evidently, there is a diversity of experiences here. What does seem to emerge persistently from many studies is that the work in the EPZ factories is subject to more discipline and may not be suited to all. Assembly lines, for instance, impose more discipline—one worker off the line for ten minutes can disrupt the work of all during that time—than work that can be done at one's own machine. Economic historians have documented how in the textile factories in nineteenth-century India, where families were assigned their own spindles and looms to work with, there was little discipline. But in the Tata steel plant at Jamshedpur, started in 1913 by a remarkable Indian entrepreneur who would go on to found one of India's progressive business dynasties, a disciplined labor force was critical, given the altogether demanding nature of the production process.[24] An example closer to home is the contrast between the leisurely style and hours of work of professors such as myself, on whom the university does not impose a strict and uniform regimen regarding hours worked and daily attendance, and the excruciatingly long hours of disciplined work imposed on the young men and women who join Wall Street firms, glued to their screens and reduced to take-out foods and a dog's life even though the collar may be diamond-studded.

Thus, in the Taiwan EPZs cited earlier, the women talked of "bells, buzzers, punch-cards, supervisors and strict monetary penalties," but this was necessary because a manager observed that, in electronics, "products are either perfect or useless" and a disciplined labor force mattered. Interestingly, the author adds: "One young woman I talked with grew up in Kaohsiung, and during the summer months, for two consecutive years, worked in the KEPZ, first in an electronics factory assembling printed circuits and later sewing in a glove factory. 'The routine nearly bored me to death,' she recalled, 'but jobs in the EPZ are easy to find, and, for a few months, you can put up with anything.'"[25]

In Bangladesh, there was evidence that "[u]nmarried girls employed in these garment factories [which, in 1995, were employing 1.2 million workers, 90 percent of them female] may endure onerous working conditions, but they also experience pride in their earnings, maintain a higher standard of dress than their unemployed counterparts and, most significantly, develop an identity apart from being a child or wife . . . legitimate income-generating work could transform the nature of girls' adolescent experience. It could provide them with a degree of autonomy, self-respect, and freedom from traditional gender work."[26]

Indeed, this account of the liberating effect of EPZ-offered work to young girls in Bangladesh underlines the necessity of judging EPZs in light of alternatives available in these poor countries. I was impressed particularly by the account by a sociologist of a woman named Eva who had left the free trade zone in the Dominican Republic and now "work[ed] as a housekeeper for a private villa adjoining a hotel complex in La Romana. She left because she could no longer stand the pressure of working in the free trade zone. . . . She earns 1000 pesos every two weeks, and not only cleans, but washes, cooks, and serves dinner when the Dominican family for whom she works or one of their guests is in town.

Though she has worked for five years, she receives no paid holidays or social security benefits, *which even free trade zone workers enjoy"* (italics added).[27]

Nonetheless, since unions are not commonplace at all in many EPZs, even when permitted, and often young girls are at work, we do need mechanisms other than the absent unions to ensure that basic safety (extending to protections against rape and sexual harassment) and re-lated health regulations are put in place by the governments and en-forced. If unions believe that temporary workers lack bargaining power, then simply having a union is not going to change that bargaining power: unions without bargaining power would be paper tigers. By contrast, the power of the government in providing the necessary regulations is immensely greater.[28] And the regulations to protect and support women should evidently be applicable nationwide, not just to EPZs, where in fact female workers are likely to be doing better!

WTO Rulings and Women

Women's Edge has also objected to the WTO Appellate Body's rulings that preferences given to the Caribbean nations on their exports of ba-nanas to the European Union violated WTO agreements and that the European Union's restrictions on the sale of hormone-fed beef were in violation of the agreed rules requiring that a scientific test must be met if such restrictions are imposed.[29] They complain that the gender effects were not analyzed by the WTO. But their critique amounts to little more than saying that those who are affected by these decisions, whether in terms of the removal of protection or preference (e.g., the banana case) or by authorized retaliation through tariffs (e.g., the hormone-fed beef case), happen to include women. But then, almost any policy change will directly affect some women.

These WTO Appellate Body decisions raise many issues, some critical to the economic well-being of the poor countries, and fixing the system for them would automatically benefit both women and men in the workforce and as consumers. But the notion that the WTO is somehow damnably deficient in not highlighting gender issues and micro-level gen-der impact each time it pronounces a decision seems to be off the wall.

A telling example of such feminist concern occurred after the EU lost its case for restrictions on American hormone-fed beef. Women's Edge complained about the effects of the ensuing tariff retaliation against Dutch tomatoes and other EU exports. This retaliation by the United

States against the EU was authorized by WTO rules because the EU could not eliminate the WTO-illegal ban. Women's Edge argued:

> The 100 percent tariffs imposed on Dutch tomatoes will affect Janice Honisberg, a woman business owner [who imports Dutch tomatoes]. She estimates that her company will lose 40 percent of its revenues as a result of the tariff and she will be forced to layoff half of her 65 employees, the majority of whom are women from low-income communities in Washington D.C. and Chicago.[30]

Tariff retaliation is a much-debated issue among economists, lawyers, and international relations scholars. To put into this important debate the sorry fate of Honisberg and her staff is to lose all proportion; it is as if a dam had burst, flooding villages and cities and destroying human life, and yet the fate of just a few women concerned you!

Aside from the gross disproportionality of such a focus, it is also misplaced. The WTO Appellate Body was exactly right to find against the legitimacy of the hormone-fed beef legislation of the European Union in light of the agreement at the Uruguay Round, which precluded such restrictions unless backed by a scientific test. And many of us are right to ask for a renegotiation of that agreement because of problems such as the hormone fed beef concerns that were not anticipated at the time of that agreement. But to demand that this agreement, and every other, be reexamined and redesigned specifically from the viewpoint of women's welfare seems about as compelling as saying that the removal of potholes from New York's roads be subjected to a prior examination of whether women are more likely to fall into them (as they well might if they wear high heels).

The proper response to demands for attention to women's welfare in a society has to be to consider ways in which women in that society and economy may be more vulnerable to the consequences of policy changes such as trade liberalization, projects such as the building of roads and railways or the provision of irrigation or drinking water, and indeed the myriad ways in which change comes. Rather than setting up roadblocks on every policy change, big and small, and demanding that each policy change be made conditional on an examination of its impact on women—a tall order in many cases, since the indirect estimates at that level of detail can only be guesstimates at best—it is more useful to think of policies that alleviate the *totality* of distress to women from the multitude of policy changes.

Women, as a class, are not destined to lose from progress any more than other groups are. To block off progress, ostensibly to help them, at every turn of the policy screw is to indulge in a policy response that is both inappropriate and likely to be counterproductive to their well-being—and men's as well.

IMF, World Bank, and Women

An equal opprobrium is assigned by several women's groups to the effects on women of the stabilization programs of the IMF, which assist countries having macroeconomic difficulties such as balance-of-payments crises, and the structural adjustment programs of the World Bank, which are generally longer-term and assist countries that are implementing economic reforms. In both cases, these institutions impose "conditionality," that is, conditions such as commitment to reducing the budget deficit or tightening monetary policy, which must be met by the assisted country.

The concerns of the women's groups are twofold. First, the typical conditionalities in these programs hurt women because when the belt is tightened, the resulting unemployment disproportionately hurts women, who will be fired ahead of the men or who are simply among the workforce that is laid off. Second, the belt-tightening often involves reducing social expenditures on health and education, which in turn forces women back into the home to provide such services instead.

But these criticisms are misdirected. The IMF hands out loans when there is a stabilization crisis. Almost always this means that the country in crisis must bring its overall expenditures in line with its income. If the IMF did not come in with loans—and this counterfactual cannot be ignored—then it is likely that matters would be worse, since the country would then have no option except to live immediately within its means. In fact, IMF support often eases the ability of the country in the stabilization crisis to borrow more funds and to make the transition to a better macroeconomic situation yet easier. This should generally assist, rather than harm, women.

It is hard to argue also that it is the IMF that systematically prefers slashing expenditures to raising revenues and that this expenditure cutting is biased against health and education expenditures. Regarding the former, it is well known, for example, that for many years the IMF was reluctant to ask countries to reduce tariffs, not because it did not believe, as it should, that the high tariffs frequently encountered in the poor countries at the time and even now were harmful, but because the IMF was worried about the potential loss of tariff revenue when a stabilization crisis required more revenue and less expenditure.[31]

As regards expenditure-cutting bias against social expenditures, the IMF and all of us would have loved to get the crisis-afflicted countries to reduce their armaments expenditures instead, for instance. But these priorities, in the end, are set by these governments themselves; the IMF sticks generally to targets that have to do with the budget deficit, that is, the difference between income and expenditure of the government, which in turn must affect the overall national imbalance that attends a stabilization crisis.

The question of removing tariffs on imports and subsidies to electricity, fertilizers, freight, and so on has been more a question of structural reforms addressed by the World Bank. These reforms have certainly been promoted in an effort to change the economic policies that have been recognized as having failed. But it is a mistake to think that these reforms have been necessarily imposed from Washington via the World Bank. Often, as I argue in Chapter 18, these reforms have been advocated and embraced by intellectuals, economists, and policy makers in these countries on their own initiative. Recognition of one's folly is often a powerful factor making for change. Foreign pressure, particularly when aid funds are at stake, can make a difference. But again, the assumption that conditionality, whether of the IMF or the World Bank, is unbending and effective is also erroneous.

Globalization: Working Abroad, Prostitution for Tourists, and Trafficking

There are, however, three critical phenomena, tangentially related to globalization, that pose unambiguous threats to women's well-being.

- Women going abroad as domestic servants—often to the Middle East, where local women are typically living in the Middle Ages and under Islamic laws as interpreted by illiterate and conservative religious leaders in countries such as Saudi Arabia—have been subjected to abuse and need protection.
- The growth of tourism has inevitably been accompanied by a rise in female and even male prostitution in countries such as Thailand.
- Trafficking in women has grown, especially with the economic distress that has attended attempts at transition in countries such as Russia and from financial crises in afflicted Asian countries.

The perils afflicting women as empires expanded and commerce increased offer a historical parallel, of course, although the precise pathologies have been diverse. Thus, Margaret Macmillan, writing in

Women of the Raj, recollects the plight of the women who followed the men into India, in words that have resonance today:

> [The employees of the East India Company] took Indian mistresses; worse, from the point of view of the Company's staunch Protestant directors, they married Catholics, daughters or widows of the Portuguese. To save the souls of its men, the Company, for a time, played matchmaker. In the later part of the seventeenth century it shipped batches of young women from Britain to India. The cargo, divided into "gentlewomen" and "others," were given one set of clothes each and were supported for a year—quite long enough, it was thought, for them to find themselves husbands. *Some did not; and the Company tried to deny that it had any obligation to look after them further.* Most unfairly it also warned them to mind their morals: "Whereas some of these women are grown scandalous to our nation, religion and Government interest," said a letter from London to the Deputy Governor of Bombay in 1675, "we require you to give them fair warning that they do apply themselves to a more sober and Christian conversation." *If that warning did not have the right effect, the women were to be fed on bread and water and shipped back to Britain.* [Italics added][32]

A more recent and less excusable example is that of the Korean "comfort women" who were forced into servicing the Japanese armed forces in the Second World War as they brutally moved westward into Korea and China—an issue that has led to continual demands for compensatory reparations by Japan.

The modern afflictions—abuse of female workers abroad, tourism-induced prostitution, and trafficking across borders—that can attend normal, empire-unrelated globalization require attention and both international and domestic action. They simply illustrate how even benign changes—such as the opportunity to earn more as a domestic, an opportunity prized and seized by hundreds of thousands of women in the Philippines, Bangladesh, India, Pakistan and Indonesia—can have some downside effects for women who are left unprotected against probable abuses by their employers. More disturbingly, these opportunities can be exploited by unscrupulous elements—traffickers and mafia such as the Japanese *yakuza*—to indulge in dreadful crimes against women such as trafficking in them for unremunerated prostitution and virtual slavery.

Fortunately, the unceasing activities of individual activists and NGOs, among them the Thailand-based ECPAT (End Child Prostitution, Child Pornography and Trafficking in Children for Sexual Purposes) and the Delhi-based STOP (Stop Trafficking, Oppression, and Prostitution of Children and Women, which works to end the traffic in women and children from Bangladesh and Nepal) have increased awareness of these problems at the international level for some years now. Many conventions have been signed and several ratified, to prevent trafficking, for instance, and the enormous gaps between laws and conventions and between laws and enforcement have been the target of continual critical scrutiny and agitation. Progress is slow, not just because of lack of political will but because of the complexity of the enforcement required. But it is relentless.

So while there are serious issues to be addressed in these specific areas, where the welfare and well-being of women can be imperiled and must be protected, I would conclude from the analysis in this chapter that the broader criticisms that many women's groups have voiced about the negative effects of globalization on women are not convincing.

8

Democracy at Bay?

In *The Merchant of Venice,* with Shylock pressing his demand for the pound of flesh to be collected from Antonio, Solanio offers Antonio the comforting assurance that "the Duke will never grant this forfeiture to hold."[1] But Antonio answers:

> The Duke cannot deny the course of law;
> For the commodity that strangers have
> With us in Venice, if it be denied,
> Will much impeach the justice of the state,
> Since that the trade and profit of the city
> Consisteth of all nations.

So Venice, because it owes its prosperity to trade with "all nations," cannot sacrifice justice and respect for the sanctity of contract to the dictates of mercy. Thus, writing five centuries ago, Shakespeare recognized that integration into the world economy via trade could constrain the freedom of domestic action.

It is precisely the growing awareness that globalization creates a web of relationships that introduce such complexity, and hence prudence and pause in the policy choices of nation-states, that has led to the charges that globalization and democracy are at odds. But the question whether democracy is enhanced or diminished by globalization is not so easily answered.

A Paradox

The principal reason is that, for reasons that reflect Shakespeare's observation, globalization constrains the exercise of sovereignty, and hence the sense and scope of democratic control, since interdependence will imply that an action by one nation-state will generally have consequences that will be affected by feedback from other nation-states.

At the same time—and herein lies a paradox—one can plausibly argue that globalization promotes the transition to democracy by regimes that are not democratic. To put the paradox starkly, globalization promotes democracy while constraining it at the same time. But the relative strengths of these conflicting forces must be assessed.

Promoting Democracy

Globalization promotes democracy both directly and indirectly. The direct link comes from the fact that rural farmers are now able to bypass the dominant classes and castes by taking their produce directly to the market thanks to modern information technology, thereby loosening the control of these traditionally hegemonic groups. In turn, this can start them on the way to becoming more-independent actors, with democratic aspirations, in the political arena.

Globalization is at the source of this phenomenon in two ways: the computers themselves are available because of trade, and the markets accessed are foreign in many cases, not just domestic. Thus, a recent report from Kamalpur village in India by the *Wall Street Journal* reporter Cris Prystay documents how the villagers are now selling their crops by computer, cutting out the middlemen.

> Soybean farmer Mohammed Arif, 24 years old, says the computer allows farmers greater control over their own goods. Farmers often get cheated at markets, or get stuck with whatever price is offered that day. With the computer, he says, they can make a considered decision at home, holding crops until prices improve.[2]

The indirect link, on the other hand, comes from a proposition vigorously advanced by the American political scientist and intellectual Seymour Martin Lipset in his 1959 classic *Some Social Requisites of Democracy*.[3] Lipset's argument was complex, in tracing the impact of economic development on democratization via the mediating effect of "social development" in the form of increased education, social equality, and changes in class structure. This led to criticism by other scholars, such as Ralf Dahrendorf and Samuel Huntington, that economic development did not necessarily lead to such social changes and that the social changes may sometimes even be destabilizing, producing anarchy and chaos rather than democracy.[4]

But Lipset's central argument has always been interpreted somewhat differently in public discourse, and properly so, since the link between these social changes and politics is perhaps far too tenuous to rest even a weak generalization on it. The thesis popularly attributed to Lipset has instead been that economic prosperity produces a middle class. This emerging middle class creates, however haltingly, an effective demand for democratization of politics: the new bourgeoisie, with wallets a little fatter, seeks a political voice, not just one in the marketplace.

So, as with the thesis successfully linking globalization with reduced poverty, we now have another two-step argument: globalization leads to prosperity, and prosperity in turn leads to democratization of politics with the rise of the middle class. The first step is supported by evidence (Chapter 5). Is the second step also?

There is no doubt that many believe it to be true. Indeed, many politicians embrace it passionately. In arguing for China's entry into the World Trade Organization, Congressman Tom DeLay confidently asserted, "Entrepreneurs, once condemned as 'counter-revolutionaries', are now the instruments of reform. . . . [T]his middle class will eventually demand broad acceptance of democratic values."[5] President Bill Clinton, also supporting China's entry, argued that "as China's people become more mobile, prosperous, and aware of alternative ways of life, they will seek greater say in the decisions that affect their lives." President George W. Bush has also spoken in the same vein: "It is important for us to trade with China to encourage the growth of an entrepreneurial class [because when we do this] you'll be amazed at how soon democracy will come."[6]

The strong belief that economic prosperity, engineered through globalization as also the fostering of economic freedoms and associated use of markets rather than central planning, will promote democracy has also been at the heart of a different impassioned debate, contrasting the Russian and the Chinese experience. Russia under Gorbachev opted for glasnost (political freedom and democracy) before perestroika (economic restructuring, including an end to autarky); China opted for economic change while keeping democratization firmly away. China's enormous success and Russia's astonishing failure have led many to think both that democratization should follow, not precede, economic reforms, and that, as Lipset would have it, the prosperity and the middle classes that follow the success of economic reforms will indeed lead to democratization down the road.

But Lipset's thesis initially ran into a lot of scholarly skepticism because the world seemed to tolerate authoritarianism even as economic development proceeded apace. As the postwar period unfolded and nearly all of the newly independent incipient democracies, with the dramatic exception of India, collapsed during the 1960s and 1970s into what seemed like a long nightmare of authoritarian regimes that seemed to be impervious to corrosion from economic development when it occurred, disillusion set in about the optimism that development would usher in democracy.

But after the massive shift to democracy that began in the 1980s, the thesis received a new lease on life. As the political scientist Sheri Berman has stated: "Wherever one looked—from Southern Europe to East Asia, from Latin America to the Soviet Union—it seemed as if transitions were the order of the day. In many cases, furthermore, the transitions seemed to follow impressive periods of economic development or correlate with a shift to a free-market economy."[7] And it is noteworthy that, after reviewing three decades of literature on the link between economic development and democracy, the political scientist Larry Diamond concluded that the evidence broadly supported Lipset's proposed link between development and the rise of democracy.[8]

But if the link between development and the rise of democracy is robust, Lipset's causation in the shape of the rise and role of the middle class is less so. There is, of course, some evidence in favor of this explanation. Middle classes, particularly today, have greater contacts with other societies by travel, video, radio, and television and hence indulge in more seditious thoughts and a diverse range of protests that include samizdat. Juan Linz and Alfred Stepan note that there is "even strong empirical evidence that increases in regional wealth increase citizens' expectations that they should be well treated by the police."[9]

Yet factors other than the rise of the middle class have played a role. Thus Linz and Stepan make the fascinating observation—based on Pinochet's regime in Chile, Brazil in the early 1970s, and two decades in Franco's Spain—that while there was willingness to put up with authoritarian regimes as long as they were delivering development, this willingness disappeared once development was delivered and prosperity seemed to be securely in place.[10] They write:

> [M]any nondemocratic regimes . . . are originally defended by the state elite and their core socioeconomic allies as necessary given the *exceptional* difficulties (often economic) the polity faces. Thus, prolonged economic prosperity, especially in an authoritarian regime, may erode the basis of the regime's justification based on exceptional circumstances. Prolonged economic success can contribute to the perception that the exceptional coercive measures of the nondemocratic regime are no longer necessary and may possibly erode the soundness of the new economic prosperity.[11]

It is also well to remember some notable recent experiences that do not really support the role-of-the-middle-class thesis. Consider the way democracy was ushered into Indonesia and South Korea in the immediate aftermath of the Asian financial crisis in 1997–98. Democracy came not as a result of orderly, gentle opening of the door as bourgeois groups increased with economic prosperity and demanded more political rights. It was instead a result of the economic upheaval that the crisis wreaked: the authoritarian elites were discredited and swept away! The mismanagement of globalization (discussed in Chapter 13) and its malign impact were what really produced the swift transition to democracy.

Then again, the benign China scenario—that rapid development will democratize China—has also been challenged, but the criticisms are frankly not persuasive. The critics draw on the work of the sociologist Barrington Moore, who had suggested that the Japanese transition to democracy as the middle classes emerged was compromised by their accommodation to the ancien régime.[12] Taking his cue from this work, the journalist Lawrence Kaplan has argued that the Chinese middle classes will be co-opted by the authoritarian regime into supporting rather than opposing it. This is certainly true if we take an immediate snapshot. The human rights activist and sinologist Andrew Nathan has written that presently "almost every ostensibly independent organization—institutes, foundations, consultancies—is linked into the party-state network."[13] The political oversight of the Communist Party over the society and the polity are evident to all who see without wearing blinkers. Yet local elections have taken place. The Internet, despite attempts at regulating it, is working its insidious way into the system. Trade and investment, though concentrated in the four dynamic coastal provinces, are creating new consumers, new producers, and new links with the outside world and its capitalist allures and democratic ways. To assert that all this will not nudge, even push, the communist regime into more political freedoms seems to be to confuse inertia with rigor mortis.

Constraining Democracy

The concern that democracy is constrained by globalization, even as globalization promotes it, takes several forms, each of which goes back much farther in time, even leaving aside Shakespeare. These various formulations range from concerns about the ability to shift policies radically to the left to lesser but still progressive concerns about the ability simply to undertake social spending, and even to maintain overall spending, in a global economy.

Radical Shift to the Left

The worry that extreme, radical shifts to the left cannot be undertaken in the presence of globalization is best understood in the somewhat different but parallel context of the Soviet Union in the early years after the 1917 revolution, splendidly discussed by the historian E. H. Carr, who wrote of the Soviet dilemma of "socialism in one country."[14]

If a single nation, even if the government is popularly elected, shifts to radical policies, financial capital may leave; even the bourgeoisie ("human capital") may emigrate, voting with its feet. At the same time, fresh foreign funds may dry up, exacerbating the crisis. Governments, contemplating such an outcome, may shun leftward policy shifts, or if they try them, they may be forced to retrace their steps amid chaos. Evidently, if such socialism obtains everywhere, rather than just in one country, the prospects are better for it to manage a sharp lurch to the left since there is no capitalist safe haven to worry about.

While Carr was writing about the Soviet Union, which was revolutionary rather than democratic, his thesis works very well indeed for Salvador Allende's ill-fated presidency in Chile and for Lula da Silva's recent presidency in Brazil. Allende was democratically elected but chose to move dramatically to the left. The effect was to galvanize the bourgeoisie against him and to induce a massive capital outflow. At the same time, the workers who had voted him into power were being rewarded with higher consumption. So Allende's government was caught in a pincer movement between shrinking resources and increasing demand for them.

When I went to Santiago in the spring of 1973, a few months before Allende's overthrow and suicide to evade capture by Pinochet's forces in the Moneda Palace, the city was in an uproar, with demonstrations, tear gas, broken shop-front windows, and a system rife with long queues for buses, shortages of essential foods, and a black market exchange rate so huge that if you exchanged your dollars at that rate, you could eat three-star meals for the price of a pizza! Then, of course, the CIA and Henry Kissinger plotted to undermine the regime as well. Evidently, socialism in one state was a dangerous, even fatal, proposition.

Lula da Silva, the populist politician who was elected in 2003 to be the president of Brazil, has evidently learned from Allende's undoing. His first steps have been to embrace tough macroeconomic discipline, to reverse his anti-trade positions, and to talk reforms, to ensure that Brazil's fragile finances do not turn into a disaster à la Allende. He has simultaneously rewarded his labor and environmental constituencies, not at the expense of the budget but by diverting resources from defense with measures such as the cancellation of expensive orders for fighter aircraft. Da Silva's and his supporters' political preferences for a sharp turn to the left have therefore been prudentially put on hold, at least for now.

One must still ask the question: would not something like this have been the outcome even if globalization were not so substantial as it is now on the dimensions of trade, investment, and foreign borrowing? Even if Brazil were a closed economy, is it not likely, for instance, that da Silva would have had to exercise fiscal and monetary prudence or risk having a failing economy on his hands? In short, we must ask: are radical shifts to the left being discounted and rejected now primarily because of a growing appreciation that they endanger the economy regardless of globalization, or mainly because of the added risks posed by globalization?

I suspect it is the former, not the latter. After all, there is by now a long list of countries that tried rather radical leftist economic policies and failed in varying degrees. Manley in Jamaica, Nkrumah in Ghana, Nasser in Egypt, and Sukarno in Indonesia come to mind. All of these were charismatic leaders; some were also of considerable intellectual ability. But economics is a jealous mistress, and you ignore her at your peril. A friend of mine in Brussels told me that he had seen François Mitterand (who had famously appointed Jacques Attali, an impressive intellectual with no knowledge of economics, as his adviser on the economy) give an interview on French television. He was standing in front of a wall full of bookshelves. The interviewer asked him if there was any book on economics among them. Mitterand thrust his chest forward and said with gusto, "Not one." And, of course, a few weeks later, France had a nice economic crisis!

Public Spending: Total and Social

A lesser worry, but one that has engaged many recently, concerns not the feasibility of a radical shift to the left but simply whether a globalized, open economy would be able to sustain postwar liberal levels of total spending, and within that total the amount dedicated to social spending. Total spending, as we well know from the attacks on it by mainstream conservatives and from the ideological pronouncements of Prime Minister Margaret Thatcher and President Ronald Reagan, is a principal contributor to the maintenance of a progressive state, whereas social spending, especially on health, education, and welfare support, is often the area within the budget that attracts the special wrath of these critics. If such spending is constrained by globalization, that is surely a blow to the possibility of a liberal (not radical) state. Why should globalization prove to be such a constraint?

The argument is that if total and social spending were maintained, leave aside increased, the effect would be to risk the country's economy because such spending would be associated with "irresponsibility" by the credit agencies and Wall Street, whose judgments about a country's economic virtue and rectitude are essential to its well-being. The proponents of this view then look at infatuation with foreign borrowing as the principal conduit through which the ability to maintain an adequate degree of autonomy in these matters may be compromised. Few believe that trade can lead to such an outcome: it is hard to imagine that increased trade penetration or interdependence will lead to such political vulnerability (except, of course, when the powers of a hegemonic or powerful state are being marshaled toward such a purpose).

But if the *ability* to maintain total and social spending is impaired thus, the *incentive* to do so may be enhanced. Why? Because, as Karl Polanyi argued in a general fashion decades ago, and as the political scientist John Ruggie has adapted the argument today to the question of whether openness promotes social spending, the embrace of what might be called the liberal international economic order, or increased openness for short, implies greater vicissitudes and volatility.[15] We then also have politicians desiring greater social spending in order to moderate the social effects of economic openness through adjustment assistance programs, for instance. Even total spending may be a stabilizing influence, as it is steadier and institutionally more insulated from volatility. Ruggie, perhaps the most creative postwar thinker on these questions, put it rather strikingly as "embedding" the liberal embrace of openness in the world economy in domestic spending.[16] It was an act of embedding liberalism in the domestically responsible state.

With the two arguments, one on ability and the other on incentives, going in contrary directions, the observed outcome will depend on the relative strength of the two effects. This creates a statistical problem: how can we use the data to identify and thus assess the empirical strength of the ability and the incentive effects if all we see is the final outcome? This identification problem is amusingly illustrated by recalling the country—you can surely guess which it is—where men are bad lovers and the women yet worse cooks. Are poor lovers penalized by bad food, or is bad food rewarded with indifferent love?

As it happens, we have some suggestive empirical support for both the contrary effects but little nuanced and compelling evidence of their relative strength. The Ruggie viewpoint is broadly buttressed by the finding of the political scientists Peter Katzenstein, who observed that many small and open states in northern Europe had developed large public budgets (which is not the same as social spending, of course), and David Cameron, who argued that countries with more openness had larger public sectors.[17] Later, the economist Dani Rodrik extended Cameron's study, which had focused only on the rich OECD countries, to a larger sample of one hundred countries and reinforced the argument that increased (trade) integration into the world economy is associated with greater spending relative to national income.

But then we also have the political scientist Geoffrey Garrett, who argues that there is evidence for the contrary proposition that globalization has forced down spending. Instead of focusing on just trade openness and *levels* of public spending, he has looked more persuasively at *changes* in trade flows and in public spending; and finds that the countries in which trade grew fastest during 1970–1995 also had slower growth in spending.[18]

While looking at changes is better than looking at levels, the problem is that *trade* is not what one ought to focus on. There is absolutely no systematic and compelling evidence that some blanket measure of trade openness is associated with problems such as increased volatility of prices or earnings, which may then cause the increase in total or social spending. Economists know well that openness may dampen, not amplify, fluctuations in prices, as when a bad harvest leads to high prices, which are then dampened by induced imports, in turn requiring fewer subsidies and less public spending to protect consumers.

In fact, medieval famines in Europe were moderated by the increasing opening of trade routes and integration precisely because food moved to famine-stricken high-price areas, dampening prices, moderating the food scarcity, and improving its accessibility to the poor. There is an interesting implication here also for the economist Amartya Sen's well-known but wrongheaded analysis of famines. He has argued that democracy is what prevents famines by allowing information about the famine to percolate up. But the nature of the democracy is crucial. In the case of the Bihar famine in India in 1967, it was democracy that made fighting the famine more, not less, difficult. I was in Delhi at the time and in close touch with the policy makers, and although we all knew that there was ample food available within the country, India had a federal democracy and a states-based food zones system. The states with surplus food would not allow it to be sent to Bihar. As it happened, it was the trucks carrying contraband food from the states with surpluses that helped (exactly as in medieval Europe where the trade was legal instead) but not sufficiently![19] In the end, Prime Minister Indira Gandhi had to go to Washington to get food for Bihar. (This option has not been exercised by China during times of famine, revealing the real asymmetry between democratic and totalitarian states: both are informed of the famine, but the latter are more able and willing to have their populations die from famine—as we have seen currently in North Korea—than to seek food aid from ideological foes abroad.)

I am more inclined to the view that it is the threat of capital out-flows that we must focus on, rather than trade, to examine whether globalization lays a heavy hand on public and social spending. But when this is done, the evidence seems to elude us.[20] I suspect that the reason is simply, as recent analyses suggest, that balanced against this pressure to hold back spending as integration into the world's capital markets proceeds is a set of strong institutions, including labor unions and social democratic parties.[21] Where strong, these institutions have nullified the globalization pressures. This is, in fact, similar to what I argue in Chapter 10 on the fear about a race to the bottom: that globalization will cause our labor standards to fall. What I find there is that our labor standards have not fallen as feared; strong institutions have turned the politics around to a push for a race to the top worldwide!

It would appear, therefore, that the fear that globalization puts total and social spending at risk because globalization punishes such spending needs to be discounted, plausible as it appears at first blush. But there is an altogether different worry that some commentators have seized upon: that globalization may reduce the ability of countries to raise revenues through their fiscal systems—that, in the words of the noted fiscal economist Vito Tanzi, globalization is growing "fiscal termites"! He cites the growth of e-commerce, which is often tax-free; the growth of tax-minimizing "transfer pricing" within multinationals, which learn to take their profits where taxes are least; use of offshore financial centers; and other such trends that pose a threat to the ability to raise revenues as economic activity gets globalized.

But there is little evidence to date that the termites have wreaked havoc. The total tax burden of the members of the OECD has in fact increased over the last thirty years, from 26 percent of GDP in 1965 to 37 percent of GDP in 1997, despite Reagan, Thatcher, and globalization.[22] So, given the ingenuity of tax authorities, the institutional obstacles to dismantling spending, and the unwillingness to run huge budget deficits over long periods, most of the developed countries are unlikely to see their budgets fall prey to Tanzi's termites.

Then again, a novel argument can be advanced in support of the beneficial effect of globalization on the ability of small nation-states to retain their autonomy of preferences and political action, and hence on the practice of democracy. Based on the analytical and empirical work of the economists Alberto Alesina, Enrico Spolaore, and Romain Wacziarg, who have explored the relationship between the number and size of nations and global integration, one can argue that without globalization a small nation will feel constrained, if it is to enjoy scale economies, to merge into a larger union and thereby submerge its preferences into the larger whole, but with worldwide globalization and the ability to access truly large markets, it can exploit scale economies at arm's length and retain its autonomy.[23] Globalization, by relieving the pressure to join into federations and larger states simply so as to enjoy scale economies in production and trade, enables small nations to retain their individuality in economics and politics.

Are Politicians Undemocratic When They Embrace Globalization?

So it would appear that the arguments that globalization will promote democracy are more robust than those that say that it will impair its exercise and efficacy. But then there is yet a different criticism: that politicians embrace globalization even when the people oppose it. This is one of the two charges that are leveled against the globalizing governments; the other is that there is a "democratic deficit" at the World Trade Organization, which is an intergovernmental institution, a question examined below.

Carl Hamilton, an elected member of the Swedish parliament and a distinguished economist to boot, has responded effectively to the first charge. Consider his response to the argument, advanced by two activist authors, that elections are rarely fought on one issue and therefore it is "rather ludicrous" for elected governments to say that they are "legitimately" pushing for trade liberalization.[24] Hamilton's principal answer, abstracted from a much fuller refutation, is best stated in his own words:

> The authors are hardly correct that "a government rarely wins or loses an election on a particular issue." There are plenty of counter examples unless one defines an "issue" in an extremely narrow sense. . . . But do isolated cases of narrowly defined "issues" belong to the set of the interesting ones? Our answer is no: the authors seem unlikely to be correct when considering the direction of policy embedded in the large number of successive decisions over some forty years on multilateral trade rounds resulting in lower trade barriers and enhanced integration.
>
> Let us consider the OECD countries . . . assuming that *on average* there has been at least 25 members per year since 1960 and that the average period between general elections has been some four years. This means that there have been at least 250 general elections [and almost certainly more] among this group. If these governments' decisions to liberalise (manufactures) trade had been in systematic conflict with the voters' preferences, it is likely that such a misrepresentation at some points in time [would have] become serious election issues in some of the 250 elections.[25]

In fact, as Hamilton notes, trade and integration have repeatedly been the fodder of elections in both Europe and the United States, and in virtually all cases trade and integration have won the day. Even the closely fought NAFTA vote was affirmative, and the EU has continued its integration and its play at the multilateral trade negotiations unabated and unabashed. True, there have always been protectionist voices, now joined by anti-globalization voices, and sometimes they are very shrill. But that cannot be a reason to say that the pro-globalization decisions by politicians have been "undemocratic."

Of course, there is a further argument that the entire democratic process is illegitimate because corporations have captured it, that freer trade and direct investment lobbies are pushing for such integration of the world economy. Yes, some are, though many are old-fashioned protectionists who would rather retreat into the safety of sheltered domestic markets. But one has also to forget the rich complexity of the political process, the fact that there are countervailing lobbies such as unions, consumers, steel users (as against steel producers), and others. And one must also consider the role that intellectuals such as myself play in influencing policy determination, a role that John Maynard Keynes summed up in these famous words: "The ideas of economists and political philosophers, both when they are right and when they are wrong, are more powerful than is commonly understood. Indeed, the world is ruled by little else. Practical men, who believe themselves exempt from any intellectual influence, are usually the slaves of some defunct economist."[26] Indeed, in a recent book titled *Going Alone,* I and my co-authors have taken a close look at the extensive unilateral trade liberalization that occurred worldwide in the last quarter of a century, and the role of ideas and intellectuals is seen to play a major role in many of these episodes.[27]

Perhaps, however, there is something to be said for the rather subtle argument that by choosing policies such as trade liberalization and signing on to agreements and institutions such as NAFTA, today's politicians are locking future politicians into continuing these policies because the economic and political costs of withdrawal are asymmetrically higher than the benefits obtained by entry. This argument is usually produced by Mexican defenders of NAFTA and their North American friends as a virtue of bilateral agreements that multilateral agreements and institutions such as the WTO ostensibly do not enjoy, but it can be seen by opponents of such policies as a vice instead: that the freedom of choice of future politicians is being compromised.[28] Short of building in provisions for withdrawal from such agreements and arrangements—as indeed the United States has done in acceding to the WTO—it is difficult to see what can be said about this issue of intergenerational conflicts, which cuts both ways, being symmetrically applicable to restricting as to liberalizing agreements.

Does the World Trade Organization Suffer from a "Democratic Deficit"?

But then is it not true that the WTO, an international organization, suffers from a democratic deficit, from illegitimacy because governmental voices do not reflect the voices of NGOs? Elections in modern, liberal states do ensure legitimacy. The question is rather whether good governance and decision making require that the civil society voices be heard even in intergovernmental institutions such as the WTO, just as many democracies function today with the executive and the legislature listening to such voices when deciding on policy and on its interpretation and execution.

As in domestic politics today, this evolution of the domestic decision-making process is inevitable at the international level. But one must distinguish among voice, vote, and veto. And one must also note that the WTO is three-faceted: it oversees trade negotiations, it has a small secretariat that services the director general and several committees of officials and examines issues before the negotiators, and it has a Dispute Settlement Mechanism that decides, in light of the agreements reached by negotiating nations, on complaints brought before it by member nations.

Evidently, the negotiations are among governments, and they are free to include in their delegations anyone they want. Some nations, such as Belgium, still have only bureaucrats and members of parliament; others, such as the United States, now also carry both businessmen and civil society groups, including labor unions; and yet others, such as India, have opened up to businessmen but not to civil society groups (though these groups are consulted prior to the negotiations). In addition, it is now common for NGOs to have their own parallel show on the road at the negotiations, and they track the day-to-day developments and seek to influence the outcomes from outside.

The WTO secretariat does interact now with NGOs, business groups, parliamentarians, and other groups on a formalized basis. There have been, for instance, annual conferences with NGOs for some years. What is not known widely is that these meetings are inadequately funded, and that while governments of the rich countries make noises about giving civil society contacts more play, they still have underfunded the WTO to a degree invoking Scrooge rather than Soros.

The Dispute Settlement Mechanism has also become more transparent than it was, but then the WTO's predecessor, the GATT, did not have a binding dispute settlement mechanism, whereas the WTO does. So the GATT worked to settle disputes through politics in smoke-filled rooms where transparency was both physically impossible and diplomatically unwise. Today the WTO is a legalistic body; like courts worldwide, the proceedings must become transparent and will.

However, the NGO demand that they be allowed to submit amicus curiae briefs sounds great but runs into the problem (identified in Chapter 4) that, for the most part, only the rich-country NGOs, with their army of lawyers and their rich-country perspectives on matters that include labor and environmental issues, will be able to submit these briefs. It is natural for the lawyers and the bureaucrats in the United States to believe that God, not politics and themselves, has sanctified their way of doing things, but others have to put these matters into an appropriate context. Poor countries will have to be satisfied that the submission of such briefs will be symmetric and balanced between the rich- and poor-country NGOs. This decision is not to be made by lawyers; it is a political one. But progress can certainly be made by ingeniously adapting the solution to respond to the legitimate worries of the poor nations.

9

Culture Imperiled or Enriched?

On August 12, 1999, José Bové, an obscure Frenchman, and a group of other farmers entered the town of Millau in southwestern France and flattened a McDonald's that was still under construction.[1] The rubble was driven, in a celebratory fashion and much like a corpse in a hearse, through the town on trucks and tractors and dumped on its outskirts. With a theatrical flourish that the French language accentuates, he proclaimed: "The object was to have a non-violent but symbolically forceful action, in broad daylight and with the largest participation possible. . . . I believe that the French people have already made a decision about this case—they are with us in this fight against junk food and against globalization."

By fusing culture and agriculture, Bové was tapping into two of France's obsessions: the American threat to French culture—and who can deny that the French cuisine is one of France's cultural triumphs, even greater than its cinema?—and the threat to French agriculture from the spread of the Anglo-Saxon-led policies on trade liberalization that have intensified globalization.

As put exquisitely by Jean-Michel Normand in *Le Monde:* "McDonald's . . . commercial hegemony threatens our agriculture and its cultural hegemony insidiously ruins alimentary behaviour—both sacred reflections of the French identity." Believe it or not, Alain Rollat of *Le Monde* joined the lament and the alarm, declaring, "Resistance to the hegemonic pretenses of hamburgers is, above all, a cultural imperative."[2]

But the leveling of McDonald's also had an immense international salience because it was simultaneously a symbolic act of defiance pandering to two of today's profound prejudices: anti-Americanism and anti-globalization. BBC News reported that Bové, the plucky Frenchman, was regarded as "the little guy versus the big guy" and was being compared to Astérix, "a Gaul who took on the might of the Roman empire." He became "an icon of French individuality refusing to be swamped by the imperial forces."[3]

Bové was taken to court and sentenced to a three-month prison term, still being appealed in the French legal system. He lost his appeal to France's highest court, the Cour de Cassation, but threatened to go to the European Court of Human Rights in Strasbourg. Manifestly, Bové will never look back. Andy Warhol's celebrated fifteen minutes of fame have turned in his case into an enduring celebrity status. He has been a cult figure at Porto Alegre.

But if Bové's protest in Millau reflected the concern that globalization threatened mainstream culture, the way of life in the very heart of his beloved France, there has been equal alarm at the prospect that globalization could kill peripheral cultures. These are, of course, the tribal, often isolated cultures whose external contacts have been negligible enough to leave them at a level of "primitive" development. Not many are left. But their day in the sun has arrived—a member of one of them, Rigberto Menchu of Guatemala, was awarded a Nobel peace prize, and the United Nations has taken up their cause now through the Permanent Forum on Indigenous Issues.

If they can link up with the anti-globalization forces, they are guaranteed attention that is otherwise hard to come by. So consider the easy and gratuitous attack on globalization and on market-oriented reforms in India by L. Jawahar Nesan of Western Michigan University at a UN meeting on indigenous peoples recently. Talking of the Dalits, the untouchables of India, who are by no stretch of the imagination to be equated with indigenous peoples, Nesan said, "As for the future, the economic reforms currently under way in India [are] becoming the main enemy of the Dalits. Reduction of subsidies, stress on export-oriented growth, corporatization of farming, and privatization and disinvestments are bound to hit the Dalits the hardest."[4]

But are Bové and the leaders of the indigenous peoples correct in claiming that economic globalization is imperiling both mainstream and indigenous cultures? In my view, this is far too simplistic and pessimistic; just as often, economic globalization is a culturally enriching process.

Activists also complain that international institutions such as the WTO are rigged with rules that further add to the destruction of these cultures through globalization. Among the chief complainants in this regard has been the feisty minister of Canadian heritage, Sheila Copps. In June 1998, she brought together ministers of culture from twenty countries at a meeting (called a "summit," of course) sounding the alarm at the perils posed by globalization and by trade rules to the national cultures worldwide. Later, Mexico hosted the meeting in 1999; Greece followed in 2000. In Canada, the witticism is that "Sheila's cops" want to weaken the limits being negotiated at the WTO on imposition of restrictions on free trade in movies and other cultural products. Yet, wit aside, the issue raised is a serious one and requires closer scrutiny.

Mainstream Culture

Consider the obsession of Bové's compatriots with the unstoppable spread of English and the near demise of French worldwide. The growing triumph of English is a result not just of economic globalization but also of the fact that English-speaking countries have dominated the world militarily in the last two centuries. Historians have long observed that if the flag sometimes follows trade (as with the East India Company and the Dutch East Indies Company, the two great monopolies of England and the Netherlands that preceded the conquest of India and Indonesia), trade more often follows the flag.

If the nineteenth century was British, a time of Pax Britannica, and the twentieth century was American, when Pax Americana prevailed, the twenty-first century, which many feared would be Japan's, a Pax Japonica, promises to be American again.[5] In fact, since Britain is the metropolitan power from which America won its freedom and from whose progeny among the first immigrants, the Founding Fathers, it derived its unique constitution, the British have always enjoyed a "special relationship" in the United States, where it is common knowledge that a BBC accent and a peerage will get you everywhere on the East Coast!

The British Empire therefore is unique among all others in history in having enjoyed two innings: one its own in the nineteenth century and another vicariously through its former colony, the United States, in the twentieth. Certainly the Spanish, Portuguese, German, and French empires in the period of European conquest and expansion, not to mention the "evil empire" of Soviet Russia more recently, left legacies of disintegration, chaos, military dictatorships, and feudal regimes. The two innings, with America sharing the same language, have certainly given English an extraordinary momentum over an extended period.

But economic globalization, not always reflective of the international power structure, has also driven the spread of English. Japan was perhaps the last holdout. Japan's policy of what the cultural historian Henry Smith has aptly called "controlled openness" gave foreigners heavily cir-

cumscribed access to Japan and simultaneously prevented the colonization that brought many other non-Western cultures and economies closer
to Western norms in modern times. Commodore Perry's "black ships"
arrived in Japan in 1853, and the first full commercial treaty was signed
with the United States in 1858. With similar treaties to follow with European powers, "treaty ports," including Nagasaki, Kanagawa, and principally Yokohama, were opened to foreign residence and trade; and the
residences of foreigners elsewhere were confined to areas set aside as
foreign settlements. An old woodcut shows Yokohama with a main street
dividing the island into two, perhaps a symbol of the uneasy coexistence
of foreigners with native Japanese, and a tiny and fragile bridge at the
northern end that connects the island to the mainland, signifying the
controlled openness! The occupation after the Second World War pushed
the acculturation further but still so slowly that when the United States
succumbed to a Japan fixation and even Japan-bashing in the 1980s,
when Japan's economic engine seemed beyond successful competition,
it was still the case that, as a wit put it, you could buy from Japan in
English but had to sell to it in Japanese. But today's Japan has gone the
way of all others, as young Japanese now write and even speak English
with a facility that once seemed beyond their abilities even if assisted by
Professor Higgins.

And so when the "global pessimists" argue that "English is a killer
language spreading like a cultural plague around the world, eliminating
distinctive voices and cultural identities," I side rather with Charles
Leadbeater, the English intellectual and author of *Up the Down Escalator: Why the Global Pessimists Are Wrong*, when he responds: "[M]any
varieties and hybrids of the language have emerged. The pessimists' black
and white world rules out the possibility of people reaching these fruit-
ful combinations in language, commerce and technology. But that is how
people increasingly seem to cope, by creating hybrids."[6]

Indeed, no better illustration of this hybridization, the co-opting
and refashioning of English idiom, grammar, and spelling to mesh with
local color, is provided than by Salman Rushdie, who extravagantly tosses
together Bombay slang and impeccable English in his novels touched by
the magic realism that, in turn, is borrowed from South America's gifted
writers. And the Indian subcontinent's maniacal mangling of metaphors
is fondly recollected by Angus Wilson in *Reflections in a Writer's Eye* when
he records his Ceylonese friend as saying: "You see, I was a bad egg, so
my parents sent me to Jaffna College" and "I like the village here, but this
house I have at present is not my cup of tea."[7] Yet more telling is the
continual mixing of metaphors, as in the apocryphal story of the malin-
gering Indian clerk asking the English manager for leave to attend his

mother's funeral. He writes: "Sir: The hand that rocked my cradle has finally kicked the bucket. Can I have leave to go to my village?" The manager rises to the occasion and responds: "Dear Mr. Chatterjee: Your mother has died once too often. So I must put my foot down with a firm hand. Your application is denied."

In fact, as one looks around the world, one sees that the local use of indigenous languages has also revived, alongside and at times in response to the spreading international use of English. The rise of multiculturalism and the celebration of ethnicity rather than its extinction are modern phenomena that defy the global pessimists' dire predictions.

The United States has even gone bilingual, for another globalization-related reason: the illegal movement of Mexicans and other Hispanics into the United States. They are often illiterate and impoverished; their illegal status also forces them to suffer an underground existence. Therefore, their extensive and exclusive use of Spanish, rather than the traditional shift to English by previous (legal) immigrant groups, is inevitable. Given the American emphasis on equal rights for all, a shift to multilingualism down the road is equally certain. Already the cash-dispensing machines of the banks have been "talking" to customers, not just in English but in Spanish and lately also in Chinese. Gujarati, Bengali, Russian, and other languages can not be far behind.

Bové's colorful assault on McDonald's will not survive scrutiny either. For every protester, there are many more who patronize McDonald's throughout France. Since 1972, when it arrived in that country, its French customers have made France McDonald's third largest market in Europe. Its Champs-Elysées branch raked in revenues of nearly $5 million in 2001 alone.[8]

The irony is not that McDonald's has destroyed French culture but how French culture and French consumers have decimated instead the mold that marks its American restaurants:

> For 50 years, a primary ingredient of the recipe for expansion at McDonald's—and the entire fast-food industry—had been consistency. A Pittsburgh McDonald's looked like a Paris McDonald's, which in turn looked like a McDonald's in Prague. Menus might vary to reflect local tastes, but the essential offering was universal: cheap food served in a bright, clean and, above all, familiar-looking setting.
>
> A dramatic departure from that formula is taking place here in France, where franchisees face increasing competition from fast baguettes. Half of this nation's 932 McDonald's outlets have been upgraded to a level that would make them almost unrecognizable to an American. Far from being cookie-cutter copies, each of the remodeled restaurants features one of at least eight different themes—such as "Mountain," complete with a wood-beam ceiling reminiscent of a ski chalet. The company has even begun to replace its tradi-

tional red-and-yellow signs with signs in muted tones of maroon and mustard. And while the basic burger offerings remain the same, there is espresso and brioche.[9]

True, the sociologist Jean-Pierre Poulain has observed:

> During my field research, I have been struck by the strange self-justification discourse used by most adults, saying that they were coming to McDonald's for the first and last time. It was as if they were coming out of an X-rated movie.[10]

But such masking behavior is all too common, of course, during a cultural or social exposure to new impulses, as is happening in France as it encounters and embraces, adopts and adapts to, American cinema, pop music, food, and television.[11]

For those who worry about the intrusive presence in their beloved locales of the McDonald's icons, the golden arches, there is a further lesson to be learned: even the most sacred icons will yield to profits. And the arches have in fact gone from many McDonald's restaurants around Paris.

Indeed, these adaptations to local cultures, and the proliferation of these assimilated and acculturated McDonald's restaurants, is so remarkable worldwide that one can appreciate the bon mot where a Swedish grandfather, long used to seeing McDonald's restaurants in Stockholm, goes to visit his granddaughter at Barnard College in New York and tells her: "Yo, yo, they even have McDonald's in New York!" In fact, the reality eerily reflects the bon mot. The *New York Times* reporter Elisabeth Rosenthal wrote recently from Beijing:

> Europeans may be wont to view every Big Mac as a terrifying sign of American cultural imperialism, but Chinese have mostly welcomed the invasion— indeed they have internalized it. In one recent survey, nearly half of all Chinese children under 12 identified McDonald's as a domestic brand, according to Beijing's Horizon Market Research.[12]

The fearful notion that the world's many cultures are doomed to be buried under an American avalanche also ignores the fact that other cultures are doing very well indeed, and even exporting their own artifacts and products to others around the world. The United Nations Educational, Scientific, and Cultural Organization (UNESCO) has estimated that for music, printed matter, visual arts, photography, radio, television, and other media, the share of just the developing countries had risen from 12 to 30 percent in the twenty years ending 1998. Of course, this is not quite the same as exporting their culture; much of it could simply be the export of music and books that were the products of rich-country artists and writers but printed and produced more cheaply in the poor countries! Still, the numbers are large enough to suggest a two-way flow. Besides, when one gets down to that detail, the facts are still reassuring to the anti-alarmists. For instance, as the economist Tyler Cowen has argued, award-winning movies have come from Iran, Hong Kong, China, Denmark, India, Britain, and France, among other nations, and the trend has been certainly cosmopolitan and two-way as far as the United States is concerned.[13]

Yet another reality check is in order. Cultures will certainly change over time, as invention, organizational innovation, political change such as democratization, and globalization on many dimensions occur. This process of decay of the old and evolution of the new always evokes nostalgia among more sensitive observers. Just read the great Japanese novelist Junichiro Tanizaki's beautiful essay "In Praise of Shadows," where he laments the passing of the old Japan. But then, Japan has also given much to the world through her literature, her cinema, and her sushi, and the cultures of others have been changed by contact with Japanese aesthetics, arts, and artifacts.

A few more observations are in order here.[14] The idyllic past whose passing one laments is based on a reconstruction that bears little relationship to the reality today. Thus the British writer George Monbiot, like many others, has advocated reversion to a "modern peasant economy, based on organic food and local markets, bypassing and disavowing the supermarkets." But that countryside is no longer the idealized version that we know from the captivating Impressionist paintings of Monet and Cézanne or from John Constable's enchanting rendering in *The Cornfield*.

It is also interesting that when these critics of globalization imagine the countryside that they want to revert to, their desired "utopia" admits elements that themselves were intrusions into the rural scene and were attended by articulate, even impassioned, protest at the time. Thus, W. G. Hoskins, who wrote eloquently in 1963 about how he would like to have England preserve and enhance Rutland, then England's smallest county, against the "incessant noise, speech and all the other acids of modernity," nonetheless allowed for the railways to intrude on his landscape. But the mere invention of the railways and their appearance in rural England had led to protests from farmers, based on fears such as that the roar of the railways would terrify cows so much that they would not yield milk! And with the fears of the past truly forgotten, today's Britain sees the railways as part of its heritage, with ninety-one steam railways and museums in England and thirty-six elsewhere.

Indeed, human beings have a complex self-identity whose mosaic draws on "horizontal" colors that come from living with others within a community and "vertical" colors that come from ethnic and historical roots and memories, often reconstructed and imagined. Nearly all societies will therefore treasure the past, seeking to freeze and recall in museums the cultural heritage they decide to hold precious. As cultures evolve and elements of them vanish, we must decide what we need to remember and retain in our midst. All of the past cannot be frozen endlessly in time. This conscious choice of the elements of one's heritage that must be preserved is precisely what happens as the old gives way to the new. And so we have the National Trust in Britain to preserve the historic castles and palaces that cannot be privately maintained, the use of public and philanthropic funds to finance museums and the arts in the United States, public support for the revival of Noh plays in Japan, and the work of UNESCO in saving great treasures in the poor countries.

Nostalgia, then, is used not to bottle up change, which in any case is inevitable, but to decide what a society really wants to remember in the context of change and then to find ways to do so. That is surely the way to go.

Indigenous Culture

As one scans the proclamations of activists such as Blanca Chancoso, president of the Confederation of Indigenous Nationalities in Ecuador, and Chief Arthur Manuel of the Neskolith band in British Columbia in Canada, as well as the writings of the social and cultural anthropologists who work with them, it is easy to see that indigenous peoples have suffered grossly at the hands of the Europeans, who swept through their lands in the Americas in a conquest that they identify as "colonialism and imperialism." Annihilation at worst and marginalization at best have been the fate of the indigenous peoples who once populated North America and Latin America.

But it is a great leap from acceptance of this history to argue that globalization is therefore an equal or at least significant threat to these communities, weakened as they are by this tragic experience. It is hard to imagine that, as with colonialism and imperialism in history, these communities face extinction from globalization. Yet that is what these activists and anthropologists seem to believe.

And so they oppose trade liberalization, for instance. When the Free Trade Agreement of the Americas (FTAA) was being discussed in Quebec City, Canada, at the Summit of the Americas in April 2001, these indigenous leaders were out in force, opposing the creation of such a trading bloc. And recall that the Zapatistas from Chiapas have opposed NAFTA as well.

Their biggest worry seems to have been that they would lose their lands because the governments of the countries in which the indigenous groups were supplanted by the intruding colonialists and settlers in the last two centuries appear to have turned to legal doctrines such as the theory of *terra nullius* (under which communal rights to "unoccupied" land are not recognized). Such doctrines have made it easier to deprive the indigenous groups of their traditional right to deny legal purchase by others of such lands. Chief Arthur Manuel has argued that his community faces forestry companies that are using "colonial-era doctrines of discovery": these doctrines "said we indigenous peoples had no property interests," thus native land "accrued" to Europeans. This ethnocentric idea "is the essence of usurping and violating the rights of indigenous peoples."[15] Chief Arthur has denounced the Canadian government's Comprehensive Claims Policy as tantamount to extinguishing claims to territory in exchange for small benefits.

But what has globalization to do with this, really? If their complaints are valid, these policies and enabling laws were put in place to seize their lands forcibly and without adequate compensation so that they could be put to use for economic activity such as building railways, dams, and factories. But they would have been, and indeed were, pursued regardless of whether the country was autarkic or outward-oriented in trade and investment, for instance. The problem has been the unequal power between the successful settlers of yesterday and the conquered tribes, between governments of today and these politically powerless indigenous peoples.[16]

There is nothing here that is a result of economic globalization. The reprehensible situation (which fortunately is in transition in many countries—for instance, Chile has since 1990 a revised law that shifts the balance more toward protecting the property rights of the indigenous communities than was the case earlier) is historically derived from conquest and subsequent exploitation through laws and processes developed to facilitate exploitation via what often were underhanded land seizures. Globalization, of course, increases the incentive to expropriate more lands in this manner. It may also, through increased economic prosperity, strengthen the ability of those who wish to expropriate the indigenous groups' lands. But I have not been able to find empirical evidence to link increased globalization with enhanced expropriation.

In fact, when multinationals are among those who seek to utilize these domestic policies on land use, that very fact seems to give more political salience and hence an extra edge to protests by the activists among the indigenous groups and can lead either to the termination of the planned takeover of the community's lands or to larger compensatory transfers of resources to the communities whose lands are to be co-opted for use. These outcomes are evident in the recent protest by a few indigenous Pehuenche Indians, in fact six families, who have protested against the building of the Ralco Dam in south-central Chile by Endesa, a Spanish power company. Refusing to sell their land to be submerged by the proposed reservoir even though ninety-three other families accepted compensation, they held up the work on the half-finished dam by arguing, "Our ancestors are buried here; we can't trade them in for money."[17]

The case that globalization, and in particular trade integration, contributes to devastation of the indigenous cultures in this fashion is therefore unproven. So when an anthropologist writes, after the Canadian government's use of armed police and tear gas to contain the protests at the Quebec summit where the proposed FTAA was on the agenda, that "the state [in its use of force] mimicked the *grotesque violence enacted through free trade policies*" (italics added), one can only gasp! And one can barely repress astonishment when the rhetoric escalates further: "The indigenous activists in Quebec were already aware that at numerous sites—streets, villages, and fields—where their communities confront globalization, prevailing economic discourse is intimately conjoined with state repression."[18]

Ironically, it is the likelihood that globalization may pass them by, rather than the fear that globalization will in fact reach them and harm their people, that has worried economists. Many of us have argued that the economic benefits from the increased prosperity that globalization will bring through trade, aid, investments, and technical change will likely bypass traditional, "primitive" groups, for instance in the tribal areas in India, because they are only tenuously connected to the mainstream economy. So special policies are necessary to bring them into the mainstream. In short, economists want to invent and then implement policies that would extend to the indigenous peoples the globalization-induced prosperity that they might be missing out on!

Thus the economist's view of the matter is diametrically opposed to that of the anthropologist and the indigenous activist. The former celebrates the integration of these peoples into the mainstream economy that is itself integrating into the world economy, and is distressed when globalization bypasses them. The latter lament it and would like to delink the indigenous peoples from the globalization phenomenon. In the end, an overwhelming source of difference lies in the fact that economists accept and indeed invite change, whereas anthropologists do not.

Much of the anthropological literature that supports the anti-globalization attitudes stresses the contrasts between modernity and the traditional values that the indigenous peoples have inherited and the activists in their ranks espouse.[19] But as modernity makes its way, one must ask: how many followers do the activist leaders represent? The pull of modernity in many ways has been the source of the outmigration of rural young people to urban areas in search of a different, more alluring lifestyle. There is surely no reason to think that it does not work in the case of the indigenous groups as well. It is perhaps a low blow, but the easy acceptance of the unpersuasive notion that the indigenous peoples generally, as distinct from the activists within them, wish to be trapped in their traditions and associated value systems and economic deprivation (by the standards of modern consumerism) has led to excessively cynical commentary such as the following from Doug Henwood, the editor of *Left Business Observer*. In reaction to a meeting of the International Forum on Globalization at Riverside Church, the famous site of anti–Vietnam War protests, in New York in 1995, where the speakers included the famous Indian activist Vandana Shiva, an accomplished physicist by training, the editor wrote:

> The ecofeminist Vandana Shiva views technology as a male disruption of the sacred woman-nature dyad, and advocates a "subsistence" economic model. ... Shiva opened her talk at the conference by noting that one of the "positive externalities" of globalization was that she'd made so many good friends around the world.... If "globalization" can produce such desirable things as friends ... perhaps it's wrong to name it as your main enemy.
>
> It's ironic that people should rack up the frequent flyer miles while touting the virtues of localism—writing books and running institutes while telling the masses that they should stay home and tend to their lentils. This recalls T. S. Eliot's remark that "on the whole it would appear to be for the best that the great majority of human beings should go on living in the place where they were born." At least Eliot, who was born in St. Louis but moved to London at age 26, was an avowed snob.[20]

In the end, the indigenous peoples will have to confront the fact that the old yields to the new. Only active nurturing of the collective memory and a selective preservation of cultural artifacts can be a response, not the impractical fossilization of traditional attitudes and values.

The International Rules of Globalization

But cultural concerns have arisen also in the context of the rules being negotiated at international institutions such as the WTO to oversee and manage globalization. Two sources of discord, between the United States and Europe in the main but with many other lesser players in the fray as well, have been (1) the American desire to eliminate trade barriers on cinema and television, in particular, and the European resistance to treating these as simply "goods and services," with the Europeans and many others arguing for a "cultural exception" to the freeing of trade; and (2) the contrasting attitudes of the Americans and the Europeans, with different nations arrayed on both sides of the divide, concerning the safety and hence the wisdom of free trade in hormone-fed beef and genetically modified products.

At the WTO and in bilateral trade negotiations, the United States made ill-disguised threats against foreign nations that were refusing to open their cinemas and televisions to free access by American movies and TV shows.[21] The French and South Koreans responded with vociferous protests.

Faced with possible capitulation by their government to such American pressures, brought by Hollywood lobbyists, several South Korean actors, clad in black, gathered in December 1998 to mourn their own deaths, staging a mock funeral marking the death of the fledgling Korean cinema. While the restrictions continued, with a quota system under which theaters are required to screen Korean movies no less than 146 days a year, the Korean government was ready by 2002, four years later, to relax or eliminate these quotas as part of a proposed bilateral investment treaty with the United States. Predictably, the protesting actors and directors objected that the decision undermined Korea's cultural identity and "should not be judged only by market principles."[22] Nearly fifty filmmakers, wearing purple and yellow bands reading "Keep the screen quota as it is," claimed that the end of the quota would be a "suicidal act."

The French government has been more than willing to go along with similar quotas, claiming that films and television shows are "cultural goods" and that this should entitle them to exemption from the rules of commerce.[23] The European Union, acting under French pressure, passed the famous TV broadcasting directive Television Without Frontiers in 1989, requiring that "when practicable" the larger share of television content must be of European origin—that is, films and programs made in Europe (joint productions must be under "preponderant control" by the European partners). The French have toughened the regulation by insisting that 60 percent of the transmissions be European and 50 percent must be in the French language.

In addition, regarding cinema, the French government has a 10 percent cinema tax surcharge, the revenue from which is used to subsidize French filmmaking.[24] This policy was also the subject of the Hollywood lobbyists' objection during the Uruguay Round negotiations, though these efforts were resisted and did not succeed in the end. The position

that Jack Valenti, the politically powerful and well-connected chief lob-
byist for Hollywood, had advanced, according to trade negotiators outside of the United States, was little short of astonishing. He had claimed
that since American films were being shown in French cinemas and raising tax revenues that subsidized French films, those revenues should be
split with producers of American films pro rata to the 57 percent share
of American films in the total shown in French theaters. At the time I
wrote sarcastically to the *New York Times,* exposing the absurdity of
Valenti's lobbying efforts: "I suggest that this remarkable new principle
of taxation be adopted symmetrically by the United States. Our toll re-
ceipts (often earmarked for our highway spending) should be shared
with Japan pro rata to the number of Japanese cars that pay road and
bridge tolls in this country."[25]

In fact, the free-traders among us do allow for a "cultural exception." While the lobbyists invoke the doctrine of free trade to advance
their agendas and designs, the fact is that we teach our students that
there are non-economic objectives in life and that, rather than disregard
these social objectives, we should minimize the economic costs of meeting them. In fact, the best textbooks on how to design and pursue the
best policies in an open economy are quite explicit on all this: the French,
South Koreans, and Canadians, among many others, have allies among
the really informed free-traders.

But that does lead one to ask: are policies such as audiovisual restrictions and quotas the response that in fact minimizes the costs of
meeting these objectives? Or do we have better policy options? As it happens, there are better options.

At the outset, it is hard to see how, with modern technology, these
restrictions can be anything but a nuisance with little effect. Today, given
the ever-increasing ease of access to movies and television programs
worldwide, and the ability to enjoy them on DVDs and the Internet at
home, where no effective constraints can apply, how can any government, including even the draconian Chinese government (which just
had to reverse its attempts at regulating and restricting access to Google),
really make restrictions effective? The history of grassroots discontent
spread by dissidents in the Soviet Union (the samizdat phenomenon)
had in fact led to the realization that, contrary to modern technology reinforcing George Orwell's dystopia where Big Brother would be watching
you, the tables had been turned on Big Brother himself. Hence the witticism that the CP (Communist Party) had been weakened, even destroyed,
but certainly not strengthened, by the PC (the personal computer).

So the policy option of restricting trade with quotas on movies and
the like is not even a feasible one, if truth be told. You buy American ill

will, but to little advantage. Suppose, however, that it were a feasible policy. It would still be an inferior choice.

If the intention is to help domestic filmmaking withstand the on-slaught of American films, the smart thing to do is to subsidize your own productions. So instead of sheltering Renoir and Rohmer from com-petition with Spielberg and Shyamalan, assist them financially to pro-duce their movies and let them compete in the French marketplace, using competition laws to ensure equal access to all films and effectively out-lawing the cornering of theater outlets, for instance, leaving it to the French audiences to view what they wish.

This policy of permitting free imports of films while subsidizing the production of local films would surely be a better option. Indeed, that is more or less what we are likely to be moving to if only the Hollywood lobbyists were not so intolerant of cultural support.[26] The "threatened" countries should also realize that such promotion, as against protection, of local films does work. It did in the case of Satyajit Ray's early films, and it has worked also for other artistic, "highbrow" films in India, sev-eral supported by the Film Institute of India, which receives state funds. South Korea has also discovered that local films, when well made, can compete with American films. *Swiri*, a local feature film (produced, in-cidentally, without subsidy), attracted, four weeks into its release, a record 1.25 million viewers in Seoul alone, promising to rival the record audi-ences for Hollywood's *Titanic*. Pessimism about both the ability of local filmmaking to survive and the assistance that can be meaningfully pro-vided when survival is an issue is surely exaggerated and often wrong.

But the American tendency to consider such cultural concerns as little more than masked manifestations of protectionism by others, a tendency that Hollywood lobbyists such as Valenti take advantage of in Washington as they pursue their agendas, also needs to be explained. The Americans certainly find it difficult to see global integration as a threat to culture, for they are truly an exceptional nation here, as in most other matters.

America is built on immigration, and immigrants are a sizeable frac-tion of the annual addition to the labor force. Multiple ethnicities are simply taken for granted, and multiculturalism has a natural constitu-ency that has only grown in recent years. In my classes at Columbia, it can be difficult to find a true "native" American, born into U.S. citizen-ship; the faculty also come from countries around the world. This trans-lates into an openness to cultures. Indian music, Chinese acupuncture, and a host of other cultural influences freely work themselves into America's kaleidoscope. These cultural imports wind up fitted into an ever-expanding mosaic; they are not seen as a threat.

At the same time, America's enormous cultural vitality and technological creativity, combined with hegemonic status in world politics, make her a net exporter of culture, giving her therefore no sense of threat from that direction either: it is *her* culture that spreads. But this spread of American culture threatens others to whom it goes. The spread of low culture, symbolized by McDonald's and Coke, accentuates intergenerational conflicts at times, leading to the older generation's nostalgia for their vanishing ways, as I have already discussed. But the problem is more acute with high culture. In particular, the United States is at the cutting edge of women's rights, children's rights, and much else that the more traditional, at times feudal or oligarchic, regimes elsewhere find threatening to their cultural and social order. America creates waves that threaten to drown them.

But that is not all. America stands out also because it is today the world's most experimental society in its attitudes toward technical

"Something's wrong with the broccoli. Please take it back to the kitchen and have it genetically modified."

© The New Yorker collection 1999 J.B. Handelsman from cartoonbank.com

change. Where Americans see technology as solving problems, others see it as creating them. That difference in attitudes, a cultural difference for sure, underlies the contrasting positions taken by the Americans and the Europeans on the issues of hormone-fed beef and genetically modified (GM) products. The widespread use of silicone implants by women and of Viagra by men in the United States, one may remark, has almost turned the nation into one where artificially enhanced women are being chased by artificially aroused men! The contrast between the Americans and the precaution-obsessed Europeans on GM products is well illustrated by a cartoon from the *New Yorker* that shows a dissatisfied customer telling the waitress to take the broccoli back to the kitchen and "have it genetically modified": instead of laying traps in your path, GM processes aid you in your pursuit of happiness.

For these cultural reasons, therefore, Americans uniquely find it difficult to see why free trade in cinema, television, GM products, and so on is considered by others to pose a threat to their culture and well-being. In consequence, Americans see the ugly hand of protectionism behind agitations and policy actions, such as the exclusion of hormone-fed beef from other markets even though the exclusion is based on fear rather than greed. And it only reinforces the efforts of lobbyists for cultural industries such as Hollywood to exploit and misuse the case for free trade to advance their own agendas.

10

Wages and Labor Standards at Stake?

arx was famously wrong when he predicted the progressive immiseration of the proletariat.[1] The real wages and living conditions of the working classes improved over the span of the nineteenth century, reducing the squalor that has been captured for posterity by social critics such as Chadwick and Hegel and by writers such as Dickens.[2] Marx got the effects of accumulation under capitalism wrong: it can, and often will, raise wages by increasing the demand for labor. But the improvement in working conditions was a result of social legislation such as the Factory Acts of England, which paved the way for the protection of workers.

Anti-globalizers fear that Marx is striking again: that, thanks to globalization, his prediction of falling wages is finally coming to pass. Labor unions in rich countries fear that trade with poor countries with low wages will drive down the real wages of their own workers and produce paupers in their midst. They also sense a threat to their labor standards, achieved through well over a century of anguish and agitation, as trade with poor countries with lower standards intensifies and some multinationals are seen to move to these low-standards locations, "taking jobs away." The resulting pressure to lower standards produces in this view a race to the bottom as these rich countries abandon their high standards to ensure competitiveness.

These fears appear plausible, no doubt about it. Yet the facts strongly suggest that they are not supported by evidence. Most studies of the real wages of workers assign to trade at best a small fraction of the decline in real wages in the 1980s and much of the 1990s. I will argue here the stronger proposition that trade has actually helped the workers, not just harmed them insignificantly, by moderating the decline that was instead caused by technical change that economized on the use of unskilled labor.

At the same time, there is no evidence for a race to the bottom. The reality is that political pressures have developed instead for imposing higher standards, whether appropriate or not, on the poor countries. So we witness paradoxically, as is demonstrated in this chapter, what is in fact a race to the top.

Globalization and Workers' Wages

It is certainly possible that closer integration by the richer nations with the poor countries, with a more abundant supply of unskilled labor, will depress the wages of the richer countries' workers. What is the intuition behind this fear? It makes sense to assume that lower prices for labor-intensive goods, among which textiles and shoes are obvious examples, brought about by imports from the poor countries, should translate into lower wages for labor. Therefore, one can legitimately regard trade with poor countries as an *indirect* way in which their impoverished masses will drive down our wages, just as their emigration to our countries will do it *directly*.

As it happens, this parallel between the effects of free immigration and of free trade in goods found an echo in political debates over immigration policy in the last century. It is interesting to recall the fierce debate that broke out in England over the proposed immigration legislation in 1905 that would have created quota restrictions on immigrants in response to the "alien invasion" by Central European Jews of London at the end of the nineteenth century. In that political fracas, the free-traders were also free-immigrationists, while the immigration restrictionists were also trade protectionists.

This intuitive parallel with immigration, which makes trade with poor countries a cause of concern by the labor unions seeking to protect their members' earnings, was also manifest in the firestorm that broke out in the United States over the inclusion of Mexico in NAFTA in the early 1990s. The influx of impoverished Mexicans across the Rio Grande— the so-called peso refugees, many illegal migrants—had already provoked calls to curtail that flow in order to safeguard American workers' wages and working conditions. The prospect of NAFTA raised similar objections: imports from Mexico would also have this adverse impact on American workers.

So while some thought that trade would improve Mexican prosperity and cut down on Mexican emigration to America eventually, many others, including the labor unions and influential Democrats such as Richard Gephardt and David Bonior, were concerned instead with the immediate pressure on American workers' wages that they expected from NAFTA. And, in a throwback to the English debate at the end of the nineteenth century, some opposed NAFTA and simultaneously proposed tougher immigration control measures.

Available evidence makes it difficult, however, to argue that trade with poor countries has been responsible for the stagnation, perhaps even a decline, in the real wages of workers in the rich countries, particularly in America. Several economists have examined this question, and the overwhelming majority, including Paul Krugman of Princeton (now a fiercely liberal *New York Times* columnist) and Robert Lawrence of Harvard, are agreed that the role of trade with poor countries in depressing wages is small, perhaps even negligible. But even they give too much away. If the evidence is examined somewhat closely, it can be argued that trade with poor countries is likely to have *improved* wages, in the sense that it has moderated the decline that would have occurred due to non-trade-related factors, chiefly labor-saving technical change.

To understand why, remember that this fear follows from the fact that the poor countries export labor-intensive goods such as textiles, garments, shoes, and toys to us. If the prices of these goods fall in trade because of increasing supplies from the poor countries, this will trigger a decline in the reward to unskilled workers: an intuitive effect, as explained earlier, going from lower prices of the goods produced to lower real wages of the workers producing them.[3] Thus the key issue is whether the prices of such goods have actually been falling, triggering the declining real wages.

Here the evidence really does not support the assertion. During the 1980s, when the real wages of American workers were stagnant, the prices of the labor-intensive goods as a group actually rose relative to the prices of the set of all other goods in world trade. And their prices actually fell during the 1970s, when American real wages, defined both as compensation per worker and as the less satisfactory average hourly earnings (which do not include non-wage benefits), rose.[4]

What happens to the prices of these goods depends on a host of factors that affect the production and consumption of those goods, chiefly in the poor countries. If their production rises faster than consumption, the effect is to increase exports of these goods. Increased exports, in turn, will reduce the world prices of these goods . The factors that affect production include capital accumulation and technical change. Economists have demonstrated that both these constituents of growth tend to reduce the production and hence the exports of labor-intensive goods.

Capital accumulation increases the supply of capital and therefore creates an extra incentive to producers of capital-intensive goods. Technical change will do the same since it is concentrated in practice in industries producing capital-intensive goods, and technical progress there tends to pull in resources from the less progressive industries that typically produce labor-intensive goods.[5] Therefore, the rapid accumulation of capital and absorption of technology in the Far East and then in the Near East have led to a progressive fall in the relative prices of labor-intensive goods, rather than in their rise, as feared by the unions.

The common mistake is to assume that trade in labor-intensive manufactures will result in exports from one poor country being piled on top of those of another in an endless process that would make them come like gangbusters into the markets of the rich countries, depressing prices and lowering real wages. In truth, because of technical change and capital accumulation in the countries that are growing out of the poor-country ranks (e.g., East Asia in the 1970s and 1980s), the entry of new exports of labor-intensive manufactures by poor countries is offset by the withdrawal of exports of labor-intensive manufactures by the rapidly growing erstwhile poor countries. The latter group of countries become exporters of capital-intensive manufactures and importers of labor-intensive manufactures instead. Therefore, the *net* exports of labor-intensive manufactures to the rich countries grow far less dramatically than if one conjured up the image of everything piling on, burying the rich countries in an avalanche of exports. The fear that the "yellow peril" (as the phenomenon of rapidly expanding exports from Japan was described in the 1930s) would be joined by the "brown peril" and eventually by the "black peril" as poor countries emerged as exporters of labor-intensive manufactures is belied by the fact that the "yellow peril" is *replaced* by the "brown peril," and so forth. International economists have long understood this phenomenon empirically, calling it the phenomenon of ladders of comparative advantage.

This more comforting picture is exactly what the Australian economist Ross Garnaut showed in 1996. Thus in the chart below one can witness how East Asia steadily increased net exports of labor-intensive manufactures in the 1970s while Japan (whose income had been growing rapidly) reduced them. The same pattern repeated itself in the period from 1980 to 1994, when the net exports of East Asian countries (the NICs, newly industrializing countries) declined from over 10 percent of world trade in labor-intensive manufactures to nearly zero, while China went in a crossing diagonal from around 2 percent to over 14 percent. The difference between the two leaves a greatly reduced net impact on what Garnaut calls the "old industrial countries," the rich nations, on average.

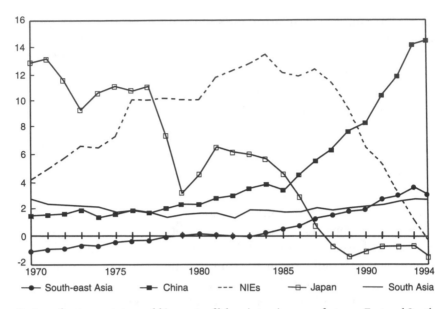

Ration of net exports to world imports of labor-intensive manufactures, East and South Asia 1970–94 (%). *Note:* South-east Asia includes ASEAN (including Singapore) and Vietnam; NIEs include Taiwan, Hong Kong, Korea, and Singapore; and South Asia includes India, Pakistan, Bangladesh, and Sri Lanka. *Source:* UN trade data, International Economic DataBank, The Australian National University, prepared by Ross Garnaut.

A recent empirical study by the economists Robert Feenstra and Gordon Hanson examined the effect on real wages of unskilled American workers as a result of outsourcing (i.e., buying components from other producers instead of producing these components oneself) to foreign suppliers of labor-intensive components in U.S. manufacturing during the period 1972–90. This study also concluded that the effect of such imports of labor-intensive goods for producers (rather than as goods for consumers, such as textiles and shoes), much of it also from poor countries, actually *raised* the real wages of the workers.[6]

So the principal cause of worry for the unions and their political allies, that a trade-driven fall in the (relative) prices of labor-intensive manufactures, whether of consumer goods or of outsourced components, will drive down the real wages of workers in rich countries is not compelling. Nor are other trade-related explanations that have been produced for this pessimistic scenario. Thus, for instance, it has been argued that labor-saving technical change, which is the real culprit, is itself induced by international competition faced by labor-intensive industries and the pressure on wages there. But think about it a little. If wages are declining, then induced technical change is likely to bias the search for technology in a direction that will use *more*, rather than less, of the cheapening labor. But the problem for real wages of the unskilled workers comes from labor-*saving* technical change.

In short, the contention that trade with the poor countries will produce wage declines in our midst is not compelling when examined: the underlying premises do not square with the facts.[7] Moreover, if we shift the focus of our analysis to how protection as presently practiced actually affects workers, we get yet another picture that portrays protection as harmful to workers. Current protection in the United States seems particularly aimed at lower-end consumer goods (such as flip-flops) that have virtually gone out of production in the United States by now and where the net effect on our workers' well-being comes not from the effect on their wages in employment, but overwhelmingly from their role as consumers.

The further findings on this question by Edward Gresser, reported in *Foreign Affairs*, are startling: "Tariff policy, without any deliberate intent, has evolved into something astonishingly tough on the poor. Young single mothers buying cheap clothes and shoes now pay tariffs five to ten times higher than middle-class or rich families pay in elite stores."[8] The removal of these tariffs would destroy this highly differentiated and inegalitarian tariff structure, which undercuts the real incomes of the poorest consumers and therefore of the working class.

Race to the Top, Not to the Bottom

The fear that the labor standards in the rich countries will be corroded by trade with, and investment in, the poor countries bothers workers and unions as much as the fear of an induced decline in wages. They are afraid that, faced with international competition or threats of employers to leave for locations where the standards are lower, employers will successfully manage politically to persuade governments to revise labor (and environmental) standards downward. Again, this seems likely, but does it happen systematically?

It generally does not seem to, at least if you look at recent American experience. Two examples suggest skepticism, if not rejection, of the race-to-the-bottom hypothesis. Take the fiercely competitive garment industry, where the politically active Union of Needletrades, Industrial, and Textile Employees (UNITE) operates. Its former president, Jay Mazur, and the current president, Bruce Raynor, have been strong proponents of the race-to-the-bottom view. But there is no evidence that this competition has led to a decline in labor and safety standards in the garment district in New York City, for instance. It is true that there are many sweatshops in the garment district. But the causes of these low standards, in violation of legislated standards, are twofold: the appalling lack of enforcement (because of a dearth of inspectors through the 1980s and 1990s) for the industry nationwide, and the presence of illegal immigrants who cannot demand legislated rights because of fear of deportation. In fact, if the degree to which standards actually fall below the legislated standards in these sweatshops has increased in the last two decades, it is surely likely to reflect the increased bipartisan agreement on introducing greater domestic enforcement (including through the use of employer sanctions) against illegal immigrants—an illiberal consensus that included the union movement itself until just recently![9]

As a contribution to the growing NAFTA debate, the General Accounting Office conducted a study of furniture firms faced with tough lead paint regulations in California and their migration across the Rio Grande.[10] The GAO estimated that a small fraction of wood products firms had moved, and concluded that their responses to questions concerning what profit-making factors had induced them to leave for Mexico were quite mixed.[11] Nonetheless, this study was widely cited at the time as evidence suggesting that a race to the bottom in lead paint regulations would follow. But a phone interview with the South Coast Air Quality Management District, southern California's agency responsible for regulation of air quality, elicited the response that emission control standards for paint coatings and solvents had "never been relaxed."[12] Evidently, the widely held perception that California's strict lead paint restrictions would induce furniture firms to cross the Rio Grande had led to no downward revision of these restrictions.

But there is little doubt that during the Reagan and first Bush administrations the Republican view that regulation had gone too far created in the public mind the fear of a race to the bottom. As scholars of the subject have noted, if you wished to deregulate for reasons that had nothing do with international competition (e.g., if cost-benefit analysis implied there was too much regulation, or if there was an ideological preference for deregulation), the smart thing nonetheless was to say that you were suffering from competition from rivals elsewhere who were less regulated.

President George H. W. Bush created in 1989 a Council on Competitiveness.[13] The council, which was headed by Vice President Dan Quayle, was intended to continue the work of the Council on Regulatory Relief, a task force that had been chaired by Bush during the Reagan administration.

The history of this council awaits careful research. But available materials indicate that its major deregulatory efforts appear to have been justified in cost-benefit terms rather than on grounds of improved competitiveness. Cost-benefit arguments were used in its many brushes with the Environmental Protection Agency on issues such as the burning of lead batteries and the softening of development restrictions on wetlands. It is hard to find significant examples where the council successfully reduced environmental or labor standards by invoking improved international competitiveness as a key reason.[14]

Recall also that if one is concerned about the decline in labor standards that might follow from the downward trend in the United States over more than a quarter century in the degree of unionization of the labor force, down by now to less than 10 percent in the private sector, globalization has not had much to do with it. It has far more to do with the draconian Taft-Hartley anti-labor legislation that goes back half a century. Under that legislation, the ability to use the strike as a weapon was seriously curtailed: sympathetic strikes by unions outside the industry were restricted, and the ability to hire replacement workers (scabs) was protected. This crippling of the right to strike, many union activists conclude, led to ineffective unions, as a union without adequate ability to strike is almost like a tiger without teeth.[15]

The political scientist Daniel Denzer, himself no captive of corporate interests nor a foe of unionism, wrote recently, in an influential article in *Foreign Policy,* that the public use of the phrase "race to the bottom" was a popular rhetorical device with negligible basis in fact.[16] Indeed, in a recent article in *Foreign Affairs,* Robert Ross and Anita Chan abandon the notion that the North suffers from a race to the bottom because of competition from the South, and try to shift focus to the notion of a race to the bottom within the South itself, producing no real evidence in support of such an intra-poor-countries race to the bottom either, plausible as it sounds.[17] Nor are they correct in implying that concern with the race to the bottom is now behind us in the rich countries. If only it were true!

Economists have also tried to get at this question from another angle. They have asked if there is evidence that multinationals are partial to investing in poor countries that have weak protection of workers' rights to unionize and to enjoy a safe workplace. Consider first, however, whether lower wages (as distinct from lower worker standards) are a magnet for investors. One needs to be careful and not just look at wages; they must be adjusted for labor productivity differences because lower wages may simply reflect lower productivity. The studies that do this adjustment, though they are focused not on poor countries but rather on investment flows among the rich countries or among different states within the United States, show that (productivity-adjusted) wages do matter to corporations that are considering where to invest.

But evidence also suggests that this is only one of many factors determining location decisions by multinationals.[18] The question of interest here, however, is whether the other factors affecting the locational decision of the firms include lower worker standards. Interestingly, cross-sectional analysis—that is, analysis of a number of countries at one point in time—of the outward investment by U.S. corporations shows that the greater the extent to which ILO workers' rights conventions are ratified by a country, the greater its share of U.S. investment tends to be.[19] Of course, the United States has in truth a better record on workers' rights, no matter how defined, than China; but China has ratified more conventions than the United States because the U.S. political and legal scene requires that ratifications lead to real obligations, whereas in China it does not. So ratifications are not a good guide to what protections exist for workers in reality. Analysts at the ILO have also found that higher unionization rates are associated with higher investment inflows, whereas fewer episodes of repression of rights of collective bargaining and association also go with higher inflows.[20] In fact, much of the other international evidence on whether the location of multinationals reflects attraction to the absence of high standards and particularly on whether multinationals use technology that is less environmentally friendly in locations where there are lower environmental standards, also shows that this is not a significant issue.[21]

In short, the evidence suggests that multinationals, generally speaking, do not go streaking to where labor rights are ignored or flouted. If true, this suggests a lack of empirical support for the notion that multinationals, by moving to where workers' rights are violated, encourage their violation by the poor governments seeking to attract those companies.

Why, then, is the race to the bottom, so easy to imagine and dread, not the dragon it is feared to be by the anti-globalization activists? For two reasons, one having to do with the economic behavior of multinationals in poor countries and the other, much the more important, relating to the political behavior of the unions and their allies in rich countries. The former (discussed at great length in Chapter 12 alongside several critiques of multinationals) is simply that just because lower standards exist in the poor countries, it does not follow that multinationals will take advantage of them. The gains to be made by doing so can be outweighed by several economic factors. Take just reputational effects. The multinationals, which account for an overwhelming percentage of direct foreign investment in the poor countries, cannot afford to be seen to dump dangerous effluents into the waters or into the air or treat their workers badly. With incipient or even full-blown democracies in many poor countries, with the growth of NGOs, with CNN and the BBC everywhere, the ability of multinationals to do something legal but offensive in terms of widely shared morality is seriously diminished. The reputational consequences of profiting from host-country laxity are sufficiently serious today to outweigh for many multinationals the extra profits that might be made by the "taking advantage" strategy.[22] Whether this means that legislative safeguards are not important is of course another matter, one of appropriate governance, which I turn to in Chapter 17.

Much the more important reason why a race to the bottom has not occurred lies instead in the fact that the effects of pressures from trade and outgoing investments on our standards are simply not substantial enough to undo the gains we have made after decades of political action. Our institutions are simply too strong to permit this. The unions, even though weaker than they were, and the environmental groups, which are stronger than ever, are politically active, not ciphers, and the Democratic Party sees them as core constituencies. Anytime rollbacks of regulations are sought on any grounds, the pro-regulatory bulbs light up and the political activists go to work. This is seen in energetic agitations against rolling back regulations on wetlands, on cutting down forests, and on the ability of unions to finance electoral campaigns of pro-union candidates for Congress and the presidency from general union dues. And while the anti-regulatory forces are abundantly financed by business lobbies such as the Chamber of Commerce and associations for specific industries such as logging, this is matched by two advantages that favor the pro-regulatory groups: their cause resonates with the public as socially responsible, and they substitute their labor for the capital they are short on, ringing doorbells, using the Internet, and working the political circuit with fervor and energy. On issues such as the rights of labor and the protection of the environment, the labor-intensive strategy has been demonstrated to be the more effective one in analysis of California referendums on such issues.

So American standards remain generally unaffected by the race to the bottom. But, paradoxically, the politics then shifts to a race to the top. Worried about international competition from producers in poor countries who have lower standards, the unions then turn to *raising* standards in these countries. Seen as a political ploy to moderate competition from rival suppliers abroad, this can be described as a form of "export protectionism" or "intrusionism," where you virtually force the exporters into accepting measures that raise their cost of production and hence cut down on their competitiveness. This is, in fact, what importing countries do when, not desiring to resort to import protection, they get the exporting countries instead to adopt export restraints (ironically called "voluntary" export restrictions), as was done, for example, when the Japanese were persuaded to limit exports of their cars to the United States to 2.2 million units in the early 1980s or face the imposition of import barriers. That export restraints are ways of reducing trade as much as import barriers are is best seen through analogy. Faced with a charging beast, you may hold it by its horns, much as import restraints do in trade, or you may reach behind the beast and catch it by its tail to break the charge, much as export restraints and forced raising of standards and hence of production costs in exporting countries do.

What is remarkable about this political process, where our lobbying groups seek to capture our all-too-powerful government to push for higher standards abroad, is that it is couched in the potent language of fair trade. They argue that we should not have to compete with, and lose to, others with lower standards. In short, we want to be virtuous but not have to pay for it! To see the morally unattractive nature of this position, consider what would happen if the United States were a closed economy. Suppose then that we raise our labor standards and ask polluters to pay. In that case, the industries that use a lot of labor and the polluting industries will contract. This is only the flip side of our labor and environmental policy choices. But when it comes to an international economy, the labor and environmental lobbies want to have the higher standards *and* not to lose the industries! In their frantic desire, they are willing to walk over the exporting countries and force on them standards that may not be appropriate or may be different from what would be desirable from their own perspective, which is often democratically determined. It is not surprising, therefore, that this political posturing by our labor and environmental groups is occasionally seen in poor countries, including by some unions and environmental NGOs there, as a kind of neo-imperialism![23]

In fact, the politics of protectionism can manifest itself in the domestic setting of the high standards themselves. Cynics go to the length of arguing that where high standards are imposed on traded goods, such as air bags in cars (as distinct from standards on how cars are produced), and are automatically extended to imported cars, the motives may be precisely to reduce the competitiveness of rivals abroad. This is because it may be more expensive for foreign car manufacturers to retool themselves for air bags.

Different Reasons for Seeking Higher Standards Elsewhere

But if it is not a race to the bottom but a race to the top (with the goal of moderating competition) that we observe, and if the poor countries generally resist this race, which they see as a dagger aimed at their export competitiveness, there are still other, moral and altruistic (rather than egoistical or self-serving competition-reducing) reasons that higher standards are sometimes sought abroad by some in the rich countries.

First, for some standards, the issue is simply one of morality, not competitiveness. If, say, goods are produced anywhere with child labor, I may not want to consume them, no matter that they are cheaper when produced in the poor countries, because I believe that they are immorally produced. Thus I may refuse to sup with the devil even though the consequence is that I miss a free meal! My position here is *not* that I am seeking with my action to produce higher standards abroad. I may well believe that my action will have absolutely no effect whatsoever on the use of child labor abroad. Yet I abstain from participating in consuming goods that use child labor, to satisfy my own conscience.

If this is the moral argument, then all it can imply is that I should have the ability in the marketplace to choose goods made without the use of child labor. This suggests that if sufficient numbers of people who think like me are willing to pay more for their principles, then positive labeling will become feasible. The Germans helped to develop the label Rugmark, which goes to firms producing rugs without the use of child labor. The new organic product label in the United States is yet another example. Somewhat differently, firms may advertise, and get a reputation for, their goodness in certain respects, catering to the moral preferences of their intended customers; this is what Ben & Jerry's does in its production of ice cream, as does the Body Shop chain of personal care product stores.

The advantage of this, as against negative labeling where goods are marked "made with child labor," is that negative lists bring with them many difficulties. They can tar a wide range of behaviors, of greatly varying degrees of offensiveness, with the same brush. The mere accusation that child labor is used, without addressing questions such as how the children are treated, whether they work just a few hours and then are escorted to school, and so on, makes it unlikely that an informed moral choice will be made. Further, a negative list would be enormously expensive and administratively difficult for poor countries to administer. Indeed, often the exports from these countries are in primitive bottles and packages where the labels would be harder to affix and may not be fully legible, whereas positive labels are more likely to be applicable to better-endowed and better-equipped firms.

But the moral argument also takes a more common form: the standards are often sought to be extended to poor nations on grounds of altruism. Thus one may take the position that, even if no trade with

Mars or outflow of investment to it could occur and hence no race to the bottom need be feared, green men from Mars should not put green children to work. One's motive may entirely be interplanetary empathy and concern for children everywhere. There is undoubtedly some of this sentiment underlying the demand for standards to be raised in the poor countries. Often the policy recommended to bring this about is the use of sanctions, chiefly trade sanctions inserted through what is now called "linkage" of standards with trade liberalization and inclusion of standards in trade treaties and trade institutions. The inadvisability of such sanctions, and the use of more efficacious non-coercive methods to advance standards worldwide are considered in Chapter 17.

11

Environment in Peril?

Environmentalists have long thought of economic globalization as a threat to the environment. Trade, advocated by economists and in consequence encouraged by the bilateral and multilateral aid and development agencies and expanded by reductions of trade barriers by both unilateral action and reciprocal bargaining by policy makers, is a frequent target of their anguish and anger. To a large extent, the conflict is inevitable. Impassioned differences often arise from the altogether different philosophies and lifestyles of trade economists and environmental activists.

The economists generally belong to the philosophical tradition that sees nature as a handmaiden to mankind. This humanity-centric view of nature is deeply rooted in the tradition that originated among the Hebrews and the Christians and spread to the Western world. As the Bible says in Genesis:

> And God said, Let us make man in our image, after our likeness: and let them have dominion over the fish of the sea, and over the fowl of the air, and over the cattle, and over all the earth, and over every creeping thing that creepeth upon the earth.[1]

The views of the ancient Greeks were also consonant with those in the Bible. Aristotle famously observed:

> Plants exist for the sake of animals, and brute beasts for the sake of man—domestic animals for his use and food, wild ones (or at any rate most of them) for food and other accessories of life, such as clothing and various tools.
>
> Since nature makes nothing purposeless or in vain, it is undeniably true that she has made all animals for the sake of man.[2]

But today's environmentalists in the West reject these views, asserting instead nature's autonomy. A loving view of the environment has been embraced by many of them. Just recollect the moving verse of the English poet Gerald Manley Hopkins, lamenting the environmental degradation wrought by human activity:

O if we but knew what we do
When we delve or hew—
Hack and rack the growing green!
Since country is so tender
To touch, her being so slender,
That, like this sleek and seeing ball
But a prick will make no eye at all,
Where we, even where we mean
To mend her we end her,
When we hew and delve:
After-comers cannot guess the beauty been.
Ten or twelve, only ten or twelve
Strokes of havoc unselve
The sweet especial scene,
Rural scene, a rural scene,
Sweet especial rural scene.[3]

The dramatic shift in sentiment about nature that has come to pass today is well reflected in the writings of the leading twentieth-century Western environmentalists. John Muir, the founder of the Sierra Club, wrote:

When we contemplate the whole globe as one great dewdrop, striped and dotted with continents and islands, flying through space with all other stars all signing and shining together as one, the whole universe appears as an infinite storm of beauty.[4]

And Rachel Carson, renowned for her *Silent Spring*, said:

It is a wholesome and necessary thing for us to turn again to the earth and in the contemplations of her beauties to know of wonder and humility.[5]

By contrast with the earlier "nature is subordinate to man" Western tradition, however, the Japanese have always viewed themselves in harmony with nature rather than exploiting it: a tradition reflected in the Nobel laureate Yasunari Kawabata's famous novel *The Old Capital,* set in Kyoto with its marvelous displays of nature's splendor.[6] I suspect that this difference of tradition partly accounts for the comparative ease with which Japan, despite having ruined its environment as badly as the West during the course of its industrialization, has found fewer roadblocks in its attempts at corrective and regulatory actions.

The environmentalists thus tend to value environment over income, whereas trade (and other) economists conventionally tend to value income over the environment. This difference lies at the heart of their conflicts in recent years. But this disparity reflects yet other contrasts.

Trade has been central to economic thinking since Adam Smith discovered the economic virtues of specialization and of the markets that sustain it. Economists therefore think of the markets as being in place and government interventions such as tariffs and other trade barriers as policies that disrupt and distort them. On the other hand, environmentalists are typically dealing with situations where markets do not exist— as when pollutants are dumped into lakes, rivers, and oceans, and into the sky above, and the polluter does not have to buy permits to do so— and therefore must be specially created. In fact, whereas environmentalists often disdain markets, prescriptions such as the regulatory imposition of "polluter pay" taxes, under which the polluter is taxed for the pollution that he causes, amount to nothing more than demands to create the missing markets. Trade therefore suggests absence of regulation, whereas environmentalism suggests its necessity.

In turn, trade is exploited and its virtues extolled by corporate and multinational interests, whereas environmental objectives have typically (though not exclusively) been embraced by non-profit organizations, which are generally wary of, if not hostile to, these interests.

The distrust that has reflected these different traditions has led some environmentalists to extraordinary assertions of hostility toward globalization, and toward international trade and the World Trade Organization and its predecessor, the GATT. GATT was attacked just over a decade ago as "GATTzilla," reminiscent of the Japanese movie monster Godzilla. GATTzilla was a monster, but this was also the time when the United States was in the throes of a national psychosis about the rise of Japan, which was widely demonized as a wicked trader, a predatory exporter, and an exclusionary importer— indeed a two-faced rival. If the GATT was feared and denounced, free trade itself was held to be a malign process, causing all manner of harm in all sorts of ways, certainly to the environment, which was rapidly becoming a key concern.

At the time, in the 1980s and early 1990s, I wound up defending free trade in debates with two leading environmentalists, Herman Daly (an American economist who is an icon of the environmental movement and used to work for the World Bank) in *Scientific American* and Edward Goldsmith (the doyen of British environmentalists) in the Cambridge Union and in the English magazine *Prospect*.[7] I recall particularly the Cambridge Union debate, where, astonished that free trade was being blamed for environmental problems and other ills in the world, I replied to Teddy Goldsmith by recalling Balzac's 1831 novella, *The Wild Ass's Skin* (*La peau de chagrin*). When the central character, Raphael, desires a beautiful woman, the talisman in shape of the ass's skin that he has been tempted into accepting shrinks, and with it his life span shrinks as well. So to go to the opera, where he cannot avoid seeing attractive women, Raphael carries a special "monocle whose microscopic lens, skillfully inserted, destroy[s] the harmony of the loveliest features and [gives] them a hideous aspect." Looking through this monocle, Raphael sees only ugly women and is able to enjoy unscathed the glorious music he loves. "Mr. Goldsmith," I added, "you seem to have with you a similar monocle, except that when you use it and see us wonderful free-traders, you find us turned into ugly monsters, our halos turning into the devil's horns!"

But even if the distrust is dissolved, serious questions remain to be addressed. The ones I examine below have been the most salient in recent years.

A Common Fallacy: Freer Trade, Without Environmental Policy in Place, Is Harmful

Thanks to the debates between free-traders and environmentalists, most sophisticated environmentalists no longer hold the view that if trade is freed without environmental policies being in place, not only will the environment be harmed but the country's economic welfare will be set back. But this misconception is still commonplace in the wider environmental community.

That this *may* happen is surely correct. That it *must* happen is incorrect. I and my GATT colleagues Richard Blackhurst and Kym Anderson addressed this issue in 1991 when I was economic policy adviser to Arthur Dunkel, the director general. The GATT Secretariat was working on a special report on trade and the environment, and we took the occasion to clarify matters.[8] In particular, we provided examples from the real world that showed that, contrary to the environmentalists' pessimistic certainties, economic welfare increased with trade liberalization even though ideal environmental policies were not in place, and that the environment improved also.[9]

The most compelling illustration came from agricultural trade liberalization contemplated in the Uruguay Round of multilateral trade negotiations. Anderson calculated that such liberalization would shift agricultural production from higher-cost, pesticide-intensive European agriculture to lower-cost, manure-using agriculture in the poor countries, so that both income and welfare would increase in each set of countries, and total environmental quality would also improve.

The GATT report also cited a study by Robert Feenstra that showed (as is illustrated in the following chart) that import quota protection had led, as economists had predicted, to increased imports of larger gas-guzzling cars from Japan and reduced imports of smaller, higher-fuel-efficiency cars because the bigger cars carried more margin of profit than the smaller ones and it paid the Japanese car manufacturers to export more of the larger cars within a given quota. So the imposition of protectionist quotas had led to both lower economic welfare and to increased pollution.

But one could equally cite cases where the freeing of trade, in the absence of an appropriate environmental policy, would lead to a deterioration in the environment. This seems to have been the case with what is called sometimes the "blue revolution" (following the "green revolution" for new seeds, which also inspired, believe it or not, the phrase "pink revolution" for improvements in raising pigs): the rapid expansion of

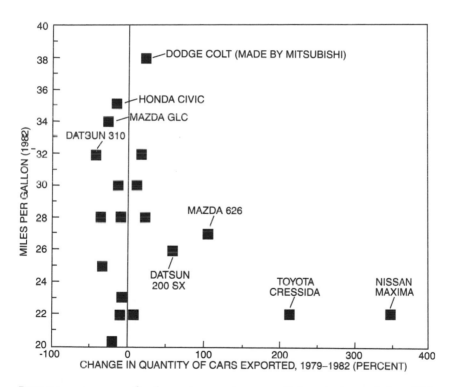

Perverse consequences for the environment may result from trade restrictions. This graph shows Japanese car exports to the United States before and after Japan's acquiescence in voluntary export restraints. Sales of small, fuel-efficient models declined, whereas those of the larger "gas guzzlers" soared. *Source:* Robert C. Feenstra, University of California, Davis.

coastal shrimp farming in the 1980s in several countries in Asia and Latin America, principally in Ecuador, Colombia, Indonesia, Thailand, the Philippines, India, Bangladesh, China, Taiwan, and Vietnam. By the early 1990s, the share of pond production of shrimp had risen to nearly a third of the total shrimp harvested.

While private domestic firms and foreign multinationals from around the world led the process, this expansion was also assisted by development specialists in the national governments and in multilateral aid agencies such as the World Bank and the Asian Development Bank. Shrimp exports constituted a growing share of export earnings, which these agencies correctly—recall Chapter 5—assumed would also accelerate the growth of the economy. But it turned out that coastal shrimp farming, often described also as "shrimp aquaculture," was creating harmful environmental spillovers regarding which no policies were in place. Three acute problems had arisen:

- The shrimp ponds produced effluents that contaminated the water supply for others (and for themselves as well).
- They used large quantities of fresh water, which then led to a drop in the water table and the intrusion of salt water.[10]
- Their expansion often led to the destruction of surrounding mangrove forests, "with serious consequences for commercially valuable fish and shrimp stocks which depend on a mangrove habitat during the juvenile stages of their life cycles, [with the result that there may be] serious reductions in marine harvests and domestic fish supply in the future."[11]

It will be immediately obvious in this example that if those who own and operate the shrimp farms were forced under a "polluter pay" principle to compensate those whom they harmed, then the environmental damage inflicted by the coastal farms would be reduced because the production of coastal shrimp—whose producers are currently not having to pay for the social costs they are imposing through spillover effects—would have to cover those social costs. Economic welfare would also improve since the policy would have raised the cost of production to reflect true social costs.

So, in the absence of an appropriate environmental policy that makes producers pay for the pollution they cause, there is no reason to say that free trade will *necessarily* do worse or better than trade restrictions on either the environmental or the economic front. The examples of agriculture and car imports were favorable to free trade; the coastal shrimp example was not. It all depends on the particular case.

The "Best" Policy: Combine Free Trade with Appropriate Environmental Policy

On the other hand, the optimal policy is to have an appropriate environmental policy in place, to look after the environment, and then to pursue free trade to reap the gains from trade. By using both policies, you get both objectives accomplished. In short, as our forefathers knew well, you cannot generally kill two birds with one stone. Those who want protection to help on the environment forget about the gains from trade that would be lost as a result of the trade protection; they are mistakenly trying to use one stone, trade policy, to kill two birds, gains from trade and an appropriate environment.[12]

Why do I say "appropriate" environment? Because, except in the limiting cases where you want to put an infinite value on an environmental outcome, you are going to have to balance income gains against environmental benefit. In the coastal shrimp case it is hardly sensible to say that the environmental considerations should be so overwhelming that no environmental damage to mangrove forests should be accepted. Rather, such damage must be balanced against the loss from shrimp export earnings. This trade-off will imply a choice somewhere between a zero pollution tax and a prohibitive one, of course. This choice will obviously reflect the societal valuation of the environment and income—a matter that requires discussion.

But before addressing that issue, it should be said that environmentalists are right to argue that growth rates must be adjusted for environmental damage. Growth that devastates the environment is surely not being correctly measured if no downside adjustment for the environmental damage is made. Keeping this in mind, the Yale University economists William Nordhaus and James Tobin (the latter was also a Nobel laureate) have long proposed a new measure of national income and its growth that subtracts for environmental degradation.[13] Reduced estimates of growth rates, so adjusted, have been made by Herman Daly.[14]

The Valuation of Environment: The Real Question

How to value the environment, however, is at the center of the questions raised by the environmentalists, and needs more scrutiny. It is best illuminated by reference to some common examples of environmental damage from trade expansion that groups such as the Defenders of Wildlife have cited in their activist agitations. These include the contention that the demand for softwood, pulp, and paper in the United States has accentuated the "over-harvesting of the boreal forest in Canada, while demand for mahogany and other precious hardwoods drives deforestation in the Brazilian Amazon," and that "in countries like Chile, millions of square miles of native and globally-unique forest have been cleared to make way for monoculture tree plantations to feed international demands for wood products."[15]

These groups write as if public policy is wrong when *any* environmental damage is observed. But this criticism is mistaken unless one puts an infinite value on saving the boreal forest in Canada or the forests in Chile. In the absence of such an extreme valuation, which puts zero weight on income and infinite weight on environment, the optimal outcome will be characterized by *some* trade gains and *some* environmental damage. Once this is recognized, it follows that, except in the few situations where it makes sense to attach an infinite weight to environmental preservation, the environmentalists are more credible if they ask, quite properly, for a rise in the relative valuation of environment to income.

Moreover, when environmental groups such as the Defenders of Wildlife condemn the harvesting of the Canadian boreal forest, their complaint is misdirected at trade. It is really about the valuation that the Canadians are putting on their boreal forests. And since Canada is a democratic society, it is up to the Canadians through their domestic political process to make that choice, and not up to the Defenders of Wildlife to impose their extraneous valuation on what Canadians should do, and not do, within their own jurisdiction with their natural resources. Democracy is not a right that people are willing to sacrifice to such groups, no matter how altruistic and selfless they might be. This is particularly so in countries that have escaped from the colonial yoke and have not been ensnared into a neocolonial embrace. The proper role for these international environmental groups is to aid and assist the domestic groups that, in turn, go legitimately through domestic political channels and attempt to shift the balance of political forces toward a higher valuation of the environment.

And it is fair to say that environmental valuation has indeed risen in the last three decades as the environmental movement has come into its own. Aside from this trend effect, there is also a demographic effect. I have long argued that the intensity of environmental preference or commitment is characterized by a U-shaped curve: if you plot intensity of preference on the vertical axis and age on the horizontal axis, the plotted curve comes down and then moves up in a U-shape, since the preference is high among the young and the old.

The very young care intensely for the environment. They rarely think in terms of trade-offs, implicitly ignoring the cost of reaching environmental goals and therefore never having to revise environmental preferences in light of knowledge about the cost of indulging them. They also have an oversimplified view of what must be done. They get upset when, confronting their parents and asking for cloth diapers to be chosen in preference to disposables, they are told that cloth diapers are likely to be washed with detergents and that, if you go yet further back in the chain of inputs, it is possible that a shift to cloth diapers may cause net environmental harm. And they are not alone: several environmental activists get agitated as well by what they call "obfuscation," which any systematic and comprehensive analysis often leads to. And that is precisely, of course, what economists bring to the table. I recall one of my Oxford teachers, Ian Little, a world-class economist, telling me when he had returned from a couple of years advising in Whitehall: "I thought we economists worked with models that sometimes abstracted too much from complexity. But I found that bureaucrats and politicians worked with even simpler, naive models: if x affected y, that was the end of the matter; whereas the economist typically argued, 'But y will affect z, which in turn will affect x and feed back on y as well.'" In fact, the iconoclastic *New York Times* columnist John Tierney once told me that the greatest amount of condemnatory e-mail he had received was over a *New York Times Magazine* article showing how recycling programs had actually worsened the garbage problem![16]

But if the very young hold intense preferences on environmental objectives, unmindful of complexity and trade-offs, the old also tend to do the same. After life's fitful fever, as they retire to Sanibel Island in Florida and other sunny climates that are kinder to their arthritic bones, they are closer to their six feet of ground. And one sees countless such old folks turning to protect turtles and ospreys, and putting money into the environmental groups.

So we have intense preferences among the young and the old, and those in the middle are the ones who worry about trade-offs and complexity. The environmental economist Matthew Kahn, to whom I suggested this U-shaped phenomenon, actually looked at the referenda on environment in California and found some evidence supportive of it.[17]

But if this is so, then there is an important implication as populations age around the world, especially in the rich countries. In Europe, already we have "35 people of pensionable age for every 100 people of working age; in Spain and Italy the ratio of pensioners to workers is projected to be one-to-one."[18] As the middle shrinks in the foreseeable future, we have an additional reason environmental valuations will rise: demographics will reinforce the trend effect from environmental activism.

Income and the Environment

But the environmentalists also argue that, especially when it comes to specific pollutants and environmental harms, growing incomes (and hence the global trade and investment that contribute to them) will be associated with deteriorating environmental outcomes. The other argument is that global trade with and investment in countries with lower environmental standards are tantamount to "unfair competition" and will destroy our industries, which are subject to higher standards. Alternatively, they will lead, as the unions fear for labor standards (a fear discussed and discounted in the preceding chapter), to a race to the bottom, destroying the higher standards with a view to ensuring competitiveness with lower-standard rivals.

The belief that specific pollutants, such as sulfur dioxide, resulting from increased economic activity will rise in urban areas as per capita income increases depends on two assumptions: that all activities expand uniformly and that pollution per unit output in an activity will not diminish. But neither assumption is realistic.

As income rises, activities that cause more pollution may contract and those that cause less pollution may expand, so the sulfur dioxide concentration may fall instead of rise. In fact, as development occurs, economies typically shift from primary production, which is often pollution-intensive, to manufactures, which are often less so, and then to traded services, which are currently even less pollution-intensive. This natural evolution itself could then reduce the pollution-intensity of income as development proceeds.

Then again, the available technology used, and technology newly invented, may become more environment-friendly over time. Both phenomena constitute an ongoing, observed process. The shift to environment-friendly technology can occur naturally as households, for example, become less poor and shift away from indoor cooking with smoke-causing coal-based fires to stoves using fuels that cause little smoke.[19] But this shift is often a result also of environment-friendly technological innovation prompted by regulation. Thus, restrictions on allowable fuel efficiency have promoted research by the car firms to produce engines that yield more miles per gallon. But these regulations are created by increased environmental consciousness, for which the environmental groups can take credit. And the rise of these environmental groups is, in turn, associated with increased incomes.

Also, revelations about the astonishing environmental degradation in the Soviet Union and its satellites underline how the absence of democratic feedback and controls is a surefire recipe for environmental neglect.

The fact that economic growth generally promotes democracy, as discussed in Chapter 8, is yet another way in which rising income creates a better environment.

In all these ways, then, increasing incomes can reduce rather than increase pollution. In fact, for several pollutants, empirical studies have found a bell-shaped curve: pollution levels first rise with income but then fall with it.[20] The economists Gene Grossman and Alan Krueger, who estimated the levels of different pollutants such as sulfur dioxide in several cities worldwide, were among the first to show this, estimating that for sulfur dioxide levels, the peak occurred in their sample at per capita incomes of $5,000–6,000.[21] Several historical examples can also be adduced: the reduction in smog today compared to what the industrial revolution produced in European cities in the nineteenth century, and the reduced deforestation of United States compared to a century ago.[22]

The only value of these examples is in their refutation of the simplistic notions that pollution will rise with income. They should not be used to argue that growth will automatically take care of pollution regardless of environmental policy. Grossman and Krueger told me that their finding of the bell-shaped curve had led to a huge demand for offprints of their article from anti-environmentalists who wanted to say that "natural forces" would take care of environmental degradation and that environmental regulation was unnecessary; the economists were somewhat aghast at this erroneous, ideological interpretation of their research findings. In fact, as I have emphasized, environmental activism has stimulated new regulations that have in turn produced environment friendly improvements. All of this has made development and environmental improvement frequent bedfellows.[23]

Competing with Others Who Have Lower Standards on Domestic Pollution

If income expansion does not automatically imply that environmental harm will rise from specific pollutants, the complaint about competition with producers in countries with lower standards is also unjustified, plausible as it appears.

It is worth stressing that the issue at stake here involves pollution that is domestic, *not* global (concerning which, as with the Kyoto treaty on global warming, wholly different issues arise; these are considered below). To see the distinction clearly, consider that if I pollute a lake that is entirely within India, the issue is domestic to India. But if I pollute the

Ganges River, which flows into Bangladesh, then the problem becomes international. If I use cars or scooters that take leaded fuel, I pollute the air in the cities where this happens, and it is the local populations that are hurt; but if my factories produce a lot of pollution in American cities close to the border between the United States and Canada, I can cause acid rain across the border in Canada, producing an international problem of spillovers. If I smoke, I will hurt those around me in New York, so Mayor Michael Bloomberg has to deal with this domestic pollution issue; but if I use aerosol cans and help destroy the ozone layer, I imperil the earth and therefore all others multilaterally.

In technical jargon, global (whether bilateral or multilateral) pollution spillovers require that they be paid for through appropriate taxes or regulations. These policies generally call for international cooperation, since no one jurisdiction can normally take the required action. But that is obviously not true for domestic pollution phenomena.

You would think that the issue of what India does with her purely domestic environmental pollution is one for the Indian democracy to resolve. That was precisely what I argued earlier.[24] This would also be the case for the public debate in the United States on whether drilling for oil in Alaska's Arctic National Wildlife Refuge should be permitted. In fact, the environmental groups and the oil lobbies, with their respective allies among the NGOs and among politicians and the media, are fighting it out over this issue. As a citizen of the United States, I weigh in on the side of the environmentalists and am rooting for them to win. Few Americans would, however, tolerate foreign groups, whether oil firms or the Greens, actively intruding into the politics of this debate; therefore hardly any foreign lobby intrudes.

Yet, ironically, it is precisely in these domestic pollution matters that much of the current agitation against trade's adverse effects is centered. In fact, the assertion is that if India chooses to adopt lower pollution tax rates in an industry than the United States does, then the resulting competition is "unfair" to American producers in that industry. If such unfair competition is allowed, then American industry will be destroyed. Or else the result will be political pressures to reduce the American standards, to "save jobs," to "level the playing field," leading to the race to the bottom that was discussed and discounted in the previous chapter in regard to the possible erosion of labor standards. Either way, the outcome would be undesirable.

In fact, a number of environmentalists have argued that such unfair competition amounts to "social dumping" and must be countervailed through trade protection. David Boren, who during his time in the U.S. Senate introduced legislation to countervail the "social dumping" allegedly resulting from lower standards abroad, proposed such a measure on the grounds that

> we can no longer stand idly by while some US manufacturers, such as the US carbon and steel alloy industry, spend as much as 250 percent more on environmental controls as a percentage of gross domestic product than do other countries. . . . I see the *unfair advantage enjoyed by other nations exploiting the environment* and public health for economic gain when I look at many industries important to my own state of Oklahoma. [Italics added][25]

But the argument that the resulting competition is "unfair" is illogical for several reasons.

First, the fact that others in the same industry abroad do not carry the same burden is in itself not a reason to cry foul. After all, different countries have different wages, capital costs, infrastructure, weather, and what have you. All of these factors lead to differential advantages of production and trade competitiveness. Diversity of environmental tax burdens is part of the immense diversity that makes for the gains from trade, in this perspective.

Second, the rates at which pollution taxes are levied in the same industry across countries should differ because they should reflect different conditions in those countries. Thus, even if Mexico and the United States were to value the environment equally, the fact that Mexico has cleaner air and fouler water than the United States would mean that in Mexico there would be a greater negative valuation put on industries that pollute water and a lesser negative valuation on industries that pollute the air than there would be in the United States. It would therefore be strange to say that Mexican and American industries should have identical tax burdens, regardless of the differences in their situations that require that these tax rates be different. And it would be stranger still if the pollution tax rates that are appropriate to the United States, in the view of Boren or Gephardt, were to be necessarily the ones chosen as those which others must converge to, rather than the other way around.

Third, there is also the fact that sometimes the standards are set deliberately at higher levels so that rivals abroad, who would have to incur great costs to meet them, are unable to produce economically with those standards and thus get to be uncompetitive. The higher standards then are being strategically set. This was the charge made against the Japanese car manufacturers in the 1980s: their frequency of mandatory safety inspections was so high that Detroit alleged that it was enacted as a trade barrier, since it added disproportionately to the costs of operating in the Japanese market for Detroit. In particular, small firms with an inadequate scale of operation are likely to find the adaptation of their products to incorporate new regulations developed elsewhere to be a serious obstacle.

This is also a reason often advanced by poor-country producers and exporters against our labeling requirements, which of course represent higher standards. They argue that, often lacking modern packaging and selling without bottles and cans in accumulated heaps in bazaars and informal markets, they are unable to comply and hence are excluded from markets where such labeling is required. As Prime Minister Indira Gandhi once remarked tellingly, it is hard to lift oneself up by one's bootstraps when one is too poor to be wearing boots.

Finally, if the "polluter pay" tax rates are different across countries in the same industry, it still does not follow that the industry in the country with a higher tax rate will lose in international competition. To understand this subtle point, remember that resource allocation will reflect the pollution tax rate differences in *other* industries as well. It is perfectly possible therefore for a tax on steel emissions to be higher in the United States but for resources to be pulled into, rather than away from, the steel industry if the pollution tax rates are differentially higher in other industries in the United States than elsewhere. A focus on just one sector is quite inappropriate, even as the differences in tax rates are legitimate in any case and attempts at making them uniform across countries within the same industry defy logic.

Race to the Bottom in Standards for Domestic Pollution

By contrast, fears of a race to the bottom in pollution standards are not analytically unsound; rather, they lack empirical salience. Some of the reasons for this lack of salience are similar to those outlined in the previous chapter for fears about a race to the bottom in terms of labor standards. Others, however, are specific to the environmental questions.

As the California lead paint example in the previous chapter illustrated, it is hard to find examples where environmental standards have been reduced in practice because of lesser standards elsewhere. More formal econometric studies also support this conclusion. In an early review of these studies and his own, the economist Arik Levinson wrote:

> The conclusion of both the international and domestic studies of industry location are that environmental regulations do not deter investment to any statistically or economically significant degree. Most authors are careful to note the limitations of their individual research and to place caveats on their counterintuitive conclusions that stringent regulations do not deter plants, nor do lax regulations attract them. But the literature as a whole presents fairly compelling evidence across a broad range of industries, time periods, and econometric specifications that regulations do not matter to site choice.[26]

In all fairness, however, we must ask whether this benign conclusion was arrived at because the differences in standards in these studies were small or because there are other compelling reasons, which outweigh even a non-negligible financial gain to be had by taking advantage of lower standards, for corporations to make location and even choice-of-technology decisions as if these lower standards were not decisive. I would conclude the latter, for a variety of reasons.[27]

First, it is possible that in practice the differences in standards across countries in many industries are not large enough to outweigh the many other factors, such as cheaper access to certain raw materials, proximity to markets, tax breaks, and so on, that typically attract investment.

Second, these economic factors include the fact that when multiplant firms invest in different locations, as multinationals often do, they tend to work uniformly with the most stringent standards they face among these locations, to reduce the transaction costs involved in making diverse choices to take advantage of the environmental regulatory diversity. Simply put, it is more cost-effective to run all of their plants with the same basic technology, so we get a race to the top.

Third, faced with differing standards, firms will tend to predict that all countries are on an escalator to higher standards and therefore decide that it is best to be ahead of the curve in the countries that have lower standards and to act as if they already have higher standards. If they do not, retooling costs will ensue over time.

Fourth, the higher-standard countries are the ones that innovate. Many such innovations lead to embodied technical change (i.e., it is built into new equipment). Environment-friendly technology is often also vastly more productive, and so its use is more profitable in almost any situation. If so, the firm is likely to use it and to disregard the alternative where it uses the less environmentally friendly technology that saves some money by exploiting the lower environmental standard but loses more by forgoing the higher productivity of the newer, more environmentally friendly technology.

Fifth, as environmentally unfriendly technology becomes obsolete with the invention of new, environmentally friendly technology, the entrepreneurs in the poor countries with lower standards are the ones who typically hold on to it. In many cases, they import it as secondhand machinery after it is discarded by the multinationals headquartered in the rich countries. The real concern, therefore, for those who object to the use of environmentally unfriendly technology in the poor countries should be about the sale of such secondhand machinery to the poor countries. Multinationals who account for the bulk of direct foreign investment are not likely candidates for indictment in terms of their own use of environmentally unfriendly technology in the poor countries.

Finally, the incentive to use environmentally friendly technology, and hence to disregard the fact that the host country has lower environmental standards, is partly due to the fact that today there would be heavy reputational costs for the big firms if they were to take advantage of the absence of environmental laws in the host countries. If you polluted the Rio Grande with mercury, even though Mexico has no laws on the books against such a practice, you can count on some NGO or investigative journalist stumbling onto it, and there go your reputation, sales, and profits! This works best when the practice you are indulging in is widely considered to be beyond the pale, but even in less egregious cases it does provide an offset to the notion that you can take full advantage of a lack of regulation without a dent in your profits.[28]

So in reality we do not have a race to the bottom in environmental standards, because while some exceptions will certainly arise, multinationals are, generally speaking, not playing the game of actively looking for locations without environmental regulation or seeking out technologies that are environmentally unfriendly. A race cannot get started unless the competitors sign up to run.

It is also worth remembering that the long-run trend in setting environmental standards is going to be favorable for environmental protection anyway, because of the growth of the environmental movement and its impact on the steadily higher valuation put by all societies on environmental objectives. But it is also relevant to note that this trend can only be reinforced by corporate-interest-driven factors. Aside from the strategic consideration I have noted, which will drive firms at times into setting higher standards for supplying their home markets so that rivals abroad have to satisfy them or lose market share, there is the more important fact that increasingly firms that are producing environmentally friendly technology are also lobbying and capturing the regulatory agencies to set the standards that mandate the use of such technology, as with higher fuel efficiency standards for cars. These lobbies then have a benign symbiotic relationship with the environmentalist lobbies, both playing the game, one for profit and the other for altruism, with the effect of pushing the world into higher standards.

Is the WTO Against the Environment?

But if free trade is not vulnerable to the current environmental critiques of globalization, environmentalists have also raised a different set of objections that relate not to trade as such but to its management by the World Trade Organization and its predecessor institution, the GATT. Here too, the criticisms are open to objection.

I will focus on two particularly irksome sources of disaffection.[29] These have to do with the fact that the WTO (and the GATT, which preceded it for forty-eight years) has rules that relate to trade in products that raise safety questions (e.g., hormone-fed beef and GM products) and to trade in goods that raise values questions instead (e.g., tuna caught with nets that kill dolphins or shrimp caught without the use of turtle-excluding devices).[30] In both cases, the environmentalists feel that the trade rules put environmental regulators at a disadvantage.

Now, generally speaking, GATT has been designed to accept whatever regulation one wants to put up, putting this within member countries' jurisdiction and exercise of autonomy. Its only requirement is that the regulation be applied equally to domestic production as to imports. Yet problems have arisen precisely because in terms of safety, values and environmental areas, regulations have been designed or operated in a fashion that has led the affected members to raise questions and even bring matters before the Dispute Settlement Mechanism. Let me explain why.

Safety Issues: Hormone-fed Beef and GM Products

The most contentious issues have related to the question of safety in agricultural trade. Here, governments occasionally have to contend with fears that are so strongly held that they prompt regulations that rule out both imports and domestic production. But then other governments complain that these fears cannot be allowed to automatically disrupt their exports, that the fears must be shown somehow to be grounded in something reasonable. As it happens, all governments share these concerns. So the Uruguay Round agreements included in the relevant sanitary and phytosanitary (SPS) section dealing with these matters the requirement that the regulatory ban must be grounded in scientific evidence. When the European Union imposed its ban on the sale of hormone-fed beef, the problem was that the ban could not pass such a scientific test. Given the SPS agreement, the WTO Dispute Settlement Mechanism had no option except to find the EU ban to be in violation of the WTO rules. Protests by environmental NGOs erupted in Europe over the ruling and were directed against the WTO, but the "culprits" were the contracting parties, the nations that had agreed on the SPS's scientific test requirement in the first place.

The GM products issue is similar but has much greater potential for disrupting trade, of course. The EU's concerns and policies, such as a five-year moratorium on the sale of GM seeds and foods containing GM inputs, cannot be justified by currently available scientific evidence. The

United States is now taking the matter to the WTO Dispute Settlement Mechanism, and it could well win because the Europeans do not have science on their side yet. More environmentalists will then protest.

The NGOs clearly think that the scientific test requirement is too demanding. They would rather go with the current EU negotiating position that the scientific test principle must be replaced by the precautionary principle. This is no principle, of course; it merely states that if I have a fear about anything but no respectable scientists will put their signatures to its credibility, then I should still be allowed to indulge it. In short, we go to an open-ended approach to safety regulation, denying science the decisive role it ought to have.

We have a clear conflict here. The EU governments, which have been at the heart of both the hormone-fed beef and GM products disputes, are clearly in a bind because they have skeptical, even hostile, populations that will not tolerate the elimination of the bans just because there is no scientific evidence to justify them. Yet, the scientific test seems to be the only way to prevent the chaos that would arise if governments could indulge their fears freely without constraint.

It seems to me that a possible solution in this situation is to introduce flexibility in terms of remedies to be applied when the WTO Appellate Body finds against legislative or executive actions that are virtually dictated by public opinion. Since such actions cannot be vacated, it is futile for the only option to be retaliation in form of tariffs that reduce the offending country's trade by gigantic amounts (the hormone-fed beef retaliation exceeds $200 million; the GM products retaliation could be in untold billions). That is the path to massive trade disruption, and one that would also bring the WTO into further disrepute.

In some cases, an option that could be introduced formally into the WTO is to make a tort payment to the injured industry.[31] Since this is better related to the profits lost rather than to sales volume affected, it could be put in the range of the sales-to-profits ratio in the industry in question. I guess this would be about 5–7 percent in the hormone-fed beef case, implying that if the EU simply made a tort payment to U.S. beef producers of $10–15 million annually, that would take care of the problem. Obviously, this approach makes sense only if reasonable sums are involved, and also if the loss of the market is not due to values-related objections (so that the EU is not making payment to producers of factory-farmed chickens, for instance), in which case the payment is likely to be regarded as paying sinners for not practicing vices!

Yet another option that serves to introduce desirable flexibility is to allow "eco-labeling." The EU has decided to shift away from a moratorium on GM products and simply ask for labels that state the GM content of every food item, leaving the consumers with the freedom to choose. Those who fear GM products will avoid buying them; those who think that genetic modification poses no risk and dismiss the objections to them as faddish or fanciful can simply ignore the label and buy freely.

Those who are fanatical enough to want to stop the production of GM foods everywhere would see this as a sellout, however, since it opens up the European market to increasing penetration as GM foods appear on the shelves and do not lead to strange happenings on full-moon nights. Their ambition is too high and impractical, considering that most of the world has already shifted hugely to GM products. But the objection to labeling of GM products gets a little more compelling if the use of GM seeds can spill over to adjacent fields (perhaps through unintended transmission by wind of the GM seeds themselves or of pollen from GM plants); if this is feared, then GM seeds should not be planted at all. At the same time, the American farm lobbies have objected to labeling because they say that it is impossible to determine meaningfully the GM content through the food chain, so that any figure for GM content displayed on a label could be challenged by litigation that could result in serious liability for damages. Then again, there is conflict over whether the labeling should be cautionary or neutral: the opponents of genetic modification would like labels that might say "Contains GM product—unsafe," whereas the proponents would insist on something like "GM content: 2 percent of total weight." Also, the proponents of genetic modification would prefer that GM-free products carry labels identifying them as such rather than requiring GM products to be labeled. This issue is not easily resolved, as the world outside the European Union is massively shifting to the adoption of GM products and it becomes plausible to claim that it is more sensible, given the lower share in world sales, for the GM-free products to carry labels, just as organic foods do rather than non-organic ones.

But none of these difficulties is beyond resolution by compromise and good sense. And labeling remains an option that introduces an element of necessary flexibility in remedies available when a legislative or executive violation of the WTO agreement has been ruled by the WTO Dispute Settlement Mechanism to have arisen.

Values-Related Products: Dolphins, Turtles, and Others

The other set of problems that have created hostility toward GATT and the WTO have come from values-related decisions affecting production and process methods (PPMs) that violate ethical preferences. Recall the classic case, initiated by Mexico, about U.S. legislation prohibiting the imports into the United States of tuna from the tropical oceans if caught by using purse seine nets, which kill dolphins. The GATT panel on the case issued a controversial ruling on August 16, 1991, finding in favor of Mexico, and triggering a massive NGO condemnation of GATT as an anti-environmental body.[32] As it happened, the report was not adopted by the GATT council, so it had no force, because Mexico did not press for its adoption. Mexico had been advised by its lobbyists that the GATT victory, if pressed, could cost Mexico the passage of NAFTA.

While the legalities are somewhat complex, and changed slightly between the initial 1991 panel and the one in 1994, the essence of the decision was that GATT discouraged interrupting market access for products on the grounds that the processes and production methods used in their manufacture were unacceptable.[33] To see why PPMs were considered to be generally out of bounds, it is important to see that the GATT originated as an institution that was primarily about reducing trade barriers.[34] It was also solidly built on the notion of non-discrimination. Its most-favored-nation (MFN) rule required that the lowest tariff rate had to be extended to all members.

But then, as is clear to all students of discrimination, a tariff can be non-discriminatory on the face of it but discriminatory in reality. This can be done readily if products are defined not just by output characteristics but also by the methods used in producing them (i.e., by PPMs). Students of international economics were long instructed by Gottfried Haberler, one of the giants of twentieth-century international economics, who cited in his celebrated treatise the possibly apocryphal story of how Germany had a high MFN tariff on a specific type of cheese produced from cattle grazing at altitudes above a thousand meters, with bells around their necks.[35] Evidently this applied to Swiss cheese, but if Tanzania or Sri Lanka were to produce cheese fitting this bill, the tariff would apply to them as well! Robert Hudec tells a similar but definitely true story in regard to the German tariff on mountain cattle, which was designed to give Switzerland a trade concession while excluding Danish cattle (because Denmark had not made reciprocal concessions as "payment").[36]

When the dolphin-tuna case was decided in 1991, the view taken by the GATT panel was that unless specific exceptions had been negotiated and agreed to, this "trade tradition" where PPMs should not be allowed to intrude and thereby facilitate de facto discrimination must be followed. As the earlier-cited GATT report on trade and the environment argued, the fear also was that an open-ended grant of exception on values-related PPMs could lead to a slippery slope and a flood of exclusions that could not be challenged as countries passed unilateral legislation and executive orders that asserted a moral objection to a practice they did not like and denied others market access. For instance, all products made with child labor, however defined, could be excluded. Dolphins might be important to many Americans, but cows are sacred to many Indians (fortunately not all!), and so beef sales and imports could be proscribed altogether. If energy was deemed too cheap in the United States, as it has long been compared to almost all other oil-importing countries, then an automatic PPM could justify ending energy-using imports from the United States (an issue I return to below). One could go on. The problem is that—unlike, for instance, SPS exclusions, which can be moderated by a scientific test—there is no practical way in which morality can be circumscribed.

But there is also the fear that such an open-ended PPM exclusion would essentially imply that the moral preferences of the powerful nations would prevail, since those of the smaller nations would not be championed in a system where only nations have the legal standing to bring disputes to the GATT. The more articulate of the poor countries with democratic politics and NGOs pointed out that this could return us to a neo-imperial order reminiscent of the days of European empires when might made right and the church marched alongside the soldiers or followed soon after. It is easy enough for the young in the countries that were freed from colonial rule in the aftermath of the Second World War to forget today that this symbiotic relationship often existed between those from the conquering European countries who pursued secular agendas and those who had the ambitions of an imperial church. They need to read, if nothing else, the poignant Nigerian novel *Things Fall Apart,* by Chinua Achebe, which tells of the tragedy that overtakes Okonkwo, its native hero, as Christianity spreads under colonial rule in the Niger delta.

These considerations would suggest that an open-ended automatic legitimation of values-related PPM-based exclusions is unwise, even if there might be legal disagreements about its GATT-inconsistency. In fact, that was very much the position of the developing countries at the mammoth Rio Conference on the Environment in June 1992, where a strong statement against the use of trade sanctions to advance environmental agendas was issued. And I might quote the Center for Science and Environment, the most radical of the pro-environmental NGOs in India today, on this issue:

> In the current world reality trade is used as an instrument entirely by northern countries to discipline environmentally errant nations. Surely, if India or Kenya were to threaten to stop trade with USA, it would hardly affect the latter. But the fact of the matter is that it is the northern countries that have

the greatest impact on the world's environment. . . . [T]he instruments that need to be devised for . . . a system of global discipline must be fair and equally accessible to all. Reinforcing [through unilateral muscle-flexing by rich-country NGOs and their governments via trade sanctions] the power that already flows in a northern direction cannot improve the world.[37]

These considerations were disregarded in the case of the WTO Appellate Body's 1998 decision on the shrimp-turtle case, brought by India and three other developing countries against the United States for its law excluding the imports of shrimp caught without the use of turtle-excluding devices (TEDs), which are nets with narrow necks.[38] In effect, although the United States lost the case on appeal on minor technicalities, the Appellate Body reversed the earlier decisions that found in favor of the developing country plaintiffs and sided with the U.S. environmentalists and legislation that imposed trade restrictions.

There is little doubt that the Appellate Body was influenced by the immense lobbying effort of the richly endowed environmental NGOs and their threat that a ruling that reaffirmed the finding in the dolphin-tuna case would put the WTO at risk. These may be, as Ralph Nader calls them, "faceless judges," but they have eyes and ears nonetheless. And the agitations of these rich-country groups carry far more visible evidence of political realities that judges inevitably reflect in their interpretations and rulings than do declarations at Rio and writings by less visible and poorly financed NGOs in the poor countries that are on the receiving end of this issue.

Astonishingly, the Appellate Body relied (partially) instead on the *preamble* to the Marrakesh Treaty establishing the WTO in 1994, where the phrase "sustainable development" is used, to justify a permissive reversal of the earlier decisions on value-related PPM-based suspensions of market access! Even God does not know what *sustainable development* means. It has become the nonsensical, anything-you-want-it-to-mean term today that *socialism* was in the 1960s and 1970s, when every concerned and committed politician in the Third World professed it while justifying his preferred agenda cynically by affixing the adjective *Arab* or *African* before it. It is surprising, therefore, that the Appellate Body relied on this vague phrase in a preamble, in preference to formal declarations at conferences on the environment such as the 1992 Rio conference, which explicitly declared against the use of trade sanctions.

It is also surprising to ask the developing countries, which cannot find the resources even to read the fine print that more and more is being thrown at them by the increasingly legalistic texts of trade treaties and instruments, to worry also about what goes into preambles. Surely most of us, and not just the developing-country negotiators, think that the preamble is like the overture at the opera: the audience is free to rustle through the libretto and even to whisper to friends until the real opera begins.

The shrimp-turtle decision has therefore left many observers in the developing countries outraged. It also is a dangerous ruling because of the possibility, which bothered the authors of the 1991 GATT report on trade and the environment, that it opens up a Pandora's box. Consider that this finding applies *fully* to the United States, which has failed to sign the Kyoto Protocol on global warming, whereas almost all other nations have. The United States is therefore producing traded products using PPMs that other nations can claim damage the environment. We would in effect be talking about a virtual embargo, as most products use energy in their manufacture! The United States is protected only by its size and its ability as a hegemon to browbeat other nation-states into not passing such legislation. But that leaves a gaping incoherence and cynicism in the world at the inherent asymmetry and injustice of a WTO Dispute Settlement Mechanism that implicitly, even if perhaps unwittingly, favors the powerful.

But one cannot rule out actions against the United States, using this precedent, in more manageable cases such as cigarettes. While the United States and Germany have managed to get exemptions from advertising restrictions in the recent anti-tobacco treaty at the WHO, the fact is that virtually all other nations have adopted such restrictions.[39] Again, using the shrimp-turtle decision as its guide, a set of nations could simply proscribe the sale in their home markets of any cigarettes produced and sold by firms using advertising, thus ruling out imports of American cigarettes. Since tobacco firms are properly considered to be venal, and cigarettes to be bad even though legal, such prohibitive legislation by foreign nations would be widely applauded, and if the United States brought a WTO case, it would have no leg to stand on because of the shrimp-turtle decision. But one must ask: how would the U.S. Congress react? Would congressmen not march down the steps of the Capitol, denouncing the WTO's arrogance and threatening withdrawal? Many other such cases can be imagined that are not entirely beyond the realm of probability.

In short, the lobbying of the environmentalists, and an apparently intimidated Appellate Body, have led to an inappropriate outcome. Is there a better solution to the values-related PPM problem? I believe that the best approach has to bypass attempts at imposing desired PPMs on other countries through what are little more than trade sanctions. Instead, the rich and powerful countries that wish to propagate their moral preferences, whether widely held or idiosyncratic, should proceed to subsidize the PPMs that they advocate (e.g., non-use of purse seine nets and use of TEDs), putting their own resources where they claim their moral preferences are. This is, in fact, exactly what the signatories to the Kyoto treaty on global warming have done: recognizing that the developing countries have resource problems, because they are poor, the rich countries have promised resources, financial and technological, to enable them to make the switch to processes emitting less carbon into the atmosphere. In the same vein, the best solution to the shrimp-turtle problem would surely have been for the United States to buy the TEDs, which presumably cost about $50 a net, and send them gratis to the developing countries for their use. I doubt if more than about $10 million would have been involved; that is less than a tenth of the money that the IMF spends on travel every year.

Besides, it would surely be a good idea to reopen CITES, the convention on international trade in endangered species, to include the PPMs where we currently see problems, with a continuing open window to consider more possibilities as they arise. CITES deals only with trade in endangered species, prohibiting trade, for instance, in tigers and tiger parts, turtles and turtle parts. But now that we have TEDs, it makes sense to extend the treaty to include PPMs such as TEDs. Although the shrimp-turtle case had nothing to do with CITES, a negotiated prohibition on the use of TEDs and provisions to subsidize their purchase (as in the Kyoto treaty, where immensely greater sums have been promised) would surely have taken the heat out of this contentious dispute.

In short, the environmentalists need to remember that their preferred use of muscle and lobbying, always justified in terms of images of their righteousness arrayed against the wicked corporate interests, is not always in defense of the best policies in cases involving a conflict between trade and the environment. The shrimp-turtle victory for them was a sad loss for the world; the battle was waged on the wrong front.

Global Pollution and the WTO

Much of the analysis so far has been addressing what I called domestic pollution problems. But something must be said about global problems such as global warming, ozone layer depletion, acid rain, and other cases where there are externalities for other countries—effects on them from what one country does within its own jurisdiction or in the global commons where no country has jurisdiction. Remember, however, that while these are global problems, they are not necessarily a consequence of globalization. Thus the ozone layer gets depleted partly because people use aerosol cans, and global warming is intensified by the carbon-emitting belching of Indian cows and by the clearing of carbon-absorbing forests, the latter often reflecting in part the traditional practice of slash-and-burn agriculture.

By now, many of the global environmental problems have been addressed through negotiated treaties and conventions, typically described as multilateral environmental agreements (MEAs).[40] They often have fewer parties than the WTO, the membership of which has steadily grown to over 145 today, with several others, including Russia, standing with hat in hand at the door. Several of these MEAs allow the use of trade restrictions against non-members, whom they describe as "free riders," and against members who become "defectors." A good example of the former concerns the use of CFCs in refrigerators. This is forbidden by the Montreal Protocol on substances that contribute to the depletion of the ozone layer. But if non-members still use them, the signatories then want to be able to use trade sanctions against such non-members, the free riders.

The question then immediately arises: what if these free riders and defectors are WTO members and are entitled to MFN treatment? Obviously, an exception would have to be formally built into the WTO to allow the selective and discriminatory use of trade restrictions, or else the exercise of such trade-restricting provisions could lead to a dispute where the WTO Dispute Settlement Mechanism would have the problem of ruling on this conflict. That potentially creates a problem for environmentalists who want a clear affirmation of the legitimacy of the use of trade sanctions by signatories to the MEAs.

Even if the WTO were not an obstacle, is the use of trade sanctions sensible in this context? In particular, it is necessary for the parties to MEAs to remember that regarding the non-signatories as free riders may not always be appropriate. It is possible that they do not want to board the bus! Each MEA has two dimensions: efficiency and fairness. Take, for instance, the Kyoto Protocol, which was created in December 1997 by several countries to grapple with the problem of global warming. Most countries have signed on, pledging to cut their greenhouse emissions by 2010. But the United States has objected to the Kyoto Protocol on grounds of efficiency *and* fairness. It does not consider the protocol's targets to be consistent with efficiency.[41] It also regards the negligible demands on the developing countries to reduce their emissions as unfair. On the other hand, if the targeted reductions of emissions by the developing countries were to be raised to accommodate the United States, the developing countries would regard that as unfair. The developing countries have been carrying the day; the United States is therefore the free rider in being the only major country out of the Kyoto Protocol. But then is it to be subjected to the protocol's trade sanctions?

Hardly. Even if power were left out of the equation, surely the correct approach should be to address and accommodate the objections and concerns of the non-signatory nations rather than resort to trade sanctions to be used against them because they do not agree with the views of a plurilateral coalition (i.e., a coalition that is more than bilateral but less than fully multilateral in membership). Often, this can be done without crippling concessions. Let me illustrate.

The fact that the Kyoto Protocol does not require the developing countries to share the burden of meeting targets to reduce carbon emissions has been the sticking point with U.S. legislators. And this is a bipartisan view. It is often forgotten that the U.S. Senate, with negligible opposition, refused to sign on to Kyoto on these grounds during the Clinton administration. The Bush administration merely resurrected the corpse and knifed it, creating with this public theater resounding applause among its anti-environmental supporters and a matching hue and cry worldwide from the environmentalists.

The objections in the U.S. Senate to the treaty, on the other hand, could have been surmounted, with virtually similar provisions in terms of distribution of burden between the rich and the poor countries, if only the treaty had been packaged in a different way. The way the packaging was done involved the use of principles that no longer appeal to U.S. legislators. It was argued that the developing countries were being exempted because of "progressivity" of burden sharing: the poor should carry less burden than the rich. But this principle is increasingly under attack as conservatism has resurrected itself in the United States. An additional justification produced to let off developing countries with no obligations to reduce carbon emissions was that the rich countries had despoiled the environment through several decades of industrialization, which had emitted huge quantities of carbon into the atmosphere; they therefore should pay, rather than developing countries.

The progressivity argument spoke to flows, the current emissions; the argument about past emissions, based vaguely on a "you were a worse culprit" notion, spoke to the stocks. Neither principle had political appeal. Besides, both were added up incoherently into the Kyoto provisions, letting off the poor countries very lightly.

But we could get a similar result if we kept stocks and flows distinct and appealed instead to principles that currently do play well in the United States. Thus, take the stocks argument. The United States currently accepts the principle of the Superfund, where companies must clean up past damage to the environment, even—and oddly, in my view—when the pollution was not scientifically considered harmful. So the United States can be asked simply to accept internationally what it accepts at home: the damage it did in the past must be paid for, with payments (which should be several hundred billions, for sure) going into an international Superfund.

This fund could be used to finance the use of carbon-free technology in the developing countries and financing research into new inventions including the carbon-trapping technology that is being developed. Here the fact that the United States leads in such research and therefore its industry can be expected to profit from this arrangement should prove to be a major motivating factor.

At the same time, as far as current emissions are concerned, each country could be charged for its net emissions of carbon minus its absorption of carbon. It would mean buying permits for *all* emissions—again, a principle that Americans love because it is market-based. This would also automatically mean that the rich countries would likely pay the largest amounts to be able to emit annually and therefore would have the greater incentive to cut emissions.

Thus, by building the treaty around two principles, the Superfund for stocks/past and permits for flows/present, Kyoto could be redesigned and repackaged in a way that both appeals to current American principles of public policy and generates results for the distribution of cost burdens between the rich and the poor countries not greatly dissimilar to what the present Kyoto treaty does.

The point of this discussion is not just to suggest how a repackaged Kyoto treaty is likely to surmount the objections from the United States, but to indicate that efficient design and distributional fairness are important. The notion, therefore, that trade sanctions are weapons to be exercised against recalcitrant free riders is not the best way to think about the problem.

In any event, there have been absolutely no cases brought at the WTO by WTO members who are not MEA members and have had trade sanctions imposed on them. The question is therefore academic, and perhaps it is best left there.

12

Corporations: Predatory or Beneficial?

I n the movie *Manhattan*, Woody Allen's character talks about the hotel where the food was dreadful, and there was not enough of it, either! The critics of multinationals often make similar complaints. They argue that multinationals must be condemned because they bypass countries that need them, accentuating the divide between those who are fortunate and those who are not. Then they also complain that the multinationals cause harm where they go, exploiting the host countries and their workers.

The complaint about bypassing needy countries is misplaced. If multinationals avoid some poor countries, that is surely not surprising. They are businesses that must survive by making a profit. Indeed, no corporation ever managed to do sustained good by continually posting losses. If a country wants to attract investment, it has to provide an attractive environment. That generally implies having political stability and economic advantages such as cheap labor or exploitable natural resources. In the game of attracting investment, therefore, some countries are going to lose simply because they lack these attributes.

For these unfortunate countries, the harsh reality is that no matter how good their politics and policies are, they may not suffice to attract multinationals. I recall a Jamaican radio program where I was being quizzed by the widow of the charismatic prime minister Michael Manley, a socialist of great conviction and charm. She was complaining to me that Jamaica had done all the right things, in particular opening herself to freer trade, but it had not helped the country to attract investment. I reminded her that the proper question to ask was: would protection have led to better results? The answer was no, because it is improbable that Jamaica could have attracted investment if it had closed its small domestic market. I also pointed out that fortunately Jamaica was not wholly lost in her quest for economic success. After all, over half of its population, among them the current U.S. secretary of state, Colin Powell, and the Harvard sociologist Orlando Patterson, worked abroad, and that too was an outward-oriented strategy that Jamaica was exploiting profitably due to its proximity to the United States. The truly unfortunate countries were those few where no routes to prosperity through exploitation of trade, inward investment, or outward migration could be found or where the ability to travel along these routes was crippled by acute problems of governance, as in the African countries ravaged by war.

It is unrealistic to expect multinationals to invest in these countries and "save" them. The only answer is to offset this private neglect by redirecting public aid, technical assistance, and corporate altruism to them so that they get the funds and know-how that will not come through the marketplace. The World Bank, for instance, should turn away from lending to countries such as India and China, which surely have the ability to develop by themselves, and focus their efforts and resources on countries that cannot hack it on their own. But, of course, the World Bank leadership seeks to maximize influence by distributing largesse to all; even altruistic institutions will occasionally be run by men whose private ambitions, rather than social good, are the primary determinants of their policies.

The real battle, however, is being fought over the multinationals that *do* go to the poor countries. In the 1950s the early development economists, among them Hans Singer, complained that multinationals created enclaves within countries, with no spillover effects, good or bad, for the host countries. There was probably something to this observation when the multinationals were in extractive industries such as diamonds and bauxite.[1] Today, however, manufacturing and, increasingly, financial and other services attract far more investment. The concern today is not about the multinationals having no effect. Rather, there is a fierce debate between those who consider multinationals to be a malign influence and those who find them to be a benign force. I will argue here that the evidence strongly suggests that the benign view is more persuasive.

Harmful Effects?

In characteristically cynical fashion, the Nobel laureate V. S. Naipaul, whose many novels do not have a single tender love scene, writes in the opening chapter of his novel *Guerrillas* of the remnants of an industrial park, "one of the failed projects of the earliest days of independence." "Tax holidays had been offered to foreign investors; many had come for the holidays and had then moved on elsewhere."[2] Naipaul darkly suggests that the multinationals had profited from the tax generosity, contributed nothing, and then moved on.

A Different Race to the Bottom

As it happens, this is precisely what many serious observers of tax breaks to attract multinationals fear: that there is a race to the bottom on tax concessions as poor countries compete among themselves to give such generous terms to foreign investors that they wind up net losers. This race is, of course, a well-known phenomenon at the level of different states under a federal government, such as in the United States; before his election as president, Bill Clinton's main exposure to the world abroad came from his joining this race as governor of Arkansas.

That, in fact, the race is so fierce that poor countries wind up net losers is doubtful, because multinationals bring many benefits that should outweigh the giveaways in tax and other benefits such as rent-free use of public lands, but such an adverse outcome cannot be ruled out. An analogy from aid policy is helpful. Aid terms are sometimes quite onerous because aid flows take the form of loans to be repaid and the interest charges on the loans are close to commercial rates (as in the early Japanese aid programs). Aid is also tied to imports from the donor countries, so the aid recipient must often import goods and accept projects from the donor at prices that exceed those that would be paid if it were allowed to import from the cheapest sources. Such tying of aid is inherent in food aid, where donor countries typically give you food produced by their own farms but not money to import food from where you want. So when the U.S. administration recently complained that the European restrictions on GM foods and seeds were preventing African countries from accepting U.S. aid to prevent famine, this was an absurd charge since it was perfectly possible for the United States to give dollar aid that could then be used to import non-GM EU food to prevent the starvation. The problem was that the United States wanted to give its own GM food to the Africans.

Given all the ways in which the value of aid dollars is typically reduced by terms and conditions imposed by the donors, it is possible that the benefits from the aid will not merely be reduced but, in some cases, may actually turn into a loss-causing proposition! Many economists have cautioned poor countries not to accept anything that is called aid just because it is so described, but to look it in the eye and to reject potential rip-offs. In short, the gift horse may well be a Trojan horse! So, indeed, may be the case with multinationals brought in by offering excessively generous tax concessions.

But often the concessions reduce rather than eliminate altogether the burden of the corporate taxes to be paid. That leaves then the presumption that the country hosting the multinational benefits because *some* taxes do get paid. Other benefits such as the employment of underemployed and unemployed labor and the occasional diffusion of technical know-how and better management practices would remain, of course, to enhance the total benefits from inward direct investments.

From the viewpoint of the multinationals, the competition among countries to attract them is a phenomenon that increases their share of the total economic gains flowing from investment in the poor countries. But, not content with that situation, multinationals have long sought to improve their bargaining power still further. To do so, they have asked for codes, even mandatory provisions (proposed by the European Union, for instance, at the WTO), to prevent the receiving countries from imposing restrictions (such as that they must use domestic components or accept export obligations) on the multinationals that come in. For instance, the OECD unsuccessfully attempted, at the urging of business groups, to devise a multilateral agreement on investment, while the European Union and Japan are trying currently to negotiate a mandatory agreement on investment in the ongoing Doha Round of multilateral trade negotiations.[3]

The efforts to get these agreements negotiated are often justified by claims that they would contribute to a more orderly and efficient allocation of the world's scarce investible resources. But if this were the true rationale for these efforts, then we would have expected these codes to eliminate not just the restrictions on multinationals but also the subsidies to them. Both restrictions and artificial encouragements (through tax breaks) equally distort world production and trade. But when the lobbying efforts of the business groups are analyzed, one finds of course that there are no provisions for ruling out such tax breaks and subsidies to themselves.

Large Companies and Small Countries

In fact, the worry about a race to the bottom is part of the more general concern that critics have when negotiations for investment occur between large companies and small countries. It is assumed that this will lead to weak, poor countries yielding to unreasonable demands from the stronger corporations.

This fear is often justified by noting that if major corporations and the world's economies are ranked together, the corporations by their sales volumes and the countries by their GDPs (a measure of their national incomes), then the corporations are half of the top one hundred performers! This dramatic statistic is misleading, however, as the two sets of data are not comparable. To see this, consider a shirt that costs $100. Its sales value (which economists would call gross value) includes the value of cloth at $70 and wages and profits (i.e., incomes earned by the productive factors in the garments industry) of $30. Economists call this $30 the value added in the garment industry. Now, GDP is simply the entire factor income or value added in all activities, including garments. So when we compare sales volumes, which are gross values, with GDP, which is value added, we are comparing oranges with apples. The comparison, while conceptually flawed, also exaggerates the role of corporations because sales figures across the entire economy will add up to numbers that will vastly exceed the GDPs of the countries where these sales occur.

The Belgian economist Paul De Grauwe and the Belgian senator Filip Camerman, who were the first to notice the illegitimacy of these types of comparisons between countries and corporations, reworked the statistics to measure corporations also by value added. That necessary correction changed the picture wholly. "In 2000, sales by General Motors were $185 billion but value added was $42 billion; sales by Ford were $170 billion but value added was $47 billion; and sales by Royal Dutch/ Shell were $149 billion but value added was only $36 billion." While leading anti-corporation activists had argued that "14 of the 50 largest economies and 51 of the 100 largest were companies, [in fact] only two of the top 50 economies, measured by value added, and 37 of the top 100 were corporations."[4]

But even if the corporations, when appropriately compared, had turned out to appear dominant, this would not necessarily support the fears of corporate rip-offs. Weak countries can also play off one giant corporation against another; and they occasionally do. Thus small countries such as Poland have recently chosen between Airbus and Boeing, both huge corporations and both in continuous and fierce competition. Enron was accused of having taken India for a ride just a few years ago, before the corporation self-destructed. But the problem was that India, because it was in a rush to get energy investments going rapidly, had foolishly failed to invite tenders and have Enron compete vigorously with other potential investors.[5]

In the end, the anti-corporation critics need to remember the chief lesson that economists learned when faced in the 1930s with John Kenneth

Galbraith's celebrated assertion that large corporations meant that there was monopoly power. The key to whether such monopoly power exists is to be found in effective barriers to entry. If new firms can enter, providing effective competition, the mere presence of large firms in an industry cannot guarantee sizeable monopoly profits. Sheer size is misleading. Giants in an industry who are enjoying abnormal profits must contend with other giants at the door, this potential entry cutting effectively into their monopoly power and keeping abnormal profits down. This is true also in political space as the smart nations play off multinationals from one country against those from others, eliminating dependence on just one source.

But these objections to the fear that small nations will be ripped off by large corporations are less compelling in the poor and small countries with weak governance. One must then contend with the fact that rulers, politicians, and bureaucrats in such countries may be bribed by corporations with deep pockets into creating artificially excessive profits at social expense by accepting terms and conditions that are detrimental to the host country's social advantage. The resulting spoils are split between the multinationals and the corrupt and corrupted officials of the host country. These possibilities are real; rumors about them are abundant, especially in African countries that have been plagued by wars and pestilence. But hard evidence is hard to come by, in the nature of the case.

However, the trend seems to be to make such possibilities less likely as governance has become a subject of concern and action by many aid agencies. There have been successful attempts at achieving transparency, as with the recent agreements requiring disclosure of oil royalty payments to governments that hitherto refused to make them public and which have a bad track record of a large fraction of these oil revenues going missing.[6] These were the handiwork of the Publish What You Pay coalition of NGOs led by the financier George Soros. Similar calls for transparency on the terms negotiated for entry by specific multinationals, and actions such as the enactment of the code at the OECD (thanks to efforts by the United States, which had pioneered in the enactment of such legislation for U.S. firms) to make bribes paid in host countries illegal, are examples of the way in which the joint rip-off model is steadily becoming less likely today.

Political Intrusion

Perhaps the critics' greatest fear has been that multinationals intrude dramatically into the political space of the host countries in nefarious ways.[7] Two classic examples come from South America and Africa. When Chile elected Salvador Allende, who began a decisive shift to the left in his policies toward foreign investment and economic policies in general, leading multinationals operating in Chile drew a line in the sand with the active assistance of the CIA and Henry Kissinger, whose Chilean record of human rights abuses has come under revived scrutiny. ITT and Pepsi are known now to have played a role in the coup against this elected president of Chile.[8] Christopher Hitchens, in his impassioned indictment of Kissinger, has recently recounted these misdeeds:

> In September 1970 . . . [there emerged in the presidential elections] a moral certainty that the Chilean Congress would . . . confirm Dr. Salvador Allende as the next president. But the very name of Allende was anathema to the extreme right in Chile, to certain powerful corporations (notably ITT, Pepsi-Cola and the Chase Manhattan Bank) which did business in Chile and the United States, and to the CIA.
>
> This loathing quickly communicated itself to President Nixon. He was personally beholden to Donald Kendall, the president of Pepsi-Cola, who had given him his first international account. . . . A series of Washington meetings, within eleven days of Allende's electoral victory, essentially settled the fate of Chilean democracy. After discussions with Kendall and with David Rockefeller of Chase Manhattan, and with CIA director Richard Helms, Kissinger went with Helms to the Oval Office. Helms's notes of the meeting show that Nixon wasted little breath in making his wishes known. Allende was not to assume office. ". . . No involvement of embassy. $10,000,000 available, more if necessary. Full-time job—best men we have. . . . Make the economy scream. 48 hours for plan of action."[9]

Then again, in 1960–61, the Belgian corporation Union Meunière was implicated in the episode in Katanga where Tshombe, a puppet, was installed after the overthrow in September 1960 and assassination in January 1961 of Patrice Lumumba, the first elected leader of Congo, which gained independence from Belgium on June 30, 1960. Lumumba's only crime had been his ardent anti-colonialism and left-wing orientation.[10]

These cases are not at all atypical when one recalls how, for instance, the elected Iranian prime minister Mohammad Mossadegh was overthrown by the CIA, partly if not principally because of the giant oil companies' interests, and how the CIA intervened in Central and South America to protect the commercial interests of multinationals such as the United Fruit Company.[11]

But are not such episodes much less likely, even highly improbable, today? This would indeed appear to be the case. The reasons are twofold. First, democracy has broken out in many underdeveloped countries, however imperfectly. Egregious political abuses come to light because democracy permits diverse non-governmental groups and individuals of conscience to point the accusing finger at offending corporations and governments. Second, the accusing finger now has more salience in the age of television and the Internet. Gorbachev uses troops in the Balkans, CNN carries the pictures, and his moral standing collapses until he quickly learns from his political blunder and changes course.

These correctives seem to have diminished greatly the incidence of gross meddling in domestic politics by foreign multinationals. The real danger lies instead in overreach against the multinationals, with demands that they in fact *should* meddle in domestic politics. Some NGOs today seem to accuse multinationals of neglect, rather than intervention, when it comes to advancing their own agendas.

One example comes from Nigeria in 1999. Royal Dutch/Shell was widely condemned by human rights and environmental NGOs for abuses by the government.[12] In Ogoniland, an oil-rich area in the Niger delta, the Nigerian government (a military dictatorship) was accused of siphoning oil revenues to uses outside of Ogoniland. The oil companies, when confronted with protests that involved seizures of property and their executives, were condemned for drawing on the often draconian enforcement resources of the Nigerian government. Moreover, the protesters complained that the oil companies were damaging the local environment.

But can the oil companies be blamed for the policies of the Nigerian government that redirect oil revenues to national priorities that, in the estimation of the Ogonis, reward the Ogonis inadequately? How export proceeds, revenue collections, oil royalties, and earnings are allocated among different claimants in the country is a decision of the Nigerian government and has nothing to do with human rights. If multinationals started interfering in decisions of this kind, that would be political intrusion that would be rejected by every government that values the independence that many nations fought for prior to their independence from colonial powers. That the Ogoni people would want to influence the outcome toward themselves is reasonable; that Royal Dutch/Shell should have no say in the resolution of these questions in Nigeria is equally reasonable. That the Nigerian government was not democratic and did not have legitimacy has some salience, but this cannot mean that a foreign multinational such as Royal Dutch/Shell, which has even less legitimacy to influence or dictate allocational choices in Nigeria, must be sanctioned to do the meddling.

The use of the state's enforcement resources to protect company property and personnel against seizure seems also to be appropriate; what other choices does a company have? When several universities called in the National Guard or the local police during the anti–Vietnam War demonstrations that led to seizure of university administrative offices, occasionally there were confrontations and violence, as at Kent State. But such violence must be distinguished from gratuitous and autonomous violence inflicted on demonstrations that do not involve unlawful seizures. The reports from Ogoniland are quite explicit on how the seizures prompted reaction from the authorities, even as they note and properly condemn how these same authorities often brutally harassed the local NGOs and individuals who were within their rights to protest whatever they wished to protest. Take just a few examples:

> In March 1997, youths captured a barge delivering goods to a Chevron installation. The crew of seventy Nigerians and twenty expatriates were held hostage for three days by youths demanding jobs on the vessel. Following negotiations, in which money was paid to the protesters, the barge was allowed to go offshore, when the navy then boarded it and rescued the hostages.
> In October 1997, the Odeama flow station in Bayelsa state was closed for several days by youths demanding that fifty of them be employed by SPDC.
> From December 13 to December 17, 1997, thirteen employees of Western Geophysical were held hostage by youths in a barge off the coast of Ondo State.
> In July 1998, SPDC reported that . . . the previous week, youths at Nembe hijacked a helicopter and forced the evacuation of staff.[13]

That the oil companies polluted without having to pay the social cost of pollution imposed on the Ogoni people is the most compelling complaint, if true. If the Nigerian government had no environmental policies, and if the oil companies then proceeded to pollute freely and knowingly, the local population certainly had an economic and moral case against the oil companies. So insofar as the protests were aimed at addressing the environmental damage (as distinct from getting the oil companies to meddle in the national policies on distribution of benefits from oil production and simply trying to extract jobs through harassment), they were justified. However, I would argue that seizures of people and property are not the way to organize the protests, but that the methods of non-violent resistance advanced by Mahatma Gandhi and practiced so well by Martin Luther King Jr. are the better way.

Exploitation of Workers?

If any conviction strongly unites the critics of multinationals today, however, it is that they exploit the workers in the poor countries. At first blush this sounds very strange, since firms that create job opportunities should be applauded, no matter that their motivation in investing abroad is to make profits, not to do good. After all, the protesters in Ogoniland were asking for more jobs from the oil companies!

So why are the critics agitated? Much of their ire has been aroused by their assumption that the multinationals, so rich and with such deep pockets, pay such low wages. Then there is also the related assertion, including by the leaders of the anti-sweatshop movement on U.S. campuses, that multinationals run sweatshops in the poor countries. Sweatshops are accused of paying "unfair" or "inadequate" or "low" wages, often of not paying a "living wage." More often, they are condemned for violating "labor rights."

Wages and Exploitation. That multinationals exploit workers in the poor countries by paying low wages is the most frequent and least persuasive charge. The typical critique asserts that if a Liz Claiborne jacket sells for $190 in New York while the female worker abroad who sews it gets only 90 cents an hour, it is obviously exploitation.[14]

But there is surely no necessary relationship between the price of a specific product and the wage paid by a company that can be interpreted in this accusatory fashion. Just for starters, for every jacket that succeeds, there are probably nine that do not. So the effective price of jacket one must consider is a tenth of the successful jacket: only $19, not $190. Then again, owing to distribution costs, and in the case of apparel tariff duties, the price of a jacket almost doubles between landing in New York and finding its way to Lord & Taylor's display hangers.

But that is not all. Consider the diamond polishing industry in the town of Surat, India, which has witnessed rising prosperity ever since Surat has become a rival to Antwerp in this business. If the final price of the diamond in Paris is a million dollars, even a wage payment of $10 an hour and total wage payment to the worker of $1,000 will appear minuscule as a fraction of the final price. But so what?

Again, I have heard people argue that wages in Jakarta or Phnom Penh are a pittance compared to Michael Jordan's multimillion-dollar advertising remuneration by Nike. But it is inappropriate to compare a company's advertising budget with the wage rate or even the wage bill: it proves nothing, certainly not exploitation under any plausible and persuasive definition.

A possible question of interest may be whether Nike and other multinationals are earning huge monopoly profits while paying their workers only a competitive wage, and whether these firms should share these "excess" profit with their workers. But, as it happens, nearly all multinationals such as Liz Claiborne and Nike are in fiercely competitive environments. A recent study of the profits performance of 214 companies in the 1999 Fortune Global 500 list showed a rather sorry performance— about 8.3 percent on foreign assets, and even a decline to 6.6 percent in 1998.[15] Where is the beef that might be shared with workers?

So let me turn to the question of low wages. Are the multinationals paying their workers wages that are *below* what these workers get in alternative occupations in what are really poor countries with low wages? This is virtually implied by the critics. We must ask if this is really true or whether the multinationals are actually paying higher wages than the workers would get elsewhere—say, from local firms in the industry or in alternative jobs.

If the wages received are actually *higher* than those available in alternative jobs, even if low according to the critics (and reflective of the poverty in the poor countries), surely it seems odd to say that the multinationals are exploiting the workers they are hiring! Now, if there were slavery elsewhere and the workers were being whipped daily, as the Romans did with the galley slaves, then the fact that multinationals were whipping them only every other day would hardly turn away the critics! But wages are another matter, obviously. So what are the facts on wage payments?

As it happens, several empirical studies do find that multinationals pay what economists now call a "wage premium": they pay an average wage that exceeds the going rate, mostly up to 10 percent and exceeding it in some cases, with affiliates of U.S. multinationals sometimes paying a premium that ranges from 40 to 100 percent.[16] The University of Michigan economist Linda Lim has reviewed much of the available evidence from a number of studies in Bangladeshi export processing zones, in Mexico, in Shanghai, in Indonesia, and in Vietnam, and reports that they overwhelmingly confirm the existence of such a premium.[17]

In one of the careful and convincing studies, the economist Paul Glewwe, using Vietnamese household data for 1997–98, was able to isolate and focus on the incomes of workers employed in foreign-owned firms, joint ventures, and wholly Vietnamese-owned enterprises. About half of the Vietnamese workers in the study worked in precisely the foreign-owned textile or leather firms that so often come in for criticism. Contrary to the steady refrain from the critics—some of whom man websites continually directed at Nike, for instance—Glewwe found that "workers in foreign-owned enterprises fare better, making an average of 42 cents per hour," almost twice that of the average wage earner. Glewwe concludes:

> Overall, the evidence shows that these workers [in foreign-owned enterprises] are better off than the average Vietnamese worker. . . . The data also show that people who obtained employment in foreign-owned enterprises and joint ventures in Vietnam in the 1990s experience increases in household income (as measured by per capita consumption expenditures) that exceeded the average increases for all Vietnamese households. This appears to contradict

the claims that foreign-owned enterprises in poor countries such as Vietnam are "sweatshops." On the other hand, it is clear that the wages paid by these enterprises . . . are a fraction of wages paid in the U.S. and other wealthy countries. Yet Vietnam is so poor that it is better for a Vietnamese person to obtain this kind of employment than almost any other kind available in Vietnam.[18]

In fact, econometric studies have tried to explain why this premium exists by controlling for scale, worker quality, age of the establishment, and other differences among the firms being compared; the premium, while diminished, still persists. There is also some evidence that this irreducible premium reflects higher productivity in firms under foreign ownership.[19]

What about subcontracting by multinationals? There does not appear to be any significant evidence, that these subcontractors pay less than the going wage in domestic firms and in alternative jobs. It is likely, however, that the wages paid are closer to these alternatives; the wage premium is possibly negligible, if it obtains at all, in subcontracted work.

In both cases, whether there is direct employment at a wage premium by the multinationals or subcontracted employment at a negligible premium, these are only direct or proximate effects. By adding to the demand for labor in the host countries, multinationals are also overwhelmingly likely to improve wages all around, thus improving the incomes of the workers in these countries.

Labor Rights. But if the wage argument against multinationals must be dismissed, there is still the accusation that these corporations violate labor rights. One view is that local labor laws are violated on safety and other working conditions. Another is that the conditions at work violate not domestic laws in the host countries but customary international law. Both critiques raise difficulties.

At the outset, it is highly unlikely that multinational firms would violate domestic regulatory laws, which generally are not particularly demanding. Since the laws are often not burdensome in poor countries, it is hard to find evidence that violations are taking place in an egregious, even substantial fashion. Ironically, sweatshops exist in the New York garment district (*not* in Guatemala, mind you), where the laws *are* demanding and simultaneously the ability of the affected workers to invoke them is impaired, as in the case of illegal immigrant workers.

Moreover, sweatshops are typically small-scale workshops, not multinationals. If the subcontractors who supply parts to the multinationals, for example, are tiny enterprises, it is possible that they, like local entrepreneurs, violate legislation from time to time. But since the problem lies with lack of effective enforcement in the host country, do we hold multinationals accountable for anything that they buy from these countries, even if it is not produced directly by the multinationals? That is tantamount to saying that the multinationals must effectively boycott anything that is produced and sold by countries where labor laws are not enforced effectively. But then why impose this obligation only on the multinationals? Surely it should apply equally to all citizens and legal entities in countries whose multinationals are being asked to indulge in the boycott of the offending country. This means going to the ILO to invoke Article 35 (which permits serious censure) or, better still, to the United Nations to invoke Article 7 on embargos. Short of that, the demands on the multinationals are incoherent.

Second, the insistence that local laws be enforced raises two questions. First, what is effective enforcement? What resources must be spent? The expenditure by the United States itself on enforcement against violations of OSHA and labor regulations has been minuscule; does that mean that multinationals investing in the United States must cease operation in this country? More important, the demand that local laws be enforced flies in the face of political practice in many democratic countries. It is important to see why.

Typically, one encounters two dominant practices in regard to social legislation: either there are no laws or there are many excessively generous ones. The lack-of-enforcement critique applies naturally to the latter situation. But then we must ask why the legislation is not enforced. The most likely reason is that there was no intention to enforce the legislation in the first place. Often extraordinarily expensive provisions are mandated simply because the enforcement is going to be negligible. Thus, as a wit once said, progressive taxes are enacted to please the Democrats and the loopholes are put in to please the Republicans. In the same spirit, countries such as India have some of the most progressive, and expensive, legislation on the books concerning even minimum wages, but with no real intention to enforce it precisely because the cost of such mandates would be forbidding. So the generosity of these provisions in the face of acutely limited resources is simply meant to produce a good feeling—the legislators mean well, but beyond that, alas . . . In fact, why not offer yet more generous benefits to the workers? I recall the Nobel laureate Robert Solow, a famous wit, being told that Harvard's highest salary was $150,000 but that no one was being paid it. In that case, he replied, why not say that the highest salary was $250,000?

Indeed, legislation may often be dated, and people may have changed their minds about its advisability, but the political battle to drop or modify it would be too expensive, so the legislation remains but is ignored. Thus, New Hampshire reportedly still has anti-adultery statutes on the books, but they are dead like a skunk in deep snow.

Often, however, it is not the violation of domestic law that is at is-sue. It is rather that the practice of multinationals, even when in confor-mity to local legislation, does not meet the demands of customary international law. When asked to explain customary international law, the activists refer to ILO conventions on workers, the covenants on civil and political rights at the United Nations, and other norms established at international agencies and conferences, whether universally adopted or not. This route to condemning multinationals is predictably quite problematic, however.

For one thing, the domestic regulation may be less demanding than these international norms for good reasons, in both economics and eth-ics. Take the case of working hours, which can be quite long in the EPZs and suggest exploitation that violates what an activist may consider to be human rights norms. But Nicholas Kristof and Sheryl WuDunn of the *New York Times* (whom I cited in Chapter 7 on the charge that young female workers were exploited in EPZs) have pointed out in an essay in the *New York Times Magazine*, provocatively titled "Two Cheers for Sweat-shops," that the young women who work long hours are often doing so voluntarily. Why? Because many want to make as quickly as possible the money they planned to earn and then return to their homes. And, like many of us who work long hours, they are not being exploited; they drive themselves. Let me quote just one account of these reporters' visit to a Chinese sweatshop:

> On our first extended trip to China, in 1987, we traveled to the Pearl River Delta in the south of the country. There we visited several factories, includ-ing one in the boomtown of Dongguan, where about 100 female workers sat at workbenches stitching together bits of leather to make purses for a Hong Kong company. We chatted with several women as their fingers flew over their work and asked them about their hours.
> "I start at about 6.30 after breakfast, and go until about 7 p.m.," explained one shy teenage girl. "We break for lunch, and I take half an hour off then."
> "You do this six days a week?"
> "Oh no. Every day."
> "Seven days a week?"
> "Yes." She laughed at our surprise. "But then I take a week or two off at Chinese New Year to go back to my village."
> The others we talked to all seemed to regard it as a plus that the factory allowed them to work long hours. Indeed, some had sought out this factory precisely because it offered them the chance to earn more.
> "It's actually pretty annoying how hard they want to work," said the fac-tory manager, a Hong Kong man. "It means we have to worry about security and have a supervisor around almost constantly."[20]

Indeed, even the restraints put on union rights in export processing zones, which are considered violations of customary international law, need to be reassessed, and possibly condoned rather than criticized, when this is done in democratic poor countries. Even governments that will not tolerate draconian mistreatment of union activists and have legislation protective and supportive of union rights such as the ability to organize will put some restraints in place in EPZs. Why? Because when unions assert rights but object to obligations, as when one cannot discipline or fire workers who hold down two jobs and collect pay while working elsewhere—a common practice in parts of India, for example—and one cannot reform them, it is tempting to think of carving out little EPZs where unions do not exist, just as the free-traders who cannot reduce trade barriers due to political obstacles then think of EPZs, where free trade obtains. As Saburo Okita, one of Japan's leading internationalists and an architect of Japan's postwar recovery, once told me when he was looking at India's self-imposed economic follies, if only India could take half a dozen small areas the size of Hong Kong and turn them into EPZs that followed the outward-oriented Hong Kong polices, while the bulk of India continued to wallow in its inward-looking inefficiencies; it would only take a couple of decades for these EPZs to overtake the rest of India!

In short, it is really the wish to escape unions, because in the country's experience they act only to enjoy rights and accept no obligations, that drives these governments to say, "Let the EPZs have no unions, for the only kind we will get are those that do harm rather than good." This is certainly not the same as saying, "We do not want unions, and we will even break them brutally!" As it happens, India, which also has gone in for EPZs, has maintained union rights but with one proviso: that wildcat strikes are not allowed in the EPZs, the rationale being that export industries are "essential" industries, an exception that is allowed even in the rich Western nations, including the United States.

What worries me also is that customary international law is often quite broadly stated (e.g., gender discrimination, which can be defined in several ways, is not permissible), much like domestic constitutions and unlike legislation and executive orders (e.g., that red mercury is not to be discharged into lakes, rivers, and oceans), which are much more narrowly stated and hence clear to follow. How is the multinational then to follow "laws" that are not legislated but are norms, and which can be interpreted in so many different ways that whether you conform to them depends on who does the interpretation?

Thus today nations have agreed to, and many have ratified, conventions dealing with so-called core labor rights. These are contained in the ILO Declaration of Fundamental Principles and Rights at Work:

- Freedom of association and the effective recognition of the right to collective bargaining
- The elimination of all forms of forced or compulsory labor
- The effective abolition of child labor
- The elimination of discrimination in respect of employment and occupation

But once one gets down to brass tacks, difficulties arise. Take the simple injunction about the freedom of association—that is, the right to unionize. How is one to cope with the fact that this right has several nuances and dimensions (and that virtually all countries could be found in violation of it in some way)? Central to this right is the ability to strike; a union without an effective right to strike is almost like a paper tiger. But, as I noted in Chapter 10, for half a century the Taft-Hartley law's provisions have allowed the hiring of replacement workers and discouraged sympathetic strikes, and this has badly crippled U.S. unions' ability to strike. The earlier-cited Human Rights Watch report concluded, therefore, that "millions of workers" in the United States were denied the "freedom of association."[21] Human Rights Watch and I consider this quite a reasonable interpretation of the violation of the core agreement to respect the right to unionize, but will this interpretation be accepted or rejected for the purpose of enforcement and litigation?[22] And who will bring action against what must be all corporations in the United States, because they are all acting under these legal provisions that are judged to violate this core right agreed at the ILO?

A similar problem can be shown to arise in the case of gender discrimination, yet another core labor right. There is no society today that is free from gender discrimination in some form. Besides, recall from Chapter 7 that even something narrower, such as pay discrimination, can be diversely defined. So how does a broad statement of these core rights, interpreted as customary international law for the purpose at hand, work?

My view is that we do need to assert these broad aspirational objectives but that, for purposes of assessing whether corporations in the poor countries are to be condemned (and even litigated against, as is beginning to happen in U.S. courts), we need to arrive at much narrower and more realistic agreements on specific practices.[23] For instance, on the right to unionize, we could reach agreement today on outlawing the killing of union leaders, but not on whether replacement workers can be hired or whether the firing of workers is allowed for economic or disciplinary reasons. Agreement could be reached, I suspect, on minimum safety provisions (e.g., the issuance of goggles to foundry workers working near blast furnaces, and enforcement of the use), though not on rich-country, OSHA standards that are very expensive for poor countries. In short, just as there is virtual agreement that torture in the shape of pulling someone's fingernails out is unacceptable (there is less on whether torture through the use of isolation and significant deprivation of sleep should be permissible), it should be possible to find areas of agreement on narrowly specific practices that may be proscribed. We could then move to bring in yet others. In short, start narrow and go broad. If you start broad and seek to use NGOs and courts to object to narrowly specific practices, you are likely to create a world of subjective interpretations and unpredictable outcomes. It will produce chaos and, in fact, imperil the flow of international investment by adding serious uncertainty and risk of expensive litigation by zealous activists peddling their preferred interpretation of the core right that they allege to have been violated by the multinational defendant.

The argument that customary international law, interpreted broadly, should be used to say that multinationals are exploiting workers in the poor countries is therefore open to serious criticism. The anti-Nike and other campaigns, which allege that these multinationals do not pay a living wage or do not have OSHA standards in their factories, are little more than assertions of what these specific critics would like a corporation to do, even when customary international law and norms are invoked to justify such accusations. It is perfectly possible and proper for others, equally motivated to do good, to say that these demands will harm rather than help the workers in these poor countries by raising the cost of production and thus making the inward flow of investment and jobs less likely. If so, these critics are themselves in unwitting violation of perhaps the most important core value: that globalization, and multinationals, should help the working class, not harm it!

Bad Domestic Policies as Cause of Harmful Effects

So the conventional criticisms of multinationals as harmful to poor countries and to their workers are not persuasive. But there are also conventional caveats about the possible harmful consequences of multinationals that economists (or "neoliberals," as they are called by the anti-globalizers) have warned against. These follow, however, from the fact that domestic policies, which the poor countries could change, are the source of the problem. As the Oxford economist Ian Little has put it well, direct foreign investment is as good or as bad as your own policies.

Perhaps the most interesting caveats, with empirical support, relate to the inflow of multinationals in the presence of high tariffs and other trade barriers. In fact, in many poor countries in the earlier anti-globalization era in the 1950s and 1960s, when outward integration was feared, multinationals were discouraged along with trade as part of what was called an import substitution (IS) or inward-looking approach, which favored substantial delinking of the economy from the world economy. But some countries feared trade yet encouraged multinationals. They even used high trade barriers as a way to get multinationals to come in and invest. The tactic was to tell a multinational that was selling its products—say, radios—in your country, "We will no longer allow you to sell the radios here. You will have to set up production facilities here to be able to sell your products." This tactic, used in the context of the IS development strategy, came to be known as one that led to "tariff-jumping" inward foreign investment by the multinationals.

The problem with this type of investment inflow was that it usually led to heavy dependence on imports of components. Faced with this tactic, firms tried to get by with as little production in the country as possible and import of the rest from more efficient factories elsewhere. So while a finished car could not be imported, the car manufacturing firm often found it possible to get away by importing nearly all of it and just adding the bumpers to it in an assembly plant in the country! So industrial development became acutely import-intensive: a little value added would necessitate an enormous import burden. The multinationals were often reduced to a battle with the governments: they wanted to assemble as little as they could, while the governments wanted them to assemble as much as they could. The resulting acrimony in these IS-strategy economies, and the inefficiencies that follow, are well illustrated in the journalist Jim Mann's account in his beautifully documented book, *Beijing Jeep*, of what happened when the American Motors Corporation (AMC) went into China to produce Jeeps for the domestic market. AMC just wanted to position itself in the Chinese market, importing as many components of the car as possible; the Chinese wanted full-scale production in Beijing instead, and to make matters worse, they wanted AMC to spend resources to adapt the Jeep for the Chinese army's use, a commercially uninteresting proposition for AMC.[24] Evidently the IS model for attracting investment was fraught with difficulties.[25]

Economists soon realized that this strategy was likely to reduce the social returns to the inward flow of direct investment to the point where it might actually immiserize, rather than enrich, a country. This is because the increased import-intensity of the process that resulted from this strategy meant that economic development was being accompanied by substantial increase in import dependence. This meant that the country had to export more to pay for these extra imports. This would generally require the country to accept lower prices for its exports, a phenomenon that economists call a terms-of-trade loss. There were added negative consequences from the fact that the import barriers that were used to attract investments by firms such as AMC would impose a cost, and all these losses could outweigh any direct gains from the firms' investment.[26]

In contrast, the export-promoting (EP), known also as outward-oriented, trade strategy was adopted in the Far Eastern economies. Where the IS-strategy countries used import barriers extensively and made domestic markets profitable and foreign sales less attractive, the EP-strategy countries pursued trade and exchange rate policies that eliminated this bias against exports and created incentives to export. The EP strategy has been demonstrated in several in-depth country studies in the 1960s through the 1980s to have produced exceptional export growth and therefore extraordinary economic performance. Just as the EP strategy was favorable to growth and the social returns from domestic investment were substantial, so were the social returns to foreign investment.

South Korea did not use inward foreign investment as a principal component of her overall development strategy, following the Japanese model. But Taiwan, Hong Kong, and Singapore certainly did. And so has China since her opening up to trade in the 1980s, when the IS variety of investment was replaced by the enormous EP type of investment in the four coastal provinces whose huge export success translated into China's impressive transformation in the two decades since.

A major study by V. N. Balasubramanyam of the University of Lancaster has carefully demonstrated what I had hypothesized earlier: that the EP variety of inward investment will also rise faster than the IS variety, which is aimed at the domestic market.[27] Investors who come in to service the domestic market because trade barriers rather than the advantages of local production are the motivating factors are certain to have high costs, whereas under the EP strategy, they come in because it is cheaper to produce there. So it is unlikely that the IS variety of investment will have much traction. Moreover, the growth of the home market is always less than the growth of world markets, especially when the possibility of increasing market shares is added to the picture.

Powerful Good Effects

Economists have noted a number of good effects that multinationals can bring in their wake. Perhaps the chief good effect is what economists call spillovers. These refer to the fact that domestic firms learn productivity-enhancing techniques from multinationals with better technology and management practices. We can identify channels through which such diffusion may occur. Managers may learn by observing or hearing about better management practices or by the experience of having previously worked at multinationals. Such diffusion may also happen with production workers, who learn better discipline, for example, when employed by the foreign firms and then take it with them to local firms, where their experience is translated into a better workforce.

That such diffusion occurs and benefits the local firms and hence the host country has been the conventional view among economist students of multinationals for some time. It owes partly to early studies that showed that the growth rate of productivity in industries with a greater share of multinational output was higher. These studies did not separate out the productivity increase of the domestic firms, which, after all, are the object of inquiry. But even when the growth of productivity in domestic firms was isolated, it was seen to be higher in the presence of multinationals.[28]

In recent years, there has been a veritable explosion of such studies. In particular, economists have probed the channels through which the spillover effects could operate.

The economists Horst Gorg and Eric Strobl of the University of Nottingham, using firm-level data for a sample of manufacturing firms in Ghana, demonstrated that spillovers occur through movement of labor because workers trained in multinationals move to local firms, often start-ups, taking with them the knowledge acquired when they worked for the foreign firm.[29] An analysis of electronics and engineering sectors in the United Kingdom underlined that diffusion tends to be greater for domestic firms within the same industry and region.[30] There is also evidence, from the analysis of firm-level data in the United Kingdom, that local firms may learn from multinationals how to export, through information spillovers, demonstration effects, and increased competition.[31]

Some studies show, however, that spillovers do not occur everywhere. In principle, we could also find instances where there are harmful spillovers. For instance, local entrepreneurship may be destroyed or inhibited. The fear that large multinationals would drive small local firms into extinction and cripple domestic entrepreneurship is widespread among the critics of multinationals. This is best reflected in a cartoon I once saw, of a tiny vendor selling hot dogs under a giant skyscraper owned by a manufacturer of packaged foods. But that cartoon also showed the weakness of the argument: the two manage to coexist perfectly well! In short, once differences in quality and in the customers targeted are taken into account, the domestic and foreign firms are likely to be catering to different markets, so that there is room for big and small. The fears are overblown, to say the least; no econometric studies have turned up significant evidence of harmful spillovers to date.

International Rule Making and Multinational Lobbying

But if the overall judgment must be that multinationals do good rather than harm, whether one considers the anti-globalization critics' indictments or the economists' concerns, there is an altogether different perspective that needs to be brought into the picture. We must consider the possibility that the multinationals have, through their interest-driven lobbying, helped set rules in the world trading, intellectual property, aid, and other regimes that are occasionally harmful to the interests of the poor countries. The answers here, I am afraid, are not as sanguine and comforting.

Intellectual Property Protection and WTO Rules

A prime example of such harmful lobbying by corporations in recent years has involved intellectual property protection (IPP). The damage inflicted on the WTO system and on the poor nations has been substantial. Let me explain.

At the outset, the main issue here relates to the collection of royalties on patents and does not belong to the WTO, which is a trade institution. But pharmaceutical and software companies muscled their way into the WTO and turned it into a royalty-collection agency simply because the WTO can apply trade sanctions. Getting IPP into the WTO means that these lobbies can use trade sanctions to collect the royalty payments they want!

How did the IPP lobbies succeed? They first pressured the United States government to pass the so-called Special 301 legislation (in the 1988 Omnibus Trade and Competitive Act). Under this legislation, any country that did not extend IPP (as legislated by the United States) to U.S. companies, even though this obligation was not negotiated in any bilateral or multilateral treaty, was subjected to tariff retaliation for an "unreasonable" practice. Then NAFTA negotiations were used to get Mexico to drop its objections to IPP and to sign on to the IPP desired by the United States. U.S. lobbyists made it clear to Mexico that admission to NAFTA was conditional on this concession.

With opposition by the developing countries being weakened by this use of punishments and inducements, the world trading system was being set up to accept IPP. In addition, pseudo-intellectual justification was adduced by pretending that IPP was a trade subject: the magic words "trade-related" were added to turn IPP into TRIPs (trade-related aspects of intellectual property rights). The U.S. trade representatives, first Carla Hills and then Mickey Kantor, promoted the propaganda (on behalf of the lobbying firms) that the poor countries would benefit from having to pay for patents they had been accessing freely until then!

And since that sounded as implausible as the Mafia telling its victims that the protection money would keep them safe from arson, they also shifted the rationale to include the notions of "theft" and "piracy," implying that the matter was really one of rights to one's property. This changed rationale made little sense for two reasons. If I have an absolute right to what I have invented, this would be in perpetuity, when in fact the lobbying companies were merely arguing about lengthening the patent period. Then again, virtually all arguments made by economists use cost-benefit analysis, which means arguing for patents and their lengths in terms of whether they do good or harm—a utilitarian form of analysis instead of a rights-based approach.

So with the conclusion of the Uruguay Round of multilateral trade negotiations and the establishment of the World Trade Organization in 1994, an astonishing capture of the WTO took place: TRIPs were introduced into the WTO integrally, as one of three legs of a tripod, the other two legs being the traditional GATT (for trade in goods) and the new GATS (General Agreement on Trade in Services). The latter two legs certainly belonged in a trade body. TRIPs, by contrast, were like the introduction of cancer cells into a healthy body. For virtually the first time, the corporate lobbies in pharmaceuticals and software had distorted and deformed an important multilateral institution, turning it away from its trade mission and rationale and transforming it into a royalty collection agency.

The consequences have been momentous. Now every lobby in the rich countries wants to put its own agenda, almost always trade-unrelated, into the WTO, following in the footsteps of the IPP lobbies. This is true, as already noted in Chapter 10, of the AFL-CIO and the ICFTU (International Confederation of Free Trade Unions), which want labor standards to be included in the WTO in the form of the Social Clause, allowing trade sanctions to kick in if the included labor standards are not met. Their principal argument is that TRIPs were allowed in for the benefit of capital, so the Social Clause must be allowed to do the same for labor; environmentalists want the same done for nature. In short, the illegitimate third leg, TRIPs, is now threatening to grow other legs, and there is a real threat that the tripod will turn into a centipede, as the poor countries fight what is evidently a process of disfigurement. It is also a threat to the poor countries in that they face rules that are no less than daggers aimed at their market access rights and possibilities.

But a further criticism must be made. The pharmaceutical firms, working through the U.S. trade representative, also managed to force two objectionable features into the TRIPs agreement. First, the optimal patent period must reflect a balance of two forces: on one hand, the protection provided by IPP provides an incentive to innovate; on the other hand, it slows down the diffusion of benefits to potential users. Under the TRIPs agreement, the pharmaceutical firms (as principal players in a service industries coalition) successfully lobbied for the patents to be uniformly extended to twenty years, a period so long that few economists of repute can be found who would call it efficient in terms of balancing the two opposing forces. Second, it built in restrictions on the ability of poor countries such as Botswana to import generic drugs cheaply from other developing countries such as India and Brazil, which were more developed and had the requisite manufacturing capacities.

The question of access to drugs is both complex and simple. To understand it, and to see why the pharmaceutical companies went wrong, it is necessary to sort out the underlying economics of patent protection when drug availability and innovation must be examined with poor countries in view.

At the outset, it must be said that the very premise that drug companies are seriously handicapped in their R&D by the lack of IPP in the poor countries is flawed. Poor countries have need but no effective demand. There is little money to be made on your invented drugs, to cover your costs and make reasonable profit, in poor-country markets. To see why the drug companies nonetheless see IPP in the poor countries as a money-spinner, it is necessary to distinguish between two types of diseases: those such as malaria, which are primarily in the poor countries, and those such as AIDS, which afflict all.

For the former, evidently IPP cannot ensure any decent return because the poor countries cannot pay. So we have several ways of getting drugs invented for them by using public and quasi-public moneys to mobilize scientists (and firms) to address the task. In the old days, one had institutions such as the Institute for Tropical Medicine in England and a similar institution in the Netherlands. Remember that the Nobel laureate Norman Borlaug was financed by foundation moneys to help invent the new seeds that made the green revolution. Michael Kremer of Harvard University has proposed the setting up of guaranteed remunerative prices for invented vaccines. All of these are variations on the use of public moneys; IPP has no role to play in this, the only solution to the invention of poor-country-specific drugs.

But everything changes when drugs to fight diseases that cut across the rich and poor nations are at stake. Here, the drug companies make money in the rich country markets; IPP in this case is clearly something they value. But then they see piffling effective demand for drugs in the poor countries. So their strategy is to sell there, producing at very low marginal costs and then charging whatever these poor markets will bear.

They would like to raise *that* return as much as they can by increasing effective demand through the use of aid moneys addressed to health programs, so that the excess of what they will charge over their marginal cost is increased, raising profitability in the poor-country markets. Medical economists have known for years that medical groups, for instance, favor insurance schemes that improve the patients' ability to pay, as under insurance programs such as Blue Cross and Blue Shield in the United States, but oppose insurance schemes such as England's National Health Service, which reduce the returns to doctors.

Pharmaceutical firms such as Pfizer want to prevent India and Brazil from selling copies of their drugs in Botswana and Gabon quite simply because their low prices would effectively put a cap on how far the drug companies can raise their prices. Their preferred solution is to get the Gates Foundation, the aid agencies, and others to give money to the poor countries to buy the drugs at higher prices instead. Hence they fulminate against Brazil and India as "pirates" and "thieves," epithets I have heard freely applied to the firms in these countries, and resolutely resist their being allowed to market their cheaper drugs in the poorer countries.

Clearly the rules sought by the pharmaceutical companies are unnecessarily harmful to the poor countries. In particular, (1) TRIPs should not be in the WTO at all, (2) twenty-year patents at the WTO are excessive, and (3) access to the generic drugs produced in developing countries, such as India and Brazil, that have manufacturing capacity should be freed for the poor countries, such as Botswana, that do not have such capacities but have medical emergencies such as AIDS, as certified by the WHO, for example. As it happens, the immense public pressure on the pharmaceutical firms during the Doha Round of multilateral trade negotiations has led to concessions by them, so that imports of drugs at lower costs by poor countries from other poor nations will be permitted more readily than earlier.

Where Corporate Lobbying Has Produced Harm

Free trade in goods (and services) is good, and except for a few economists whose dissent is loud but robust, this proposition is conceded widely. However, consider other types of trade where corporate lobbying to promote them produces harm.

Bads. Suppose that we are talking about free trade in "bads"—for instance, in heroin today or the opium trade yesterday (remember that it was forced on China during the period of European colonization). Evidently, such trade is harmful to the importing nation, while it produces profits and economic gain to the exporting nation. And if multinationals put their lobbying behind such trade, asking for it to be permitted, they are to be condemned, not applauded.

The issue of trade in bads has particular salience since U.S. multinationals lobbied intensively to deny automatic extension of Food and Drug Administration (FDA) prohibitions on banned drugs to sales abroad, including in poor countries. Their objection was twofold. First, if the United States did this, then the French and the British could make money by exporting these drugs instead, since the FDA's writ does not apply there or in the poor, importing countries. Second, the lobbies say that it is up to the importing nations, not the exporting countries, to prohibit imports if they think something is harmful. Both arguments are readily refuted.

If the United States thinks and legislates (or rules through administrative action) that something is harmful and hazardous for Americans, exporting it to others is reprehensible. That others might do it is surely no excuse. My virtue should not depend on whether others are virtuous; I should be prepared to go it alone. In fact, U.S. leadership itself could put pressure on other recalcitrant nations, through NGO actions for instance, to move once the United States has taken the lead.

Next, it is naive to think that the poor nations will follow the FDA ruling and prevent imports, as they would be permitted to under WTO rules. Often these nations are not well informed. Occasionally their governance is so weak, and their politicians and bureaucrats at such low levels of income, that it is not at all inconceivable that they can be seduced, in ways that skillfully skirt the legislative bans on bribes, or through concessions obtained through lobbying in the United States (as discussed below), into accepting bads. The only surefire way to prevent such outcomes is to extend the FDA ban to both domestic and foreign sales.

Bads Here and Goods There. But a bad here may be a good there. Thus the use of DDT has been proscribed in the rich nations, where its damage to the environment has been considered decisive ever since Rachel Carson famously documented it. In the poor countries such as India, where malaria has not been successfully eradicated, DDT offers health benefits that are judged to outweigh the environmental damage. In such a case, a blanket denunciation of DDT, as some environmental lobbies would have it, is as pernicious as corporate lobbying to enable bads to be exported. In these instances, it is indeed true that automatic extension of proscriptions on sales at home should not be extended abroad, as is desirable in the case of what are bads universally.

Goods Here and Bads There. We also have products that may be goods here but bads there. A classic example that made waves was provided by baby formula, produced by Nestlé, Abbott Laboratories, and other firms, and infant foods, such as those produced by Gerber. It sounds odd that these household products, produced by reputable firms, could be bads anywhere. And yet it turned out that, marketed in poor countries and used by poor women, they were.

Two factors operated to transform them from goods into bads. First, baby formulas were distributed in the poor countries the way they were distributed in the rich countries. Typically, a particular formula will be fed to the newborn baby in the hospital and a free box will be supplied to the new mother to take home, so that she gets in the habit of using this brand and will therefore become a loyal customer, since there is little to choose among different brands and practice makes for continued purchase. When our daughter was born in the Boston Lying-in Hospital, my wife returned home with free samples of Similac; sure enough, we continued with Similac. But in poor countries, the mother is often in no position to buy formula, and many such mothers tried to stretch their free samples as far as possible, diluting the formula with unboiled water, killing their babies. Evidently, a good product, marketed with rich-country techniques, became a dangerous bad.

Second, if the mothers had continued breast-feeding, that would have conferred immunity for six months. Shifting to the formula, even if the water had been boiled, removed this naturally endowed immunity.

The result was a massive campaign against the infant formulas, with off-the-wall accusations that Nestlé and other manufacturing firms were "baby killers," when in fact this was a genuine case of a costly failure to adapt marketing strategies to local conditions. But could they be faulted also for selling a product that substituted for breast milk and seduced mothers away from breast-feeding infants, thus depriving the infants of the natural immunity from breast-feeding?

No and yes. When my wife could not breast-feed our baby daughter, a wise old friend of ours said: "Darling, do not worry; God did not intend you to be a dairy." Well, why should working women who want formula, which frees them from having to breast-feed their infants, and who have the education and the means to use formula to advantage not be able to make that choice? There was certainly a powerful subset of women's groups that failed to see this and equated breast-feeding with bra burning—a feminist breast fixation to rival the masculine breast fetishism!

But others certainly had a valid point. Among poorer mothers being targeted, especially in the poor countries, formula was a potentially dangerous product; as with cigarettes, advertising had to be regulated and designed in ways that did not encourage the use of formula and other infant milk substitutes without necessary information as to the immunity advantage conferred by sticking to breast-feeding. In fact, this is how, in the end, the WHO worked up its International Code of Marketing of Breast-Milk Substitutes, with virtually universal approbation and agreement.

Yet when you see what some firms have actually done to sell according to this code, you see continuing avoidance. In the case of the United States, which remained the strongest objector to the code, the office of the trade representative even used its muscle to threaten smaller countries into not enforcing the code. Gerber was the firm that stood out in lobbying against the code, with Guatemala the victim.

The WHO code states that "neither the container nor the label should have pictures of infants, nor should they have other pictures or text which may idealize the use of infant formula." In 1983, the Guatemalans took this as a minimum standard: "All information must state that breast milk is the best food for children under two years; none may have photos or other representations of children under two years."

Gerber, which had introduced baby foods as long ago as 1928, used the "Gerber baby" face for its advertising campaigns worldwide. Parents in Guatemala even had been found naming their children Gerber, illustrating the power of such cheerful images in selling one's wares. Alone among the foreign firms, therefore, Gerber objected to the new law. The matter went up before the Guatemalan Administrative Tribunal, which ruled in favor of the Ministry of Health. But then an obliging U.S. government threatened to take away Guatemala's MFN status for violating trademark agreements. Faced with such threats, the Guatemalan government was under serious pressure; not surprisingly, Guatemala's supreme court found in favor of Gerber.[32] This outcome naturally failed to arouse in Washington the usual complaint that the judiciary was not independent because, after all, the beneficiary was a highly visible U.S. firm (and possibly, like the tobacco firms discussed next, a contributor to the PACs of one or both political parties).

What is equally distressing is that the Interagency Group on Breast-feeding Monitoring claimed in 1998 that manufacturers in thirty-nine countries were still giving free samples to mothers, breaking and stretching the rules created by the WHO and approved by the World Health Assembly in May 1981.[33]

"Ambiguous" Goods: Legal but Lethal. Finally, there is the large class of goods, such as cigarettes, that are legal but lethal, where society is politically schizophrenic: the sales are legal but growing restrictions are placed on their sale and use. In the case of cigarettes, subsidies continue to be paid for growing tobacco!

In such cases, corporate lobbying to countervail efforts to change rules so as to restrict the use of such harmful substances properly invites opprobrium. Thus, the recent attempt by the World Health Organization under the remarkable leadership of Gro Brundtland, former prime minister of Norway, to have a treaty on tobacco use, outlawing cigarette advertising and putting other restrictions on promotion, led to a virtually unanimous agreement as of January 2003. But the resistance of the cigarette companies, especially in the United States, had been considerable.

In fact, the corporate lobbies have also successfully used existing rules on trade in goods, with the aid of their governments, to spread the use of cigarettes in a legal but harmful fashion. Thus, in the famous case filed at the GATT by the U.S. trade representative against Thailand in 1990, and decided by GATT in favor of the United States, the American tobacco companies managed to overturn Thai entry restrictions on foreign cigarette firms because they amounted, the panel correctly held, to GATT-inconsistent measures aimed at ensuring equivalence of treatment between domestic and foreign suppliers.[34] The Thai authorities, however, were correct, not in law but in the truth of the matter, in arguing that even if advertising was prohibited, the sophisticated foreign cigarette manufacturers would be far more efficient at marketing cigarettes than would the inefficient Thai state monopoly, and that the Thai cigarettes had not managed to seduce children and women into its dragnet, whereas the foreign ones would. In addition, the entry of foreign firms would greatly expand the cigarette market instead of just switching the existing sales from the Thai monopoly to themselves, contrary to what the cigarette firms claimed. The GATT rules were therefore incompatible with the way one would really want the rules written for legal but lethal goods, and the cigarette firms were of course wedded to the continuation and exploitation of the inappropriate rules. In fact, as a series of reports in the *Washington Post* pointed out, they had been actively lobbying with their congressional supporters—it has often been remarked that elsewhere we call this bribery, but in the United States we call it lobbying—and with the U.S. trade representative to effectively change the rules so as to make them explicitly consistent with their view that "tobacco export policy is an economic issue, not a health issue." Indeed, the U.S. trade representative had been petitioned by the Cigarette Export Association to have "US trade officials negotiate with Thailand to end the advertising ban," whereas the existing rules seemed to imply that the ban was all right as long as it did not discriminate between domestic and foreign cigarettes.[35] A report in the *Los Angeles Times* pointed out that

> U.S. trade negotiators [had] pressured Japan, South Korea, Taiwan and Thailand—which all had tobacco monopolies—to open their markets to American cigarettes. *At the industry's insistence, trade officials further demanded that U.S. firms be free to advertise their brands, even though cigarette advertising in the four countries had been virtually nonexistent.* [Italics added] [36]

The article also noted:

> In Hungary, as in Russia, companies have found ways around the ban on cigarette advertising. Dressed in the stripes and colors of Western brands, young women distribute free samples in cafes and bars. In the capital, Budapest, brand names such as Marlboro and Lucky Strike, sold by British-based BAT [British American Tobacco] Industries, have been incorporated in the names of pubs and coffeehouses. . . . Meanwhile, though, the industry is seeking more freedom to promote its brands. The head of corporate relations for Phillip Morris in Hungary wrote the local heads of rival firms in December, 1992, suggesting that an industry delegation "should try to test the limits of the flexibility of the government and have a better understanding about the relation of power among ministries." "The industry should continue to talk to high-level politicians to maintain pressure on the bureaucracy," said the letter, whose contents were confirmed by company officials. . . . "They are buying political influence by going into these countries and saying, 'We want to help you with your economy,'" said Scott Ballin, chairman of the Coalition on Smoking or Health, a U.S. anti-smoking group. "You don't bite the hand that feeds you."

Need anything more be said?

To conclude: given the rules of the game, multinationals cannot be seriously faulted at the level of their practices, as the anti-globalizers and more conventional critics would have it. In fact, they bring much good to the workers they employ and to the poor nations they happen to invest in. But they cannot be exempted from criticism and hence require the utmost scrutiny when they organize and spend in order to set, and to exploit, the rules of the game. This legitimate critique therefore is different from the most popular critiques.

Corporate Social Responsibility

If corporations help rather than harm the poor countries and their workers—aside from their role in defining rules that occasionally help them at the expense of the poor countries—then the case for responsible corporate social action cannot be plausibly based on the argument that the harm that corporations do must be offset by the assumption of compensatory social responsibility.

It would appear, therefore, that the true, indeed only, compelling reason for corporations to assume social responsibility is that it is the right thing to do. For in so doing, they will *enhance* the social good that their economic activities promote when they invest in these developing countries, and for which there is now much evidence. Indeed, such acts of altruism are precisely what characterized many of the socially committed families that made fortunes in trade and industry. They came from different religious and cultural traditions that encouraged philanthropic action. The principal examples are the Dutch burghers (chronicled beautifully by Simon Schama), the Jains of Gujarat in India, the Quakers (among them the Wilberforces, who led the fight against slavery), and Jewish families (perhaps most prominently the Rothschilds).[37] With the rise of corporations delinked from families, there is now a growing perception that the corporations too, and not just the floating crowd of shareholders in their personal capacities, should commit themselves to such altruism, playing their role in contributing to the public good as each corporation best sees fit.

The edifice of corporate social responsibility, however, must rest on two foundations. One has to be altruism, which deals with what corporations *should* do. But the other must deal with regulation that defines what corporations *should not* do. In fact, once this is recognized, it is apparent that, in the main, voluntary codes must characterize what corporations should do (because firms will have different preferences regarding the good they want to do, just as we do not all agree on which charities to support) and mandatory codes must address what they should not do. This also implies that we need three complementary approaches.

Social Norming

Secretary General Kofi Annan's Global Compact at the United Nations, first proposed by him in Davos three years ago, is what economists call a social-norming proposition. By signing on to it, corporations agree to uphold certain broad values such as human rights, which of course include rights as workers, as consumers, as voters, as children, and as women. The compact has now been endorsed by several leading NGOs, such as Amnesty International, and by union federations such as the ICFTU. However, as it has no monitoring, certification, or enforcement mechanism, it has been rejected by some unions and NGO activists. But they miss the point.

The very act of signing on to such a compact focuses the signatory corporations, as well as potential critics, on what they do and plan to do to achieve progress toward the objectives. These consist of widely shared and internationally affirmed social values broadly stated (such as removal of gender discrimination and child labor). Given the broad general nature of the compact's objectives, however, the specific steps they take are best left to the corporations, working with the democratic countries in which they operate.

For instance, signatory corporations operating in the United States—where, it may be recalled, a recent Human Rights Watch report has found that millions of workers in nearly all industries are denied full freedom to associate and form unions (largely but not exclusively because of restrictions that make it difficult to organize strikes effectively)—can be expected to follow national legislation and act within their national rights. They would, for example, exercise their right to hire replacement workers freely, even though that helps cripple the right to strike. But they would be expected to reduce wage discrimination against women because the United States accepts that objective explicitly and enforces it.

The complexity of the issue is illustrated further by the fact that there are both narrow and broad definitions of gender discrimination with regard to equal pay. What U.S. corporations do with regard to implementing equal pay for women to ensure conformity to workers' rights objectives will depend, therefore, on the prevalent U.S. legislation. Thus, what socially responsible American corporations do in the United States may well differ from what Sweden or India accepts as a sensible way to proceed, although all three nations accept the general concepts of granting the freedom of association and eliminating gender discrimination.

Despite this inevitable, and indeed desirable, diversity of detail, the compact will help diffuse good practices in a flexible fashion. Once corporations with reputations to protect have signed on, they are in the public view. Pressure to make some progress, no matter how diverse and situation-specific, will arise, leading the corporations to move in one way or another toward the norms they have affirmed.

The same can be said of a growing number of codes developed by industry associations. They are criticized as cop-outs, as dodges designed to mislead and misdirect watchdogs by pretending to take action. But these criticisms seem to me to miss the dynamics of social norming, which promises more over time than is immediately delivered.

Voluntary Codes

We now also have several social-accountability codes that are offered by organizations that have been set up specifically to propagate corporate social standards. Leading examples include the pioneering New York–based Social Accountability International (on whose board I have served), the UK-based Ethical Trading Initiative, the Washington-based Fair Labor Association, and others. Unlike the Global Compact, they involve specific obligations and, equally as important, include monitoring prior to and after certification. Consequences can also follow: Social Accountability International has been known to decertify factories. These codes are voluntary and can be ignored, but once signed on to, they entail well-defined obligations.

The proponents of each voluntary code would prefer to have theirs as the only one available. But this would be fundamentally wrong. The codes can and do contain so many different requirements that diversity is desirable. In fact, since virtually all codes currently available are from developed countries, I believe it is essential that some be drafted by developing countries. That would bring very different perspectives into the fray. For example, there is a great push for a living-wage requirement in nearly all of these codes. But this, according to many intellectuals and NGOs in developing countries, is misguided since, as already discussed earlier, multinationals typically pay a premium over the alternative market wage available to their workers. Why raise that further by pretending that workers are being exploited because they are not earning even more? A code that explicitly excludes a living wage requirement but includes other stipulations should also be available. But it will likely not come from the developed world.

The element of choice and the need to keep the perspectives of developing countries in view are factors underemphasized by the anti-sweatshop movement on U.S. university campuses. In fact, I believe that the currently available codes overemphasize developed-country perspectives on issues such as workers' rights and neglect developing-country perspectives. The codes reflect a certain degree of paternalism as well as the deep influence of Western labor unions, whose own perspectives are often colored by the increasingly fierce competition from poor countries.

These issues have surfaced in the efforts led by the anti-sweatshop activists on American university campuses to define social responsibility by textile firms abroad and to exclude their universities from contracting with firms that do not sign on to specific codes.[38]

Mandatory Codes

National mandatory codes have been proposed to complement the Global Compact and the voluntary codes. These codes, and the rules and regulations that define at home what the corporations cannot do as good citizens, would extend to a nation's multinational operations abroad. These mandatory national codes will naturally vary across nations (because different nations will have different ideas and laws concerning what is hugely egregious and should be disallowed and what is not), whereas the voluntary codes are obviously uniform worldwide. I suggested such a mandatory code for American firms operating in Mexico over a decade ago in the *New York Times*, in the context of the NAFTA debate: it would ask American firms abroad to "do in Rome, not as Romans do, but as New Yorkers do."[39] In short, U.S. firms must abide abroad by the basic principles that are expected at home.

Thus, under this approach, if a U.S. firm had been in South Africa when apartheid was practiced, it would have been subject to the U.S. mandate not to implement the same policy. Or if Mexico did not have legislation forbidding the dumping of mercury into its waters, American firms would be expected by the United States not to take advantage of that. Yes, some American firms will move to the Bahamas to escape these codes, but then if they get into political trouble, the U.S. marines or U.S. diplomatic muscle will not be available to help them.

Will these diverse mandatory codes imply that a universal mandatory code is to be denied? On the contrary. As these national mandatory codes come into play, the mere juxtaposition of good and bad practices will create pressures over time for convergence to good practices, given civil society and democracy today. The convergence to universal mandatory codes, as with the recent tobacco treaty at the WHO, came after decades of national legislation where some nations moved ahead of others, while the laggards caught up under the pressures generated by the good practices of the pioneers. The reverse model of starting, rather than ending, with uniform and universalist mandatory codes seems to be unrealistic except for practices that all agree are morally reprehensible, such as slavery and forced labor.

A tapestry woven in three colors, one of social-norming codes, another of a multiplicity of voluntary codes, and a third of diverse mandatory national codes, would then appear to define a nuanced and desirable approach to the question of social responsibility by global corporations today. Multinationals, unfairly accused of predation, can embrace these approaches to corporate social responsibility to emerge even more effectively in the global economy and society as institutions that truly advance the economic and social good in the countries they invest in.

III

Other Dimensions
of Globalization

13

The Perils of Gung-ho International Financial Capitalism

tarting in Thailand in the summer of 1997, the Asian financial crisis swept through Indonesia, Malaysia, and South Korea, turning
the region's economic miracle into a debacle. Capital, which had
been flowing in, flew out in huge amounts. Where these four economies
and the Philippines had attracted inflows of over $65 billion in 1996, the
annual outflows during 1997 and 1998 were almost $20 billion, amount-
ing to an annual resource crunch of over $85 billion—a staggering
amount indeed! This caused currencies to collapse, stock prices to crash,
and economies to go into a tailspin.[1] This was not all. The fear of ruination by contagion sent shock waves worldwide. The Russian ruble went
into turmoil in August 1998; the Brazilian real did so in January 1999.

Per capita incomes tumbled to almost one-third their 1996 level in
Indonesia, with the other crisis-stricken Asian countries showing declines ranging from a quarter to nearly half of the 1996 levels. The devastation was reminiscent of the Great Crash of 1929, a searing experience
that ushered in the New Deal in the United States and led to competitive
escalation of tariffs worldwide. Writing about this crisis that had spread
ruin within almost a hundred days, I thought of Octavio Paz's famous
lines from "Happiness in Herat":

> I met the wind of the hundred days.
> It covered all the nights with sand,
> Badgered my forehead, scorched my lids.[2]

This crisis, precipitated by panic-fueled outflows of capital, was a
product of hasty and imprudent financial liberalization, almost always
under foreign pressure, allowing free international flows of short-term
capital without adequate attention to the potentially potent downside

of such globalization. There has been no shortage of excuses and strained explanations scapegoating the victims, suggesting they committed hara-kiri instead of being slaughtered. It is hard not to conclude that the motivation underlying these specious explanations is a desire to continue to maintain ideological positions in favor of a policy of free capital flows or to escape responsibility for playing a central role in pushing for what one might aptly call gung-ho international financial capitalism. Let me consider first the wrong explanations and then the right ones.

The Wrong Explanations

A benign but wrongheaded explanation was that the Asian crisis was a result of these countries' long-standing economic miracle running out of steam. That miracle, it may be recalled, was a result of long-sustained and phenomenally high rates of productive investment at levels that had no precedent in history. But if rapid accumulation of capital through rates of high investment was the source of growth, economists would fear that the growth would slow down because of diminishing returns—that is, as capital accumulated relative to labor, further investment would produce progressively less output. A man with a spade could plow an acre a day, but an extra spade, with the man not given a comrade, would add little to the work done. Economists know that this gloomy scenario can be foiled if there is technical progress that adds to output what diminishing returns subtract from it: instead of an extra spade, imagine that a motor is added to the man's spade. But my Columbia student Allwyn Young had estimated that the Asian countries had no technical change to speak of.

The lay person is bound to wonder how this could possibly be true. After all, these countries had registered huge advances in technology by importing foreign equipment embodying massive advances in technology. Just contrast the images of the hamlets and rickshaws in South Korea at the time of the Korean War, for instance, with the skyscrapers in Seoul, built no doubt with the latest cranes, that filled our screens when Korea advanced to the quarterfinals of the World Cup, to national delirium. Or look at the flood in Western markets of Hyundai cars and Samsung TVs, which cannot have been manufactured except with sophisticated technology.

The way economists calculate productivity change, however, is to attribute to investment the effects of technical change embodied in newer equipment, as in the example of the motorized spade earlier. They virtually assume that new and more productive equipment must be treated as if investment had increased: that a spade twice as productive is to be treated as if it were two spades. But the consequence is that it is somewhat startling to those who are not economists to say that the region had "no technical change"! So the pessimistic conclusions about diminishing returns are somewhat exaggerated when such equipment-embodied technical change is quite dramatic, as it has been and continues to be in Asia.

But even if the Asian economic miracle had been based on investment rather than technical progress, it is hardly plausible that the miracle would have vanished precipitously. As capital accumulated relative to labor, the future return to capital would decline only slowly, except in the most singular circumstances. But what happened in reality was that the economies *crashed*. Instead of slowly winding down, they went rapidly, within a matter of months, into negative growth rates. If you were to draw a chart of the actual growth rates of per capita incomes in the affected Asian countries, with the growth rates on the vertical axis and the years on the horizontal axis, that chart would go not into a gentle flattening out and then a steady fall, but dramatically into what everyone should remember from their geometry classes as the second quadrant, which plots negative growth rates.

The parallel with the Soviet Union was eerie. There economists had seen per capita income growth rates decline over almost two decades, and the favored explanation was diminishing returns to capital accumulation. But with the arrival of President Gorbachev and his adoption of perestroika (economic restructuring) and glasnost (political reform), the economy went crashing into negative growth rates.

The sharp, discontinuous reversal of fortune was mind-boggling in both cases. In the case of East Asia, the economists who had predicted a decline were happy to claim foresight. But to claim credit for having foreseen a crash when all one had asserted was that a decline would soon set in was not exactly persuasive. The question still remained: why did a financial crisis, and then an economic one, break out when these countries had been doing so well until then?[3]

Yet another argument, albeit a lame one, was that these countries were afflicted by crony capitalism, which led to malfeasance that produced the financial crisis under financial liberalization. As many experts on East Asia remarked, however, crony capitalism had produced the economic miracle earlier; why was it now a cancer that killed the patient? Besides, it is indeed true that many of these leaders had cronies, but which politicians do not? Are President Suharto's entourage "cronies," whereas people at Bechtel and Halliburton are Vice President Dick Cheney's "friends"? Are Barbra Streisand and Steven Spielberg President Clinton's "friends," while President Mahathir's celebrity friends are his "cronies"?

What is the difference? If it is about patronage in exchange for contributions, is it not true that Hollywood has managed to get extraordinary rewards from its lobbying in opening foreign markets for its movies (a matter I discussed in Chapter 9)?

I wrote at the time in Singapore an op-ed essay titled "A Friend in the United States, but a Crony in Asia," which drew attention to the self-serving rhetoric that was coming out of Washington as the ideologues who had pushed for international financial liberalization without adequate safeguards were rushing for cover.[4] This type of talk also fueled the notion that corruption was to be found there, not here. James Wolfensohn, president of the World Bank, took to attacking corruption around the same time, an activity that I warmly welcome, and I noticed that his staff's attention was selectively focused away from the rich countries. So I suggested that if he opened his window in Washington, D.C., and looked out, Wolfensohn would see plenty of the corruption that he and his staff were looking for in the poor countries instead. But I fully understand that it is hard to look in the face the ones whose money you must accept in order to stay in business; morality is more easily thrown at those who borrow than at those who lend.

But if these explanations of the crisis were implausible, then one had a puzzle on one's hands. After all, these economies had excellent fundamentals. Between 1991 and 1996, budgets generally showed surpluses, the investment and growth rates were as impressive as they had been since the 1960s, the inflation rate was in single digits, and current account (i.e., trade) deficits were extremely small as a percentage of national income.[5] In November 1994, when the Mexican peso crisis erupted, requiring extensive rescue efforts by the United States, the fundamentals were unsound, and the turmoil that came was not entirely surprising. East Asia was exemplary; Latin America rarely has been.

Problems with Free Capital Flows

The reason why capital inflows are tricky is simply because when confidence is shaken, the fact that the situation is inherently one of imperfect information implies that the actions of a few can initiate herd action by others.

Economists have amusingly instructive models of herd behavior under imperfect information now. If you do not know which of three restaurants in a mall is good, you could pick one at random and hope for the best. But then you see that two are empty and the third has a table taken by a well-dressed couple. You will think that they know something you don't, and therefore you will go in. The next fellow deciding on which restaurant to pick will now see two tables taken, so he will go in too, occupying a third. And pretty soon, you will have herd behavior benefiting that restaurant generously, even if it is, objectively speaking, not the best one.

This is probably the best explanation of what happened in Asia despite the splendid fundamentals. The huge borrowing of short-term capital was perhaps manageable, objectively speaking, but its sheer size had within it the seeds of panic behavior. Since there was no transparency on how much had been borrowed, the panic spread fast, feeding on itself.

The other problem with the Asian economies was that their institutional practices had not been suitably modified for transition to a regime of free capital flows. In South Korea, for instance, the debt-equity ratios in the industrial enterprises, including the big conglomerates known as *chaebols,* were traditionally twice as high as in the developed countries, where corporations relied for financing far more on equity. If the financing was with debt in wons, a panic-fed crisis could be met by conventional intervention by the central bank extending necessary cash as a lender of last resort. But if the debt was borrowed from abroad and denominated in foreign currency, this meant that there would be a balance-of-payments crisis: dollars to pay the recalled loans cannot be printed in Seoul. This should have been anticipated, and regulations to monitor and prevent massive accumulation of short-term foreign debt to dangerous levels should have been put in place before South Korea was encouraged by the IMF, and required by the OECD as a price of membership, to turn to the free-capital-mobility regime.

At the same time, a lack of banking and financial regulation compounded the problem. Many commercial banks borrowed short-term from abroad, given the new ability to do so as capital flows were freed from control, and lent the borrowed funds long-term to domestic private investors, often in real estate, without adequate safeguards. "In the five . . . economies, short-term borrowing amounted to almost a quarter of bank loans to the private sector in 1996."[6] So when the panic set in and capital began to flow out rather than in, the banks were forced to recall their loans. The central banks also cut the money supply as their foreign exchange reserves shrank due to the capital outflow. Both factors led to closing businesses and, in turn, to collapsing banks.

By contrast, India and China, which had been chalking up high growth rates through the decade prior to the Asian crisis while rejecting the calls for the elimination of capital controls, escaped the crisis altogether. One must therefore ask why the crisis-afflicted countries undertook this shift, which would soon prove expensive, to fulsome integration into the world's financial markets.

The Wall Street–Treasury Complex

The rush to abandon controls on international capital flows—economists call this a policy of capital account convertibility—was hardly a consequence of finance ministers and other policy makers in the developing countries suddenly acknowledging the folly of their ways. It reflected instead external pressures.

These came from both the IMF and the U.S. Treasury (where the leadership was doubtless provided by Treasury secretary Robert Rubin, the most influential financial figure in the Clinton administration). The economists in leadership positions in these institutions were among the most accomplished today. They could not be accused of unfamiliarity with the need for caution and prudence when it came to leaning on countries to free capital flows.

In fact, in 1989, Lawrence Summers (who was deputy to Rubin and succeeded him as Treasury secretary) and his lawyer wife, Victoria, had written a classic article about "excessive speculation," quoting with approbation statements such as:

> The freeing of financial markets to pursue their casino instincts heightens the odds of crises. . . . Because unlike a casino, the financial markets are inextricably linked with the world outside, the real economy pays the price.[7]

and the celebrated words in 1936 of John Maynard Keynes:

> As the organization of investment markets improves, the risk of the predominance of speculation does increase. In one of the greatest investment markets in the world, namely New York, the influence of speculation is enormous. Speculators may do no harm as bubbles on a steady stream of enterprise. But the position is serious when enterprise becomes the bubble on a whirlpool of speculation. When the capital development of a country becomes the by-product of the activities of a casino, the job is likely to be ill-done. The measure of success attained by Wall Street, regarded as an institution of which the proper social purpose is to direct new investment into the most profitable channels in terms of future yield cannot be claimed as one of the outstanding triumphs of laissez-faire capitalism, which is not surprising if I am right in thinking that the best brains of Wall Street have been in fact directed towards a different object.[8]

If Summers had been eloquent about free capital mobility's downside, Stanley Fischer, who was the main theoretician at the IMF as its first deputy managing director, was surely familiar with the scholarly work on financial and currency crises. So why did they go along optimistically with the notion that the time had come to hasten the elimination of barriers to capital mobility worldwide?

I suspect that this had much to do with the general shift to markets and away from controls that had occurred in the 1970s and 1980s as disillusionment grew with knee-jerk interventions worldwide. They were likely caught in the usual swing of the pendulum—one extreme follows the other. So, I am sure, was Secretary Rubin. But the explanation of his complacency is possibly more complex. His working life had been on Wall Street, with Goldman Sachs. He clearly believed that America's financial markets had brought unusual venture-capital-financed prosperity to the United States. It was natural for him to see that countries practicing capital account inconvertibility, and regulating and inhibiting the inflows of capital, were denying themselves these benefits. It was inevitable that, as with most of us, his outlook was shaped by his experience.

Then again, one must reckon with the energetic lobbying of Wall Street firms to pry open financial markets worldwide. These firms argued that their profits and social good were in sync. If they had any doubts, these were carefully concealed!

The euphoria was widespread. In the exasperated words of the Nobel laureate James Tobin, a great figure in macroeconomics:

> U.S. leadership . . . gives the mobility of capital priority over all other considerations.

And Paul Volcker, the legendary chairman of the Federal Reserve whom Alan Greenspan succeeded, remarked in consternation:

> The visual image of a vast sea of liquid capital strikes me as apt—the big and inevitable storms through which a great liner like the U.S.S. United States of America can safely sail will surely capsize even the sturdiest South Pacific canoe.[9]

It was impossible to puncture the balloon because few with dissenting opinions could penetrate what I have called the Wall Street–Treasury complex.[10] This is the loose but still fairly coherent group of Wall Street firms in New York and the political elite in Washington, the latter embracing not just the Treasury but also the State Department, the IMF, the World Bank, and so on. There is constant to-and-fro between these two groups. For instance, Rubin moved from Wall Street to the Treasury and back; Wolfensohn at the World Bank moved there from his investment firm in New York; Stanley Fischer has moved in the reverse direction from the IMF to Citigroup; Ernest Stern, the senior vice president and acting president of the World Bank, moved to Morgan Stanley; and one could go on.

I think of the Wall Street–Treasury complex not as a conspiracy but very much in the spirit of C. Wright Mills's "power elite."[11] They wear similar suits, not just similar ties; they interact on boards and in clubs;

they wind up sharing the same sentiments, reinforced by one another's wisdom. So on capital mobility, like lemmings, they took other lemmings, and us, merrily down a dangerous path.

The phrase "Wall Street–Treasury complex" has proven popular not just among radical critics or NGOs. Robert Wade, an influential writer on financial crises who teaches at the London School of Economics, has adopted it, calling it the "Wall Street–Treasury–IMF complex."[12] But "Treasury" in my phrasing stood for Washington; adding just the IMF therefore unwittingly narrows, not widens, the meaning. Barry Eichengreen, a noted economic historian and occasional consultant to the IMF, has instead called it diplomatically the "Wall Street complex," but this is to leave out half of the culpable parties![13]

In a lighter vein, remember that Dwight Eisenhower, who surprisingly launched the radical phrase "military-industrial complex," was the president of Columbia University.[14] C. Wright Mills, the author of *The Power Elite*, taught sociology at Columbia. It was at Columbia also that I wrote about the Wall Street–Treasury complex. Consequently many talk now of the "Columbia trio." I suppose this is the next best to being 'N Sync!

The Question of Malaysian Capital Controls

But the Asian crisis called into question not just the wisdom of a rapid freeing of capital flows in countries that still had capital controls. It also raised the somewhat separate question of whether a country that *already* had this freedom would be wise to temporarily abandon it and to adopt capital controls in response to panic-fueled capital flows.

As it happens, Malaysia did just that, imposing selective exchange controls in September 1998.[15] Though the IMF disapproved, Prime Minister Mahathir stuck to his guns, therefore losing IMF support but gaining freedom from its conditionality. Most observers agree that IMF conditionality was in error, requiring deflation when an expansionary response was called for. So the other crisis-afflicted Asian economies went into a deep dive and recovered later, but Malaysia managed to get to the correct, expansionary policies earlier and avoided the gratuitous deepening of the downturn.

Economists have debated whether Malaysian controls played a significant role in allowing Dr. Mahathir to expand when others were contracting under the wrong IMF medicine. That is certainly what theory would say. Just as an import tariff enables you to segment domestic from foreign markets and to raise the domestic price above the foreign price, capital controls segment the domestic capital market from the world market and this can enable you to lower interest rates (to inflate the economy) without fearing further outflows of capital because interest rates are higher abroad. The theory is not far removed from reality, in my view.[16]

Where Do We Stand?

By now, the IMF has abandoned its excessive pre-crisis enthusiasm for free capital mobility.[17] It has learned the role of prudence in opening domestic financial markets to global integration, and the need to strengthen banking structures and practices prior to the opening. It has informally accepted the possible wisdom of measures such as a tax on incoming capital flows (an innovation of Chile) if they get too large. Finally, it has painfully learned the need for diversity of responses and conditionalities should crises erupt despite the prudence and safeguards. In short, while a watchful eye over the Wall Street–Treasury complex remains a necessity, the days of gung-ho international financial capitalism are probably past.

I can do no better than to cite *The Economist,* the most influential opinion magazine today on economics and finance:

> If any cause commands the unswerving support of *The Economist,* it is that of liberal trade. For as long as it has existed, this newspaper has championed freedom of commerce across borders. Liberal trade, we have always argued, advances prosperity, encourages peace among nations and is an indispensable part of individual liberty. It seems natural to suppose that what goes for trade in goods must go for trade in capital, in which case capital controls would offend us as violently as, say, an import quota on bananas. The issues have much in common, but they are not the same. Untidy as it may be, economic liberals should acknowledge that capital controls—of a certain restricted sort, and in certain cases—have a role.[18]

14

International Flows of Humanity

I n the 1970s, with their economies in a tailspin following big oil price
hikes of 1973, even the more forbidding among the West European
governments could not bring themselves to expel the *gastarbeiters*
(the foreign "guest workers") despite their contractual right to do so.[1]
The Swiss novelist Max Frisch remarked at the time, "We imported workers and got men instead."[2]

Frisch captured beautifully the fact that economics and ethics are
inseparable in the way we must consider international flows of humanity and seek to devise policies to manage them, enhancing the benefits
and containing the problems that they entail.

Migration Today

Migration across national borders has rapidly come to the forefront of
public debates, even as it was neglected by most of the critics of globalization. Long regarded as an issue that could be addressed only gingerly
because the right to exclude has traditionally been considered the essential defining aspect of national sovereignty, it has now taken on dimensions and a legitimacy that put it alongside the more conventional
international phenomena such as trade, macroeconomics, development,
and health. Nor is the phenomenon, and its causes and consequences,
any longer on the fringe of the major academic disciplines in social sciences such as economics, political science, and international relations,
and in other fields such as ethics and literary theory.[3]

Human flows occur in diverse ways and have prompted corresponding concerns and policy actions worldwide. Three types of disaggregation

of total flows are useful in analyzing migration problems today and ways of managing them. First, we must distinguish between the poor and rich countries. Migrations from poor to rich nations, for instance, are very different in their implications from migrations that are the other way around. Next, it is important to distinguish between the flows of skilled and unskilled migrants. The former can raise brain-drain-type problems for poor countries, while the latter are far more likely to be treated as an opportunity by them. Finally, we must distinguish between legal and illegal flows, and then again between those that are voluntary and those that reflect involuntary movements prompted by strife and persecution (the latter, delimited by treaty, being the defining characteristic of a refugee, who is then assigned certain rights with corresponding obligations imposed on the receiving countries).

Some observers think that the total international migration flows today are still rather small. Approximately 175 million people, amounting to only 3 percent of the world's population, currently move across borders to live longer than a year. But this understates the phenomenon and its importance for two reasons: (1) because of border controls, however porous, such movements are not free and the desire to move must exceed significantly the ability to do so; and (2) the effects of a small phenomenon can be quite large.

Historians also contend that migration was more common and substantial in the nineteenth century, adding up to 10 percent of the population then. Several new "areas of recent settlement" were populated thus. Drawing on the research of the historians Timothy Hutton and Jeffrey Williamson, Martin Wolf has written, "In the 40 years before the first world war, migration raised the New World labor force by a third and lowered the European labor force by an eighth, figures that have not been exceeded even for California and Mexico over the past 40 years."[4] Yet precisely because they are now occurring from the poor countries to the rich ones instead of from the old to the new, the flows today carry within themselves new seeds of discord and concerns that must be confronted.

Factors Affecting International Migration

Why have migration flows grown and why are they likely to grow yet further? As always, there are supply and demand factors, the former affecting the decision of emigrants to leave and the latter influencing the entry of immigrants. The former are often called the push factors, the latter the pull factors.

With the systematic rise of immigration controls in the twentieth century, these factors operate not just through the market, as in the case of purely internal phenomena such as rural-to-urban migration, but through either tightening or relaxation of quotas and controls *and* through evasion in the form of illegal immigration and filing of false asylum claims.

Supply Factors

The improvement of one's standard of living, enhancement of educational and other opportunities for one's children, and attraction of better professional facilities in the case of skilled migrants are among the principal economic drivers of emigration. This is true principally for emigration from poor to rich countries. But it also applies to migrants who move between rich countries. The brain drain originated as an issue in the 1960s when European scientists were leaving for the United States, and it was only later that the issue traveled to the poor countries, which began to see their scarce stocks and flows of skilled people go off to, or stay on after studies abroad in, the rich countries.

Economic factors have a role even when the proximate causes for emigration are not necessarily economic. For instance, refugees almost always prefer an economically more attractive final destination. Thus refugees will often want to travel on: Central Americans move into Mexico but have their eyes set on the United States. Doctors from the Commonwealth countries often treat the United Kingdom as only an intermediate country to get into, with smaller rewards because of its National Health Service, and they mean to enter the United States in one way or another.

Increasing inequality among nations could then be seen as adding to the incentive to emigrate, providing a reason for migration flows to increase. But then, as I argued in Chapter 5, the evidence of the last two decades is just the opposite: inequality among nations has fallen. Besides, the differentials in incomes are already so high that changes in them, unless dramatic, will probably have negligible effect.

On the other hand, the most effective constraint on emigration is likely to be financial ability to undertake the journey: a factor of great importance to the poor seeking to migrate illegally, such as those from south of the U.S. border who must pay large amounts to *coyotes,* those who arrange to smuggle migrants into the United States. If so, improvement in incomes in the poor countries, as has happened in India and China with massive population and poverty, may lead to greater emigration.[5]

The common presumption, therefore, that we must provide aid and trade to the poor countries so that they will become more prosperous and hence there will be lesser numbers seeking to cross the border illegally is correct when incomes have risen a lot and are closer to levels of the richer countries across the border and beyond. But in the short and medium runs, it could be very wrong.

Then again, emigration is typically facilitated by earlier emigration, and so it has a built-in momentum to grow larger. You see that at the micro level as Korean greengrocers open up one store after another in New York, the Indians take over the newsstands, Pakistanis take over the little drugstores, and Bangladeshis turn up as waiters. As immigrants arrive from one area and into one occupation, they trigger further flows of their compatriots in the same line of work. The flip side is that the mere fact that there is El Dorado here and Dante's inferno there is not sufficient to get major flows occurring; migration has to start before it begins to gather volume. Thus, the huge Mexican inflows today are historically a result of the time when, East Asians having been excluded in California at the turn of the century, American employers sent scouts across the Rio Grande to import Mexican workers in their place, creating the stream that is now a mighty river. This widening and deepening of the stream happens because of information networks. It also occurs because the earlier immigrants provide protective coloring (if illegal immigrant status, subject to detection and expulsion, is at stake) and financial support to their families and friends to enable them to make the same journey to a better life.

The cost of legal migration is also continuing to fall due to technological factors. Travel and telecommunications progressively get easier and cheaper. Information on jobs becomes more readily available, whereas in the past the potential migrant had to rely on less reliable informal networks. Mobility is therefore getting steadily more manageable. It can only add to the migration flows.

Demand Factors

The demand for immigrants has increased in the rich countries, and should even surge, for two economic reasons.

One reflects the heavy hand of demographics in the rich countries, noted in Chapter 11. The aging of populations concomitant with sharp increases in longevity plus the drastic declines in birth rates that are turning Malthusian fears of overpopulation into today's realities of shrinking growth in populations are expected to lead to a substantial hunger for immigrants, unskilled and skilled, to supplement the domestic labor force and also to ensure that the social security systems do not wind up bankrupt because of too many claimants and too few contributors.

The other factor is specific to skilled labor. The demand for skilled workers has exploded (with a temporary disruption because of the collapse of the high-tech stocks) in the rich countries worldwide as the information technology revolution has created a huge need for computer scientists, programmers, and others in economies that are being overhauled by the new developments.[6] But one may well ask: does this necessarily translate into demand for these people's services through their immigration? The need to get the suppliers of these services, whether high-tech or low-tech, to where the users of these services are has been moderated to the extent that one can use modern technology to get these services on the wire. With technology making it possible often to get many services without having to bring the providers and users of services physically together in one location, the pressure to increase immigration can ease.

In fact, such outsourcing has exploded as all kinds of services are now being supplied from overseas. Many of us have had our calls to solve computer problems answered by technicians working in India. But I came across an amusing example where old folks in a retirement home in New York now carry beepers on which someone from Bangalore reminds them to take their medicines: "Mrs. Stein, it is time for your Mevacor"!

But I am certain that the demand for skilled immigrants also will be on a rising trend. Proximity of personnel is often indispensable. Masses of computer users today simply cannot understand what the troubleshooter in Bangalore is telling them; that includes me! The technician to fix your problem has to be here doing it *for* you, rather than doing it *with* you from overseas. The joke about the parent who calls in his ten-year-old son and says, "I do not understand how to put this chip into our TV so that you cannot see the X-rated shows; can you please do it for me?" reflects a tragic reality today. That many of us ignoramuses are old folks does not make our demand negligible—certainly not in an aging society! And there are services that simply cannot be done long distance. You cannot get a haircut unless the barber is where you are. Doctors can diagnose on TV screens from elsewhere, but nurses have to be in the hospital where you are, with tubes in your arms and your nostrils and your windpipe. All this means that the demand for skilled and semi-skilled services of all kinds will continue and will grow. And some, if not much, of it will translate into demand for skilled immigrants.

An Asymmetry

And so today we have an interesting asymmetry. The rich countries want skilled immigrants and are busy changing their immigration policies to bias them away from unskilled to skilled migrants. The poor countries, on the other hand, have an interest in having their unskilled citizens migrate, and their attitude toward the outflow of their skilled citizens, unless they have an ample and renewable supply of them, is not so clear. In consequence, one could almost say that in regard to the unskilled, supply of immigrants exceeds demand in the rich countries, and this feeds illegal immigration and flooding of false asylum entries into them; whereas in regard to the skilled, demand exceeds supply in the rich countries, and the poor countries generally worry about having too many leave (legally) and what the resulting brain drain signifies about their development prospects.

These constitute the two most critical issues today, with the protection of the rights of migrants and definition of their obligations defining the ethical dimensions that must be kept in view.

Software Engineers, Not Huddled Masses

Let me first explain further why and how the developed countries' appetite for skilled migrants has grown. Just look at Silicon Valley's large supply of successful Indian and Taiwanese computer scientists and venture capitalists. The enhanced appetite for such professionals reflects the shift to a globalized economy in which countries compete for markets by creating and attracting technically skilled talent. Governments also perceive these workers to be more likely to assimilate quickly into their new societies.

This heightened demand is matched by a supply that is augmented for old reasons that have intensified over time. Less developed countries cannot offer modern professionals the economic rewards or the social conditions they seek. Europe and the United States also offer opportunities for immigrant children's education and career prospects that are nonexistent at home.

These asymmetries of opportunity reveal themselves not just through cinema and television but through the immediacy of experience. Increasingly, emigration occurs after study abroad. The number of foreign students at U.S. universities, for example, has grown dramatically; so has the number who stay on. In 1990, 62 percent of engineering doctorates in the United States were given to foreign-born students, mainly

Asians. The figures are almost as high in mathematics, computer science, and the physical sciences. In economics, which at the graduate level is a fairly math-intensive subject, 54 percent of the Ph.D.'s awarded went to foreign students, according to a 1990 report of the American Economic Association.

Many of these students come from India, China, and South Korea. For example, India produces about twenty-five thousand engineers annually. Of these, about two thousand come from the Indian Institutes of Technology (IIT), which are modeled on MIT and the California Institute of Technology. Graduates of IIT accounted for 78 percent of U.S. engineering Ph.D.'s granted to Indians in 1990. And almost half of all Taiwanese awarded similar Ph.D.'s had previously attended two prestigious institutions: the National Taiwan University and the National Cheng Kung University. Even more telling, 65 percent of the Korean students who received science and engineering Ph.D.'s in the United States were graduates of Seoul National University. The numbers were almost as high for Beijing University and Tsinghua University, elite schools of the People's Republic of China.

These students, once graduated from American universities, often stay on in the United States. Not only is U.S. graduate education ranked highest in the world, but it also offers an easy way of immigrating. In fact, it has been estimated that more than 70 percent of newly minted foreign-born Ph.D.'s remain in the United States, many becoming citizens eventually.

Less developed countries can do little to restrict the numbers of those who stay on as immigrants. They will, particularly in a situation of high demand for their skills, find ways to escape any dragnet that their home country may devise. And the same difficulty applies, only a little less starkly, to countries trying to hold on to those citizens who have only domestic training but are offered better jobs abroad.

Let me also say that even were it possible to force the professionals to stay at home, it would be a foolish policy. Lack of congenial working conditions, absence of peer professionals to interact with, and resentment at being deprived of the chance to emigrate can lead to a wholly unproductive situation in which one has the body but not the brain. The brain is not a static thing; it can drain away faster sitting in the wrong place than when traveling abroad to Cambridge or Paris! So the only practical policy is to accommodate to the fact that the outmigration of one's skilled citizens will surely occur.

But how should the developing countries do that? The answer to that question must distinguish between countries such as India, South Korea, the Philippines, Taiwan, and China, which have large populations and a substantial capacity to generate skilled professionals at home and by education abroad, to whom therefore the outmigration of professional citizens is an *opportunity,* and those countries, especially in Africa, where the populations are small, the educational systems are inadequate, and the outmigration of the few skilled professionals they have is a *threat.* The brain drain worries apply only to the latter group of countries, and these worries are real.

In the former case, the developing countries seek ways of protecting and enhancing the outflows and of profiting from the many good spillover effects they expect to benefit from as their own citizens settle in prestigious places in the rich countries. India, for example, is profiting from the emigration of its highly skilled workers to the United States, where Indians are now in leadership positions in nearly all the sciences and also are successful in the arts. The Trojan horse principle is at work here: India's increasing friendship with the United States and the economic and diplomatic rewards that come with it owe largely to the Indians who have come to the United States and work there.

Enhancing these good effects requires that countries such as India and Taiwan adopt the diaspora model, extending a warmer embrace to their nationals abroad, so that these spillover effects can be increased. A diaspora policy would integrate present and past citizens into a web of rights and obligations in the extended community, defined with the home country as the center. The diaspora approach is also superior from a human rights viewpoint because it builds on the right to emigrate, rather than trying to restrict it. Besides, dual loyalty, where migrants retain their loyalty to their home country alongside their loyalty to the country they have come to, is increasingly judged to be acceptable. Nearly thirty countries now offer dual citizenship. Others are inching their way to similar options. Many less developed countries, such as Mexico and India, are in the process of granting citizens living abroad hitherto denied benefits such as the right to hold property and to vote via absentee ballot.

However, the diaspora approach is incomplete unless the benefits are balanced by some obligations, such as the taxation of citizens living abroad. The United States already employs this practice. I first recommended this approach for developing countries during the 1960s, and this so-called Bhagwati tax proposal has been revived today. Estimates made by the scholars Mihir Desai, Devesh Kapur, and John McHale demonstrate that even a slight tax on Indian nationals abroad would substantially raise Indian government revenues. The revenue potential is vast because the aggregate income of Indian-born residents in the United States is 10 percent of India's national income, even though such residents account for just 0.1 percent of the American population.

The diaspora model is equally applicable to the poor countries that face the outflow of their all-too-few skilled professionals. But it can take these countries only so far; we also need policies to ensure that needed skills are somehow made available in alternative ways here and now. Here we need to consider measures such as technical assistance, intensive use of the Peace Corps, corporate programs of apprenticeship and mentoring of local communities, rapid building of educational facilities at all levels, and financial aid to natives to be trained in the sciences and engineering skills abroad. This way, foreigners with skills would substitute for the nonexistent or outmigrated native professionals, even as new natives are to be trained. In a few cases of crippling outflow of critical manpower, it may even be financially not too demanding for aid agencies to pay the difference between home and foreign salaries to retain skilled professionals at home, though one has to be careful here not to do this across the board since that would create other difficulties by establishing high salary structures in poor countries and would help push domestic salaries out of line with what the country can afford. This policy has been tried with nurses leaving Malawi for South Africa, but it would not apply to professionals who want better working conditions, not just better salaries.[7]

Illegal Immigration

The more developed countries also face a situation in regard to the influx of illegal economic immigrants and fraudulent asylum seekers where accommodation, rather than impossible curtailment, must be the goal. Inducements or punishments for immigrants' countries of origin are not working to stem the flows, nor are stiffer border control measures, sanctions on employers, or harsher penalties for the illegals themselves.

Several factors are behind this. First, civil society organizations, such as Human Rights Watch, the ACLU, and the International Rescue Committee, have proliferated and gained in prominence and influence. They provide a serious constraint on all forms of restrictive action. For example, it is impossible to incarcerate migrants caught crossing borders illegally without raising an outcry over humane treatment. So authorities generally send people back across the border, with the result that they cross again and again until they finally get in.

More than 50 percent of illegals, however, now enter not by crossing the Rio Grande but by legal means, such as tourist visas, and then stay on illegally. Thus enforcement has become more difficult without invading privacy through such measures as identity cards, which continue to draw strong protests from civil liberties groups. A notable example of both ineffectual policy and successful civil resistance is the 1986 Sanctuary movement, which surfaced in response to evidence that U.S. authorities were returning desperate refugees from war-torn El Salvador and Guatemala to virtually certain death in their home countries. (They were turned back because they did not meet the internationally agreed-upon definition for a refugee.) Sanctuary members, with the aid of hundreds of church groups, took the law into their own hands and organized an underground railroad to spirit endangered refugees to safe havens. Federal indictments and convictions followed, with five Sanctuary members given three- to five-year sentences. Yet, in response to a public outcry and an appeal from Arizona senator Dennis DeConcini, the trial judge merely placed the defendants on probation.

Sanctions on employers, such as fines, do not fully work either. The General Accounting Office, during the debate over the 1986 immigration legislation that introduced employer sanctions, studied how they had worked in Switzerland and Germany and found that they had failed. Judges could not bring themselves to punish severely those employers whose violation consisted solely of giving jobs to illegal workers. The U.S. experience with employer sanctions has not been much different.

Finally, the sociology and politics of ethnicity also undercut enforcement efforts. Ethnic groups can provide protective cover to their members and allow illegals to disappear into their midst. The ultimate constraint, however, is political and results from expanding numbers. Fellow ethnics who are U.S. citizens, legal immigrants, or amnesty beneficiaries bring to bear growing political clout that precludes tough action against illegal immigrants. Nothing matters more than the vote in democratic societies. Thus the Bush administration, anxious to gain Hispanic votes, has embraced an amnesty confined solely to Mexican illegal immigrants, discarding the principle of nondiscrimination enshrined in the 1965 Immigration and Nationality Act.

Coping with Immigration, Rather Than Trying to Restrict It

If it is not possible to effectively restrict illegal immigration, then governments in the developed countries must turn to policies that will integrate migrants into their new homes in ways that will minimize the social costs and maximize the economic benefits. These policies should include children's education and grants of limited civic rights such as participation in school board elections and parent-teacher associations. Governments should also assist immigrants in settling throughout a country, to avoid depressing wages in any one region.

Some nations will grasp this reality and creatively work with migrants and migration. Others will lag behind, still seeking restrictive measures to control and cut the level of migration. The future certainly belongs to the former. But to accelerate the progress of the laggards, new institutional architecture is needed at the international level. Because immigration restrictions are the flip side of sovereignty, there is no international organization today to oversee and monitor each nation's policies toward migrants, whether inward- or outward-bound.[8]

The world badly needs enlightened immigration policies and best practices to be spread and codified. For over a decade, I have called for a World Migration Organization which would begin to do that by juxtaposing each nation's entry, exit, and residence policies toward migrants, whether legal or illegal, economic or political, skilled or unskilled.[9] Such a project is well worth putting finally at the center of policy makers' concerns.

IV

Appropriate Governance: Making Globalization Work Better

15

Appropriate Governance: An Overview

I have concluded that economic globalization, which offers economic prosperity to those who embrace it for the opportunity it presents instead of renouncing it due to the peril they fear it poses, is also generally speaking a force for advancing several social agendas. In short, in the popular phrasing of the politicians who join the anti-globalizers in the refrain that globalization needs a human face, globalization *has* a human face. Or, if I may borrow from the Aspen Institute's initiative for "ethical globalization," led by Mary Robinson, a former UN commissioner for human rights, globalization *already* has profound ethical dimensions. The alarm to the contrary is therefore false at worst, exaggerated to excess and hence error at best.

Yet this does not mean that globalization, left to itself, will produce the best, as distinct from generally good, results. If what I have written so far has been read with care, it should be clear that, in many ways, globalization will yield better results if it is managed. How and by whom it must be managed is the important question that I must now address.

A Trinity of Critical Policy Issues

It is worth repeating that the most critical aspect of appropriate governance depends on the view that is taken as to whether economic globalization needs, or has, a human face.[1] If we opt for the former view, then it is evident that we will want to limit and offset the effects of globalization. But if we embrace the latter view, as argued in Part II, then we will want to enhance its effects instead. Chapter 17 will address the question as to precisely how such benefits-enhancing policies might be devised, by drawing illustratively on the question of promoting international labor standards and on the current debates over the relative merits of trade sanctions and approaches that rely instead on moral suasion and working with agencies such as the International Labor Organization that do not levy sanctions.

But that is not enough either. Since globalization will not always ensure the advancement of economic and social agendas, we also need a second leg for the policy tripod that defines appropriate governance. We need to put into place institutional mechanisms to cope with the occasional downsides: this is the concern of Chapter 16.

The third leg of the policy tripod relates to managing transitions to globalization. While globalization can bring economic and social benefits once the transition to it is made, this leaves open the question of how rapidly the transition to globalization should be made. Indeed, some of the hostility to globalization stems not from globalization per se but from the speed with which it is pushed as policy makers liberalize trade, capital flows, and so on, and to the occasional lack of institutional mechanisms to make such a transition smooth. Thus the Asian financial crisis could possibly have been avoided if the financial liberalization had been less hasty *and* if the banking structures in many of the affected countries had been strengthened. Much too often, because of ideological and lobbying pressures, the speed of transition tends to be maximal rather than optimal, as discussed in Chapter 18.

More Perspectives on Managing Globalization

It is also necessary to remember that the management required for different kinds of economic globalization varies in both degree and kind. Thus, managing short-term capital flows is a far more difficult task than managing trade. The volume and speed with which capital can flow is larger and more precipitous, generally speaking, than fluctuations in trade are (except in the increasingly fewer cases where a country is wholly specialized in one or two primary products characterized by mutually reinforcing volatility of prices and earnings).

An important distinction must also be made between globalization that must be managed because it creates endogenous, intrinsic problems, as with short-term capital flows, and globalization that requires management because of problems that follow from policy actions, as when large numbers of economic migrants are expelled because of an economic downturn or when asylum is tightened by governments or severe crackdowns on illegal migrants are undertaken because of alleged security concerns. In the former case, it is the absence of corrective or supportive problem-solving action and governance that must be addressed. In the latter case, it is the presence of problem-creating action and governance that must be confronted.

Then again, virtually every component of globalization's governance will have both domestic and international dimensions, each linked to the other to provide the institutional support for enhanced benefits from globalization. Thus when poor countries have embraced free trade, they will want to have domestic adjustment assistance programs to assist import-competing industries that experience disruption from international competition, as in fact the rich countries have long had. But since they do not have the resources to finance such programs, international aid agencies such as the World Bank should be mobilized to provide the necessary finance. Thus domestic and international institutional action would have to be joined to facilitate the poor countries' beneficial trade integration into the world economy.

A Shared Success

But perhaps the most significant observation concerning the design of appropriate governance today comes from the recognition that the two great forces of the twenty-first century are economic globalization and the huge growth in civil society within most countries, rich and poor, and the possibility that they can be jointly harnessed in the cause of appropriate governance for managing globalization in ways that would create what I like to call a shared success.

Civil society, in the domestic sphere and reflecting national mobilization, values, culture, and political sensibilities, offers opportunities for better governance to manage globalization in the democratic societies that have increasingly come to prevail worldwide and where NGOs have proliferated hugely (as discussed in Chapter 4).

Often governments, particularly in the poor countries, adopt legislation such as the enactment of the "polluter pay" principle but do not have the means to monitor compliance. This is where NGOs on the ground become important as the eyes and ears of the legislation. For instance, until the NGOs in India brought up complaints about the environmental spillovers from coastal shrimp farming, the environmental ministry was unaware of it. The same holds for vast swaths of legislation in many poor countries: it sits there with little impact, since the information does not percolate up.

In arguing for this role for the NGOs, I am providing a liberal adaptation of the conservative argument by the Nobel laureate Friedrich

Hayek. He famously argued for leaving economic decisions to the private entrepreneurs because they had the necessary micro-level knowledge and they also had the commitment to efficiency that followed from their investment of capital.[2] Similarly, on the social issues, the NGOs have the micro-level knowledge (since they work close to the ground) and they have the commitment (provided by strong altruism focused on the cause they champion).

Second, even where governments have the information, they may be unable to act on it since the implementation of the legislation is impeded by powerful lobbies that capture the political process to the exclusion of the adversely affected but marginalized groups. Democratic politics does not always allow for equal play to all groups, of course. NGOs will often act to empower less powerful constituencies, bringing their voices into play when their vote does not accomplish this. Judicial innovation in India, where NGOs have been given by an activist judiciary the legal standing to bring cases before the supreme court on behalf of impoverished plaintiffs with no resources of their own, has translated this role of the NGOs into an effective channel of empowerment. The result has been a more effective implementation of legislation against bonded labor and exploitative child labor, for instance. This has complemented and enhanced the benefits that globalization generally brings in regard to poverty reduction and related social agendas.[3]

Increasingly, corporations—these are also non-governmental entities but need to be distinguished from NGOs for clarity of analysis—have also begun to play a role in providing appropriate governance as part of what is now called "corporate social responsibility." Thus, the Merck CEO Raymond Gilmartin has provided invaluable input into the response to the AIDS crisis in Botswana, alongside the Gates Foundation, which has committed big sums (in nine digits) to the same cause.

These different strands will be interwoven as I proceed now to a more substantive treatment of the trinity of policy and institutional design that defines the essential elements of the appropriate governance for globalization that will add yet greater glow to its human face.

But let me enter one disclaimer before I do that. I have neglected an exhortation, all too common in writings on globalization today, that an interdependent globalized world economy requires policy coordination among governments, as we just witnessed regarding the SARS epidemic. This prescription is so obvious and commonplace that it is almost a cliché; it would seem to hardly need more than a mention.[4] Yet perhaps some observations, often overlooked, are in order.

Historically, of course, this interdependence has long existed, predating modern globalization. It is common knowledge that diseases traveled with migrations, often decimating vast populations. What SARS was threatening to do today, as people traveled out of China and Hong Kong to Toronto and Singapore, was done with devastating impact when the Spanish conquistadors arrived in Mexico City and brought death from European diseases to over a third of the invaded city's population. Jared Diamond has written:

> Smallpox, measles, influenza, typhus, bubonic plague, and other infectious diseases endemic in Europe played a decisive role in European conquests, by decimating many peoples on other continents. For example, a smallpox epidemic devastated the Aztecs after the failure of the first Spanish attack in 1520 and killed Cuitláhuac, the Aztec emperor who briefly succeeded Montezuma. Throughout the Americas, diseases introduced with Europeans spread from tribe to tribe far in advance of the Europeans themselves, killing an estimated 95 percent of the pre-Columbian native American population.[5]

The same would have happened with European expansion into Africa, except that the Arab traders who came earlier had already immunized the local populations against many of the same diseases. Today the scale of travel, as distinct from long-term migrations, is so immense, however, that the risks of spreading epidemics have grown immensely with it. But then, so has the growth of international institutions and of attempted policy coordination.

Richard Cooper has described in great detail the critical role played by international policy coordination, and the enormous difficulties that had to be surmounted, in coping with cholera, plague, and smallpox in the last century.[6] Today the institutions that do this kind of work are many more and far more robust, and the necessary scientific tools and abilities are far more developed. In fact, where interdependence plays a major role in posing a risk to their own populations, one can confidently expect that the richer countries will devote resources to the problem of policy formulation and coordination because self-interest kicks in. Thus, for tropical diseases, the great colonial empires that sent their civil servants abroad and saw some of the colonials travel to the metropolitan country devoted resources to investigating the tropical diseases, since mosquitoes and tsetse flies do not distinguish between colonials and masters! Thus we had the legendary Institute for Tropical Medicine in London and the Royal Tropical Institute in Amsterdam.[7] In the same vein today, the resources devoted by the rich countries to discovering remedies for AIDS, which afflicted the rich first before spreading massively to the poor countries, have been huge compared to those devoted to diseases such as malaria, which are seen to be predominantly poor-country afflictions (though in the world of enhanced mobility today, such a distinction is increasingly fragile). Where such a distinction between universal and poor-country-specific diseases can be made, international policy coordination and innovation are far more likely to arise in the former case relative to the latter. In the former case, self-interest reinforces the altruism that does lie behind such remedial and preventive actions in public health.

Of course, such self-interest has to be plausible. Too often, U.S. proponents of aid to poor countries have tried to hide the altruism and sought to justify aid flows on grounds of enlightened self-interest, arguing that it is good not for our souls but really for our material well-being. This rationale is amusingly illustrated by the story where a rich man and a poor one are praying in church. The rich man asks the Lord for a million dollars so that he can meet a loan that is coming due. The poor man wants only a dollar so that he can buy some bread. The rich man pulls out a hundred dollars from his wallet and gives the money to the poor man, saying, "Buy as much bread as you want with this hundred dollars, but get out of here. I need the Lord's undivided attention!" Now *there* is enlightened self-interest for you.

First the cold war provided a justification for aid flows. Then it was the argument that if we did not give aid to the poor countries, they would pour across our borders like the "peso refugees" across the Rio Grande. And the latest twist—in defiance of all facts, which show that it is the educated in the more prosperous middle class who seem to fly planes into skyscrapers and drive cars with bombs into embassies—is that our security requires that aid be given to bring people out of poverty!

But the observation that policy coordination seems to be logical when there is increased interdependence must be attended by some caution and caveats. As economists have learned painfully, coordination can be counterproductive. The economists Jeffrey Frenkel and Katharine Rockett showed rather pointedly in 1988 that coordinated macroeconomic policy could produce worse outcomes for macro-level stability than lack of such coordination.[8] This can happen occasionally (and in some areas of policy even frequently) in cases where there is no objectively clear and dominant model of the working of the economy on which everyone is agreed, so that the coordination is founded on different and at times even conflicting assumptions by different actors regarding what works and why. The authors showed that, allowing for differences among international policy makers as to what was the "correct" macroeconomic model to use from among ten leading econometric models, monetary coordination improved U.S. welfare in only 546 cases out of 1,000.

Or consider that everyone is pushed by a dominant country into giving up their sensible approach, instead adopting exactly the wrong policy around which to converge! This is, for instance, the appropriate way to see how a "selfish hegemon" such as the United States, reflecting its own lobbies' agendas, pushed for a common, coordinated policy of excessive intellectual property protection at the WTO. In short, a socially harmful policy may be imposed, under the pretext of coordination or the provision of what economists call public goods, by powerful nations in an interdependent world. It is useful to remember that *interdependence* is a normatively attractive, soothing word, but when nations are unequal, it also leads to dependence and hence to possibilities of perverse policy interventions and aggressively imposed coordination of policies with outcomes that harm the social good and the welfare of the dependent nations while advancing the interests of the powerful nations.

So when I read about interdependence, a red light goes on inside my head that flashes *dependence.* Also, when my friends in international agencies talk of providing international public goods, I worry about these sometimes masking international public "bads." Moreover, when good-spirited political scientists talk of "altruistic hegemons" providing public goods to the world economy, my sixth sense tells me to worry about "selfish hegemons," an idea that I have raised in my more academic writing.[9] And when naive admonitions are made not to look gift horses in the mouth, I urge the caution that a gift horse may in truth be a Trojan horse. So my approach to this whole subject of interdependence, and the policy coordination it seems so obviously to call for, is cautionary: go ahead, but temper your enthusiasm with both a small degree of skepticism and a large dose of caveat emptor.

16

Coping with Downsides

It is not sufficient that, by and large, globalization advances both economic and social agendas. Everything does not necessarily improve every time! There are occasional downsides. And we must be prepared to cope with them with appropriate policy responses. If the policy maker retreats behind the unpersuasive claim that—more or less, and over time—the difficulties will always be surmounted and the globalization tide will surely lift all boats, she is on treacherous ground.

Blocking Efficient Change to Kill Potential Downside versus Creating Institutions to Address It If and When It Occurs

After half a century of experimentation with planning, some in the form of detailed Kafkaesque restrictions and commands on the basis of inherently fragile forecasts and plans, as happened disastrously in the case of the Soviet Union and in developing countries such as India and Egypt, we have learned that, generally speaking, the way to address potential downsides is not to act on the pretense that we can forecast their occurrence with certainty. Rather, the smart way to cope with downsides is to devise institutions and policy responses that kick in if and when the potential downside occurs.

In the city of Ahmedabad in the state of Gujarat in India, where my forefathers came from and where Mahatma Gandhi had his famous ashram, one sees today a monumental victim of the thinking, common to many in civil society today, that downsides must be eliminated fully at their source. Indian planners began a series of five-year plans in 1951. They were worried that the expansion of the large-scale cotton mills in

Ahmedabad, a city that had earned the reputation of being the Lancashire of the East, would kill the small-scale sector. So they prevented the mills in the large-scale sector from expanding and modernizing. Consequently, they became uncompetitive in the world markets and were declared "sick," a quaint Indian description that entitles the owners to a handout! Even the restrictive quotas that India had been assigned under the Multi-Fiber Agreement (which had been allocating export quotas to different supplying nations starting from earlier arrangements beginning in 1961) were often unfilled because Indian exports, produced in outdated mills, could not compete. And now with the Multi-Fiber Agreement scheduled to end in 2005, there is panic in India that mills in China will prove to be a deadly competitor, reducing yet further India's exports unless this disastrous Indian policy is abandoned.

The tragedy is that the policy made little sense to begin with. The kind of textiles and garments that are produced in India's mills, particularly with modern techniques and materials, are very distinct and distant from the products made in the small-scale sector, often in households. Economists have long talked of a continuum of goods, each of different quality and with different characteristics even though all are called "textiles" or "soap." They coexist, and the expanded availability of one quality does not necessarily spell the demise of another at the other end of this continuum or spectrum. Soap produced in rural households for rural households is not soap to urban consumers, who go for the quality and consistency produced by Unilever and Procter & Gamble. To block the expanded production of the latter to protect the former is faintly ludicrous and surely foolish.

But what can we do in the few cases when things do go wrong for the small-scale sector because the large-scale sector expands? What should be the appropriate institutional response? Evidence shows that the best way to handle this kind of downside is to make available programs that are triggered if and when things do go wrong. You do not shut off the expansion and modernization of modern mills and factories to handle this potential downside. To do that would be like cutting off your nose to handle an occasional nasal drip.

Complexity and Difficulty of Anticipation of Adverse Downsides

The notion that policy must be framed on the assumption that bureaucrats will necessarily be able to predict correctly the adverse outcomes for specific sectors, illustrated in the rather simple examples I gave above, is further seen to be implausible in the far more complex cases where we deal with a policy change that, even within the confines of a certain area such as trade policy, has several components, or with a package of policies on several dimensions such as exchange rate change, tax policy reform, trade measures, privatization, and price reforms.

I am always astonished when, in relation to trade policy, groups such as the environmental NGOs demand that environmental impact statements for major and wide-ranging agreements, such as the one concluding the seven-year negotiations at the Uruguay Round, be submitted before the agreements are approved. What nonsense this is, in truth, good as it sounds. For a project such as the Three Gorges Dam, one can attempt this. But to ask that a trade agreement's environmental impact be assessed is like asking that the environmental impact of the United States budget be examined and approved! These NGOs might say: "Ah, but you do not hesitate to cite the trade impact of the trade agreements!" Well, in fact I consider many of the estimates of trade expansion and of gains from trade—produced at great expense by number-crunching at institutions such as the World Bank with the aid of huge computable models, and then fed into the public policy domain with the aid of earnest journalists—as little more than flights of fancy in contrived flying machines.

In fact, the doyen of the economists who produce these complex models, John Whalley of the University of Western Ontario in Canada, was asked recently by the United Nations Conference on Trade and Development (UNCTAD), the agency that is meant to be a think tank for the developing countries, to evaluate what the developing nations could infer from the models that had been produced to examine the effects of the prospective Uruguay Round trade concessions on them. His frank conclusions, based on a comparison of eight such models, are worth repeating:

> The paper argues that there are substantial, and at times hard to explain inconsistencies across model results. One model shows most of the gains come from agricultural liberalization, another from textiles, and yet another from tariff cuts. One model shows developing countries losing from elimination of the MFA, another shows them as large gainers. . . . These differences occur even where similar data sets, and benchmark years are used.[1]

From the viewpoint of coping with downsides, the key trade negotiations have the particularly difficult, even impossible task of predicting the net impact on specific industries and sectors. The reason is that the effects of several negotiated changes must be worked out. Thus if agricultural subsidies are being reduced on production of corn, so are tariffs on corn imports abroad, and subsidies abroad too; simultaneous changes in incentives to produce and trade in products that are substitutes for corn in production and in consumption will also affect what happens to corn farmers. Figuring out all this, which means that economists must make all kinds of assumptions regarding which model to use and which parameters to put into it, among other things, is a devilish and unreliable business, as Whalley frankly admits.

And so we are back to the caveat I outlined at the outset: what is required is a set of institutions in place that, if and when a downside occurs in specific sectors and activities that are often beyond the powers of plausible prediction by economists and bureaucrats, can be activated to enable the afflicted to cope with the unleashed difficulties.

Designing Appropriate Institutional Safeguards

As openness, particularly to trade, has increased steadily and substantially in the rich countries in the sixty years since the Second World War, so has the evolution of institutions and policies to cope with its downsides. In fact, given the democratic politics of these countries, it was inevitable that those fearing the possibility that these downsides could come their way would be asking for such institutions and policies if openness was to be allowed to intensify. But this has not happened with the poor countries.

The principal reason why many developing countries do not have these institutions and policies to handle openness quite simply is that they were not opening their economies and hence did not have to cope with its occasional downsides. These countries were generally exempt from having to open their markets to match the rich countries' reductions of trade barriers, partly because they wrongly believed that protectionism was not bad for them because they were poor, and partly because they represented such small markets that the rich countries, who were keen on reciprocal openness concerning one another, were willing to let them close their markets even when the rich countries were opening theirs. Their reaction to continued protectionism in most of the poor countries therefore was: "Well, if you want to protect your markets, we will indulge you. Feel free to shoot yourself in the foot, should you choose to do so."

As the postwar reduction of trade barriers proceeded apace under seven successive multilateral trade negotiations conducted under GATT auspices, the last being the Uruguay Round, which concluded almost ten years ago, there opened up an inherited asymmetry between the average industrial tariffs of the rich countries and of the poor countries.

And this asymmetry, as I observed in Chapter 1 when commenting on the claims of some NGOs about the double standards in the world trading system, runs exactly in the opposite direction from that assumed by them.[2] Lest this not be found credible, since many people have been bamboozled by repeated assertions to the contrary, the chart below, on the average industrial tariffs in these two groups of countries, shows unambiguously the situation as it currently exists.

In the last decade, many poor countries have begun to see the folly of their own protectionism. Many have unilaterally begun to lower their tariffs, among the chief examples being Chile (which has very low tariffs now) and India (which has massively reduced protection but is still among the highest-tariff countries in the world).[3]

Pressure from the IMF and the World Bank has played a role in some cases also, but it is too simplistic to argue that the conversion of these institutions to the view that protectionism is a folly even in the poor countries has not been matched by a receptive set of policy makers in their client countries: they have often read the same books and learned from the same experience that underlined the folly of postwar protectionism.

Several countries are now reducing their trade barriers multilaterally as well. Since the Uruguay Round, the poor countries have begun to

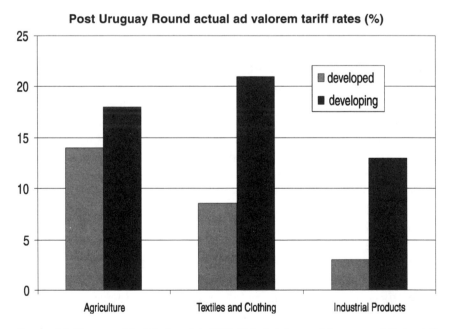

Post Uruguay Round actual ad valorem tariff rates (%)

Source: M. Finger and L. Schuknecht, 1999, "Market Access Advances and Retreats," World Bank Working Paper WPS 2232, Table SF3.

offer trade concessions to match in some degree those of the rich countries, so that the GATT game of exchanging trade concessions is no longer played only by the rich countries.

But now that they are beginning to open up their economies, the poor countries find themselves without the institutions and policies that evolved over a long period of increasing openness in the rich countries. So we need to put in place those institutions and policies, part of what I call in this book "appropriate governance," if we are to support, and increase support for, global integration of the poor countries, as we should. Indeed, if we do not, the pro-globalization policies and attitudes that I reported earlier as commonplace in the poor countries and their governments will be at risk. These institutional and policy innovations can take several forms, some good and others adequate but not as good. I will illustrate with examples from trade.

Adjustment Assistance

The idea that we should provide adjustment assistance to workers and industries affected by import competition is not new. Economics itself tells us that free trade (like each policy) can be unambiguously declared to be welfare-enhancing only if those who lose from it can be compensated by taking income from the winners while leaving the winners still better off. Most economists will not be satisfied with this potential-compensation criterion; they will want the compensation to be actually made. To see this clearly, imagine a strongly conservative administration saying, "Free trade is fine because the poor, who have gotten poorer, can be compensated by the rich, who have gotten richer," and then leaving the poor poorer. Not too many people would buy that!

Of course, one cannot do this compensation policy by policy; that would leave lots of policies captive to compensation schemes that actually cut into the policies' beneficial effects through taxes and transfers. Since it is also politically unlikely that such compensation can be attached to every policy change in practice, it is surely more sensible, generally speaking, to go for more general and comprehensive schemes such as unemployment insurance and retraining programs for all workers who are laid off, for instance.

But then politics kicks in also. In a world where "us" and "them" distinctions between domestic and foreign communities and nations had disappeared and total cosmopolitanism in a borderless world had taken its place, one could settle for fully general unemployment relief and adjustment assistance programs aimed at relief regardless of the source of the distress. Then one would agree with President Ronald Reagan, who complained that the Trade Adjustment Assistance program introduced by President Kennedy in 1962 was in error "because these benefits are paid out on top of normal unemployment benefits, [and therefore] we wind up paying greater benefits to those who lose their jobs because of foreign competition. Anyone must agree that this is unfair."[4]

But, as it happens, workers and citizens generally do not seem to believe that they should be allowed to go to the wall if they lose their jobs to foreign competition, though they are generally less outraged when the job loss is to domestic competition. If a steel mill closes down in Pennsylvania because steel in California has become cheaper, workers tend to accept that as something that happens, and the general unemployment insurance seems to be an adequate way to deal with the bad hand that an unpredictable fate has dealt one. But the same workers get indignant when the loss is to a steel producer in Korea or Brazil, and they go off agitating for anti-dumping action (which has happened often in the past) or a safeguards tariff (as happened recently, under the George W. Bush administration). Or they ask for special relief in the form of additional unemployment compensation, with or without retraining benefits and requirements. With import competition hitting you, the reaction is like that to a natural disaster: the government must intervene with special support. This quasi-xenophobia is just a fact of life. If trade liberalization is to occur and be sustained, one or more of these special programs and policies have to be considered, and working with adjustment assistance rather than protection is the better way to go, since the latter is more expensive.[5]

In fact, President Kennedy introduced the Trade Adjustment Assistance program precisely to ensure union support for congressional approval for launching the Kennedy Round of multilateral trade negotiations. The program helped the president to get the critical AFL-CIO support. As the union's president, George Meany, said: "There is no question whatever that adjustment assistance is essential to the success of trade expansion. And as we have said many times, it is indispensable to our support of the trade program as a whole."[6]

So if the rich countries have these programs, we surely need them in the poor countries as well, and even more so, as the workers who might be laid off are more likely to be close to malnourishment and are often unable to manage and finance transitions to new jobs. Trade liberalization occurs typically without systematic adjustment assistance, and this creates both economic and political risks to its success.

But how is one to finance such adjustment assistance, whatever form it takes? Poor countries typically can ill afford adjustment programs.

Many argue that these countries should start by eliminating the defense expenditures that can absorb scarce resources to excess, but hardly any country follows this precept to the degree required.

So we need to think of institutional programs of adjustment assistance that can be domestically implemented but financed externally. The obvious candidate for this task is the World Bank, which should put its money where its pro-globalization mouth is. In some cases, it may even be possible to get such financing from the corporate sector: exporting firms may well be willing to buy out opposition from import-competing workers by providing adjustment assistance to the poor governments whose markets they seek to export to. Then again, we know that industries such as the shoe industry in the United States often adjusted to imports by being bought out by the exporting firms, which then offered to use their sales network to turn them into distributive outlets. Such accommodation, which reduces the pain of adjusting to import competition, may also be encouraged by governments where appropriate.

Dispute Settlement Mechanism at the WTO

In 1999, small Caribbean countries that had been enjoying preferential entry into the European markets found themselves facing the prospect of a major loss of markets and export earnings to South American nations. The WTO Dispute Settlement Mechanism had little choice except to find against these preferential schemes, as they violated, without legitimate foundation in WTO law, the MFN principle, which requires that imports from all WTO members must enjoy the most favorable tariff extended to other members.[7]

But while such a finding was absolutely correct in law, its impact was to leave these small and poor Caribbean nations with an estimated loss in their national incomes of up to 15 percent! When oil prices went up almost fourfold in 1973, the effect was a near macroeconomic disaster in the rich countries for almost a decade (and these countries have highly developed institutions and labor markets to facilitate flexible response). But small Caribbean nations are not so blessed. So I telephoned my contacts at the World Bank to see if the Bank was creating a program of special aid to compensate and otherwise assist these countries facing huge losses. While the aid sums would be large for these small countries, they would be negligible as a fraction of what the World Bank spends and disburses. I found that nothing was in the works.

In my view, the Bank should automatically trigger support when the WTO's Dispute Settlement Mechanism brings a significant loss of income and attending adjustment problem for producers in poor countries who have lost market access. Regrettably, the World Bank, which is crippled now by overreach into everything under its so-called comprehensive development strategy, appears to suffer from a lack of appropriate prioritization.

Handling Volatility in Agriculture

The focus of the preceding arguments was on adjustment problems, regardless of which activity they related to. But agriculture (and dependence on one or two primary products for the bulk of exports and often of national income as well), poses special problems related to volatility of prices and earnings, especially in the poor countries of Africa.

These concerns are long-standing and, if anything, have somewhat faded from view. Because they were the principal focus of attention almost a quarter of a century ago, when many poor countries happened to be dependent on a few agricultural and primary exports, there had indeed been some institutional response at the international level. Unfortunately, much international effort went into thinking up so-called commodity schemes aimed at stabilizing prices. But these did not get anywhere in the end because the producing countries were interested in them when prices were down while consuming countries were interested in them when prices were up, the two sets of countries rarely working together. Besides, it is not even clear that prices should be stabilized. If there is a supply disturbance such as a harvest failure, the rise in prices offsets the fall in production and hence is good, not bad, for the farmers in the producing countries.

The international effort to develop commodity schemes, whether to stabilize prices or incomes, was therefore soon seen to be not an optimal or even feasible way to set about the business of handling commodity problems. The result was that the central corrective effort was addressed not to eliminating the volatility of export earnings but to coping with its consequences. Hence, the IMF developed "facilities" in the 1960s and 1970s to extend special loans to the poor countries when their export earnings declined, to be repaid when they went up. The IMF set up its Extended Fund Facility in 1974 to assist countries suffering from balance-of-payments imbalances, whereas the Compensatory Financing Facility, established in the 1960s, was meant to assist countries experiencing an export shortfall or excess import cost that was of a short-term nature and attributable to factors beyond the country's control.[8] It would therefore be incorrect to argue that institutions do not exist today to assist the poor countries to cope with volatility and the economic insecurity that can follow from it.

The question of volatility must be distinguished, however, from the fear that the terms of trade of poor countries' exports are declining over time—that is, that the prices of their primary exports, relative to the prices of their imports of manufactures, are in free fall and therefore these countries face in the world economy a tightening noose round their emaciated necks. The assertion of a historic downward trend was not warranted by the facts, nor was the inference that this non-existing decline would continue! The alleged decline was a product of fallacious comparisons, among them a specious choice of periods such as taking the peak prices of primary products during the Korean War and then looking at their decline in the years thereafter. It is unworthy of attention, leave aside remedial action.

Economic Insecurity and Domestic Institutional Support

But there is a different problem of economic security, most acutely applicable to farmers in the poor countries, where institutional support is necessary but lacking. It arises from the intensification of competition today and the thinning of competitive advantage so that, as I discussed in Chapter 1 on the distinctive nature of globalization today, we have knife-edge situations where sudden loss of a market to foreign rivals can occur. A number of potential and actual competitors are in the market today; and small changes in conditions abroad can make them more deadly rivals. I say therefore that comparative advantage today has become kaleidoscopic: a small turn of the instrument and you get a different image, a configuration of costs and prices that suddenly and swiftly turns you from a winner into a loser.

We sometimes hear stories from the field about how farmers turned to commercial crops for sale in world markets, borrowing and investing, only to find themselves suddenly overcome by competitors and pushed into starvation. Similar stories are told, unrelated to globalization, where investments in raising production have led to gluts that ruin the farmers, leading in turn to reduced plantings, which produce shortages and even famines. Economists have for over a century called this particular phenomenon a "cobweb cycle," where increased production leads to lower prices, which trigger lower production, which then leads to higher prices, which then cause more production, and the wheels of the cycle keep turning. The cobweb metaphor is unwittingly apt and ghastly because the cobweb draws into itself the hapless farmers in these countries.

Consider the recent experience in Ethiopia, reported in the *Wall Street Journal*, where farmers responded to market incentives, reinforced by governmental exhortations, to boost production to the point where grain harvests in the latter half of the 1990s averaged 11 million tons annually, about 4 million tons more than in the 1980s. In the bumper years of 2000 and 2001, harvests hit more than 13 million tons.[9] Because the emphasis was on "let's just produce," according to one observer, and there was no thought given to the possibility of a glut, the result was an economic disaster for the farmers. As the *Wall Street Journal* commented:

> In more-developed farming markets, meshing aspects of both the free market and government support, storage facilities would allow grain to be held until prices improved, and crops could be sold on a futures market. Loans might be guaranteed by the government, and farmers protected by crop insurance. Ethiopia's farmers had none of this."[10]

The astonishing and tragic fact is that none of this should have happened since countless numbers of people warned against this risk and highlighted the need to contain it with appropriate policies at the time of the green revolution in India three decades earlier. The Indian government put price support schemes in place, heeding the argument that if the green revolution was allowed to occur without supporting mechanisms to maintain prices as output increased, the price fall could devastate all, and would certainly ruin those who had not been able to produce more, and that an untended green revolution could then usher in a red revolution! One wonders therefore why these obvious caveats were forgotten thirty years later, when the World Bank had a resident mission in Ethiopia. Indeed, one may ask in anger why several million dollars are being spent on lucrative salaries for an immense professional staff when even elementary lessons can be forgotten at great cost to the poor countries.

But to return to the theme of globalization, we need to keep in view the possibility that a shift to internationally traded crops can put farmers at risk. Farmers in the poor countries are often small peasants and are unaware that the shift to global markets carries risks as well. They cannot therefore be expected to ensure that they are sufficiently hedged against such possibilities. It is really up to the governments to provide the required institutional support to handle the downside if and when it arises. As before, given the potentially large scale of assistance involved and given that it must span both import and export commodities, this will require several policy measures: some to provide temporary protection (as in the case of GATT Article 19, often called the Safeguards Clause, which permits countries that run into unanticipated difficulties with negotiated trade tariff reductions to withdraw these concessions) and adjustment assistance instead for export industries that lose external markets and which therefore cannot be helped by temporary import restrictions. Insofar as adjustment assistance requires financial resources, again, the role of aid agencies such as the World Bank becomes relevant to the provision of such appropriate governance.

To conclude: Appropriate handling of the downsides that will undoubtedly occur with integration into the world economy, and in the course of transition to such integration as well, requires a complex set of new policies and institutions. While many of the rich countries, which have gone through a substantial shift to openness in the postwar decades, have already made much of the institutional transition to handle the downside of openness, the poor countries typically have not developed the necessary institutions to handle the intensified challenges of increasing openness to the world economy. But the design and financing of these new institutions and policies cannot be left simply to the governments in these nations. International developmental agencies and rich-country donors also have a role to play, particularly in financing cash-strapped governments when these policies require disbursements of funds and in ensuring that institutional support to manage the downside of openness is rapidly created in the poor countries as well.

17

Accelerating the Achievement
of Social Agendas

I magine a car with a manual transmission. Those who claim that globalization lacks a human face are saying that the car is in reverse gear. I have argued here that this is wrong; in fact, the car is moving forward. But where globalization takes it into the third gear, appropriate governance can be devised to move it yet faster in fourth gear, and even into fifth if it is a sports car, where you shift again at something like ninety miles per hour (as I discovered once to my alarm on a narrow French road when my host, an affable but shy economist who turned out to have been a test pilot for the Royal Air Force during the Second World War, was driving an Alfa Romeo with a gusto that I had never seen him display before).

The debate, then, should be not about whether we should be content with the pace at which economic prosperity, aided by globalization, proceeds to reduce, say, child labor, but about what additional policy instruments we can deploy to accelerate that pace.

To use an apt analogy, if a woman is crying for help, saying, "Help, help, my husband is beating me," you would not say to her, "Hang in there—economic growth will take care of you in a couple of decades." Yes, a growing economy with more jobs should help eventually, because it would probably increase the likelihood that she could walk out on her husband since she could likely find a job and be able to support herself. But you will want to rush in and nail the beastly fellow *immediately* to the wall! The question before us is what exactly this analogy implies in terms of concrete social-outcomes-enhancing policy actions for a variety of social agendas.

The best way to sketch the nature of the debate today on appropriate instruments is to hang my remarks on the peg provided by the agitation against the lower labor (and environmental) standards and alleged human rights violations in the poor countries.[1] The general view in the United States and among many labor and NGO groups is that the appropriate and necessary instruments must consist of linkage between trade treaties and the implementation of standards on social agendas. This linkage would make market access for these countries' exporters subject to sanctions, preferably trade sanctions, if the standards were not implemented. The NGOs justify their preference for such linkage by arguing that all other means, such as the use of moral suasion and civil society agitation, lack teeth. And so, particularly in the U.S. Congress and in the political activism of the civil society groups in the American political arena, we see a desire and a determined effort to capture the political process so as to "crack the whip" to accelerate these agendas. I happen to think this is a fundamentally unsound and counterproductive choice of policy instruments, surprising as this claim may appear.[2]

Two Different Types of Linkage Issues

The demands for trade linkage address two different types of issues that seem identical but are in fact dissimilar enough to warrant separate treatment: (1) the use of *generalized* trade sanctions against offending countries, and (2) the use of tactics such as suspension or denial of market access for *particular products* that offend, such as the use of child labor or of prison labor in the manufacture of a product (an issue raised in Chapter 10).

Generalized Trade Sanctions

The embargoes against South Africa over apartheid and against Ian Smith's unilateral declaration of independence in Southern Rhodesia were multilateral and UN-sanctioned. So were the sanctions against Iraq in the years prior to the Anglo-American invasion by coalition forces. On the other hand, unilateral sanctions by major powers are not uncommon. The United States has long had an embargo against Cuba, and there were also sanctions in the shape, for instance, of denial of MFN status to the Soviet Union over its emigration policies and to China over the state of human rights.

When we apply such trade sanctions, recall that we may not necessarily be sanguine about their efficacy in eliminating the perceived lapses in moral rectitude. We may even be willing to suffer economic harm—for that is what the denial of a trade opportunity would do to oneself—even while achieving no results. Thus, when the extension of MFN rights to China was being debated in the United States, critics such as Abe Rosenthal of the *New York Times* wrote columns in this vein.

But most of us are not entirely moral absolutists. We are also consequentialists. We seek results; we want sanctions that will work. But then we must ask two questions: (1) can sanctions work, and (2) even if they do, are there not other methods that would work better, in more cost-efficient ways? In fact, the answers to both questions leave me skeptical about the use of sanctions.

Efficacy of Sanctions

Evidently, trade sanctions can work. Even when they are evaded, as is common, they can put moral pressure on offending regimes, as in the case of the embargo on South Africa. The effect of the ancillary, embargo-induced boycotts in sports and cultural events were probably even more effective in building up dissent from within the country itself. But the conditions for embargoes to work are fairly stringent and infrequently satisfied.

Embargoes are unlikely to succeed unless the offending values are universal rather than idiosyncratic. Moral pressure works better when universally abhorred slavery or apartheid is at issue rather than the provision of a living wage, a demand that many consider to be altogether ill-defined and even wrongheaded. Similarly, the preservation of an endangered species such as the tiger is more likely to attract widespread condemnation than the elimination of dolphin-unsafe tuna fishing, which reflects concern for dolphins that is not grounded in a wider moral principle but reflects simply the aesthetic fact that many Americans find dolphins cute. Except in egregious cases such as apartheid, the achievement of a multilateral consensus is therefore improbable. So unilateral embargoes become the most realistic tool if sanctions are to be used. But these have serious problems of their own.

To begin with, unilateral embargoes have less moral clout than multilateral ones: since the embargoing nation does not carry other nations with it, the claim that such acts are driven by moral rather than strategic considerations is harder to sustain. It is also harder to maintain an embargo when the targeted country can exercise the option of trade with non-embargoing countries to break the stranglehold of the unilateral embargo.

In fact, unilateral embargoes will drive a wedge between human rights and business groups because the business lost by the unilaterally embargoing country will invariably be taken up by business rivals in the non-embargoing countries, making the business groups particularly frustrated that they lose business while the targeted country is only marginally inconvenienced. In democratic countries where both groups have a voice, unilateral embargoes suffer from the defect that they cannot attract the fulsome support necessary to have them satisfactorily implemented, if they are adopted at all. One should then look for alternative measures around which the necessary democratic consensus can be built with support from both groups.

Efficacy of Alternative Measures

In the modern world, with the phenomenal growth of civil society and of media coverage, our ability to zero in on morally offensive practices has increased hugely. Embarrassment, if not shame and even guilt, allow tremendous leverage. The relentless scrutiny of Myanmar's junta today, in the press and at institutions such as the ILO, has brought even the hesitant Southeast Asian nations to condemn the junta's violations of human rights because these are violations of universally approved rather than idiosyncratic norms. They will certainly lead to results.

The effectiveness of these methods, which do not carry sanctions, in prompting change cannot be overestimated. Instances abound, crowding our newspapers almost daily. A recent example is the influence exercised by women's groups on the all-male hiring practice of the Vienna Philharmonic Orchestra by threatening to boycott their U.S. concert tour. Faced with humiliation, and perhaps also a threat to their pocketbook, the orchestra caved in and hired a female member, changing a long-standing but dishonorable practice.

Such pressure could not have been exercised effectively by the U.S. government. Aside from diplomacy, which government has a clean record on gender discrimination? Prime Minister Morarji Desai of India told me once that America's demand that India not acquire nuclear weapons was like "a drunk telling others to keep away from a single glass of wine." On the other hand, if an anti-nuclear NGO was telling *all* to keep away from nuclear weapons, it would at least have moral integrity and therefore plausibility.

The active encouragement of NGOs that militate against the offending countries on human rights appears, then, to be a superior policy to the use of embargoes. This would appear to be true also, as I shall argue below, when sanctions in regard to specific products, using unacceptable methods of production, are considered.

Sanctions for Not Meeting Preconditions
for Trade in Specific Products

Embargoes relate to all trade and are therefore a mega-weapon. By contrast, demands such as that certain labor standards be met in manufacture or else products using the proscribed processes would be denied market access relate only to specific products. These demands are of a different character on another important dimension: they are inevitably mixed up with protectionism in a way that makes their credibility and appropriateness suspect.

While one cannot altogether rule out some lobbies being interested in embargoing Chinese exports simply so as to protect themselves from Chinese competition, rather than because of their massive violations of human rights nationwide, it is hard to say that human rights activists are driven by competitive considerations. Even were this true for China, it is palpably fantastic to assert this for the agitations against South Africa earlier and against Myanmar now.

When it comes to specific products being subjected to sanctions because they do not meet labor standards, we do run right into the question of competitiveness considerations as important drivers, as I discussed in Chapter 10. As noted there, the demands for labor standards abroad come from two sets of motivations: the egoistical or self-serving ones, where the lower standards abroad are deplored because they are believed to make for lower costs abroad and hence to lead to greater competitiveness of foreign producers, and the altruistic ones, where the motivation is simply solidarity with workers abroad, an expression of trans-border moral empathy and obligation.

It is useful to distinguish between these two motivations even though a single individual or group may have both objectives. One cannot rule out, however, that some who are egoistic in their demands are strategically adopting the altruistic rhetoric in their lobbying efforts. The development economist T. N. Srinivasan has suggested, somewhat cynically, that if unions were truly altruistic about workers abroad, they would be agitating for their immigration to work alongside them, with the standards that they themselves enjoy; but the unions have often been opposed to immigration. At best, therefore, the altruism they express is a constrained one: it must be pursued in a way that will not hurt their own welfare and in fact even promote it (while hurting the employment of the workers abroad) if it reduces competition!

The labor economist Alan Krueger has argued—based on statistical analysis of the constituency characteristics of congressmen who sponsored the Harkin bill on deterring the use of child labor—that constituencies with a greater share of workers likely to suffer from increased competition were less likely to have sponsors, and that this suggests that they do not have egoistical, protectionist motives. But this analysis basically ignores the central fact that, with misleading and persistent propagation of the view that all child labor is automatically exploitative, the debate has been cleverly presented by those seeking relief from competition as one that equally derives from overriding morality. It is as if anti-abortion groups saturated the media with pictures of aborted fetuses to distort and define the debate on abortion rights, to the exclusion of the nuances that are at the heart of the debate. A statistical analysis of congressmen's sponsorship without going beyond the veil to ask pointedly whether their moral concerns have themselves been the result of clever lobbying by labor and other groups worried about competitiveness is to miss the point, since the objective is precisely to investigate whether protectionism is playing a principal role in their sponsorship. Just as Sherlock Holmes asked why the dog didn't bark, here we must ask why these congressmen acquired this particular moral concern and why that concern has taken the form of trade sanctions, which, if they kick in, would restrict imports and help U.S. firms to compete better.

Nonetheless, there is little doubt that many activists do act out of altruistic motives and have little sympathy for competitiveness outcomes. But the substantial intrusion of protectionist motivation makes the use of trade sanctions less than credible as a tool to be used in advancing labor standards: after all, the public policy scene is marked far too often by lobbies claiming social good while advancing their own self-serving agendas. Since labor standards are typically asserted to be lower in the poor countries, whose exports of labor-intensive and agricultural goods are usually the ones that protectionists in the rich countries are concerned about, it is inevitable that their governments tend to see attempts at linking trade access to labor standards as daggers aimed at their exports.

If you think about it, the unions in the poor countries face a lose-lose situation if trade sanctions are used as a tool. If higher standards are implemented and raise the cost of production (as several would), then exports and jobs will be adversely affected in the marketplace. But if they are not implemented, then trade sanctions will kick in—that is, exports will be undermined by induced protection. Either way, exports are at risk. But look at the matter from the viewpoint of the unions in the rich countries: they face a win-win situation as far as *their* jobs are concerned.

This seems to me to be the essential reason why the efforts of the AFL-CIO (and the ICFTU) to insert the Social Clause into the WTO have failed to gather the support of the Indian unions. Many unions from other poor countries support the AFL-CIO efforts because they want solidarity from the organized unions in the United States in their struggle to win civil and political rights, including the right to organize. The economic aspects that threaten their jobs are far less important to them than the fight for their rights. But the Indian unions already enjoy these civil and political rights; for them, the economic implications of specific tools such as trade sanctions, as desired by the AFL-CIO, are far more important, just as they are for the AFL-CIO, which also can focus only on economic aspects. And trade sanctions create conflicting and opposed consequences for the two sets of unions.

Then again, the poor countries see sanctions being used to deny market access as an asymmetric tool that will likely affect the poor countries and spare the rich ones. They are not paranoid. Legal standing to bring cases is available only to governments in trade institutions, such as the WTO, where the Social Clause is desired. It is improbable that the poor countries would be able to take the United States to the WTO Dispute Settlement Mechanism and succeed in getting trade sanctions authorized against this country for violating standards the way it can happen the other way around. Hegemonic powers are protected by the fact that retaliation for such behavior can occur on other dimensions such as aid and preferential market access through free trade agreements and many other policy instruments of punishment and inducement. It is interesting, therefore, that while, as I remarked in Chapter 11 on the environment, the United States in effect won the right to impose on foreign nations the use of turtle-excluding devices as a way of fishing for shrimp in the oceans, no case has yet been filed against the United States by any nation saying that the same ruling fully justifies the wholesale exclusion of any energy-using U.S. exports because the United States has failed to sign the Kyoto Protocol, and the United States can safely assume that none will be filed.

But even if there was to be symmetry between big and small countries on the willingness to file such cases (as against more conventional cases involving, say, the legitimacy of taxes and anti-dumping actions), the poor countries are handicapped in imposing retaliatory trade tariffs against the big countries, which may lose a case but not change their offending laws and actions. Why? Simply because the small countries feel that by restricting imports they will impose more cost on themselves than they will on the big offending nations, so the trade retaliation will be like shooting yourself in the foot while annoying your adversary only insofar as the shooting makes for a foul air for some fleeting moments.

True, these asymmetries obtain in regard to the enforcement of conventional agreements of the WTO. They are unavoidable. But that is precisely why the poor countries do not wish to yield to the pressure from the bigger of the rich countries, reflecting their domestic lobbying pressures, to expand the scope of the WTO to include yet other areas, essentially unrelated to trade, simply because the use of trade sanctions (enforced through the Dispute Settlement Mechanism) will kick in.

Some of the critics have also remarked that the narrowing down of the labor standards linkage demands to the core labor rights set out in Chapter 12 is no help to the poor countries. They are simply too broad; particularly because trade sanctions can follow, the poor countries feel they are signing on to potential trouble. I argued in Chapters 10 and 12 how the right to unionize, for instance, can be interpreted at different levels. If all that was proscribed was the killing of labor union organizers or their dismissal from employment, that would be specific enough and would probably get a consensus. But the right to organize is critically affected by the right to strike, without which unions are not effective even if they are allowed. It is also qualified by exceptions for "essential" services, which are variously defined by different countries in regard to both industries and what is allowed in lieu of strikes.

Recall that many labor and human rights lawyers and activists in the United States itself have complained that the relative emasculation of the ability to strike in the United States implies that, in the words of the earlier-cited Human Rights Watch report, millions of workers are denied the right to unionize effectively in the country. In fact, considering how my own university, like many other liberal educational institutions in the United States, actively prevents unionization of the campus staff, and noting that there are many reported cases of routine discouragement of union formation, one must admit that the United States is in violation of the right to unionize. It could be plausibly argued that wherever unions do not exist—and less than 12 percent of the U.S. labor force is unionized in the private sector—and there have been efforts at unionization, there is prima facie evidence that the right to organize has been curtailed. And yet this would not be acceptable to the United States, one can be sure.

If there were a Social Clause on the core labor rights, with its broad and generic language, it would then permit other nations to exclude products made in the United States on the grounds that it is not honoring the right to unionize. Would the ability of the United States to define the specifics of its own labor laws then be subject to the specific interpretations applied to these broad concepts, such as the right to unionize, by the members of the WTO Appellate Body? It sounds like a prescription for chaos and ruination of the WTO itself. But that is because I used the example of the United States.

However, nearly all the poor nations lack America's clout, so they feel apprehensive that they will be subjected to all sorts of cases, reflecting domestic protectionist pressures abroad, for violation of these broadly defined, indeed undefined, obligations in the Social Clause. What would prevent cases being filed against the export processing zones of poor countries where the right to unionize is restricted because of restrictions on strikes in some ways (e.g., India allows for labor rights but not the right to organize wildcat strikes, a provision that applies to "essential" industries, just as the United States imposes restrictions on strikes in what it defines as essential industries such as airlines)?

Labor legislation typically runs into thousands of pages in virtually every rich country, and participants in the domestic political process debate and define these specifics against the constitutional background of broadly defined rights. To believe that the WTO can be endowed with undefined rights, much the way the constitution of a nation or a deeply integrating union such as the EU does, and then its members should be subject to sanctions depending on how these undefined obligations are interpreted in regard to specific practices by an unelected body of judges, is startling, to say the least. It certainly raises fears among the poor nations, which expect that, particularly given the focus on them by the union activists, they will be the ones at the receiving end of cases brought under the Social Clause.

The sheer inability of a trade institution, especially one with a severely limited budget, to handle such complex social issues also needs to be underlined. Often the proponents of the Social Clause refer to the "precedent" established by the fact that the GATT, the WTO's predecessor, included from the time of its founding a provision for exclusion from market access for prison-made products. But that provision is indicative instead of what is wrong with the entire approach of having a trade institution deal with this type of subject. Can anyone seriously maintain that this proscription makes any sense when in countries such as the United States prisoners are typically engaged in work producing a multitude of products, not just car plates? Actually, that is a *good* thing. Today, we *want* prisoners to work rather than to be simply incarcerated. We just do not want gulag conditions. Also, with prisons being run by private corporations in the United States, we have prisoners working without minimum wages and under conditions of forced labor; we need to discuss and define what safeguards must be placed to ensure that prison labor meets minimum labor standards. The WTO is hardly the place to discuss these complex questions, but the ILO is (because it is the special agency set up to discuss precisely such issues in all their complexity and to develop norms in regard thereto, and does so with active participation from unions, employers and governments). These complexities must be addressed, and narrow specifics set out and agreed to, *before* sanctions are sought through inclusion of these matters as preconditions for market access in trade treaties and institutions.

Again, trade often accounts for a tiny fraction of the sales of products made with offending processes such as the use of child labor. Only 5 percent of the output of child labor is estimated to enter trade, so trade sanctions are not even an appropriately targeted policy. To return to prison labor, nearly all of the output produced these days in prisons worldwide is for sale in domestic markets, so what use is a GATT provision if your real aim is to accelerate the removal of prison labor?

But if the Social Clause at the WTO is inappropriate, does it not make sense nonetheless to reach a compromise with the labor lobbies and to get them off one's back by inserting into trade treaties the simpler provision that each country uphold its own labor laws, and that standards should not be revised downward in order to gain competitive advantage? This is the way in which the U.S. Congress has proceeded in its bilateral free trade agreements recently; it is also what has been incorporated in the latest fast-track legislation enabling the president to negotiate trade agreements and offer them to the Congress for approval on a straight up-or-down vote without amendments.

True, this compromise seems quite innocuous. But there are three serious problems with it. First, the unions clearly see it as a foot in the door. They are already escalating their demands in the Central American free trade agreement negotiations that these countries *raise* their standards, not just uphold them. Second, the revision of standards down or up is something that should be a result of national decisions reached democratically in light of domestic evaluations of what is good or bad for the society. Standards may well have been set at levels that are later seen to be unaffordable; they may also be seen as less important compared to newly perceived needs elsewhere. The setting of social standards, like most legislation, is a ceaselessly interactive process of experimentation and change, undertaken against the backdrop of ideas and practices that have domestic and international salience. Restrictions on the flexibility of standards setting, even if hedged by safeguards, are not a good idea compared to dialogue and persuasion, which are certainly possible in most countries today. Third, as discussed in Chapter 12, the laws and standards on the books of most countries, and certainly the poor ones, have been enacted without any intention to implement them. So they are often feel-good statements, in effect, and therefore are pitched so high as to make it ridiculous to say that they must be implemented or else sanctions, whether trade or financial, will be applied.

But if sanctions seem to raise these objections as a way of advancing desired standards in the manufacture of imported products, how should we assess the usual objection that unless sanctions are imposed we cannot get anything done—that sanctions have teeth, whereas moral suasion and exhortations do not, and that the WTO has teeth and the ILO does not because the former can use trade sanctions, whereas the latter cannot?

I think that this is the same as saying that the Pope has no troops. Surely one does not need the rack to spread Christianity. And if you do use it, the chances are great that, like Spain's Jews who broke under torture and converted but returned to Judaism in later decades, many will return to the fold when the tyrant is gone. If your cause is morally appealing, diffusion has great potential today, whereas coercion, particularly coming from the rich and mighty who fear for their pocketbooks rather than for your soul, is hardly likely to gain true converts.

Indeed, we must remember that God gave us not just teeth but also a tongue. And a good tongue-lashing on a moral cause is more likely to work today than a bite. Recall that, with NGOs and CNN, we have the possibility now of using shame and embarrassment to great advantage. In various and varying ways, these techniques can unleash what I have called the Dracula effect: expose evil to sunlight and it will shrivel up and die.[3] I must confess that I have been surprised at the skepticism that some of my friends in the NGO community display toward the efficacy of methods that do not use trade sanctions; it seems ironic that the activists should underestimate the power of their own activities to produce a better world.

I argued earlier that the ILO is the agency that can address meaningfully these questions, in all their complexity. But it is also the agency that can provide an objective and impartial review of a member country's practices and laws in regard to labor standards. It already has a Committee of Experts on the Application of Conventions and Recommendations, whose distinguished members monitor annually the compliance of member states with the conventions that they have ratified, while also taking up (one at a time) individual conventions and the examining of member states' conformity to them regardless of ratification. The Trade Policy Review Mechanism at the WTO does pretty much the same thing, taking up a few member countries at a time and examining the entire gamut of their trade policies. These reviews have provided impartial, objective, and comprehensive views of a country's policies. They have proven to be invaluable documents that NGOs and others have been able to turn to in order to provide substance to their agitations.

This is because these reviews, unlike the reviews of human rights issued by the U.S. State Department, which conveniently omits the violations within the United States itself, are considered to be truly objective: they apply universally to all nations, playing no favorites. This is in fact also the practice of the best human rights NGOs: Human Rights Watch will not turn a blind eye toward abuses of workers' rights in the United States and focus only on Guatemala and China. We can confidently expect the ILO evaluations to look at the sweatshops in the garment district of New York and at the virtual slavery among some of the migrant labor in the southern United States as much as it documents the prevalence of child labor in hazardous occupations such as rug making in Pakistan and glass making in India.

But the conventions or codes on specific practices that suitable agencies such as the ILO evolve are also likely today to translate in democratic countries into domestic legislation that domestic NGOs can help to monitor and enforce. And, in an interesting development that has gone unnoticed by the media in the rich countries, judicial activism has begun to translate these norms and conventions into effective domestic law. This new trend can be traced to what legal activists call the Bangalore Principles. In 1988, a colloquium was organized by the Commonwealth Secretariat on the Domestic Application of International Human Rights Norms under the chairmanship of the chief justice of India (P. N. Bhagwati), with the participants including Ruth Bader Ginsburg (now on the U.S. Supreme Court), Anthony Lester (a leading human rights lawyer in England), and Michael Kirby (an Australian judge). In their communiqué, they expounded principles that have had a huge impact on judicial thinking worldwide. They cited and approved the "growing tendency for national courts to have regard to [evolving] international norms for the purpose of deciding cases where the domestic law— whether constitutional, statute or common law—is uncertain or incomplete." They proceeded to define principles that should guide the judiciary, including an admonition that "this process must fully take into account local laws, traditions, circumstances and needs."[4]

Conservative judges will indeed regard this development with alarm. In fact, when I once met Antonin Scalia of the U.S. Supreme Court, arguably the most effective conservative voice on the Court today, at Vice President Al Gore's dinner for the Indian prime minister Atal Bihari Vajpayee, I was carrying my name on the lapel of my jacket. Justice Scalia took one look at my name and asked, "Do you know Justice Bhagwati?" I said, "Yes, he happens to be my brother," at which point he exclaimed, "Good grief, he is to the left of Brennan," a strong liberal voice on the U.S. Supreme Court!

I am entirely in favor of the Bangalore Principles because the judicial activism they propose and the safeguards for its appropriate practice they define represent an ideal way to set out to work with the norms that are evolving. They are grounded in domestic democratic governance. They therefore have legitimacy and robustness.

By contrast, the outburst of cases brought by activists in the United States since 1980 using the 1789 Alien Torts Act, under which aliens can even sue aliens in the U.S. courts for a tort committed in violation of international law, is exactly the wrong way to go.[5] It amounts to judicial activism being imposed on others outside the United States. It has no legitimacy since no one recognizes U.S. courts' self-asserted right to such universal jurisdiction, unlike in the cases where such universal jurisdiction is negotiated and granted to, say, the International Criminal Court for war crimes *or* where there is a bilateral treaty conferring mutual jurisdiction of this kind to each other's courts.

Not surprisingly, the latter has been denounced by many thoughtful critics as judicial imperialism, and even the most distinguished non-American human rights lawyers that I have talked to consider this to reflect the moral arrogance and hubris that Americans are far too often accused of. It also raises the question of whether U.S. activists and the judges who are admitting these cases, instead of throwing them out forthwith, would allow U.S. nationals to be sued by other U.S. nationals in Indonesian or Indian courts when these countries have literally nothing to do with the United States in the matter at hand.

To conclude: the linkage of labor standards (and human rights) to market access to trade is generally not an appropriate way to proceed, whether one thinks of embargoes or manufacturing methods for specific products.[6] The use of moral suasion and the strengthening of the review and monitoring functions of the appropriate international agencies that have been created to address these agendas with nuance and sophistication, and even the increased probability that democratic politics and judicial activism will translate international norms into effective domestic legislation or enforcement with all the required nuances and with attention to local traditions and circumstances, offer greater promise as ways of accelerating the achievement of these social objectives.

18

Managing Transitions: Optimal, Not Maximal, Speed

E ven though globalization is beneficial, an important question remains: how quickly should an economy move toward increased integration into the world economy? It is tempting to argue, as some influential reformers proposed in Russia, that a program aimed at extremely rapid transition is the answer. The consequences in that case were severe and it took Russia years, and much dislocation and anguish, to get back on track. Since such "shock therapy" had presumably worked in Poland, and was being tried in Russia because of that success, with encouragement from the same foreign advisers, led by the economist Jeffrey Sachs, who advocated its use in Poland, I wryly remarked at the time that Poland, courtesy of Sachs, had finally managed to repay Russia for all the trouble that Russia had visited upon Poland in the past!

The debate over the speed of economic reform often becomes an angry exchange of analogies. One side claims that you cannot cross a chasm in two leaps. The other side retorts that you cannot cross it in one leap either unless you are Indiana Jones, so you should instead drop a bridge.[1] Then again, shock therapists argue, if you want to cut a dog's tail, you do it with one slash of the knife, not bit by bit. The gradualists reply that you train a dog by setting incrementally escalating heights for him to jump. Or yet again, when the shock therapists say that you have to kick a door open, the gradualists retort that if you do, the door is likely to rebound shut, whereas a gentle pressure on the door is certain to succeed in opening it wide.

Today, the shock therapists have retreated, given the havoc that many feel that they wreaked in Russia. Few now share the enthusiastic, almost technocratic belief that equates full speed ahead with sensibly paced reform policies. In fact, if one looks back at the great economists in the past, they have uniformly been against shock therapy. Adam Smith, whose credentials on the subjects of freeing trade and of the use of markets are naturally indisputable, wrote in *The Wealth of Nations:*

> It may sometimes be a matter of deliberation, how far, or in what manner it is proper to restore the free importation of foreign goods . . . when particular manufacturers, by means of high duties or prohibitions upon all foreign goods which come into competition with them, have been so far extended as to employ a great multitude of hands. Humanity may in this case require that freedom of trade should be restored only by slow graduations, and with a good deal of reserve and circumspection.[2]

In a similar spirit, Keynes wrote in 1933 of the danger of haste, citing, ironically enough, the example of Russia moving *toward* socialism:

> Paul Valery's aphorism is worth quoting—"Political conflicts distort and disturb the people's sense of distinction between matters of importance and matters of urgency." The economic transition of a society is a thing to be accomplished slowly. . . . We have a fearful example in Russia today of the evils of insane and unnecessary haste. The sacrifices and losses of transition will be vastly greater if the pace is forced. . . . For it is of the nature of economic processes to be rooted in time. A rapid transition will involve so much pure destruction of wealth that the new state of affairs will be, at first, worse than the old, and the grand experiment will be discredited.[3]

How Slow, How Fast?

When it comes to globalization, the transition question relates in the public domain to trade liberalization and to capital account liberalization (i.e., to the question of liberalizing the movements of capital). That the latter needs caution and careful preparation is now manifest; nothing needs to be added here to what was said at length in Chapter 13 on the perils of gung-ho financial capitalism.

But the question of trade liberalization merits some attention. Here the consequences of hasty liberalization are unlikely to be as disastrous as they are with freeing capital flows. Trade economists in the last half century have analyzed how circumstances can arise when a rapid shift to freer trade may be immiserizing rather than enriching. As it happens, however, these situations are not likely.

Economists generally argue that as trade liberalizes, consumers will gain from the lower prices of the imported goods, and this consumption gain is always ensured since it is extraordinarily unlikely that opening to trade will raise, rather than reduce, domestic prices of imported goods. True, a monopoly may be created through a big foreign firm dominating a small domestic market. But open trade means that higher monopolistic prices cannot be maintained by the big firm against cheaper imports. In fact, all evidence shows that when markets are closed and only domestic producers are allowed to exist, the small markets will support very few firms, occasionally just one, and that such protectionist policies are themselves the cause of monopoly. Trade is in fact the best antidote to monopoly, especially in developing countries!

But with the freeing of trade, lower prices may lead to unemployment in the import-competing industries. The economist Joseph Stiglitz, a critic of globalization, has argued that the developing countries have very large rates of unemployment, so we would wind up adding to this unemployment with the freeing of trade. The human rights activists also focus on the human rights of workers in the import-competing industries being violated by their being thrown into unemployment.

But both objections are inappropriate. Even if the workers who are fired happen to get into the pool of the unemployed, others who were unemployed would get jobs in the exporting sectors, which would expand with the freeing of trade. Thus the overall rate of unemployment could remain unchanged, some workers losing jobs and others gaining them. So there would be no loss of national income from a net increase in overall unemployment, and there is a production gain—a technical phrase used by economists to signify that resources have moved away from less efficient sectors and increased in the more efficient sectors. The human rights activists must also confront the fact that while the human rights of those who lose jobs are violated, the human rights of those who get jobs are enhanced. But even if unemployment were to increase, that would only produce a loss of income that must still be put against the gains to consumers, so the net effect of the trade liberalization can still be favorable.

Nonetheless, very rapid and large-scale trade liberalization could backfire politically, as workers in import competing industries are likely to mobilize against the adjustment being imposed on them. Politicians in democratic countries are also unlikely to be impervious to their complaints, especially as those who lose are more likely to vote to punish you than those who win are likely to reward you, an asymmetry that seems to be fairly common.

This is why the pace at which trade liberalization takes place is likely to be higher the greater the economic prosperity and state of overall employment when the liberalization is attempted. Trade liberalization therefore has traditionally proceeded faster in times of prosperity than in times of distress. Equally, the more the politicians are able to provide adjustment programs to take special care of those who might be displaced in import-competing industries by trade liberalization, the less difficult it has been to secure political consent for trade liberalization, as shown by the numerous adjustment assistance programs that have been included in virtually every piece of trade legislation in the United States in recent years, including the fast-track legislation of 2002 under the current Bush administration.[4]

Bretton Woods Conditionality: Excessively Rapid Opening?

It is often alleged that the World Bank and the IMF, the twin Bretton Woods institutions that dispense long-run aid and short-run stabilization assistance, respectively, to member countries, require an excessively rapid shift to trade liberalization as part of the conditionality that goes with the provision of funds. But the matter is far more complex than the allegation, and the reality is far more benign.

To start with, the conditionalities of the two institutions used to be contradictory, rather than mutually reinforcing, on trade liberalization. When a country comes to the IMF for assistance, it is usually in a balance-of-payments crisis, which requires a stabilization program. This means that more revenues help to relieve the pressure on resources that is reflected in the balance-of-payments difficulties. This implies that tariffs that raise revenues will be seen as a help, not as a hindrance, at least in the short-run responses to the immediate crisis. Therefore, the IMF has traditionally been keen not to reduce trade tariffs (except when a serious tax alternative has been implemented that is more efficient) because of the fear that this may lead to loss of revenue at a time when every dollar collected counts. The World Bank, on the other hand, has usually pushed for tariff reduction during a crisis on the grounds that a crisis is a good time to get governments to see the folly of their ways and to adopt long-term reforms. The result has been cross-conditionality, with the Bank favoring tariff reductions while the IMF cautions against them.

The fear of losing revenues when tariffs are reduced is not justified, of course, if the duties are so high that they are avoided or evaded in such a significant way that reducing duties may have a large response and revenues may actually rise. This is a situation where economists say that the elasticity of response exceeds unity. In the case of tariffs, evasion takes the form of outright smuggling through porous borders or bribing customs officials to accept faked invoices. On the other hand, avoidance takes the form of substituting imports that are burdened with higher duties with those that carry lower duties. An excellent example is when, faced with high U.S. import duties on jackets, South Korean exporters proceeded to take the jackets apart at the sleeves, exporting sleeves at zero duty and the remaining "vest" at low duties, and then assembling the two back into jackets in Manhattan's garment district.

In fact, this is what the debate over so-called supply-side economics has been. The supply-siders, who came to prominence in the Reagan administration, believed in the responsiveness of the economic system to incentives, the way all good economists do. They were bad economists because they typically assumed that the response would be so large that policy makers could cut taxes and get more revenues; this led to irresponsible policies that fed deficits that were brought under control only later, in the Clinton administration. The deficits are now being revived under a renewed acceptance of the supply-side make-believe economics that the elder Bush once decried as "voodoo economics."

On trade liberalization's revenue effects, until the tariff cuts brought the developing countries to tariff levels on industrial products that are still higher than the average industrial tariffs in the rich countries but are much lower than they used to be, there was reason to believe that the tariffs were so high, and hence the attendant evasion and avoidance were so great, that tariff reduction would result in less than a one-to-one reduction in revenue collected, and in some instances even in an increase in revenue, unlike the IMF's worst fears. The economists Lants Pritchett and Geeta Sethi examined the experience of Jamaica, Kenya, and Pakistan on their tariff reductions and found that revenues often fell substantially less than tariff rates did.[5] Part of the reason, of course, was that very high tariff levels are usually prohibitive and kill imports, so that bringing them down into the range where imports materialize again is a surefire way to increase revenues from the tariff reform. Yet another reason is that, in practice, the tariff rates being reduced are subject to exemptions that make the reductions effectively less than what they appear to be.

But one must still ask whether the trade liberalization being advocated by the World Bank—this happened in the 1980s once many academic research projects had established persuasively that protectionist trade policies were harmful to one's health (Chapter 5)—was being forced on the client states at a harmful speed. This criticism sounds persuasive but is not.

For one thing, through much of the postwar period the developing countries were treated with kid gloves on trade liberalization because of the pervasive doctrine of infant industry protection and the notion that the benefits of open trade did not apply to countries that were behind the curve in development. These countries often had balance-of-payments difficulties, and these, in turn, were attributed wrongly at the time to their underdevelopment; this meant that trade liberalization was not supposed to be beneficial to the developing countries. Both these doctrines were in fact built into the GATT's articles, giving the developing countries virtually blanket exemptions from any real obligations. Then again, these countries were too poor to be attractive as markets to corporate interests; they were thus permitted to keep their markets closed even as the rich countries opened theirs through successive rounds of multilateral trade liberalization in the postwar years.

But, coming to the latter 1980s and 1990s, when the thinking on the benefits of trade liberalization had changed and some developing countries were also developed enough to be of interest to the exporting corporations of the rich countries, and even the IMF (whose conditionality related primarily to macroeconomic policies rather than to trade policies) was more accommodating on the need for trade liberalization, was trade liberalization pushed too fast under conditionality by the World Bank? There is no doubt that there was pressure insofar as funds are rarely given without conditionality, and conditionality must embody the dominant thinking of the time. But we must still ask:

- To what extent was the pressure welcomed by the reformers within the ranks of these governments?
- Where it was not welcome, how difficult was it to resist the pressure?
- Were reversals allowed when political difficulties or unanticipated economic complications arose down the road?

Welcome Pressure

Occasionally the pressure was seen as a desirable input into the policy process by the reformers, as a way in which the margin might shift in the political balance of forces toward the reformers. Perhaps the most telling example of such foreign pressure, or *gaiatsu,* as the Japanese call it, has been the pressure put on Japan to ensure that the openness was accompanied by successful penetration of the Japanese market by American exporters. In that instance, the United States pushed for changes in retail distribution system laws that made it difficult to open big stores— a move that happened to coincide with the view of many Japanese commentators themselves that the system made retail distribution inefficient and costly. Then again, in India, where successive governments had stoutly held on to autarkic policies, with modest reforms in the 1980s, the reformers who spearheaded the more robust trade liberalization and other reforms beginning in 1991, when a balance-of-payments crisis forced India into borrowing from the Bretton Woods institutions, were in sync with the conditionality in favor of these changes. Domestic critics charged both that the trade liberalization was bad and that the pace of liberalization was too fast, but the reformers disagreed. Besides, the sustained acceleration in the country's performance, and hence the success in its attack on poverty, proved the reformers right.

Resistance or Non-Compliance

It is again simplistic to assert that the conditionality from the Bretton Woods institutions is enforced without any give. In truth, most nations realize that the World Bank (not the IMF) is judged mainly by how much it spends. If the World Bank ends the year without lending for development, it is a failure. That creates a dilemma: if the Bank holds up spending because conditionality is not accepted or complied with, then it fails to spend; if it spends without adequate compliance, then it fails to enforce conditionality, which it believes is needed for good use of the funds. It is a commonplace observation among those who know the Bank that this has effectively diluted the Bank's ability to force conditionality on its client states.

The wide net cast by the World Bank, where countless things are looked at (including prices charged, subsidies paid, and a whole range of policies), also enables a country to say: "Look, on trade liberalization, we are running into political opposition, so we cannot comply. But we will raise the cost of electricity this year, privatize a loss-making public sector firm, and reduce administrative bottlenecks in licensing new investments." The Bank jumps at such outs. The very proliferation of conditionalities, now extending to governance, makes non-compliance in key areas such as trade liberalization a distinct possibility.

Why, then, do splendid economists such as Stiglitz, who was senior vice president of the World Bank, think of conditionality as stifling, as if what is written is what is done? I suspect that this is because they misinterpret as a huge influence the stroking that they receive when they visit these client countries. They are met with excessive courtesy and protocol at the airport, stay in penthouse executive suites, meet with prime ministers and presidents, and wind up feeling that they are more important than they really are. The notion that these countries are playing the game and manipulating them because they carry bags of cash is beyond the egos that rise like helium-filled balloons in the higher-level echelons of the Bretton Woods institutions.

Policy Reversals

Then again, remember the old adage: you can catch a tiger by the tail and not be able to let go. Once the World Bank lends to a country, it often takes a huge amount of non-compliance and recalcitrance, and the displeasure of Washington for sure, to turn the tap off. The spigot was kept open for Russia despite many disappointments on conditionality. The IMF's continuing support for Argentina during the years of the currency board, which the finance minister, Domingo Cavallo, persisted with despite advice to the contrary from the IMF and many others, is yet another example.

But a more detailed examination by my student Ravi Yatawara of the IMF's record over several years also shows that several policy reversals have occurred, with trade liberalization suspended or turned back as difficulties appeared.[6] But this is not surprising. In fact, the wisdom of allowing policy reversals when a policy runs into unanticipated problems has even been formally built into the working of leading international institutions. Thus the GATT's architects, who included distinguished economists such as James Meade, who later won the Nobel prize, created Article 19 precisely to allow for reversal of negotiated trade liberalization if it runs into rough weather.

Since no one can really anticipate fully what difficulties may materialize, and since the pace of liberalization may turn out unexpectedly to be too swift, such safeguards and reversals are already in the policy domain, and the Bretton Woods institutions are no striking exception in practice. Good sense in these matters is commonplace, since occasionally misjudgments are made and course corrections have to be undertaken. Perhaps the most dramatic such instance was the IMF's reversal of its wrongheaded deflationary prescription in the East Asian crisis—recall Chapter 12—when it realized that it had been counterproductive.

This reality also speaks to the common criticism that the Bretton Woods institutions have been guilty of hawking the doctrine that "one size fits all." This is a silly critique. After all, there is no escape from the need to decide whether you are going to wear shoes or go barefoot. So you must make up your mind whether you are going to move in the direction of freeing trade or move backward into further protection. And once you have decided, as you should, that freeing trade is the option you want, then the shoe sizes will inevitably vary, no matter what the written word on conditionality or your original intentions if you were liberalizing trade on your own initiative (as is often the case).

When I was young, there was a fierce debate in development economics between those who wanted balanced growth and those who wanted unbalanced growth. The first group, led by Paul Rosenstein-Rodan, prescribed that governments should try to balance investment in several industries, carefully calculating how much each would buy from the others, so that each industry was ensured demand and spared the situation of excess production. The latter group, led by Albert Hirschman, argued instead that unbalanced investment would produce imbalances that would turn into "creative disequilibria," spurring investments and accelerating growth. I told Hirschman that the war between the two groups was entirely unnecessary; he did not have to worry, since he would always win. Why? Because even if you started with a plan for balanced growth, it would soon become unbalanced as it hit the ground. In the same vein, let me recall the bachelor's cookbook of yesteryear when bachelors were incompetent cooks. Its recipe for scrambling eggs was just one line: "Start frying an egg."

What About the WTO?

A final word about the WTO. The WTO does not give cash. Its director general, Supachai Panitchpakdi, is more like the Pope, working by moral suasion; unlike the Pope, he does not even have the funny little fellows with spears outside the WTO building on the shores of Lake Geneva. In what sense, then, could one argue that the WTO pushes for excessively speedy trade liberalization? As it happens, the WTO itself does not.

The appropriate question is: do the negotiating rich countries manage to impose on the negotiating poor countries haste in the trade liberalization that is negotiated? The answer has to be yes, in the sense that a concerted negotiation will put pressure on all negotiating members to make concessions so that the negotiation is a success. Witness the concessions that are beginning to be wrung out of a very reluctant EU on agricultural subsidies and tariffs as the Doha Round winds its way forward. In the end, however, whatever the pressures applied and felt, both rich and poor countries can go only so fast, reflecting political difficulties at either end. In any event, recall that multilateral trade liberalization over nearly six decades has left the average protection levels higher in the poor countries—so the pressure on the poor countries to abandon their trade barriers cannot have been so fierce!

The real problem with pressure to speed up liberalization arises in a different way at the WTO. The conditions negotiated for WTO entry can witness real toughness by lobbies seeking market access to the countries seeking membership. In the case of both China and Russia, the United States has allowed domestic lobbies in the financial sector to push

for excessively rapid opening of markets prior to WTO entry. U.S. influence in this regard has been somewhat deplorable; what we are dealing
with here is the clout of what I have called in Chapter 13 the Wall Street–
Treasury complex.

Particularly onerous problems arise for the poor countries, in my
view, not over opening their markets through trade concessions, but when
the pressures are applied on them to consent to extraneous and harmful
demands aimed at appeasing the domestic lobbies in the rich countries
on trade-unrelated issues such as intellectual property protection and
labor issues, matters that I have discussed fully in Chapters 12 and 10,
respectively.

V

In Conclusion

19

And So, Let Us Begin Anew

The German poet Rainer Maria Rilke wrote:

> All of you undisturbed cities,
> haven't you ever longed for the Enemy?

He sought the force that would break the routine of our bourgeois lives, the "husk that blocks anything fresh from coming in." But he searched within:

> I live my life in growing orbits
> which move out over the things of the world.
> Perhaps I can never achieve the last,
> but that will be my attempt.
>
> I am circling around God, around the ancient tower,
> and I have been circling for a thousand years,
> and I still don't know if I am a falcon, or a storm,
> or a great song.[1]

The critics of globalization think of themselves as breaking the husk too: they seek to wake us from what they see as our complacency and to disturb our comfort with the process of globalization. But they would replace Rilke's life in "growing orbits," a spiritual pilgrimage into our inner space, with a secular journey into the outer space of public action.

Public action, however, will not succeed unless it reflects not only passions but also reason. Reason and analysis require that we abandon the conviction that globalization lacks a human face, an assertion that is tantamount to a false alarm, and embrace the view that it *has* one. Public action must reflect that change in assessment, and I have sketched here the elements of such appropriate governance. The rest is up to the reader.

Afterword

*I*n Defense of Globalization was written against the background of the massive demonstrations that erupted in Seattle in November 1999 when the World Trade Organization (WTO) was meeting to launch a new Round of multilateral Trade Negotiations. If launched, the Seattle Round would have been the first under the auspices of the WTO as distinct from the seven Rounds that had been successfully concluded under GATT, the General Agreement on Tariffs and Trade, which was the predecessor of the WTO. The protests were about the alleged adverse social implications of the economic globalization that trade typified in the minds—or perhaps I should say the hearts—of many of the militating critics.

I believe that, by examining carefully and sympathetically the many worries in this regard, *In Defense of Globalization* successfully laid many of them to rest. But, while it managed to defuse these worries, we now have a more profound set of worries, not about the *social* implications of economic globalization, but about its *economic* implications.

These newly acute worries—I should say fears—have arisen with particular political salience in the larger, rich countries. Their workers and labor unions now show palpable fear that trade with the poor countries, and investment in them, undermines both economic prosperity in the rich countries and, more important, depresses their wages and working conditions—a fear that certainly was embraced in the November 2006 elections to the U.S. Congress where Democrats embracing these fears and making anti-trade noises were handily elected. *In Defense of Globalization* did not exactly ignore these concerns: Chapter 10 addressed these fears but not with the comprehensiveness that they now demand. They occupy a place in the pantheon of anti-globalization views that matches in importance that occupied by the critics who worry instead about social implications.

This Afterword, therefore, seeks to contrast and put into perspective the two different sets of critiques, so that the reader can situate *In Defense of Globalization* properly into the current context. It also brings into focus, and counters systematically, the recent writings on the subject by the prominent journalist Thomas Friedman and the Nobel Laureate economist Paul Samuelson that have unwittingly provided ammunition to those who fear the economic implications of globalization.

Two Critiques of Globalization

At the outset, I can do no better than to recall what Rabbi Hillel, who lived in the time of Herod, said: "If I am not for myself, then who will be for me? And when I am only for myself, what am I?" What the Rabbi was saying was that we have, or must have, both altruism and self-interest to define our lives. But, in truth, on this spectrum, few lie in the center but tend to gravitate toward one end or the other. And this is just what we find among the critics of globalization. Several are *altruistic*; they proceed from *empathy*, thinking that globalization is malign in its impact on humanity, on what might be called "social issues." But a large number are also proceeding instead from *self-interest*, actuated by *fear*. These include mainly the labor unions that fear their wages and standards will collapse with globalization, and others who fear that the overall prosperity of their nation is also at risk.

I find, far too often, that many who proceed from self-interest and fear also mask their concerns by claiming to be altruistic as well. Thus, one will often come across arguments from union leaders or some NGOs that protectionism of the rich countries is also beneficial to the poor countries, as when some opponents of NAFTA claim that freer trade between the United States and Mexico has hurt both countries and also the poor in each of them.[1] This makes them more comfortable, to be sure. But beyond exposing these arguments as specious so that our public policy discourse gets more informed as is necessary for a well-functioning democracy, the only thing one can suggest to those who advance them is to admit, with Rabbi Hillel, that the pursuit of self-interest is part of our nature, but that pretense at altruism, as distinct from actual altruism, should not be.

As it happens, both sets of critics are mistaken; and so let me treat each separately, starting briefly with the criticisms based on altruism and empathy, which I have addressed fully in this book, *In Defense of Globalization*, and then proceed to a more substantial discussion of the current arguments that are based instead on self-interest and fear.

Altruism and Empathy

In Defense of Globalization met with a huge response precisely because it uniquely addressed the "social impact" questions which the young students and the civil society groups were raising.[2] The book itself was prompted by the 1999 WTO Ministerial Meeting, which sank under the onslaught of massive disruptive demonstrations that were only matched by the Clinton Administration's lack of preparation to confront and contain the mayhem. As I debated civil society leaders, including Ralph Nader in the town hall, and appeared on the opening panel for NGOs (which had to be postponed to the afternoon because of a bomb threat) with Pascal Lamy, Clare Short, Charlene Barshefsky, Alec Erwin and other trade ministers, and then talked with the demonstrators on the streets, I felt that these were not people who were worried about whether free trade was good for aggregate GNP and prosperity or whether protection was more appropriate. Rather, they were concerned with what might be called the social implications of economic globalization. They were concerned, indeed were convinced, that globalization put us behind on several "citizens' issues" such as the environment, indigenous culture (à la President Evo Morales) and mainstream culture (à la Monsieur Bove), democracy, poverty in the poor countries, and child labor there as well. To use the phraseology that Bill Clinton, Gerhard Schroeder, and Tony Blair made fashionable, they claimed that *globalization lacks a human face*. But was this true?

In *Defense of Globalization* was precisely addressed to this overriding issue. Before analyzing this issue, however, I tried to understand what had brought about the remarkable growth of altruistic concerns, much of it from the idealistic young. I found the explanation largely in what I called the "inversion of Hume's concentric circles." David Hume and Adam Smith were both members of the Scottish Enlightenment. Both had written how distance diminished empathy. In a classic passage, quoted and discussed in *In Defense of Globalization*, Adam Smith had written in *The Theory of Moral Sentiments* in 1760 that a European man of sensibility would continue to snore through the loss of a hundred million Chinese in an earthquake "provided he never saw them," but "if he was to lose his little finger to-morrow, he would not sleep to-night."

David Hume had written of concentric circles of empathy, which declined as one went further from the center. Today, however, we have the death of distance; and television brings ever closer to us the hitherto-hidden pestilence, famine, and tragic afflictions of the countless in misery. At the same time, as the political scientist Robert Putnam has argued, there is increasing tendency for civic life to decline in communities, that Americans in particular no longer "bowl together." So, the outermost circle has become the innermost circle, whereas the innermost circle is now beginning to be the outermost circle. The idealist young therefore are agitated and animated by the distant afflictions that they witness close at hand today; and they cry out for solutions, which they often find in anti-globalization rhetoric and advocacy.

By looking at virtually every social concern I could lay my hands on, I argued that globalization, by and large, advanced these social agendas instead of handicapping them. In short, globalization *has* a human face. I can only illustrate with one compelling example the kind of argumentation and evidence that I marshaled to arrive at this startling conclusion: the reader has the entire book to judge for herself the case I build, patiently and without an ideological straitjacket, against the entire range of current anti-globalization critiques.

Thus, take the wage differential against women. Take the phenomenon that, for the same type of work and the same qualifications, a firm pays men more than women. Using Gary Becker's theory of price and prejudice, we may hypothesize that the willingness of firms to pay more for equally qualified men will begin to shrink once they face stiff international competition. So, in traded industries, you would see the wage differential closing faster than in non-traded industries. Lo and behold, that is just what two splendid women economists found to be the case in the United States over a long period. Globalization, in the shape of trade, was a force for good, not harm.

But take the differential in pay that comes, not at the level of the firm, but because women traditionally have been confined to jobs that pay less: like teaching and nursing. But even here, take the example of Japanese multinationals. In Japan the glass ceiling beyond which women cannot go used to be so low that women could barely stand up! One went to Japan and found that, in a land that produced the world's first great female novelist (Lady Murasaki in the eleventh century), today the women typically were either housewives or in jobs such as serving tea to male executives who did all of the talking and negotiating. When Japanese multinationals started going abroad in massive numbers in the late 1980s, the men, of course, remained executives. Their wives who lived in New York, Paris, Rome, and London, suddenly saw how Western men

treated their wives differently and how the women were upwardly mobile in business and other occupations. That turned them into powerful
agents of change when they returned. And so now we have had Madame
Ogata as the UN High Commissioner for Refugees, Madame Tanaka as
the Foreign Minister and many women getting into the Diet and also
rising in executive ranks. Japanese investment abroad was among the
phenomena that fostered the change in attitudes that led to the promotion of equality for Japanese women.[3]

Self-interest and Fear

If the concerns about globalization that proceed from altruism and empathy can be laid to rest, those arising from self-interest and fear are not
so easily dismissed, though they are even less grounded in objective reality. As the Russian proverb goes: fear has big eyes. But it also has deaf ears.

The fear of trade and multinationals today particularly afflicts the
rich countries, where many are afraid that economic prosperity is imperiled by trade with the poor countries. Additionally, the working classes
and the unions typically fear that their wages and standards are in peril
from trade with poor countries. But it was only a few decades ago that
the fear was rampant among the poor countries that were in such peril
from trade with the rich countries: how ironic this seems. A few economists and some cash-rich NGOs have worked hard to renew the fear
among the poor countries as well. Let me, therefore, urge the reader to
work through the extended analysis and empirical evidence that I have
produced, on the benefits of trade for prosperity in the poor countries
(Chapter 5 of my book), and on the need to discount the alleged adverse
effect of trade on wages and labor standards in the rich countries (in the
earlier cited Chapter 10). But let me add a few salient points here, on the
question of the relationship between trade and prosperity, while dealing with the question of wages and labor standards more robustly later.
I will also start with conventional worries; and then I will address worries (such as the fear of India and China) that have emerged in recent
years, reinforcing the old concerns, in regard to both overall prosperity
and wages.

1. *Prosperity from Trade.*   First, my colleague Professor Arvind
Panagariya has noted that, if one examines the growth and trade record
(where available) of rich and poor countries for nearly forty years in the
postwar period, you see a remarkable phenomenon. The "economic
miracle" countries which averaged a high annual growth rate of per capita
income at about 3 percent, also showed similar growth in their trade;

and the "economic debacle" countries that experienced negligible or even negative growth rates were also characterized by similarly dismal trade performance.[4] Now, this does not necessarily imply that trade led to growth instead of the other way around. Anyone who has studied the experience of developing countries in depth knows—and I know because I have participated in two major projects (one where I was a country co-author and one which I co-directed) in the 1960s and 1970s on the trade and development policies of several countries—the argument that growth happened independently of trade, which simply followed as a "trickle-down" effect of growth, is little short of crazy.[5] But this area does invite entry by crazy people, or people who are not crazy but act as if they were because the market incentives, as I argue below, are such today that they reward craziness.

Second, note that it is possible to observe periods, which may last over almost two decades in rare cases, where autarky and high growth rates may be observed together. But it is impossible to find cases where this has been a "sustainable" relationship over very long periods. The Soviet Union collapsed after making many economists, including me at one stage, believe that its autarky was no barrier. Well, just look at a chart on Soviet Russia's steadily declining growth rate in the face of huge investment rates.[6] You see a decline in productivity that must be at least partly attributed to a virtually closed economy and rigid central planning laced with massive restrictions on production and investment. After a huge spurt in the 1920s and 1930s, these ill-advised policies finally caught up with them.

Let me also recall a funny, and true, story about my Cambridge teacher Joan Robinson. In the mid-1960s, she and Gus Ranis of Yale, one a radical and the other a mainstream economist, were overheard agreeing that Korea was an economic miracle. How could this harmony have arisen? It turned out that she was thinking of North Korea whereas Ranis was talking about South Korea! Now, after over a quarter of a century, we know who was right: North Korea simply failed to sustain its high growth rate. Autarky, and total lack of political and economic freedoms, turned the short-run miracle into a debacle.[7]

Third, much is made these days of the cliché that "one (shoe) size does not fit all," implying that general advice that trade is good is unsound and that we must vary the prescription with each country, presumably advocating protection here and there, on an ad hoc basis, and without an overarching philosophy that progress towards freeing trade is desirable. This sounds so right; but it is downright shallow and silly. Science, and good policy, require that certain general propositions be taken as guiding principles, as distinct from reliance on ad hoc prescriptions. One has to decide whether one wants to go barefoot or wear shoes. And once one decides to wear shoes, the shoe size will inevitably tend to vary, as the policy gets grounded in reality. Thus, one has to decide whether the central policy has to be openness or autarky. After the postwar experience, it is clearly possible to argue that good policymaking requires a policy of freer trade. But this does not mean that the actual freeing of trade must not take into account the political and economic difficulties that may attend the transition from one system to another: the transition to freer trade, and working with an open economy, require policy and institutional support that have in fact been the subject of rich analysis by trade economists for decades.[8]

2. *Globalization: Trade, Immigration and Wages.* The long-standing stagnation, or at best very sluggish rise, in workers' earnings in the United States has given rise to the fear that globalization, involving trade with the poor countries and also illegal unskilled immigration from them, is at the heart of the problem. Yet, this causation should not be taken at face value, no matter how plausible it seems to many in the rich countries.

First, all empirical studies, including those done by some of today's top trade economists (such as Paul Krugman and Robert Feenstra), show that the adverse effect of trade on wages is not substantial. My own empirical investigation, reported also in Chapter 10 in this book, in fact argues that the effect of trade with poor countries may even have been to moderate the downward pressure on wages that rapid unskilled-labor-saving technical change would have caused.[9]

Second, the same goes for the econometric studies by the best labor economists today, regarding the effects of the influx of unskilled illegal immigrants into the United States. The latest study by George Borjas (no friend of illegal immigrants) and Larry Katz, both of Harvard, once necessary adjustments are made, also shows a virtually negligible impact on U.S. workers' wages.

So, despite the popular fears, globalization does not appear to be the cause of the problem. What then explains the disturbing situation regarding wages? Can it be that globalization has significantly reduced the bargaining ability of workers and thus puts a downward pressure on wages? I strongly doubt this. First, the argument is not relevant when employers and workers are in a competitive market and workers must be paid the going wage. As it happens, less than 10 percent of the workers in the private sector in the United States are now unionized. Second, if it is claimed that acceleration in globalization has decimated unionization, that is dubious. The decline in unionization has been going on for longer than the last two decades of globalization, shows no dramatic acceleration in the last two decades, and is to be attributed to the union-unfriendly provisions of the half-century-old Taft-Hartley provisions that crippled the ability to strike. Third, it seems plausible that unionization has also suffered because fewer workers now expect that unions can deliver higher wages. In the public sector, the wages are squeezed because of budget constraints: as the recent New York Transit strike showed, the public utilities are increasingly unable to raise the price of services or to get more subsidies to finance losses and therefore the ability of unions in such a situation to get more for their workers is crippled. Again, increasing numbers work at home, in no small measure due to technical change such as on-line transactions, that facilitates such decentralized work, in a return to the pre-factory-work era, and are therefore less amenable to unionization.

Again, can we turn to yet another element of globalization for an explanation? Has the outflow of Direct Foreign Investment (DFI) to the poor countries with cheap labor caused a decline in the capital which works at home with unskilled labor and hence to a decline in wages? As I look at the data, the United States has received more or less as much equity investment as it has lost over the last two decades. One cannot just look at one side of the ledger; I might add that I was once in a BBC radio debate with the Mayor of the French town, which had lost its Hoover factory to England. He was lamenting the loss and holding up multinationals as somewhat wicked in their pursuit of profits. So, I told him: Mr. Mayor, Hoover is an American firm. When it came to your town, you applauded. Now that they have traveled on, you are agitated. You cannot have it both ways. Again, as I argue below, the econometric evidence on location by multinationals does not show that cheap labor is a big draw; and many other factors producing competitiveness are at play, making the rich countries also major attractions for the inflow of equity investments by multinationals.

So, in lieu of globalization as the culprit, one has to fall back on the argument that substantial unskilled-labor-saving technical change is putting pressure on the wages of the unskilled. Technical change (except for the Green Revolution, where the new seeds led to increases in both the demand for landless labor and real wages because the application of irrigation and fertilizers to the new seeds led to more intensive land use with multiple shifts) happens to be continually economizing on the use of unskilled labor. Much empirical argumentation and evidence exists on this, coming from world-class economists such as Alan Krueger of Princeton. But, as always, anecdotes (which obviously cannot substitute for systematic evidence) can make this point come alive.[10] The effect of technical change in increasing the demand for skilled and reducing that for unskilled labor today can be illustrated by two examples.

First, to take an example from my own professorial life, secretaries are increasingly hard to get from the university administration on campuses. Instead, universities now offer you computers. Whereas secretaries are generally semi-skilled—though in the past highly educated and gifted females often became secretaries because they had few other options—the computers have to be looked after, and fixed frequently due to failure (especially when one has a deadline), by "electronic plumbers" who are skilled and get paid much more. So the rapid spread of computers is steadily reducing demand for secretaries and increasing the demand for the electronic plumbers.

A more striking example comes from Charlie Chaplin's famous film, *Modern Times*. You will recall how he goes berserk on the assembly line, the mechanical motion of turning the spanner finally getting to him (illustrating Adam Smith's famous observation that the division of labor, and concentration on repetitive, narrow tasks could turn workers into morons and that education for them had to provide the antidote). Suppose that you take your child to see the film and she asks you: Daddy, take me to see an assembly line so I can actually see the people working at it. Well, it is going to be increasingly difficult to find such an assembly line for your child to see. Yes, there are assembly lines today; but they are without workers; they are managed by computers in a glass cage above, with highly skilled engineers in charge. The disoriented Charlie Chaplins have increasingly disappeared, at least from the assembly lines. Amusingly, this was brought home to Americans when, having decided to investigate the production of potato and semiconductor chips because of the widespread perception that potato chips were produced by primitive techniques and semiconductors were made with advanced technology, a reporter found that the facts were the other way around. He visited a factory that produced semiconductors and found that it involved moronic fitting of little wires onto small boards, whereas the Pringles factory he visited for potato chips was fully automated on its assembly line, with Pringles fitting beautifully on one another, each a total replica of the other, in the red and green boxes one finds in hotel mini-bars.

The facts are that this is rapidly occurring in the United States, and in other rich countries, as technical change is quickly spreading through the system. This naturally creates, in the short-run, pressure on the jobs and wages of the workers being displaced. But we know from past experience with technical change that we usually get a J-curve where, as productivity increase takes hold, it will (except in cases where macroeconomic difficulties may occur and are not addressed by macroeconomic remedies) result in wage increases. A Luddite response, therefore, is hardly called for. So, why has there been no such effect—or at least a significant effect—in the statistics on wages for almost two decades?

I suspect that the answer lies in the intensity of displacement of unskilled labor by IT-based technical change—its potency is dramatic, as is evident from nearly everyone's daily experience—and in the fact that it is continuous now, unlike such discrete changes as the invention of the steam engine. Before the workers get on to the rising part of the J-curve, they run into yet more such technical change, so that the working class gets to go from one declining segment of the J-curve to another, to yet another. The pressure on wages gets to be relentless, lasting over longer periods than in earlier experience with unskilled-labor-saving technical change. But this technical change, which proceeds like a tsunami, has nothing to do with globalization.

New Arguments Raising Fear of Globalization

Recently, however, there have been renewed fears of globalization that need to be addressed. They come, and not wittingly, from the most unlikely sources. One is paradoxically from the greatest economist alive today, Paul Samuelson, a proponent of free trade; the other comes from the prolific pro-globalization journalist Tom Friedman.

The Samuelson Question

Writing in the *Journal of Economic Perspectives*, Professor Samuelson chided the proponents of globalization as failing to realize that external changes, such as the growth of China and India, could diminish the gains from trade and hence be harmful. He is doubtless right that external, exogenous changes can harm; equally, they can help. Imagine you are in Miami and the hurricane arrives, creating devastation. But you can also imagine that in India, the monsoon is good and leads to an abundant harvest. Trade economists have long discussed the likelihood of these opposed possibilities. The issues were at the forefront during the years of the dollar shortage after the Second World War when Europeans thought that external, exogenous growth of U.S. productivity was a source of pressure on European incomes and the exchange rate. The downside possibility resurfaced in the 1980s when the fear of a rising Japan created similar fears in the United States. Now, the rise of India and China has resurrected similar fears. Will their accumulation of capital and of know-how reduce our gains from trade since we specialize in producing and exporting goods that use skills and capital intensively?

Professor Samuelson is dead right in raising this question; perhaps in the public debate on globalization, this possibility has been downplayed. Where he was misinterpreted widely is in the assumption that, when gains from trade diminish because of such exogenous changes abroad, the policy response must be to abandon free trade and to embrace protection. Take the Miami example. If its response to the devastation from the hurricane is to shut off trade with the world, the anguish of its citizens will only worsen. It is astonishing, but not surprising, how the protectionists flocked to him, a free trader, with no comprehension of Samuelson's argumentation, contending that the world's most eminent economist had "conceded" that free trade was problematic.

However, if Samuelson certainly does not advocate protectionism, he does raise the question, which bothers many who fear the rise of India and China and the effect of this, if not on our wages, at least on our economic prosperity. For, if the gains from trade diminish, that does mean reduced prosperity. Here, let me say that there are reasons to think that his downside scenario is not likely.

To see this perhaps most clearly, get back to the argument that, as India and China (the chief among the developing countries who strike fear in this regard) accumulate capital and know-how, i.e. as the rich countries and the erstwhile poor countries get to be "more similar" in their factor endowments, the gains from trade will diminish because the rich countries' exports will fall in price. But what happens, in fact, as countries become similar? Trade now breaks out in "similar goods"; what we economists call "intra-industry trade" grows.

Yet another way of putting it is to say that trade in "variety" breaks out. You can see it in the fashion trade, for example. Walk down Madison Avenue in New York, for example, and you see, cheek by jowl, Giorgio Armani, Calvin Klein, Pierre Cardin, Yves St Laurent and Kenzo, competing and co-existing: none, incidentally, seeks protection from its "home country". Or go down Broadway for women's fashions; and you see Ann Klein on one side and then, a few yards down the road, Victoria's Secret on the other side. There is much trade in similar products, with producers across countries often at different places on the spectrum of products that we call an industry.

But we have not merely casual empiricism on the issue. Pioneering empirical work by Robert Feenstra and David Weinstein has demonstrated that these gains from similar products are huge today. Once this is factored in, Professor Samuelson's fears of the downside to our prosperity from the rise of China and India seem implausible.[11]

Tom Friedman: The Earth Is Not Flat

Yet another source of recent worries about the risk to the rich countries from the rise of India and China has come from Tom Friedman's latest book, *The World is Flat,* which, despite some critical reviews, has been a bestseller for months. Friedman essentially conjures up a vision where he has these countries, with high technology and low wages, come marching down a flat road like Russell Crowe's Roman legions and take every job away from the rich countries. He often quotes the remarkable entrepreneurs in India's Silicon Valley in Bangalore, who say, quite correctly: we can do anything that Americans can do, which is no idle boast. But the reader translates that as the altogether different and erroneous proposition: Indians will therefore wind up doing everything that the Americans presently do. The latter scares the hell out of Americans. But it abolishes the notion of comparative advantage and therefore is totally wrong.

Let me put this criticism in a way that you can see at once. Do we really have a flat road? What ever happened to potholes and to mountains that the road has to skirt around or tunnel through? Take just two examples as to why countries do not travel on the same flat road. One example concerns China and India. Both countries have dramatically improved their growth rates, and reduced their poverty, by abandoning the old policy framework that included autarkic attitudes regarding trade and inward direct equity investments. You would expect them to have similar performance levels in modern sectors like IT software. But India is way ahead on it. Why? The answer surely lies in the differential politics of India and China. Democratic India rejoices in IT software and already is a major force in world commerce in it. Authoritarian China, on the other hand, is fearful of the seditious implications of letting free information flow and has put up roadblocks that inhibit the growth of this sector. To reiterate, the PC (personal computer) is incompatible with the CP (the Communist Party).

If this lack of "flatness," or difference in comparative advantage, arises from political diversity, I suspect that the case of Japan illustrates the differences that arise culturally.[12] Japan in the 1980s and early 1990s aroused similar fears: that they would take over everything we were doing in the rich countries. The fears were differently premised and had little to do with huge size (for it is an island economy) or with "low" wages, which are the fears that arise regarding India and China. The fear of Japan instead had much to do with the nation's meteoric rise in world trade and performance just as India and China's dazzling performance does today. But, in the end, they could not master the financial sector, while retaining their prowess in manufacturing. The reason seems to be cultural. Excellence in design, attention to craftsmanship, meticulous attention to consumer satisfaction, belying the previous notion that Japan could only produce shoddy products, have led to continuing dominance at the upper end of quality production. These qualities do not help you in fast-moving modern finance where dithering and dilatory responses mean that you lose to others whose responses are faster. For nearly two decades, Japan has faltered because its way of doing business has not given it comparative advantage in managing the financial sector. This has spilled over into macroeconomic failure as well. Now, Japan is busy addressing this issue by opening up its financial sector to foreign banks and investment, hoping to learn through foreign infusion the different culture that the modern financial sector requires.

So, contrary to what is feared, there is no reason to think that comparative advantage is going to disappear: that the world is flat! Two further points need to be made. As Paul Krugman has emphasized, national competitiveness is a fallacious construct. If India and China have low wages, the exchange rate can adjust to offset that advantage; or, with fixed exchange rates, other (not so good) mechanisms will be triggered to adjust the trade balance and to have comparative advantage resurface. But there is also the important point that econometric studies on the location decisions of multinationals (when all industries are considered) typically show that factors other than cheap labour are important; concern about lower wages is simply a fetish.

Moreover, it is a mistake to think that, just because wages are low, the sheer size of the population of India and China will ensure that they will remain low despite rapid growth. All observers, whatever their political persuasion, are agreed that over two decades of two-digit growth in the four provinces on the east coast of China have seen a rapid increase in the demand for labor, whereas the kicking-in of the one-child policy and the slow influx of workers from the hinterland (partly because there are many obstacles put in the path of rural-urban migration by the authorities) have combined to raise wages and improve working conditions. Equally, in India, when the outsourcing of "long distance" or arm's-length services such as call-answer services is considered, the wages have been rising there too. In fact, if you look at the population in the age cohort for college, only about a tenth actually goes to college. Of that, still a smaller fraction studies in English.[13] Of that, only a small fraction can speak English. Of that, again, a small fraction can speak English in a way we can understand. Yes, the lines outside call centers are long; but queuing up does not guarantee that you can do the job that is available.

Then again, whereas Richard Freeman of Harvard University talks these days of the large numbers of engineers graduating in India and China—more than in the United States—this does not factor in the quality of the education they have received. It will be many years before even a small fraction of these will come up to snuff. Besides, there are lots of local tasks such as bridge repairs, road-building, and construction, which absorb a gigantic fraction of these engineers. Moreover, in China, the stock of engineers was badly depleted by the Cultural Revolution, and a sizeable fraction of the current graduates must go toward rebuilding this stock. In short, both the alarmist interpretations and predictions of the growth of skilled personnel in China and India, as well as the threat it poses to rich-country jobs through diminished gains from trade, should be seriously discounted. Our comparative advantage in skill-intensive jobs is by no means going to disappear in the foreseeable future.

A Different Metaphor:
Kaleidoscopic Comparative Advantage

If comparative advantage is not dead—indeed it cannot die in the world as we know it—the real problem is that it has become volatile. Friedman's metaphor is wrong: the world is not flat any more than it was when the flat-earthers of antiquity were challenged by Pythagoras in sixth century BC. The appropriate metaphor is different: the world is now characterized by what I call "kaleidoscopic comparative advantage."

As it happens, this volatility, or "knife-edge" property of specialization—where you have it one day, lose it toa rival tomorrow, and possibly get it back the day after tomorrow—is itself due to the fact that almost no CEO in traded services and goods leads a comfortable life now. The "thick" margins of competitive advantage have practically disappeared. When William of Orange and Queen Mary grew oranges in the greenhouses at Hampton Court, no one lost sleep in Haifa, where the oranges grew naturally in abundance. Today, the competitive margins have shrunk for several reasons.[14] To cite some principal phenomena, multinationals could now go to many locations, which would thereby obtain access to their technology; interest rates were increasingly similar due to the growing integration of financial markets; many more countries were building educational institutions where students could read the same textbooks; and increasingly, students were studying abroad and acquiring technical know-how at the world level. At the same time, many countries had become actively involved in the international markets because trade barriers had been gradually dismantled, either through reciprocal cuts in trade negotiations or due to unilateral actions inspired by the realization that protectionism was harmful to one's economic health.

Where the readers of Friedman are likely to think that competition comes from India and China, however, my analysis focuses on the fact that it can come from almost anywhere. CEOs, looking behind them, are very likely to see *some* rival stealing up on them. But that rival need not be from India or China. It can be from Brazil, from Poland, from France, indeed from a number of trading countries. But there is certainly going to be someone stealing up on you today; and you had better be on your toes.

To illustrate again with an anecdote: In 1991, I was at my daughter's music camp for a Parents' Weekend. That evening, I started talking to a father who told me that he was from Silicon Valley and that competition from Japan was enormous. I knew all about it, especially as Silicon Valley had been embraced politically by the Japan-bashing Clinton Presidential campaign. So I moved to the father standing with us and asked him what he did. He said he was growing mushrooms. So, I said: ah, you must be leading a happier life. No, he said, pulling his hair out: Taiwan is killing me! In short, everyone is in fierce competition if they are in international trade. Or take a recent example: the competition between Airbus and Boeing. Both are essentially neck and neck. Boeing had been slipping behind, but then Airbus made a major blunder on its A380 and fell behind. But when Boeing makes the next mistake, Airbus could get back into first place. The competition is knife-edge.

Two consequences follow. First, faced with this ferocity of competition, the temptation to ask for protection is great. But that is a difficult road to travel, as policymakers rarely oblige. Then one can always ask for a different kind of protection: one can try to "level the playing field" by requiring the rivals from poorer countries with lower labor and other standards to raise them to our levels, so they do not get an "unfair" advantage—that is, one can ask for "fair trade." To put it in terms of the flat world metaphor, the response to import competition can take the form of raising the cost of production of your rivals abroad, so that we do *not* have a flat world. Rather, we have firms under competitive pressure trying to flatten the world! It is what I call "export protectionism."

Second, it is a mug's game. Even if poor countries equalized their labor and domestic environmental standards to ours, it would never eliminate the problem of fierce competition today. It is like putting a finger in the dyke.

Coping with Kaleidoscopic Comparative Advantage Requires Several Policy and Institutional Changes

Friedman is wrong in suggesting that the world is flat and comparative advantage has disappeared relative to India and China, I am afraid. And so are the unions and other NGOs who think that raising standards elsewhere up to those in the rich countries (where standards, incidentally, vary greatly and, in the case of the United States, are nothing to write home about, for that matter) will moderate competition and lead to a more comfortable life.

What then should be our response to globalization when it is characterized by rapidly shifting comparative advantages? The gains from trade are real; but the volatility requires institutional response and reconstruction of inherited ways of doing things.

Security for Workers, No Longer through Specific Jobs. If volatility is now a dominant fact of life, unions cannot expect to define security for their unskilled workers in terms of specific jobs. Specific jobs are increasingly subject to demise and disappearance. So, the unions must define security in terms of workers themselves. This means that the unions must now get active in getting their members to acquire the tools of mobility from one job to another. This requires that the unions must now go back to the old tenets of socialists such as G.D.H. Cole, who emphasized the importance of educating the workers. Workers may enjoy, like many of us, sitting in front of television sets and drinking beer and eating potato chips as they watch soccer or baseball with frenzied attention. But they must be persuaded to go to a union school on Saturday or Sunday, when they can learn a language, computers, or some other new skill for two to three hours every week. This addition to their "portfolio of assets" will increase their chance of being able to go from a lost job to a new one.

Consider as well the fact that unskilled labor's wage profile over a lifetime typically showed a mild rise, an upward slope, because the firms tended to impart human capital on the job to workers who would stay in the job over long periods. Now, that wage profile is likely to be flatter because, faced with impermanence, the firm's incentive to add human capital to the unskilled workers it is employing currently is going to be reduced.[15] This argument also calls for initiatives to add human capital through appropriate education for the unskilled workers today.

Skilled Labor: Assisted Trajectories of Transition. The same goes for skilled labor. Strangely enough, while the "skill premium" has grown, also due to technical change that economizes on unskilled labor but favors skilled labor, the fear of globalization has spread even to the skilled who see their jobs being imperiled by the phenomenon. This alarm spread rapidly through the United States when a radiologist sent out X rays digitally to India to be read there: it was then assumed that all radiologists (and then doctors in all medical specialties) would lose their jobs. But the fact is that no radiologist has lost his job to date. The outsourcing has been largely to India and Australia, where the time zone differences have made it possible to get X rays read while the American doctors sleep or enjoy their weekends (so that these foreign firms are aptly called "nighthawks").

In fact, it is hard to think of a net loss of jobs in the skilled categories as technical change and shifting circumstances continually throw up demands for new skills. Thus, even if radiology were to be lost through outsourcing, can it be doubted that the spread of obesity has led to a vastly increased demand for doctors in diabetes and cardiology? Besides, the ageing of the population has led to a hugely increased demand for cosmetic surgery that is now spreading from women to men. I have wagered that even Clint Eastwood will some day get a face lift, though I doubt if I (and he) will live long enough for me to win the bet.

The real problem again is how to facilitate the movement of the skilled from declining to rising skills. I have proposed that the professional associations, like the American Medical Association, assist the process by working out "assisted trajectories of transition" so that if radiologists lose out, then they do not have to go back to the beginning and work for years to shift to the specialties rising in demand. Rather, the AMA would work with the doctors to see how the length of the transition path can be minimized.

Education: Reducing Excessive Specialization.   Again, education— whether at a university, less exalted institutions such as the community colleges in the United States, or vocational institutions—must ensure that the ratio of specialized to general technical education is shifted in favor of the latter. Thus, engineers should not spend the greatest amount of time learning mechanical engineering and the least amount of time on general engineering, which would embrace more of chemical and electrical engineering, for instance. In the Soviet Union, where there was *no* change, engineers were trained for very specific specializations where they spent their lives in an inflexible job assignment in a rigidly planned economy. We now have the problem that we must educate people in skills that no longer have a guarantee of being in permanent demand, and hence they must be endowed with a good general base, a platform from which they can reassign themselves from obsolete skills to those in new demand.

The Question of Ageing Societies.   I might add that, in ageing societies such as those in many parts of Europe, the ageing phenomenon creates both opportunities and problems. On the opportunity side, consider that it leads to new demands for a variety of medical skills: among them, cosmetic surgery, which has witnessed a huge surge. But, on the problems side, enabling older professionals to transit to new skills can be quite difficult. If the demand for Professors of Economics were to fall off, and there were no tenure, and I lost my job at the age of 55, for example, I would hate to be told that there were a lot of opportunities for Professorships in Theoretical Physics: it would be pretty well impossible for me to become a Professor of Theoretical Physics at that age! In some cases, therefore, the challenge of transiting to new skills will be daunting. It is clear, therefore, that one element of adjustment that would be useful is to make import-competition-related adjustment assistance amounts and time periods age-linked.[16]

Differential Demographics: A Gray Peace Corps.   I also see in both modern demographics and the asymmetrical endowment of skills worldwide an opportunity to find new and fulfilling jobs for the ageing skilled workers of the rich countries. Countries such as Germany and Italy are no longer reproducing themselves: their women no longer see themselves as manufacturing babies. At least two consequences follow.

First, these European countries find themselves in the same position that they were in at the end of the Second World War. The war had decimated their population of young men, and they responded by developing the *gastarbeiter* (guest-worker) programs. If properly managed, this provides an interesting opportunity for the poor countries with workers who cannot be gainfully employed to send them to the rich countries that have more jobs than people. I used this fact to advantage when asked on U.S. television how I felt that Mrs. Sonia Gandhi, an Italian, might become India's Prime Minister. I ducked the issue by saying: "Italy is not reproducing itself; in about 30 years, a quarter of the Italian workforce is expected to be immigrants; of these, a large fraction will obviously be Indians; given the high rate of turnover of Italian Prime Ministers, I can therefore confidently expect that there will soon be an Indian Prime Minister of Italy; we will then have taken our revenge!"

Second, regarding skilled workers, ageing populations (and accompanying retirements), and the difficult adjustment problems facing the old thanks to skill obsolescence due to kaleidoscopic comparative advantage, Europe and the United States can fill the huge needs of African nations for skills of virtually every type. As we train more Africans, most will surely leave to work in the rich countries: indeed, while Indians and Shirley MacLaine believe in a multiplicity of lifetimes, they maximize their welfare in the current life like everybody else. Eventually, these Africans will return when political governance has improved, economic growth has taken root and social conditions have changed for the better.

In the meantime, we will long have glaring needs for skills in Africa. I have argued that these needs can be met by creating a Gray Peace Corps where retired doctors, agronomists, teachers, nurses, doctors, and people with many other skills can be sent for periods of two and more years at suitably high compensation to work in African countries. Again, therefore, supply and need can meet through cross-border flows, properly organized and managed, easing in turn the adjustment problems of ageing populations.

Labor Markets.   Then again, in a world of kaleidoscopic comparative advantage, with increased volatility in specialization, labor market flexibility in hiring and firing becomes important. When comparative advantage is lost, if workers cannot be laid off, the cost to the firm rises significantly. So, if the firms can invest abroad where labor can be fired when demand fails, the margin will shift in favor of investing abroad rather than at home. So, we will get the phenomenon—observable in France and Germany, which both have stringent restrictions or penalties for firing workers—of competitive French and German firms that do not create jobs in their home countries. This seems to be the case also in Sweden: the Report by the Swedish Confederation of Industry highlights this problem persuasively.

Again, when entire firms disappear and workers enter the search process, the question arises as to the optimal length of relief and assistance before the next job is found. Evidently, a safety net has to be provided, on both political and economic grounds. But if the workers are supported at high compensation rates and for long periods, the safety net may turn into a hammock, delaying beyond the optimal the provision of assistance during the search process for new jobs.

Innovation: From Basic Science to Engineering.   One final thought is necessary. Globalization today reflects knife-edge, volatile comparative advantage for several reasons, which I have already detailed. But one important reason is that when firms go from basic science, which is largely unpatented, to engineering new products and processes, which can be patented, the diffusion of that know-how is very swift today. Thus, software diffuses very rapidly; and intellectual property protection is sought merely with a view to getting royalties on what cannot be prevented from being diffused.

But when the Schumpeterian monopoly advantages that innovation brings are eroded rapidly today, the only way to survive and prosper in the globalized world is to be *continually innovative.* Innovation policy then becomes part of the portfolio of policies to cope with globalization today. Hence I told Leif Pagrotsky, who had gone from the Trade to the Education portfolio in the Social Democratic government of Swedish Prime Minister Göran Persson, that his change of portfolio had not taken him too far away from trade: education (as I have already discussed) and policies to encourage innovation are critical to success in seizing the opportunities posed by globalization today.

So, I conclude with the observation that globalization poses institutional and policy challenges that require a coherent and holistic treatment. The large, rich countries like the United States, France and Germany, are drifting from one *ad hoc* response to another. The globalization phenomenon, however, is not one where you can muddle through. That is a luxury that even the large, rich countries cannot afford.

November 2006   New York

Glossary

Acronyms

AFL-CIO The American Federation of Labor–Congress of Industrial Organizations is a voluntary federation of America's unions, representing more than thirteen million men and women nationwide. The AFL-CIO was formed in 1955 by the merger of the American Federation of Labor and the Congress of Industrial Organizations. Headquarters are located in Washington, D.C.

AI Amnesty International is a worldwide movement of people who campaign for internationally recognized human rights. Amnesty International was founded in 1961 by British lawyer Peter Benenson and is independent of any government, political ideology, economic interests, or religion. At the latest count, there are more than 1.5 million members, supporters, and subscribers worldwide.

CITES The Convention on International Trade in Endangered Species of Wild Fauna and Flora sets controls on the international trade and movement of animal and plant species that have been, or may be, threatened due to excessive commercial exploitation. This United Nations Environment Programme convention came into effect in 1975 as a result of growing awareness that international trade was endangering more and more wild species everywhere on the planet. CITES is an international consensus on sustainable mutual management of natural resources. More than a quarter of a century later, in November 2001, it included 155 member states, called parties. One of the first countries to ratify the convention was Canada, where it came into effect on July 3, 1975. The CITES secretariat is based in Geneva, Switzerland.

CUTS Established in 1983, the Consumer Unity and Trust Society started off as a consumer protection organization in Rajasthan, India. Since then it has been working in several areas of public interest at the grassroots, national, subcontinental, and international levels.

EPA The U.S. Environmental Protection Agency was created in July 1970 in response to the growing public demand for cleaner water, air, and land. The White House and Congress worked together to establish the EPA. Its headquarters are located in Washington, D.C.

FDI   Foreign direct investment; investment that is usually large enough in an enterprise to get control.

GATS   The General Agreement on Trade and Services is among the World Trade Organization's most important agreements. The accord, which came into force in January 1995, is the first and only set of multilateral rules covering international trade in services.

GATT   The General Agreement on Tariffs and Trade was first signed in 1947. The agreement was designed to provide an international forum that encouraged free trade between member states by regulating and reducing tariffs on traded goods and by providing a common mechanism for resolving trade disputes. GATT was folded into the World Trade Organization, its successor.

HRW   Human Rights Watch is the largest human rights organization based in the United States. The NGO started in 1978 as Helsinki Watch. Human Rights Watch researchers conduct fact-finding investigations into human rights abuses in all regions of the world. The organization then publishes those findings in dozens of books and reports every year, generating extensive coverage in local and international media. Human Rights Watch is based in New York, with offices in Brussels, London, Moscow, Hong Kong, Los Angeles, San Francisco, and Washington, D.C.

IBRD   The International Bank for Reconstruction and Development, also known as the World Bank, was established on July 22, 1944, and came into effect on December 27, 1945. Its aim is to provide economic development loans to countries in need.

ICFTU   The International Confederation of Free Trade Unions was set up in 1949 and has 231 affiliated organizations in 150 countries, with a membership of 150 million. Its head-quarters is located in Brussels, Belgium.

ILO   The International Labor Organization is a UN agency that seeks the promotion of social justice and internationally recognized human and labor rights. It was founded in 1919 and is the only surviving major creation of the Treaty of Versailles, which brought the League of Nations into being. It became the first specialized agency of the UN in 1946. The ILO formulates international labor standards in the form of conventions and recommendations setting minimum standards of basic labor rights: freedom of association, the right to organize, collective bargaining, abolition of forced labor, equality of opportunity and treatment, and other standards regulating conditions across the entire spectrum of work related issues.

IMF   The decision to establish the International Monetary Fund was made at a conference held in Bretton Woods, N.H., in July 1944. The IMF came into official existence on December 27, 1945. The IMF is an international organization of 184 member countries. It was established to promote international monetary cooperation, exchange stability, and orderly exchange arrangements; to foster economic growth and high levels of employment; and to provide temporary financial assistance to countries to help ease balance of payments adjustment.

MAI   Multilateral agreement on investment; being negotiated at the OECD.

MFN   The most-favored-nation principle is embodied in the GATT (and some other trade treaties). It requires every member of the GATT to extend to all other members the lowest tariff that it has in place on a product. Specific exceptions are allowed in the GATT; for example, Article 24 permits members to deny MFN status to non-members of free trade agreements and customs unions.

NAFTA   The North American Free Trade Agreement took effect on January 1, 1994.

NGO   Non-governmental organizations are private organizations that pursue activities to relieve suffering, promote the interests of the poor, protect the environment, provide basic social services, or undertake community development. In wider usage, the term can be applied to any non-profit organization that is independent from government.

OECD   The Organization for Economic Cooperation and Development groups thirty member countries in a unique forum to discuss, develop, and refine economic and social policies. The OECD grew out of the Organization for European Economic Cooperation (OEEC), which was formed to administer American and Canadian aid under the Marshall Plan for the reconstruction of Europe after World War II. OECD took over from OEEC in 1961.

POCOs   Post-colonialists.

POMOs   Post-modernists.

TAA   Trade Adjustment Assistance for Firms is a federal program that provides financial assistance to manufacturers affected by import competition. It was established in 1974. Funded by the U.S. Department of Commerce, TAA is a network of twelve regional non-profit organizations that manage the program.

TRIMS   The Agreement on Trade-Related Investment Measures is one of the three main areas of work in the WTO on trade and investment. It prohibits trade-related investment measures, such as local-content requirements, that are inconsistent with basic provisions of GATT 1994.

TRIPS   The Agreement on Trade-Related Aspects of Intellectual Property Rights is Annex 1C of the Marrakesh Agreement establishing the World Trade Organization on April 15, 1994.

UNCHR   The United Nations Commission on Human Rights, composed of fifty-three states, meets each year in regular session in March/April for six weeks in Geneva. Over three thousand delegates from member and observer states and non-governmental organizations participate. One of the most important tasks entrusted to the commission has been the elaboration of human rights standards. In 1948 it concluded work on the landmark Universal Declaration of Human Rights.

UNDP   The United Nations Development Programme works globally to reduce poverty, preserve energy resources and the environment, combat AIDS, and promote communications technology. It has also undertaken the key tasks of promoting democracy, building peace, and preventing disasters whenever possible.

UNEP   The United Nations Environment Programme was established in 1972 and is the voice for the environment within the United Nations system. UNEP works with a wide range of partners, including United Nations entities, international organizations, national governments, non-governmental organizations, the private sector, and civil society.

UNHCR   The Office of the United Nations High Commissioner for Refugees was established on December 14, 1950, by the United Nations General Assembly. The agency is mandated to lead and coordinate international action to protect refugees and resolve refugee problems worldwide.

USTR   The Office of the United States Trade Representative is America's principal trade negotiator and the chief trade policy adviser to the president of the United States. USTR has permanent offices at the World Trade Organization in Geneva, as well as in Washington, D.C.

WTO   The World Trade Organization is the only global international organization dealing with the rules of trade between nations. The WTO was created by the Uruguay Round negotiations between 1986 and 1994 and was established January 1, 1995. At its heart are the general trade agreements, negotiated and signed by the bulk of the world's trading nations and ratified in their parliaments. As of April 4, 2003, its membership extends to 146 countries. The organization is based in Geneva, Switzerland.

Phrases and Concepts

Alien Torts Act

Enacted in 1789 and dormant for nearly two hundred years, this statute has been revived by activists in the United States. It grants jurisdiction to the U.S. federal courts for civil action by an alien, even against other aliens, for a tort committed in violation of international law.

Bangalore Principles

These principles were set out during February 1988 in Bangalore, India, at the Colloquium on the Domestic Application of International Human Rights Norms, under the chairmanship of Chief Justice P. N. Bhagwati of the Indian Supreme Court and the sponsorship of the Commonwealth Secretariat, London.

Bretton Woods Institutions

The World Bank and its sister organization, the International Monetary Fund, were created at Bretton Woods, New Hampshire, in 1944. Together they are referred to as the Bretton Woods Institutions (BWIs).

Civil Society

In the definition used by the London School of Economics, "*Civil Society* refers to the set of institutions, organizations, and behavior situated between the state, the business world, and the family. Specifically, this includes voluntary and non-profit organizations of many different kinds, philanthropic institutions, social and political movements, other forms of social participation and engagement and the values and cultural patterns associated with them." Popularly, and as used in the book, it is used more narrowly to refer to non-governmental organizations.

Cobweb Cycles

These are phenomena in commodity markets studied by economists. Price falls, which leads to reduced investment in the next period, which in turn leads to a price rise in the period after, which again leads to increased investment and then to price falls, and the cycle gets repeated.

Core Labor Rights (or Standards)

ILO Declaration of Fundamental Principles and Rights at Work:

- freedom of association and the effective recognition of the right to collective bargaining
- the elimination of all forms of forced or compulsory labor
- the effective abolition of child labor
- the elimination of discrimination in respect of employment and occupation

Domestic NGOs

Domestic NGOs are non-governmental organizations that address primarily domestic issues, such as quality of water, pesticides, dowry payment, and so on. The Center for Science and Environment in India is an example.

Global NGOs

Global NGOs are non-governmental organizations that address global issues, including those raised by the activities of international institutions such as the IMF, WTO, and World Bank.

Kyoto Protocol

The accord's exact name is United Nations Framework Convention on Climate Change (UNFCCC) and was launched at the Earth Summit in 1992 in Rio de Janeiro, Brazil. The Kyoto Protocol, also known as the Kyoto treaty, is a step forward from the original Framework Treaty binding emission targets reductions; its text was adopted at the Kyoto Conference of the Parties to the Climate Treaty, December 1997 in Japan.

Millennium Summit

The Millennium Summit of the United Nations was held September 6–8, 2000, in New York City at the United Nations headquarters. Heads of states and governments of member states participated in the opportunity to agree on a process for fundamental review of the role of the United Nations and challenges facing the organization in the new century. The Millennium Goals are the targets that were approved at the summit.

Montreal Protocol

The Montreal Protocol on Substances That Deplete the Ozone Layer is an international agreement designed to protect the stratospheric ozone layer. The treaty was originally signed in 1987 and substantially amended in 1990 and 1992. The Montreal Protocol stipulates that the production and consumption of compounds that deplete ozone in the stratosphere—chlorofluorocarbons (CFCs), halons, carbon tetrachloride, and methyl chloroform—are to be phased out by 2000 (2005 for methyl chloroform).

"Polluter Pay" Principle

The "polluter pay" principle requires polluters to pay for the pollution they discharge. When they do not have to pay this tax, the true social cost of what they produce will not be reflected in their actual cost, and the result will be overproduction of the pollution-creating products.

Portfolio Capital

Portfolio capital flows relate to investment that provides the investor with a return on equity but without control over the company, a control that is generally not sought either. Short-term capital flows, such as those whose outflow precipitated the Asian financial crisis, are typically composed of portfolio capital.

Tradable Permits

When pollution results from an economic activity, it should be paid for or else the social and private costs of production will diverge. "Polluter pay" taxes would remedy this. A similar policy would be to get polluters to buy permits. When these permits are allowed to be traded among different polluters, economic efficiency results: the cost of reducing pollution to desired levels will fall. The Kyoto Protocol permits some trading.

Notes

Preface

1. Among the polls, I have been struck by one commissioned by the World Economic Forum and presented at its New York meetings in February 2002. It surveyed an urban sample of one thousand individuals in each of twenty-five countries, and virtually everywhere a majority viewed globalization favorably. But, exactly as I have argued for some time, there was evidence of an ironic reversal: the developing countries showed greater majorities in favor of globalization, whereas the opposite would have been true earlier. Thus while there was much skepticism about globalization in the developing countries in the nearly three decades following the end of the Second World War, and an opposite pro-globalization attitude in the developed countries, this has now turned upside down. I discuss all this later in the book.

2. But let me also say, not to advertise myself but to protect my flank, that I have written about both short-term capital flows and international migration far more extensively elsewhere and propose to write yet more in the future. I have in fact said much that has set off controversy on the question of short-term capital flows, and many of my writings, including a much-cited and translated 1999 article in *Foreign Affairs*, are reprinted in my last collection of public policy writings, *The Wind of the Hundred Days: How Washington Mismanaged Globalization* (Cambridge: MIT Press, 2001).

   As for immigration, I have written extensively on it now for some thirty years, with some recent writings reprinted in my recent collections of public policy essays, *A Stream of Windows: Unsettling Reflections on Trade, Immigration and Democracy* (Cambridge: MIT Press, 1998) and *The Wind of the Hundred Days*. I also plan to follow the present book with two others on international immigration, one an intellectual, economic, and philosophical analysis of immigration restrictions, and the other a benign look at illegal immigration into the United States.

Chapter 1

1. There is extreme sensitivity on the part of the critics of globalization to being described as "anti-globalizers." It is fashionable now to assert that the anti-globalizers are not against globalization but are rather for alternatives, but surely that is only the flip side of their attacks on globalization as they interpret it. Then again, it has become fashionable to say, as

the Yale anthropologist David Graeber has recently asserted, that the "phrase 'antiglobali- zation' movement was coined by the corporate media," and since corporations are anath- ema to most such critics, as I argue in the text, that damns the phrase at one remove, but with passion. Compare David Graeber, "The Globalization Movement: Some Points of Clari- fication," *Items & Issues* 2, 3–4 (2001), 12–14.

2. This trilogy is discussed in depth later in the chapter.

3. I am deeply indebted to Blair Hoxby of Yale for flagging to my attention these additional sources of intellectual opposition to globalization.

4. I have written on the issue, noting how the facts on asymmetry of protection are the oppo- site of what is alleged by the critics charging double standards and hypocrisy, in several places. See, for example, Jagdish Bhagwati and Arvind Panagariya, "Wanted Jubilee 2010: Dismantling Protection," *OECD Observer*, May 27–29, 2002; and "The Truth About Protec- tionism," *Financial Times*, March 29, 2001. A focus only on protectionism of the rich coun- tries, to the exclusion of protectionism in the poor countries, is also dangerous and self-defeating, as I argue in "Targeting Rich-Country Protectionism: Jubilee 2010 et al.," *Finance & Development*, September 2001.

5. I had isolated this "unfair trade" virus in my 1990 Harry Johnson Lecture, published as *The World Trading System at Risk* (Princeton: Princeton University Press, 1991). Martin Wolf, writing in the *Financial Times* on Oxfam's foray into world trade policy with a report citing unfair trade and double standards, had a similar critical commentary.

6. I base my remarks on the much-cited Oxfam report *Rigged Rules and Double Standards: Trade, Globalization and the Fight Against Poverty* (Oxford: Oxfam, 2002). Oxfam spokes- men have written extensively in this vein in newspapers and magazines. I was also on a panel of trade ministers and trade experts at the last Davos meeting where a senior Oxfam representative spoke along the same lines with passion but little else.

7. In fact, even a sophisticated anti-globalization economist such as Dani Rodrik of the Kennedy School at Harvard University may have helped to spread this confusion; see Rodrik's "The Global Fix," *The New Republic*, November 2, 1998, on proposed changes in the world trad- ing system. The article starts illogically with the financial crisis as the cause of the world malaise that needed attention.

8. The polling firm is based in Toronto; the results can be accessed at http:// www.environicsinternational.com/global/press_inside.html. Lest the reader think wrongly that this report is not credible because it was commissioned by the World Economic Forum, I also cite below the pro-globalization findings of other polls that are not similarly handi- capped.

9. Cf. Jagdish Bhagwati, ed., *The New International Economic Order* (Cambridge: MIT Press, 1978), Chapter 1.

10. The poll also suggested that the developing countries such as Indonesia and Argentina, which were badly hit by financial crises just prior to the poll, were less enthusiastic about globalization. I comment on that later when I discuss how the sins of one form of globaliza- tion tend to be visited on the virtues of another, and that this "fallacy of aggregation" com- plicates the task of assessing globalization's consequences meaningfully.

11. See http://www.americans-world.org/digest/global_issues/globalization/gz_summary.cfm.

12. Pew Research Center for the People and the Press, "Views of a Changing World," June 2003, 71; http://people-press.org/reports/display.php3?ReportID=185.

13. Martin Wolf, "Will the Nation-State Survive Globalization?" *Foreign Affairs* 80, 1 (2001), 181–82.

14. Ibid., 182.

15. Francis Fukuyama, *The End of History and the Last Man* (New York: Free Press, 1992).

16. This meeting in Porto Alegre has now become an annual, parallel affair and describes itself as the World Social Forum, in contrast to the World Economic Forum of Davos. The con- trasting choice of terminology is clearly intended to suggest that they are for social out- comes and for humanity, whereas their opponents are for profits and against humanity.

17. See http://www.globalexchange.org/campaigns/rulemakers/topTenReasons.html.

18. Jagdish Bhagwati, *The Economics of Underdeveloped Countries* (London: Weidenfeld and Nicolson, 1966), Chapter 1. I must add two vignettes about this first book of mine. First, its Chapter 1 is titled "Poverty and Income Distribution." Second, I had the curious satisfaction of getting back at a social-democratic critic, Dr. Louis Emmerij, when I gave a keynote speech at Antwerp many years ago. When I had talked about poverty and how to address it, he got up and said that it was good to see that Professor Bhagwati was "finally" turning to poverty. So I retorted, "As it happens, I was rereading my 1966 book on underdeveloped countries last week to write my speech today, and I am sorry to have to tell you that the first chapter was concerned precisely with poverty."

    Besides, I must say that the book contained a moving photograph of a malnourished, starving child in Africa. At a time when it was fashionable to equate developmental analysis with esoteric questions such as the optimal choice of techniques, where the modeling was used to arrive at the disastrous conclusion that capital-intensive techniques were appropriate in poor countries, as they would raise savings and lead to faster growth, it seemed like heresy and a betrayal of economics to focus directly on poverty and pestilence and to concretize them with telling pictorial evidence. In fact, John Chipman, a world-class economist at the University of Minnesota and a fine friend, wrote to me at the time that he had heard a colleague exclaim: "Bhagwati has gone bananas; he has published a book with a picture of a starving child in it!"

19. Terry Eagleton, *Literary Theory: An Introduction*, 2nd. ed. (Minneapolis: University of Minnesota Press, 2001), 128.

20. See also the quote from Edward Said further below. Blair Hoxby has reminded me that, earlier than Foucault, these antirational views may be traced to Theodor Adorno and Max Horkheimer's *Dialectic of Enlightenment,* first published in German in 1944.

21. V. S. Naipaul, *Beyond Belief: Islamic Excursions Among Converted Peoples* (New York: Vintage, 1999), 276.

22. Today social anthropology has moved into a more liberal stance, under the influence of postcolonial and postmodern theorists. Nonetheless, it is not free from its status quo bias on culture, which seeks to value rather than vanquish the old, and to be skeptical and suspicious of change. The influence on policy of this discipline has revived as social anthropologists have found their way into foundations, the World Bank, and several NGOs.

23. David Hume, *A Treatise of Human Nature* (London: J. M. Dent, 1911), 2:128. See also David Hume, *An Enquiry Concerning the Principles of Morals,* ed. J. B. Schneewind (Indianapolis: Hackett, 1983): "Sympathy, we shall allow, is much fainter than our concern for ourselves, and sympathy with persons remote from us, much fainter than with persons near and contiguous" (49); and "It is wisely ordained by nature, that private connexions should commonly prevail over universal views and considerations; otherwise our affections and actions would be dissipated and lost, for want of a proper limited object. Thus a small benefit done to ourselves, and our near friends, excites more lively sentiments of love and approbation than a great benefit done to a distant commonwealth" (49).

24. Adam Smith, *The Theory of Moral Sentiments,* ed. D. Raphael and A. L. Macfie (Oxford: Clarendon, 1976), 136–37.

25. This new consciousness of ills elsewhere, and the aroused conscience that often goes with it, does not imply that remedial action will necessarily follow. Famines, pestilence, war crimes, and much else that plagues humanity has continued to our great embarrassment and sorrow.

26. Hierocles, in A. A. Long and D. N. Sedley, eds., *The Hellenistic Philosophers* (Cambridge: Cambridge University Press, 1987). The quote from Hierocles is from Fonna Forman-Barzilai, "Adam Smith as Globalization Theorist," available at http://www.ciaonet.org/olj/cr/cr_v14_4_fof01.pdf, 4.

27. This delightful story has been reprinted as the lead story in Roald Dahl's collection *The Wonderful Story of Henry Sugar* (New York: Puffin, 1988).

28. Edward W. Said, "The Public Role of Writers and Intellectuals," *The Nation,* September 17, 2001, no. 8, vol. 273, 27.

29. Ibid.

30. Immanuel Wallerstein, "Development: Lodestar or Illusion?" in Leslie Sklair, ed., *Capitalism and Development* (London: Routledge, 1994).

31. V. I. Lenin, *Imperialism: The Highest Stage of Capitalism* (Moscow, USSR: Progress Publishers, 1982; 18th printing) chapter 8, titled "Parasitism and Decay of Capitalism," 96.
32. Nikolai Bukharin, *Imperialism and World Economy* (New York: Howard Fertig, 1966), 169.
33. Chapter 12 offers a comprehensive analysis of corporations and their role in today's globalized economy. Arguments such as effects on local culture are addressed in Chapter 9.
34. Alan Wolfe, "The Snake: Globalization, America, and the Wretched Earth," *The New Republic*, October 1, 2001, 31.
35. Naomi Klein, *No Logo: No Space, No Choice, No Jobs* (New York: Picador, 2002).
36. Nicaragua Solidarity Network.
37. Elmer Edgar Stoll, "Shylock," *Shakespeare Studies* (New York: Stechert, 1927). Quoted in *The Merchant of Venice*, ed. Kenneth Myrick (New York: Signet Classic, 1987), 165.
38. See my op-ed article "What Buchanan Owes Clinton," *New York Times*, February 22, 1996. The melodramatic title, chosen (as always) by the newspaper, reflected the fact that I was pointing to some parallels between Buchanan's demands and the Clinton administration's Japan-bashing attitudes and the proposals of some of the administration's supporters who had in fact asked for even higher tariffs against the Japanese. The situation was ironic, in my view: a liberal administration sharing the views of a xenophobe!
39. Michael Sandel, "It's Immoral to Buy the Right to Pollute," *New York Times*, December 15, 1997.

Chapter 2

1. In contrast to Prime Minister Tony Blair's forthright condemnation, described in the text, President Bill Clinton could not bring himself to denounce the demonstrators in Seattle in 1999. Aside from his indulgence, Clinton perhaps carried the memory of the Chicago riots that scarred and virtually killed Hubert Humphrey's presidential bid.
2. Or one could say wittily that the former wished to be heard, while the latter wanted to be listened to. The former were in jeans, the latter in suits. The former were in the streets, the latter in corridors. One could go on.
3. Of course, nothing is ever altogether new. Thus there was the famous antislavery movement organized by the great Quaker families such as the Wilberforces of England in the eighteenth century; the abolition of slavery was surely a global concern, since slaves were transported across the oceans and put to work in the colonies.
4. Not all economists will concede this, of course. While I do not directly refute their views in this book, though I have done so in many other places, the book does offer some explicit analysis of the link between globalization and economic prosperity. This is because, as will be seen with some of the questions I address in this book, greater economic prosperity serves to advance the social agendas as well. Thus, in Chapter 5, on poverty, and Chapter 6, on child labor, the fact that globalization increases economic prosperity is an important factor in asserting that globalization reduces both poverty and the use of child labor.
5. From John Stuart Mill, *The Principles of Political Economy*, Part 3, Chapter 17, Section 14; quoted in Charles Calomoris, "A Globalist Manifesto for Public Policy," Hayek Memorial Lecture, occasional paper no. 124, Institute for Economic Affairs, London, April 2002, 21.

Chapter 3

1. I serve on its Academic Advisory Board for Asia.
2. It is not entirely clear whether this was an unanticipated problem or whether the shrimp firms were unaware of these consequences and caught flatfooted; the latter seems to have been the case, and I proceed in the text on that assumption.
3. See the discussion of this evidence in Chapter 1 of my *A Stream of Windows: Unsettling Reflections on Trade, Immigration and Democracy* (Cambridge: MIT Press, 1998).

4. See, in particular, my book *Protectionism* (Cambridge: MIT Press, 1988), and an earlier volume I edited, *Import Competition and Response* (Chicago: University of Chicago Press, 1978).

5. The pertinent arguments need to be looked at in the original and are available in several places. My own are reprinted, for the most part, in my collections *A Stream of Windows* and *The Wind of the Hundred Days: How Washington Mismanaged Globalization* (Cambridge: MIT Press, 2001). See also my testimony on the U.S.-Jordan free trade agreement, where the central questions related to the inclusion of labor standards in trade treaties and institutions are analyzed; it is available at http://www.columbia.edu/~jb38/papers/jordan.pdf.

Chapter 4

1. Lester Salamon, "The Rise of the Nonprofit Sector," *Foreign Affairs* 73, 4 (1994), 109–22.

2. The World Bank defines NGOs more functionally from the viewpoint of its own interests as "private organizations that pursue activities to relieve suffering, promote the interests of the poor, protect the environment, provide basic social services, or undertake community development." See the Bank's Operational Directive 14.70, cited in http://docs.lib.duke.edu/igo/guides/ngo/define.htm.

3. As I will argue later, both Khor and Mehta, two of the developing-country NGO chiefs, are strongly against linking labor standards to trade, and both therefore oppose the social clause at the WTO. So do the Indian and Singapore trade unions. Thirteen of the biggest Indian trade unions, which uniformly oppose linkage regardless of where they are on the political spectrum, have a membership of 8.3 million, which brings them neck and neck with the AFL-CIO, which gets all the press and also publicity for John J. Sweeney, head of the American labor federation, while the Indian unions leaders remain faceless to the public in the OECD countries because neither they nor their views make it to the press.

4. Examples of this Southern perspective may be found in Chapter 10, on labor standards, and in Chapter 11, on environment and globalization.

5. In my own experience, I encountered some of these people, including my father-in-law, a Cambridge graduate in English literature who spent his entire life working for a meager salary in a small college in Surat, then a small town and now in the throes of prosperity because of globalization in the form of an outbreak of trade in polished diamonds. Surat and Antwerp are now two big names in the trade; and Surat polishes diamonds like no one else does!

6. For a sympathetic account of the agitation, see the website of the International Rivers Network, an NGO that actively opposes big dams: http://www.irn.org.

7. As Fareed Zakaria once remarked about Robert Putnam's book *Bowling Alone* (New York: Simon and Schuster, 2000): whereas the author was complaining about how people were no longer bowling together, suggesting a breakdown of the communitarian spirit that traditionally glued American democracy together, the Oklahoma City bombers had hatched their evil plot while bowling together! Technology can be used for good and for bad; the prior question, as in the text, is why it has been used for good.

8. I owe this witticism to Michael Edwards, one of the world's leading experts on NGOs.

9. Václav Havel et al., *The Power of the Powerless*, ed. John Keane (London: Hutchinson, 1985), 49–50.

10. Quoted in Mikkio Kivikoski, "'Anti-Politics' and Civil Society," in Markku Kangaspuro, ed., *Russia: More Different Than Most* (Helsinki: Kikimora, 1999), 64. I have found this article immensely useful, aside from the direct reading of Václav Havel, Václav Benda, Miroslav Kusy, and other dissident intellectuals. Steven Lukes' introduction to Havel et al., *Power of the Powerless*, is worth reading for its analysis of how different intellectuals debated the way in which Havel's ideas could actually translate into effective antipolitics in the post-totalitarian regimes within which they were conceived.

11. Quoted in Kivikoski, "'Anti-Politics' and Civil Society," 68.

12. György Konrád, *The Melancholy of Rebirth: Essays from Post-Communist Central Europe, 1989–1994* (San Diego: Harcourt Brace, 1995). Quoted in Kivikoski, "'Anti-Politics' and Civil Society," 68.
13. Salamon, "The Rise of the Nonprofit Sector," 111.
14. By one estimate, the number of transnational NGOs increased more than tenfold between 1960 and 1997, to roughly sixteen thousand. See Union of International Associations, *Yearbook of International Organizations 1997/98*, vol. 1 (Munich: Saur, 1997), cited in Jan Aart Scholte, "The WTO and Civil Society," CSGR Working Paper No. 14/98, University of Warwick, England.
15. For a sympathetic treatment of these globalized NGOs, see Margaret Keck and Kathryn Sikkink, *Activists Beyond Borders: Advocacy Networks in International Politics* (Ithaca: Cornell University Press, 1998); and Jackie Smith, Charles Chatfield, and Ron Pagnucco, eds., *Transnational Social Movements and Global Politics: Solidarity Beyond the State* (Syracuse: Syracuse University Press, 1997).
16. See the work of the British political scientists Grant Jordan and William Maloney, *The Protest Business? Mobilizing Campaign Groups* (London: Routledge, 1999).
17. In this context, I found particularly interesting Linda Spalding's sympathetic but still disillusioned account of the not-exactly-exemplary activities of Birute Galdikas, the third of Leakey's "three angels" (the other two being Jane Goodall and Dian Fossey), in saving the orangutan in Borneo. See Spalding, *The Follow* (London: Bloomsbury, 1998). But is this really surprising? We all combine in our personalities and our activities different degrees of altruism and self-interest. And many of us are susceptible to seeking self-interest while claiming to be altruistic.
18. W. H. Auden, "Base Words Are Uttered," in W. H. Auden, *Collected Poems*, edited by Edward Mendelson (New York: Random House, Vintage International, February 1971), 298.
19. It should be noted that the *New Republic* was a strong supporter of Al Gore in the 2000 presidential campaign and considered Ralph Nader to be a spoiler who cost Gore the election.
20. See "The Man Behind the Anti-Free-Trade Revolt," *New Republic*, January 10, 2000.
21. Norimitsu Onishi, "African Numbers, Problems and Number Problems," *New York Times*, Week in Review section, August 18, 2002, 5. It is of course possible that later investigations may uncover other undesirable features of the use of child labor on the cocoa plantations.
22. Alison Maitland, "Accountability 'Vital' if NGOs Are to Retain Trust," *Financial Times*, June 25, 2003, front page, first section. In a letter to the editor on June 30, 2003, in response to this report, Stuart Etherington, CEO of the National Council for Voluntary Organizations, based in the United Kingdom, mentions the pioneering work of Guidestar in providing the public an analysis of the finances of NGOs, 18.
23. This case is referenced and discussed in Chapter 11, on the environment.
24. This theme has been developed recently also by the brilliant young lawyer from the University of Wisconsin's law school, Gregory Schaffer, in a number of recent papers. My own work, reported below when I come to Part III, also develops this theme in depth.
25. See http://www.urbanreflex.com/monopoly.html.

Chapter 5

1. See http://www.un.org/millennium/declaration/htm, 5.
2. I owe this quote to T. N. Srinivasan and used it earlier in my convocation address at Panjab University, Chandigarh, India, when receiving an honorary degree in December 2000. The convocation address is available from my website, http://www.columbia.edu/~jb38.
3. See W. S. Churchill, *Lord Randolph Churchill* (New York, 1906), 268–69; and Jacob Viner, *Essays in the Intellectual History of Economics*, ed. Douglas Irwin (Princeton: Princeton University Press, 1991).
4. Tomas Larsson, *The Race to the Top* (Washington, D.C.: Cato Institute, 2001), 133–34.
5. Adam Smith, *The Wealth of Nations*, ed. Edwin Cannan (New York: Modern Library, 1937), 81.

6. Jawaharlal Nehru, *Discovery of India* (New York: John Day, 1946), 402–3.

7. For many years *immiseration* was not in the dictionary, and often I had difficulty convincing editors to allow me to use the word. By now it has entered the economists' usage, and no editor has bothered me in a decade or so. William Safire, if he runs out of ideas, can surely do a column in the *New York Times Magazine*.

8. My use of the phrase "immiserizing growth" also endeared me to the intellectuals in Sorbonne, where there is a soft corner for me, I am told, because of this early paper of mine.

9. See Jagdish Bhagwati, "Immiserizing Growth: A Geometric Note," *Review of Economic Studies*, June 1958.

10. Economists can demonstrate that the best way to do this is to impose an "optimal tariff," an argument that goes back to David Ricardo's contemporary Torrens, who produced this objection to Prime Minister Robert Peel's policy of repealing Britain's Corn Laws with a view to taking Britain unilaterally into a free trade policy. For a full statement of the theory of commercial policy and its application to conventional and modern objections to free trade, see my *Free Trade Today* (Princeton: Princeton University Press, 2002).

11. Norman Borlaug was responsible for the innovation in wheat.

12. I have discussed the role of influential economists in supporting and rationalizing these erroneous policies that proved costly for growth and for poverty reduction in my Radhakrishnan Lectures, published as *India in Transition* (Oxford: Clarendon Press, 1993). Ironically, some of these economists are among those today lamenting the growth of poverty, failing to recognize that they are among those who caused it!

13. The economist Anne Krueger, currently the first deputy managing director at the International Monetary Fund, directed a substantial research project when she was vice president and chief economist at the World Bank, the findings of which broadly support what I say in the text. See Anne Krueger, *Trade and Employment in Developing Countries: Synthesis and Conclusions* (Chicago: University of Chicago Press, 1982). Also see the extended discussion in my "Export-Promoting Trade Strategy: Issues and Evidence," *World Bank Research Observer* 3, 1 (1988): 27–57.

14. The credit for this innovation has gone to the Bangladeshi economist Mohammed Yunus, who founded the Grameen Bank. But the original experiment was by the remarkable Ilabehn Bhatt, who founded SEWA, the Self-Employed Women's Association, in Ahmedabad. The general failure to recognize her pioneering role in microcredit is perhaps yet another instance of gender discrimination.

15. Hernando de Soto, *The Mystery of Capital* (New York: Basic Books, 2001).

16. Padma Desai and I documented these effects in India in *India: Planning for Industrialization* (London: Oxford University Press, 1970). Similar documentation and analysis exists for many countries by now.

17. A comparable feat belongs to Gary, Indiana, which also has produced two Nobel laureates: my teacher Paul Samuelson and Joe Stiglitz. I gather that St. Lucia and Gary are not that different in the size of their populations.

18. I and Padma Desai documented at length in *India: Planning for Industrialization* the enormous delays and corruption being spawned by the bureaucratic restriction and licensing requirements in India. Hernando de Soto has also tirelessly documented these delays in country after poor country. And, as I argue, these delays hurt the poor far more than the rich and the connected.

19. What I say about the role of democracy, NGOs, and others factors in giving empowerment to the poor and the peripheral groups has been argued by me in several writings over the last two decades.

　　On democracy, for example, see my 1993 Rajiv Gandhi Memorial Lecture, titled "Democracy and Development: New Thinking on an Old Question," reprinted in my collection *A Stream of Windows: Unsettling Reflections on Trade, Immigration and Democracy* (Cambridge: MIT Press, 1998).

20. As it happens, the lead in this was given by my brother, P. N. Bhagwati, a former chief justice of India, who also helped set up India's Legal Aid Program.

21. This literature has been reviewed splendidly by Jere Behrman and Anil Deolalikar, "Will Developing Country Nutrition Improve with Income? A Case Study for Rural South India," *Journal of Political Economy* 95, 3 (1987).

22. This is the Vikram Sarabhai Lecture given in Ahmedabad and has been reprinted as Chapter 25 in my *Political Economy and International Economics*, ed. Douglas Irwin (Cambridge: MIT Press, 1991); the quotes below are from 545–46.

23. I remarked at the time that "distribution within the household may be such as to deprive the weaker members such as females, of an adequate access to the consumption basket. In the 1970s I was somewhat isolated . . . as an economist in being seriously interested in the sex-bias that was visible in the statistics on educational enrollments, literacy, infant mortality, and nutritional levels, much of the evidence coming from anthropological findings and other surveys" (ibid., 546).

24. For a formal discussion of alternative theoretical models, see T. N. Srinivasan and Jagdish Bhagwati, "Outward Orientation and Development: Are Revisionists Right?" in Deepak Lal and Richard Snape, eds., *Trade, Development and Political Economy: Essays in Honour of Anne Krueger* (London: Palgrave, 2001); a fuller version is available at http://www.columbia.edu/~jb38.

25. Quoted in Douglas Irwin, "Interpreting the Tariff-Growth Correlation in the Late Nineteenth Century," Dartmouth College. A revision was published in *American Economic Review Papers and Proceedings*, May 2002, and this is the version that I use in the text.

26. See Michael Clemens and Jeffrey Williamson, "A Tariff-Growth Paradox? Protection's Impact the World Around," National Bureau of Economic Research Working Paper No. 8459, Cambridge, Mass., September 2001; and Kevin O'Rourke, "Tariffs and Growth in the Late 19th Century," *Economic Journal* 110 (2000): 456–83.

27. Irwin, "Interpreting the Tariff-Growth Correlation."

28. Douglas Irwin, "Did Late-Nineteenth-Century U.S. Tariffs Promote Infant Industries? Evidence from the Tinplate Industry," *The Journal of Economic History* 60, 2 (2000): 335–60.

29. The OECD project was directed by the Oxford economists Ian Little and Maurice Scott along with the Stanford economist Tibor Scitovsky. The National Bureau of Economic Research project, which followed it, was directed by me with Anne Krueger.

30. The results from these projects, including one from the World Bank by the late Bela Balassa, a pioneer in the field, are reviewed in Bhagwati, "Export-Promoting Trade Strategy."

31. These were among the conclusions that I drew in my synthesis volume on the findings of the National Bureau of Economic Research project, codirected with Anne Krueger. Aside from them, there are many that have been discussed in the recent literature, including the role of new products and variety when an economy opens up, the absorption of (disembodied) know-how that can come from diffusion of new methods as trade and direct foreign investment bring the new methods to one's attention, etc. Among the economists who have contributed to this literature creatively is Paul Romer of Stanford, an illustrious son of the illustrious Governor Romer, who has also gone on to argue that the cost of protection is likely to be far higher than has been commonly believed by many economists.

32. New computers embody more-advanced technology than old ones. Economists therefore talk of "new-vintage" capital equipment. This is also embodied technical change, as distinct from disembodied technical change, where—with, say, better organization—you get more productivity from the same equipment and manpower.

33. I have developed this argument at length in Bhagwati, "East Asian Growth: The Miracle that Did Happen," keynote address at a Cornell University conference, reprinted in my collected public policy essays, *The Wind of the Hundred Days: How Washington Mismanaged Globalization* (Cambridge: MIT Press, 2001).

34. There are several writings by these two authors. The latest is "Spreading the Wealth," *Foreign Affairs* 81, 1 (2002): 120–33. The findings on trade and growth are discussed on 126.

35. Again, the higher globalization on trade and investment flows may have been the result of a mix of policies such as infrastructure development and not exclusively due to outward orientation in trade policy. But without such outward orientation, the globalizers would surely not have achieved the high globalization and the accompanying high growth rates.

36. Xavier Sala-i-Martin, "The World Distribution of Income Estimated from Individual Country Distributions," National Bureau of Economic Research Working Paper No. 8933, Cambridge, Mass., May 2002, 31.

37. Simon Schama, *The Embarrassment of Riches: An Interpretation of Dutch Culture in the Golden Age* (New York: Vintage, 1997).

38. See the studies of the World Bank economist Branko Milanovic.

39. See Surjit Bhalla, *Imagine There's No Country: Poverty, Inequality, and Growth in the Era of Globalization* (Washington, D.C.: Institute for International Economics, 2002). These findings are receiving huge attention, and scrutiny, since they tear at the guts of the fashionable pessimism on the subject of trends in global inequality. Also see a related exchange in *Foreign Affairs*, July–August 2002, on the subject of inequality among nations.

Chapter 6

1. See International Labor Organization, *Child Labor Surveys: Results of Methodological Experiments in Four Countries, 1992–1993* (Geneva: International Programme on the Eradication of Child Labor, ILO, 2002).

2. *Invisible Slaves* (New Delhi: SAACS, 1999).

3. See Priya Ranjan, "An Economic Analysis of Child Labor," *Economics Letters* 64 (1999): 99–105. Ranjan also builds an interesting model formalizing this insight.

4. See Rajeev Dehejia and Roberta Gatti, "Child Labor: The Role of Income Variability and Access to Credit Across Countries," National Bureau of Economic Research, Working Paper No. 9018, Cambridge, Mass., June 2002.

5. Cf. Kathleen Beegle, Rajeev Dehejia, and Roberta Gatti, "Do Households Resort to Child Labor to Cope with Income Shocks?" Department of Economics, Columbia University, Discussion Paper No. 0203-12, 2002.

6. Kaushik Basu, who agrees with this policy conclusion, has argued that in some circumstances there may be two equilibria, one where children cannot be hired and so the adults find demand for them rising, and the other where they can be. In that case, the prohibition of child labor could push the economy into the other equilibrium, which may be welfare-enhancing. He thinks that only one equilibrium is likely in the poor countries, however, and in that case a ban on the use of child labor would be welfare-worsening. See Kaushik Basu and Pham Hoang Van, "The Economics of Child Labor," *American Economic Review* 88, 3 (1998): 417–27.

7. See "Ethical Shopping; Human Rights," *The Economist*, June 3, 1995, 58.

8. This price increase was relative to the consumer price index.

9. See Eric Edmonds and Nina Pavcnik, "Does Globalization Increase Child Labor? Evidence from Vietnam," National Bureau of Economic Research Working Paper No. 8760, Cambridge, Mass., January 2002; available from http://www.nber.org/papers/w8760.

Chapter 7

1. The threat from strength was seen as coming from our inability to compete with the Japanese in industry. The threat from weakness is seen as coming from their inability to revive the economy.

2. "Samurais No More," *Foreign Affairs*, May–June 1994, 7–12.

3. Sandra Black and Elizabeth Brainerd, "Importing Equality? The Impact of Globalization on Gender Discrimination," November 2000; available at http://econpapers.hhs.se/paper/izaizadps/dp556.htm.

4. Becker analyzes discrimination reflecting employers' prejudice, as explored by Black and Brainerd, and also prejudice by fellow workers and by customers. See Gary Stanley Becker, *The Economic Approach to Human Behavior* (Chicago: University of Chicago Press, 1978).

5. Arlie Russell Hochschild, "Global Care Chains and Emotional Surplus Value," in Anthony Giddens and Will Hutton, eds., *On the Edge: Living with Global Capitalism* (London: Vintage, 2001), 130–46.

6. Ibid., 136.

7. Ibid., 135.

8. When the migration is long-lasting, even extended over decades, the deleterious emotional and social effects on the migrants' families, if they are left behind and if occasional return visits are too expensive to manage, can be very different, of course. Yet countervailing these effects are the definite economic benefits that such migration often brings to the families. In a fascinating story on the Persian Gulf oil boom and the long-term emigration of workers that it inspired from the state of Kerala in India, Amy Waldman wrote in the *New York Times* that the women left behind talked of "loneliness," recalling "moments they ached for their husband's presence." Then she adds: "But they sutured their longing and kept living. Were the years of separation worth it? Pullar Umar's wife and son were asked. Yes, they replied, for without the sacrifice, they could not have built the house they moved into— without him—last week." Amy Waldman, "Gulf Bounty Is Drying Up in Southern India," *New York Times,* February 24, 2003.

9. Hochschild, "Global Care Chains," 144.

10. "Women and Trade," Testimony for Hill Briefing on Women and the WTO, June 28, 1999, by Marceline White, Women's Edge, 2.

11. "Women and Trade: Investing in Women: FTAA Investment Policies and Women," Trade Fact Sheet, Women's Edge, October 21, 2001.

12. Ibid., 3.

13. Reported in "How Today's Trading System Hurts Women," *Human Rights for Workers,* June 3, 2002. This newsletter, put out by Robert Senser (http://www.senser.com), is very useful.

14. Oxfam, *Rigged Rules and Double Standards* (Oxford: Oxfam, 2002), 85; also quoted in "How Today's Trading System Hurts Women."

15. Whether workers are exploited in ways other than poverty-level wages being paid to them is a wider question that is also considered in Chapter 12.

16. "Women Declare That Trade Is an Instrument of Development Not Profit," press release by the regional representatives attending the Strategic Planning Seminar in Cape Town, South Africa, August 12–18.

17. Ibid.

18. Ibid.

19. James Shapiro, "Taiwan," *Multinational Monitor,* June 1981, 11–12.

20. V. Spike Peterson and Anne Sisson Runyan, *Global Gender Issues,* 2nd ed. (Boulder: Westview, 1999), 82.

21. See the latest analysis of the reasons for this decline by Robert Baldwin, *The Decline of US Labor Unions and the Role of Trade* (Washington, D.C.: Institute for International Economics, 2003). This study argues that trade has contributed only modestly to the general decline in unionization though greater incidence is noted for uneducated labor.

22. H. Safa, "Free Markets and the Marriage Market: Structural Adjustment, Gender Relations, and Working Conditions Among Dominican Workers," *Environment and Planning* 31 (1999): 294. This is a fascinating sociological analysis of the effects of structural changes in the economy on gender roles and relations.

23. Their work is cited in Chapter 12 .

24. See the fascinating work of Morris D. Morris et al., *Indian Economy in the Nineteenth Century: A Symposium* (Delhi: Indian Economic and Social History Association, 1969).

25. Shapiro, "Taiwan."

26. Barbara S. Mensch, Judith Bruce, and Margaret E. Greene, *The Uncharted Passage: Girls' Adolescence in the Developing World* (New York: Population Council, 1998), 39–40. I thank Judith Bruce for extensive comments on an early draft of this chapter.

27. Safa, "Free Markets and the Marriage Market," 294.

28. Its efficacy would increase if NGOs were also present to bring violations of these regulations to public attention. In this context, the legal standing given by an activist Indian su-

preme court to NGOs to bring such violations to court on behalf of those lacking the ability themselves is a useful innovation. The role of civil society in the design of appropriate governance today is a theme developed in Part IV.

29. See the WTO Dispute Settlement Report, "European Communities-Regime for the Importation, Sale and Distribution of Bananas-Recourse to Article 21.5 by Ecuador," WT/DS27/RW/ECU 99-1443.

30. "Women and Trade," Testimony for Hill Briefing on Women and the WTO, June 28, 1999, by Marceline White, Women's Edge, 4.

31. But the IMF did think that, ultimately, these countries should replace their reliance on tariffs for revenue with other more efficient methods of taxation.

32. Margaret Macmillan, *Women of the Raj* (New York: Thames and Hudson, 1996), 16–17.

Chapter 8

1. William Shakespeare, *The Merchant of Venice* (New York: Signet Classic, 1965), Act III, Scene III.

2. "Companies Market to India's Have-Littles," *Wall Street Journal,* Thursday, June 5, 2003, B1, B12. At the heart of this phenomenon is, of course, access to knowledge of prices and buyers that the computers provide. In the old days, this was done in admittedly a far smaller way by newspapers specializing in printing and providing information on prices that was inaccessible earlier. Thus the Japanese novelist Junichiro Tanizaki writes in his autobiography, *Childhood Years: A Memoir* (Tokyo: Kodansha International, 1988), about his grandfather: "Grandfather had chosen to locate his printing establishments near the rice merchants' quarter because he thought it might be highly profitable to publish news of the daily fluctuations in the price of rice every evening for sale to the dealers. There were still very few newspapers then, and certainly no evening editions; and Grandfather's plan succeeded wonderfully. The "Tanizaki Daily Price List," as the sheets were known, made a lot of money for the print shop; and, in effect, Grandfather had established his own small-scale evening paper" (5).

3. Seymour Martin Lipset, *Some Social Requisites of Democracy: Economic Development and Political Legitimacy* (Indianapolis: Bobbs-Merrill, 1959). Also see his *Political Man* (New York: Anchor, 1963). See, too, some of the writings of Ralf Dahrendorf on the subject, especially in regard to historical German experience with the emergence of democracy there.

4. See Ralf Dahrendorf, *Society and Democracy in Germany* (New York: Doubleday, 1969), which was published in Germany in 1965, and Samuel Huntington, *Political Order in Changing Societies* (New Haven: Yale University Press, 1968). Fareed Zakaria's new and wildly successful book, *The Future of Freedom* (New York: W. W. Norton, 2003), on the other hand, buys into the Lipset thesis.

5. Quoted in Lawrence F. Kaplan, "Why Trade Won't Bring Democracy to China," *The New Republic,* July 9–16, 2001, 24.

6. Both quotes are from Sheri Berman, "Modernization in Historical Perspective: The Case of Imperial Germany," *World Politics* 53 (2001): 431.

7. Ibid., 434–35.

8. See "Economic Development and Democracy Reconsidered," in Gary Marks and Larry Diamond, *Reexamining Democracy* (Newbury Park: Sage, 1992), 93–139; cited in Juan Linz and Alfred Stepan, *Problems of Democratic Transition and Consolidation* (Baltimore: Johns Hopkins University Press, 1996), 77.

9. Linz and Stepan, *Problems of Democratic Transition and Consolidation,* 78; also see n. 18.

10. Ibid., 76–81.

11. Ibid., 77–78.

12. Barrington Moore, *Social Origins of Dictatorship and Democracy: Lord and Peasant in the Making of the Modern World* (Boston: Beacon, 1990).

13. Quoted in Kaplan, "Why Trade Won't Bring Democracy to China," 26.

14. E. H. Carr, *Socialism in One Country, 1924–1926* (London: Penguin, 1970).

15. Karl Polanyi, *The Great Transformation* (New York: Farrar and Reinhart, 1944).
16. John Ruggie, "International Regimes, Transactions and Change: Embedded Liberalism in the Postwar Economic Order," *International Organization* 36, 2 (1982).
17. Peter Katzenstein, *Small States in World Markets* (Ithaca: Cornell University Press, 1985); David Cameron, "The Expansion of the Public Economy: A Comparative Analysis," *American Political Science Review* 72, 4 (1978): 1243–61. Also see Dani Rodrik, "Why Do More Open Economies Have Bigger Governments?" *Journal of Political Economy* 106, 5 (1998).
18. Geoffrey Garrett, "Globalization and Government Spending Around the World," July 2000, esp. 27; www.yale.edu/leitner/pdf/1999-06.pdf.
19. I have addressed these issues, and the errors in Sen's arguments centered on availability of information as the key to why democracy will prevent famines, in my 1993 Rajiv Gandhi Memorial Lecture "Democracy and Development," reprinted in my collection *A Stream of Windows: Unsettling Reflections on Trade, Immigration and Democracy* (Cambridge: MIT Press, 2000).
20. See, for instance, D. Swank, "Political Institutions and Welfare State Restructuring: The Impact of Institutions on Social Policy Change in Developed Democracies," in P. Pierson, ed., *The New Politics of the Welfare State* (London: Oxford University Press, 2001), and other articles by him on the subject of capital mobility in particular.
21. See, in particular, the interesting work of Umea University (Sweden) political scientist Cynthia Kite, "The Political Stability of the Globalized Welfare State," paper presented to the Symposium on Globalization and the Welfare State, Jonkoping, Sweden, May 31–June 1, 2002.
22. Vito Tanzi, "Globalization and the Work of Fiscal Termites," *Finance and Development*, March 2001, 34–37.
23. Alberto Alesina, Enrico Spolaore, and Romain Wacziarg, "Economic Integration and Political Disintegration," *American Economic Review* 90, 3 (2000): 1276–96.
24. See N. Woods and A. Narlikar, "Governance and the Limit of Accountability: The WTO, the IMF and the World Bank," *International Social Science Journal*, November 2001.
25. Carl Hamilton, "Globalisation and Democracy," paper presented to the International Seminar on International Trade on "Challenges to Globalisation," May 24–25, 2002, Stockholm.
26. J. M. Keynes, *The General Theory of Interest, Employment and Money* (London: Macmillan, 1936), 383.
27. Jagdish Bhagwati, ed., *Going Alone: The Case for Relaxed Reciprocity in Freeing Trade* (Cambridge: MIT Press, 2002).
28. See my essay "Globalization, Sovereignty and Democracy," in *The Wind of the Hundred Days: How Washington Mismanaged Globalization* (Cambridge: MIT Press, 2000), for a discussion of this problem.

Chapter 9

1. I consider here only the issues raised in the public policy debate on the effect of economic globalization on culture. There are, of course, at least two other major questions of interest that culture has raised in the scholarly and policy literature. One relates to the extensive debates prompted by Samuel Huntington's classic *Foreign Affairs* article "The Clash of Civilizations" concerning whether future conflicts between nation-states will be prompted by culture (embracing religion) now that ideology is dead, à la Fukuyama. The other relates to the perennial question of whether culture determines economic development. On the latter question, raised anew by David Landes and Lawrence Harrison, see my review essay, "The West's Triumph: Did Culture Do It?" *The New Republic*, May 25, 1998; reprinted in *The Wind of the Hundred Days: How Washington Mismanaged Globalization* (Cambridge: MIT Press, 2000).
2. The quotes are from Philip Gordon and Sophie Meunier, *The French Challenge* (Washington, D.C.: Brookings Institution Press, 2001), 53. I am indebted to Niah Shepherd for research on the facts of this episode and much else in this chapter.

3. BBC News, June 30, 2000, available at http://news.bbc.co.uk/2/hi/europe/812995.stm.

4. Quoted in *News India-Times* (USA), June 14, 2002, 21. The truth is exactly the opposite: that the acceleration of prosperity due to globalization and economic reforms will help reduce India's poverty faster, as argued in Chapter 5, and thus help the Dalits, who suffer more acutely from poverty.

5. See note 1 to this chapter.

6. I have argued that this is because the United States has a unique and enduring advantage: that it is a country of immigrants who, whether skilled or unskilled, continually provide renewal. It also attracts, because of its universities and research institutes and its spirit of freedom and equality that is hardly matched elsewhere, talented people from around the world.

7. Charles Leadbeater, *Up the Down Escalator: Why the Global Pessimists Are Wrong* (London: Viking, 2002), 108.

8. Angus Wilson, *Reflections in a Writer's Eye* (New York: Viking, 1986), 160.

9. These facts, plus others below, come from a delightful *Wall Street Journal* article, "Armchairs, TVs and Espresso—Is It McDonald's?" by Shirley Leung, August 30, 2002, A1.

10. Ibid.

11. Quoted in Gordon and Meunier, *The French Challenge*, 30–31.

12. Thus, rap music has become a commercial success, with groups such as IAM and 113 moving upscale and hip-hop jostling English pop music successfully on the French scene. Cf. "Parlez-Vous Verlan," BBC News, March 26, 2002, at http://news.bbc.co.uk/2/hi/europe/1892853.stm. For interesting documentation of this spread and its tenuous relationship to the Dwight MacDonald and Theodor Adorno theories that suggested an imperialist exercise of "oppressive power" and "psychological control" by a dominant culture, see Edward Rothstein, "Damning (Yet Desiring) Mickey and the Big Mac," *New York Times*, March 2, 2002, B9.

13. Elisabeth Rosenthal, "Buicks, Starbucks and Fried Chicken. Still China?" *New York Times*, February 25, 2002, A4.

14. See Tyler Cowen and Eric Crampton, "Uncommon Culture," *Foreign Policy*, July-August 2001; and Tyler Cowen, *Creative Destruction: How Globalization Is Changing the World's Cultures* (Princeton: Princeton University Press, 2002).

15. The two observations I make here are stimulated by the excellent discussion in Leadbeater, *Up the Down Escalator*, 59–63; the quotes from Monbiot and Hoskins are from Leadbeater.

16. I quote much of what I say from an extremely informative paper by Ajay Gandhi, "Indigenous Resistance to New Colonialism," *Cultural Survival Quarterly*, fall 2001, 32–34.

17. This perspective is a product of many postcolonial and Marxist writings, of course. For an interesting essay on the broader and profound questions for anthropology that these and other writings have raised, see Edward Said, "Representing the Colonized: Anthropology's Interlocutors," *Critical Inquiry* 15, 2 (1989).

18. This story, and the quotes, are from "People Matter Too," *The Economist*, June 8, 2002, 35. The report also includes interesting details on another such protest in Tambo Grande, Peru, not by indigenous groups but by traditional local growers of limes and mangos who have objected through their local council vote to the proposed entry into their valley by the Canadian multinational Manhattan Minerals, which presumably intends to mine copper, silver, and gold in the region.

19. Gandhi, "Indigenous Resistance to New Colonialism," 34.

20. See, for instance, the contributions in Dawn Hill, ed., *Indigenous Knowledge Conference Proceedings* (Hamilton: Indigenous Studies, McMaster University, 1999), and Stanley Diamond, ed., *Primitive Views of the World* (New York: Columbia University Press, 1960).

21. Doug Henwood, "Antiglobalization," *Left Business Observer* 71 (1996).

22. Some of the arguments here have been developed by me in my essay "Trade and Culture," in *The Wind of the Hundred Days: How Washington Mismanaged Globalization*. The Korean examples were produced by my student Kyung Kim.

23. The quotes and the details are from "South Korean Stars Defend Film Quotas," BBC, January 28, 2002, at http://news.bbc.co.uk/2/hi/entertainment/1786453.stm.

24. The facts below are from Gordon and Meunier, *The French Challenge*, 28–29.
25. The details on the way in which the subsidy was handed out to French filmmakers are nicely summarized in Gordon and Meunier, *The French Challenge*, 48–53.
26. Jagdish Bhagwati, letter to the editor, *New York Times*, December 24, 1993; reprinted in my collection *A Stream of Windows: Unsettling Reflections on Trade, Immigration and Democracy* (Cambridge: MIT Press, 1998), 477–78. The letter was inspired by a story in the newspaper by Karl E. Meyer, supporting the French view. In his reply Valenti asserted erroneously that his lobbying had to do with a totally different and more defensible question: that the tax levied on blank tapes and cassettes to recover revenues lost through unauthorized copying be pro rated to the United States on the basis of an estimated share of copying of America movies and TV programs.

Chapter 10

1. Scholars of Marx are divided over the question whether, in addition to his celebrated prediction of a falling rate of profit, Marx did indeed predict a falling real wage for the proletariat. But several scholars, and much of the public, believe that he did.
2. Real wages are nominal (i.e., dollar) wages divided by some appropriate price index, usually of what the wages are spent on.
3. This effect actually requires a number of stringent conditions in order to be made watertight. It is called in the technical literature the Stolper-Samuelson theorem.
4. For details, see Figure 11.2 in Jagdish Bhagwati, "Play It Again Sam: A New Look at Trade and Wages," in *The Wind of the Hundred Days: How Washington Mismanaged Globalization* (Cambridge: MIT Press, 2000), 127. A comprehensive statement of my optimistic thesis on the effect of trade on wages will be found there.
5. These are technically proven results of research on the effects of growth on trade that were produced in the mid-1950s and 1960s.
6. Robert Feenstra and Gordon Hanson, "Productivity Measurement and the Impact of Trade and Technology on Wages: Estimates for the U.S., 1972–1990," National Bureau of Economic Research Working Paper No. 6052, 1997. This paper focuses on the impact of outsourcing on relative wages of skilled to unskilled workers and that ratio rises. But the effect on the absolute real wages of the unskilled workers shows an increase, the relative fall coming from a disproportionate rise in the real wages of the skilled workers. The calculation of the absolute real wages of was done by Robert Feenstra in a private communication, at my request.
7. I have confined myself to the most influential arguments linking trade with poor countries to our workers' wages. For a full-scale analysis, see Bhagwati, "Play It Again Sam," and the many references therein.
8. See Edward Gresser, "Toughest on the Poor: America's Flawed Tariff System," *Foreign Affairs* 81, 6 (2002), 9–14. Gresser seems to present his findings without explaining why they have come about. The explanation lies, however, in the nature of tariff cutting. Poor countries, and hence the lower-end consumer products, missed out because the poor countries were not playing the reciprocity game, offering their own concessions in exchange for ours. I have considered this explanation, drawing on Michael Finger's insights, in "The Poor's Best Hope," *The Economist*, June 22, 2002.
9. Today, the AFL-CIO sees greater gain in embracing the illegals through yet another amnesty since these legalized immigrants are now seen as potential union members, whereas illegals clearly cannot be. Equally, the Catholic Church sees both God's grace and membership benefits in amnesty, since a sizeable fraction of the illegal population in America is Hispanic, Catholic, and devout.
10. See "U.S.-Mexico Trade: Some U.S. Wood Furniture Firms Relocated from Los Angeles Area to Mexico," United States General Accounting Office, GAO/NSAID-91-191, Washington, D.C.

11. Such responses, in any event, must be treated with caution, as they do not measure appropriately the relative weights assigned to different factors and are subject to many well-known errors.

12. The phone call was made by my research associate Michael Punzalan, an undergraduate student at New York University.

13. The creation of this council was announced by him during the State of the Union address on February 9, 1989.

14. I discussed this question with Marina Whitman, who was the chief economist for General Motors and a member of the Council of Economic Advisers. Her view was also that the competitiveness argument seemed like a good strategy to remove objectionable regulations, but that industry had rarely been able to invoke it successfully.

15. Human Rights Watch in its 2000 report *Unfair Advantage: Workers' Freedom of Association in the United States Under International Human Rights Standards* concludes that "millions of workers" in the United States are denied this key freedom and that the chief cause lies in the restrictions placed by American labor legislation itself way before modern globalization kicked in.

16. Daniel Drezner, "Bottom Feeders," *Foreign Policy,* November-December 2000.

17. Robert J. S. Ross and Anita Chan, "From North-South to South-South: The True Face of Global Competition," *Foreign Affairs* 81, 5 (2002).

18. These studies are reviewed in Drusilla Brown, Alan Deardorff, and Robert Stern, "The Effects of Multinational Enterprises on Wages and Working Conditions in Developing Countries," March 11, 2002, 24–27; available at http://www.econ.kuleuven.ac.be/ew/academic/intecon/home/WorkingGroupSeminars/Files/Deardorff.pdf.

19. William Cooke and Deborah Noble, "Industrial Relations Systems and U.S. Foreign Direct Investment Abroad," *British Journal of Industrial Relations* 34 (1998): 581–609.

20. David Kucera, "The Effects of Core Worker Rights on Labor Costs and Foreign Direct Investment: Evaluating the Conventional Wisdom," International Labor Organization, Geneva, 2001.

21. See, for instance, Beata K. Smarzyska and Shang-Jin Wei, "Pollution Havens and Foreign Direct Investment: Dirty Secret or Popular Myth?" World Bank Policy Research Working Paper No. 2673, 2001; and Arik Levinson, "Environmental Regulations and Industry Location: International and Domestic Evidence," in Jagdish Bhagwati and Robert Hudec, eds., *Fair Trade and Harmonization,* vol. 1 (Cambridge: MIT Press, 1996). The only exception that I know is recent work by Levinson showing that inside the United States, where the regulations differ by state, differences in environmental regulation in adjacent locations have some influence on the choice of location (though the actual choice of technology may not have been affected, so that the difference in regulatory restriction may be a proxy for something else, e.g., whether the location is business-friendly, for example).

22. It does not follow that legislative safeguards are unimportant. Whether they are will depend on the issue at hand, as discussed in Chapter 17.

23. This is true of Indian unions, which uniformly oppose linking labor standards to trade treaties and institutions in a manner that would imply trade sanctions, and of Indian environmental groups such as the world-renowned Center for Science and Technology, which opposed the unilateral imposition by U.S. law of the requirement to use turtle-excluding devices on foreign exporters of shrimp.

Chapter 11

1. This well-known passage from the Bible is quoted aptly by the philosopher Peter Singer in his essay "Environmental Values," reprinted in *Writings on an Ethical Life* (New York: Ecco, 2000), 88.

2. Quoted in ibid., 88.

3. Gerald Manley Hopkins, "Binsey Poplars," *Poems of Gerard Manley Hopkins* (London: Humphrey Milford, 1918).

4. From http://www.wisdomquotes.com.

5. Ibid.

6. Yasunari Kawabata, *The Old Capital,* trans. J. Martin Holman (San Francisco: North Point Press, 1987). The opening paragraphs already show this love for and harmony with nature, when Chieko, the young girl, is observing the violets flowering on the trunk of the old maple tree in her garden, and Kawabata writes: "Sometimes she was moved by the 'life' of the violets on the tree. Other times their 'loneliness' touched her heart" (3).

7. The *Scientific American* debate with Daly and the *Prospect* debate with Goldsmith are reprinted in my collected essays, *A Stream of Windows: Unsettling Reflections on Trade, Immigration and Democracy* (Cambridge: MIT Press, 1998) and *The Wind of the Hundred Days: How Washington Mismanaged Globalism* (Cambridge: MIT Press, 2000), respectively.

8. This report was issued as part of GATT, *Annual Report* (Geneva: GATT, 1991). It was designed and the research for it was organized by Blackhurst, who was at the time the chief economist for the GATT, with Anderson as his deputy.

9. See GATT, *Annual Report* (Geneva: GATT, 1991).

10. I owe these points to Derek Hall, "Explaining the Diversity of Southeast Asian Shrimp Aquaculture," Trent University, Ontario, Canada, 2003.

11. Conner Bailey and Mike Skladany, "Aquacultural Development in Tropical Asia," *Natural Resources Forum,* February 1991, 69.

12. The economics of what I am arguing has been set out more fully and rigorously in my Stockholm Lectures, published as *Free Trade Today* (Princeton: Princeton University Press, 2002), Chapters 1 and 2.

13. See, in particular, William Nordhaus and James Tobin, "Is Growth Obsolete?" *Income and Wealth* 38 (1973). Also see William Nordhaus and Edward Kokkelenberg, eds., *Nature's Numbers: Expanding the National Economic Accounts to Include the Environment* (Washington, D.C.: National Academy Press, 1999).

14. See Herman Daly, *Beyond Growth* (Boston: Beacon Press, 1989), particularly Chapters 6 and 7. Also see the Appendix in Herman Daly and John Cobb Jr., *For the Common Good,* 2nd ed. (Boston: Beacon Press, 1994).

15. The quotes are from an unpublished memorandum, "The Link Between Trade and the Environment," January 17, 2003, from an executive of a major environmental group, which was shared with me by an environmentalist friend. They are fairly typical, however, of several environmental groups.

16. See John Tierney, "Recycling Is Garbage," *New York Times Magazine,* June 30, 1996.

17. Matthew Kahn was once my colleague at Columbia University, where we worked on this idea; he is now at Tufts University. The research has not yet been published.

18. See Charlemagne, "Europe's Population Implosion," *The Economist,* July 19, 2003, 42.

19. For this example, I am indebted to my colleagues Alexander Pfaff and Shubham Chaudhuri, who have written on the effects of increased household income on fuel choice and hence on indoor air quality.

20. The per capita income levels are on the horizontal axis; the pollution levels on the vertical axis. The curve can be converted into a U-shaped curve if cleanliness rather than pollution levels are plotted. In parallel with the U-shaped curve suggested by Simon Kuznets for income inequality and incomes—that inequality would rise and then fall—the environmental curve is also called sometimes the Kuznets environmental curve.

21. Gene Grossman and Alan Krueger, "Economic Growth and the Environment," *Quarterly Journal of Economics* 110 (1995), 353–77.

22. I am indebted to an unpublished paper by Jeffrey Frankel ("The Environment and Economic Globalization," Council on Foreign Relations, New York, 2003) for these historical examples.

23. There are also some econometric studies that explore the association between trade (rather than income) and the environment, showing positive rather than negative association. For instance, see Ana Eiras and Brett Schaefer, "Trade: The Best Way to Protect the Environment," Backgrounder No. 1480, The Heritage Foundation, Washington D.C., September

2001, available at http://www.heritage.org/Research/TradeandForeignAid/BG1480.cfm; and William Harbaugh, Arik Levinson, and David Wilson, "Reexamining the Empirical Evidence for an Environmental Kuznets Curve," National Bureau of Economic Research, Working Paper No. 7711, May 2000.

24. This is not to say that in matters such as humanitarian intervention to save lives, an active role by foreign NGOs and individuals should be discounted or deplored. In fact, among the important activities of Amnesty International has been agitation to identify and work for the release of political prisoners, an activity I have myself participated in when embracing the cause of Dr. Joseph Mensah, minister of finance in Ghana, when he was arbitrarily imprisoned.

25. Quoted in Jagdish Bhagwati and T. N. Srinivasan, "Trade and the Environment: Does Environmental Diversity Detract from the Case of Free Trade?" in Jagdish Bhagwati and Robert Hudec, eds., *Fair Trade and Harmonization: Prerequisites for Free Trade?* (Cambridge: MIT Press, 1996), 162–63. This article contains a far more comprehensive treatment of several trade-versus-environment issues than I have been able to present in this chapter; it should be read in its entirety by anyone who seeks a more technical and comprehensive discussion of the issues. Of importance is also C. Ford Runge, *Free Trade, Protected Environment* (New York: Council on Foreign Relations, 1994).

26. Arik Levinson, "Environmental Regulations and Industry Location: International and Domestic Evidence" in Jagdish Bhagwati and Robert Hudec, eds., *Fair Trade and Harmonization: Prerequisites for Free Trade?* (Cambridge: MIT Press, 1996), 450.

27. These are set out in Bhagwati and Srinivasan, "Trade and the Environment," 173–75. Several have been cited, in turn, by the environment lawyer Daniel Esty in many of his recent writings. See, in particular, Carolyn Deere and Daniel Esty, eds., *Greening the Americas* (Cambridge: MIT Press, 2002).

28. This ties into the issue of corporate social responsibility, which was discussed in Chapter 12, and to the tactics of NGOs, which were discussed also in Chapters 1 and 4.

29. For a comprehensive treatment, see Bhagwati and Srinivasan, "Trade and the Environment."

30. Yet another class of problems has related to direct environmental regulations such as the ban on the sale of beer in cans instead of bottles. This was at issue in the Ontario legislation on beer, which the United States objected to as disguised protectionism. After two GATT panels had found against Canada and in favor of the United States, the two countries finally reached agreement on a resolution of the dispute in April 1992. But then, five days later, the Ontario government placed an "environmental tax" of 10 percent on beer cans. As it happened, there was no such tax on other aluminum cans, and Ontario beer was sold in bottles, while imported beer was sold in cans. Obviously, the environmental regulation chosen by the Ontario authorities seemed tailor-made to protect the Canadian beer producers, and the authorities had ignored alternative environmental regulations that would have not been so directly aimed at beer imports. It is not surprising, therefore, that the United States accused the Ontario government of hiding its protectionist intent behind the virtuous mask of environmentalism and proceeded to indulge in retaliation.

The underlying rationale for objecting to environmental legislations such as Ontario's is the traditional trade-legal view (embodied, in the view of many, in GATT's Article 20, which permits measures deemed necessary to protect human, animal, or plant life or health) that if the same environmental objective can be obtained by two environmental regulations with different levels of disruptions to market access, then the method that causes less trade disruption should be preferred. Other cases also confirm the prevalence of this sensible approach, which allows countries to pursue environmental objectives of their choice but simply urges them to choose methods that minimize the adverse effect on market access and hence on the gains from trade while guaranteeing the environmental outcome at the same level. This principle is broadly followed in other matters as well, such as by the GATT panel in the 1992 decision on alcoholic beverages where five states required a common carrier to enforce their tax and alcohol policies. There the United States lost because "the United States has not demonstrated that the common carrier requirement is the least trade restrictive enforcement measure available to the various states and that less restrictive measures, e.g. record-keeping requirements of retailers and importers, are not sufficient for tax administration purposes."

I am indebted to Steve Charnowitz for directing me to an excellent study of this Ontario environmental beer tax case by Jim Lee of American University. I have drawn copiously on this reference in writing this note.

31. I made such a proposal in a paper presented at a Columbia University conference held July 22–23, 1999, just prior to the famous Seattle ministerial meeting of the WTO. The paper has been reprinted as "An Economic Perspective on the Dispute Settlement Mechanism," in *The Wind of the Hundred Days: How Washington Mismanaged Globalism* (Cambridge: MIT Press, 2000).

32. Two panel reports were issued ("United States—Restrictions on Imports of Tuna"), one on August 16, 1991 and the other on June 16, 1994. Both remained unadopted by the GATT Council. They are available from several legal sources, including 30 *ILM* at page 1594 for the 1991 ruling and 33 *ILM* at page 839 for the 1994 ruling. *ILM* is the abbreviation for *International Legal Materials*, published by the American Society of International Law.

33. GATT Article 20 does provide for exceptions on grounds such as health and safety, but these were deemed inapplicable.

34. This does not mean that it does not have internal institutions and arrangements altogether excluded. Thus there are provisions about how to handle state trading; there is recognition that domestic measures can be deployed to nullify trade concessions; and goods made with prison labor can be excluded from trade by members. But none of this adds up to a negation of the statement that predominantly GATT deals with reduction of border measures to restrict or distort trade and with rules concerning trade.

35. See Gottfried Haberler, *Theory of International Trade with its Applications to Commercial Policy* (London: William Hodge, 1936). This is an English translation of the original German edition from 1933.

36. The famous cattle concession was granted by Germany to Switzerland in the Swiss-German Commercial Treaty of April 12, 1904. For the German text of the concession and its translation, see Gerard Curzon, *Multilateral Commercial Diplomacy* (Geneva: M. Joseph, 1965).

37. "Trade Control Is Not a Fair Instrument," editorial, *Down to Earth*, August 15, 1992, 4. The magazine is published in New Delhi and enjoys a large circulation. The NGO is the Center for Science and Environment, based in New Delhi.

38. The panel report in the case "United States—Import Prohibition of Certain Shrimp and Shrimp Products" is dated May 15, 1998, and is excerpted in 37 *ILM* at page 832, 1998; the Appellate Body decision is dated October 12, 1998, and is reported in 38 *ILM*, page 118, 1999. See the discussion of these rulings in my "Afterword: The Question of Linkage," *American Journal of International Law* 96, 1 (2002): 126–34.

39. See WHO Web site, http://www.who.org, for details on the tobacco treaty.

40. Aside from CITES, they include several others. Among them are the Montreal Protocol on Substances that Deplete the Ozone Layer, adopted September 16, 1987; the Basel Convention on the Control of Transboundary Movements of Hazardous Wastes and Their Disposal, March 27, 1989; the Kyoto Protocol; and the Convention on Biological Diversity.

41. This is a viewpoint that is not ideological but reflects some real concerns with the design of the Kyoto Protocol. For persuasive criticism of the Kyoto design, see the excellent essay by Richard Cooper (a world-class economist and Democrat), "Toward a Real Global Warming Treaty," *Foreign Affairs* 77, 2 (1998): 66–79.

Chapter 12

1. Evidently, these economists were thinking of what might be called "linkage" effects in terms of demands for local materials. Effects on the host country can arise in all sorts of other economic and political ways, as when oil royalties or shares in diamond sales accrue to local rulers, who can then indulge in wars and devastation.

2. V. S. Naipaul, *Guerrillas* (New York: Alfred A. Knopf, 1975), 5.

3. The OECD is the "rich nations' club" and only two developing countries, South Korea and Mexico, have been admitted to it.

4. This and the following quote are from Martin Wolf's column "Countries Still Rule the World," *Financial Times,* February 6, 2002, reporting on the Belgian study.

5. There were accusations of bribery by opposition parties in India and by some journalists; but they remained both implausible and unproven.

6. See Florian Gimbel, "Corporate Transparency: Time to Publish and Be Praised," *Financial Times,* June 2, 2003.

7. For an early discussion of the political issue, see my Ninth V. K. Ramswami Lecture, "International Factor Movements and National Advantage," delivered in New Delhi, 1979; reprinted in Jagdish Bhagwati, *International Factor Mobility,* ed. Robert Feenstra (Cambridge: MIT Press, 1983).

8. President Allende took his own life, rather than surrender to the armed forces that were certain to capture him in the Moneda Palace. Technically, therefore, he died at his own hand; in reality, he was assassinated, since what he expected by way of retribution and quasi-legal murder was exactly what countless numbers of Chileans, many his supporters, suffered summarily and brutally without even a pretense of legality at the hands of Pinochet's armed forces.

9. Christopher Hitchens, "The Case Against Henry Kissinger," at http://archive.8m.net/hitchens.htm, 6.

10. The most persuasive account of the atrocities directed at Patrice Lumumba, and of the active collaboration of the Belgian authorities in this murderous violation of democracy and an elected head of state, is in Ludo de Witte, *The Assassination of Lumumba* (London: Verso, 2001). Kwame Nkrumah, who also showed considerable independence in foreign policy, was also destabilized by the CIA but fortunately did not lose his life. It is hard today not to be agitated about these brutal suppressions by the United States and the European powers such as Belgium, with the encouragement of multinationals fearful of left-wing regimes, of democratically elected leaders in the early decades of postwar independence of the former colonies.

11. See the account of the coup against Mossadegh in Stephen Kinzer, *All the Shah's Men: An American Coup and the Roots of Terror in the Middle East* (Hoboken: John Wiley and Sons, 2003). Kinzer was a reporter for the *New York Times.*

12. I am indebted to an excellent account by Human Rights Watch on "Protest and Repression in the Niger Delta," available at http://www.hrw.org/reports/1999/nigeria/Nigew991-08.htm.

13. The examples are taken from ibid., 7–8.

14. This precise estimate, and the inference of exploitation, were the central contention, in a letter to the editor in the *Financial Times* (written in response to my defense of Nike in an op-ed piece in the same newspaper) by Eileen Applebaum, who held a senior professional position on the staff of the Economic Policy Institute, a liberal-left think tank in Washington D.C. See Eileen Applebaum, "Unsuitable Wages Comparison," *Financial Times,* May 5, 2000.

15. The study was conducted at Templeton College, Oxford University.

16. See Edward M. Graham, *Fighting the Wrong Enemy: Antiglobal Activists and Multinational Enterprises* (Washington, D.C.: Institute for International Economics, 2000).

17. Linda Lim, *The Globalization Debate: Issues and Challenges* (Geneva: International Labor Organization, 2001). In addition, there are several econometric studies of the reasons for the wage premium, which also produce further evidence of a wage premium in Mexico, Venezuela, and Indonesia, by economists such as Robert Feenstra, Gordon Hanson, and Ann Harrison. These econometric studies are reviewed in Drusilla Brown, Alan Deardorff, and Robert Stern, "The Effects of Multinational Enterprises on Wages and Working Conditions in Developing Countries," March 11, 2002, available at http://www.econ.kuleuven.ac.be/ew/academic/intecon/home/WorkingGroupSeminars/Files/Deardorff.pdf.

18. Paul Glewwe, "Are Foreign-Owned Businesses in Viet Nam Really Sweatshops?" University of Minnesota, 1999.

19. For Venezuela, see Brian Aiken and Ann Harrison, "Does Proximity to Foreign Firms Induce Technology Spillover?" PRD Working Paper, World Bank, Washington, D.C., 1993; and for Morocco, see M. Haddad and Ann Harrison, "Are There Positive Spillovers from Direct Foreign Investment? Evidence from Panel Data for Morocco," *Journal of Development Economics,* October 1993. Brown, Deardorff, and Stern, "The Effects of Multinational Enterprises," discuss further evidence.

20. September 24, 2000. The article is adapted from their latest book, *Thunder from the East: Portrait of a Rising Asia* (New York: Alfred A. Knopf, 2000).

21. *Unfair Advantage: Workers' Freedom of Association in the United States Under International Human Rights Standards,* Human Rights Watch, August 2000.

22. As it happens, the AFL-CIO has argued plausibly that massive direct violations of the right to organize are widespread in the United States as well, with employers often firing workers who attempt to form unions, for instance. For the disturbing documentation of this reality, see David Moberg, "Labor Fights for Rights," *The Nation,* September 15, 2003, 24–28.

23. The growing numbers of such lawsuits (under the 1789 Alien Torts Act) against U.S. corporations in U.S. courts by plaintiffs, mostly workers, who were employed elsewhere than in the United States, is being listed at http://www.worldmonitors.com. I am indebted to Elliot J. Schrage for providing this reference.

24. AMC found it more profitable to export the Jeeps to China than to manufacture them there. So the more of the car they could make in the United States and the less they had to assemble in China, the more profit they would make.

25. See Jim Mann, *Beijing Jeep* (New York: Simon and Schuster, 1989), and my review of it in *The New Leader,* 1989.

26. There is a huge literature on the possibility of immiserizing foreign investment, a possibility noted by several authors including myself, but beautifully demonstrated by the economists Carlos Diaz Alejandro and Richard Brecher in their classic article "Tariffs, Foreign Capital and Immiserizing Growth," *Journal of International Economics* 7 (1977).

27. See V. N. Balasubramanyam and M. Salisu, "Export Promotion, Import Substitution and Direct Foreign Investment in Less Developed Countries," in A. Koekkoek and L. Mennes, eds., *International Trade and Global Development: Essays in Honour of Jagdish Bhagwati* (London: Routledge, 1991); and V. N. Balasubramanyam, M. Salisu, and D. Sapsford, "Foreign Direct Investment and Growth in EP and IS Countries," *Economic Journal* 106 (1996), 92–105.

28. Several of these early studies, including the very first by Jorge Katz, which used Argentine data, have been reviewed by Magnus Blomstrom and Ariel Kokko of the Stockholm School of Economics in various publications.

29. "Spillovers from Foreign Firms Through Worker Mobility: An Empirical Investigation," Leverhulme Centre for Research on Globalization and Economic Policy, University of Nottingham, 2002.

30. S. Girma and H. Gorg, "Foreign Direct Investment, Spillovers and Absorptive Capacity: Evidence from Quantile Regressions," Leverhulme Center, University of Nottingham, 2002.

31. David Greenaway, Nuno Sousa, and Katharine Wakelin, "Do Domestic Firms Learn to Export from Multinationals?" Leverhulme Center, University of Nottingham, 2002.

32. These details are from "The Gerber Baby—Trademark or Con Artist," http://www.infactcanada.ca/gerbbaby.htm, among other sources consulted by Olivia Carballo.

33. "Accountability for the Progress of Women: Women Demanding Action," *Progress of the World's Women 2000: A New Biennial Report,* 125, available at http://www.unifem.undp.org/progressww/2000.

34. See Report of the Panel, "Thailand—Restrictions on Importation of and Internal Taxes on Cigarettes," October 5, 1990, GATT, Geneva, Switzerland; "Accountability for the Progress of Women," 125.

35. Susan Okie, "Cigarette Ads Smoking Rise Abroad Linked; Foreign Countries Lowering Barriers to U. S. Tobacco," *Washington Post,* May 5, 1990.

36. Myron Levin, "Targeting Foreign Smokers," *Los Angeles Times,* November 17, 1994.

37. See Niall Ferguson, *The House of Rothschild: The World's Banker, 1849–1999* (New York: Viking, 1999).
38. Several economists, organized under the Academic Consortium of International Trade Scholars (ACIT), formed recently by myself and several others at the University of Michigan, joined the debate on these questions and had some success in bringing them to the forefront. This was done not with a view to rejecting the notion of social responsibility, but rather with a view to bringing reasoned debate, and needed diversity, to the definition of social responsibility.
39. "American Rules, Mexican Jobs," *New York Times,* March 24, 1993.

Chapter 13

1. By far the most informed and informative account of the course of the Asian financial crisis, and its causes and aftermath, is to be found in Padma Desai, *Financial Crisis, Contagion and Containment* (Princeton: Princeton University Press, 2003); the reader who is interested in probing this all-too-important topic further can do no better than to read this book in its entirety. I have drawn extensively on this splendid book in this chapter; the chart is from this book, 134. The estimates of declines in national incomes (GDP) per capita are in her Figure 6.2, 132; the reversals of capital outflows are illustrated in her Figure 6.4, 134.
2. This is also the title of my latest collection of policy essays, *The Wind of the Hundred Days: How Washington Mismanaged Globalization* (Cambridge: MIT Press, 2001).
3. The issues raised in the text are fully discussed by me in Chapters 4–6 in *The Wind of the Hundred Days.*
4. Published in *Business Times* (Singapore), May 25, 2000, reprinted in *The Wind of the Hundred Days.* In this article, I have also distinguished between different ways in which our politicians reward their cronies and Asian politicians typically do. The former ways are socially less expensive, I argue.
5. For further details and insightful analysis, see Desai, *Financial Crisis,* 89–91.
6. Ibid., 94.
7. See Lawrence Summers and Victoria Summers, "When Financial Markets Work Too Well: A Case for a Securities Transaction Tax," *Journal of Financial Services Research* 3 (1989).
8. The Keynes quotation is taken, as cited, from Summers and Summers, ibid. The exact quote can be found in J. M. Keynes, *General Theory, Collected Writings,* vol. 7, 158–59. The preceding quote in the text taken from Summers and Summers is from First Boston's Albert Wojnilower.
9. Both quotes are from Desai, *Financial Crisis,* 96.
10. Jagdish Bhagwati, "The Capital Myth: The Difference Between Trade in Widgets and Dollars," *Foreign Affairs,* May-June 1998.
11. See C. Wright Mills, *The Power Elite* (London: Oxford University Press, 1956).
12. See Robert Wade, "The Asian Crisis: The High Debt Model Versus the Wall Street–Treasury–IMF Complex," *New Left Review,* March-April 1998, 3–23.
13. Barry Eichengreen, "Capital Mobility: Ties Need Not Bind," *Milken Institute Review* first quarter 1999, 29–37.
14. The phrase is in his famous 1961 speech. For detailed citation, see *The Wind of the Hundred Days,* 10 n. 2.
15. For details, see Desai, *Financial Crisis,* 122–24.
16. I have been persuaded by the fine analysis in Ethan Kaplan and Dani Rodrik, "Did the Malaysian Capital Controls Work?" NBER Working Paper No. w8142, February 2001.
17. See, for instance, Easwar Prasad, Kenneth Rogoff, Shang-Jin Wei, and M. Ayhan Rose, "Effects of Financial Globalization on Developing Countries: Some Empirical Evidence," IMF, Washington D.C., March 17, 2003.
18. "A Place for Capital Controls," editorial, *The Economist,* May 3, 2003. The thoughts about the asymmetry between free trade and free capital mobility, and the arguments in support, are just what I expressed in my article "The Capital Myth." I am flattered.

Chapter 14

1. These workers were brought in from Turkey, Yugoslavia, and other countries. For a description and economic analysis of the *gastarbeiter* system, see Jagdish Bhagwati, Klaus-Werner Schatz, and Kar-yiu Wong, "The West German *Gastarbeiter* System of Immigration," *European Economic Review* 26, 3 (1984): 277–94; reprinted in Jagdish Bhagwati, *Political Economy and International Economics*, ed. Douglas Irwin (Cambridge: MIT Press, 1991).
2. In the original German, he said: "Man rief Arbeitskräfte, und es kamen Menschen." See http://www.auslaender.rlp.de/themen/treff302/302-27.html.
3. When I started working on immigration problems over three decades ago, it was a rather exotic subject for the better economists to get mixed up in. Today, it has become one of the favored topics of research among the younger economists. Literary theory and law are also rife with serious scholars addressing issues dealing with immigration questions. The World Economic Forum in 2003 at Davos also had immigration as one of its six main topics, signifying the arrival of this topic on the world agenda. Homi Bhabha (a literary theorist at Harvard), Susan Martin, and I were the organizing committee; and some of what I write here owes to the stimulating discussions we had among ourselves and at the Davos sessions.
4. Martin Wolf, "Humanity on the Move: The Myths and Realities of International Migration," *Financial Times*, July 30, 2003, 11. See Timothy Hatton and Jeffrey Williamson, *The Age of Mass Migration: Causes and Economic Impact* (New York: Oxford University Press, 1998).
5. This too was documented in Chapter 5.
6. This issue is discussed further in the subsection on technology below.
7. I am indebted to Maurice Templesman for pointing this example out to me.
8. Migration institutions at the UN level are fragmented. The UNHCR looks after refugees, the ILO after workers' rights, and the WTO under GATS agreement after the ability of providers of services to enter the countries where the users are, under the so-called Mode IV. There is an International Organization for Migration, but it does not have a UN status and is more of a hands-on institution that provides consultancy on migration-related matters to member countries and undertakes in-the-field assistance to migrants.
9. See Bhagwati, "A Champion for Migrating Peoples," *Christian Science Monitor*, February 28, 1992; reprinted in Bhagwati, *A Stream of Windows*, 315–17.

Chapter 15

1. These issues have been described briefly in Chapter 3.
2. See F. Hayek, "The Use of Knowledge in Society," *American Economic Review* 35, 4 (1945): 519–30.
3. The grant of legal standing to NGOs by the Supreme Court of India came from Chief Justice P. N. Bhagwati—transparency requires that I disclose that he is my brother—and is described as public interest litigation in India. His work in greatly expanding legal aid has provided yet another element in the substantial architecture that permits greater empowerment of the poor in India today.
4. In fact, at least since the influential writings of the economist Richard Cooper starting in 1973, when he delivered the Wicksell Lectures in Stockholm on the subject of economic policy in an interdependent world, no serious policy analyst of globalization has forgotten the need for carefully designed coordinated action. See Richard Cooper, *Economic Mobility and National Economic Policy* (Uppsala: Almqvist and Wiksell, 1974).
5. Jared Diamond, *Guns, Germs and Steel* (New York: W. W. Norton, 1997), 77–78.
6. See Richard Cooper, "International Cooperation in Public Health as a Prologue to Macroeconomic Cooperation," in Richard Cooper et al., *Can Nations Agree? Issues in International Economic Cooperation* (Washington, D.C.: Brookings Institution, 1989). The story that Cooper tells is fascinating; so is his analysis of the interplay between contrasting scientific theories and national self-interest in delaying by decades effective policy coordination.

7. The institute in Amsterdam was set up in 1910 and had a famous section on tropical medicine where work was carried out on diseases such as malaria by eminent authorities such as Nicholas Swellengrebel, a great-uncle, as it happens, of the noted Dutch economist Jan Gunning at the University of Amsterdam today.

8. See Jeffrey Frankel and Katharine Rockett, "International Macroeconomic Policy Coordination When Policymakers Do Not Agree on the True Model," *American Economic Review* 78, 3 (1988): 318–40.

9. See Jagdish Bhagwati, "Threats to the World Trading System: Income Distribution and the Selfish Hegemon," *Journal of International Affairs* 48 (1994): 279–85; reprinted with slight editing in *A Stream of Windows: Unsettling Reflections on Trade, Immigration and Democracy* (Cambridge: MIT Press, 1998). The notion of an altruistic hegemon providing public goods, on the other hand, is most associated with my teacher Charles P. Kindleberger, who wrote of the British playing that role in the 19th century and the Americans in the 20th century in regard to the international economic system.

Chapter 16

1. John Whalley, "What Can the Developing Countries Infer from the Uruguay Round Models for Future Negotiations," Policy Issues in International Trade and Commodities Study Series No. 4, UNCTAD, Geneva, 2000, 1.

2. This asymmetry was discussed in Chapter 1; see Jagdish Bhagwati and Arvind Panagariya, "Wanted Jubilee 2010: Dismantling Protection," *OECD Observer,* May 27–29, 2002; and "The Truth About Protectionism," *Financial Times,* March 29, 2001. The chart is from the latter article.

3. Much of this unilateral trade liberalization has been documented, and its causes analyzed, in Jagdish Bhagwati, ed., *Going Alone: The Case for Relaxed Reciprocity in Freeing Trade* (Cambridge: MIT Press, 2002).

4. Quoted in Steve Charnowitz, "Worker Adjustment: The Missing Ingredient in Trade Policy," *California Management Review* 28, 2 (1986): 163. This excellent article has a most useful history of American efforts at providing adjustment assistance. There have, of course, been changes and yet newer measures since the article was written.

5. This view is developed by me in *Protectionism* (Cambridge: MIT Press, 1988).

6. Quoted in Charnowitz, "Worker Adjustment," 158.

7. All articles related to the case can be found on the Web site of the United States mission to the European Union: http://www.useu.be/issues/bananadossier.html.

8. See *Financial Organization and Operations of the IMF,* Treasurer's Department, International Monetary Fund: Washington D.C., 2001, 42–45.

9. See Roger Thurow, "Behind the Famine in Ethiopia: Glut and Aid Policies Gone Bad," *Wall Street Journal,* July 1, 2003, A1, A4.

10. Ibid., A4.

Chapter 17

1. I have already considered these issues from somewhat different perspectives in Chapter 10, on labor, and in Chapter 11, on the environment.

2. I have written extensively on this issue over the last decade. Aside from papers reprinted in my two collections of public policy essays, *A Stream of Windows: Unsettling Reflections on Trade, Immigration and Democracy* (Cambridge: MIT Press, 1998) and *The Wind of the Hundred Days: How Washington Mismanaged Globalization* (Cambridge: MIT Press, 2001), see in particular my "Afterword: The Question of Linkage," *American Journal of International Law* 96, 1 (2002): 126–34, which deals with labor standards in particular. I draw here especially on

"Trade Linkage and Human Rights" in *The Wind of the Hundred Days,* reprinted from Jagdish Bhagwati and Matthew Hirsch, eds., *The Uruguay Round and Beyond: Essays in Honor of Arthur Dunkel* (Ann Arbor: University of Michigan Press, 1999).

3. See my *Protectionism.*

4. Quoted from the text of the Bangalore Principles sent in a private communication with Justice P. N. Bhagwati, April 2003.

5. Though many cases have been brought by aliens against U.S. corporations operating in the country where the alien is a citizen, the very first case in 1980 involved two alien parties. The Second Circuit Court of Appeals in New York permitted the family of a young Paraguayan who had been kidnapped, tortured, and murdered to sue the alleged torturer (a Paraguayan police officer who had emigrated to the United States) in a U.S. court. The alleged crime had occurred when the defendant and the plaintiff were aliens, and courts outside the United States would not do what the Second Circuit Court did. Mind you, it would be perfectly appropriate, on the other hand, for the United States to expel the defendant if indeed he was convicted of such torture, as the immigration statute permits this.

6. Additional suggestions such as the use of labeling rather than sanctions, for both environmental and some labor issues such as the use of child labor, have been discussed by me in Chapter 11 in the analysis of values-related PPMs.

Chapter 18

1. I owe this retort to Padma Desai, who argued against shock therapy in Russia from the outset.

2. Adam Smith, *An Inquiry into the Nature and Causes of the Wealth of Nations* (New York: Random House, The Modern Library, 1937), 96.

3. The quotation appears in J. M. Keynes, *Collected Writings*, vol. 21, 245; it is from two articles published by Keynes on "National Self-sufficiency," in *The New Statesman* and *Nation*, 8 and 15 July 1933.

4. Chapter 15 already examined the adjustment assistance issue from the viewpoint of addressing the occasional downside of globalization.

5. See Lant Pritchett and Geeta Sethi, "Tariff Rates, Tariff Revenue, and Tariff Reform: Some New Facts," *The World Bank Economic Review* 8, 1 (1994): 1–16. The authors point to a number of reasons why the analysis of revenue effects of tariff reductions is a complex task.

6. Ravi A. Yatawara, "Timing Is Everything: On the Determinants of Commercial Policy Changes," in *Essays on the Reform of Trade and Exchange*, Ph.D. dissertation submitted to Columbia University, May 2000.

Chapter 19

1. The quotes are from Robert Bly, *Selected Poems of Rainer Maria Rilke* (New York: Harper & Row, 1981), 12. In German, the words are even more moving:

Ich lebe mein Leben in wachsenden Ringen,
die sich über die Dinge ziehn.
Ich werde den letzten vielleicht nicht vollbringen,
aber versuchen will ich ihn.

Ich kreise um Gott, um den uralten Turm,
und ich kreise jahrtausendelang
und ich weiss noch nicht: ich bin ein Falke, ein Sturm
oder ein grosser Gesang."

Afterword

1. See, for instance, Chapters 4 and 7 in a polemical book by a U.S. Democrat, Congressman Sherrod Brown, *Myths of Free Trade*, (New York: The New Press, 2004). Unfortunately, at the time of this essay going to press, Mr. Brown was elected to the new U.S. Congress and can be expected to bring his misguided views assiduously to the floor in that legislative body.

2. The earlier work of my Columbia University colleague Joe Stiglitz promised much but delivered little: it was focused largely, and then again with little nuance, on the policies and conditionalities of the Bretton Woods institutions, the IMF and the World Bank, with little bearing on the issues that ailed most of the agitated. See Joseph Stiglitz, *Globalization and Its Discontents* (New York: W.W. Norton, 2002). Strangely enough, Nancy Birdsall has argued that the Stiglitz book deals with "social justice," whereas mine does not, because the indexes of the two books show minimal references to the phrase in my book unlike his. The absurdity of this conclusion, and the fact that my book deals with virtually all social-justice issues whereas his uses the phrase without addressing any of these issues meaningfully, if at all, is demonstrated in my note, "In Defense of *In Defense of Globalization*," posted on my website www.columbia.edu/~jb38.

3. This trend has also been helped by the increasing flow of Japanese students to the West, where they learn our way of life and our values. Thus, the early Japanese students used to be deferential and called me "sensei," the revered teacher: I sometimes joke that I used to love it as no American students would ever do that! But now, they put their feet on the table like the American students and even blow those horrid bubbles from their chewing gums. This "acculturation" of Japan is a gathering force that shows itself up in several ways. I have described the phenomenon by titling a 1994 *Foreign Affairs* article of mine, on the U.S.-Japan trade negotiations where the Japanese refused to accept demands for import targets, "Samurai No More": our negotiators thought they were dealing with the samurai when, in fact, they were dealing with GIs. Another apt metaphor is: "Crossing Against the Light": whereas the traditional Japanese dutifully waited for the green traffic light to flash before they crossed a road, now they are like New Yorkers dashing across despite red and yellow lights.

4. See Arvind Panagariya, "Miracles and Debacles: In Defense of Trade Openness," *The World Economy*, Vol.27 (8), August 2004, pp. 1149–71.

5. I use the word "crazy," which is not very polite, in the tradition of Keynes who wrote famously that it would be crazy to prefer bilateral trade agreements to multilateralism in trade.

6. See, for instance, the chart on the Soviet growth rates in Padma Desai's introductory chapter in her *Soviet Economy: Problems and Prospects* (Oxford: Basil Blackwell, 1987), Chart 1.1.

7. There is consensus now that the cocktail made with three liqueurs—greater reliance on markets, political democracy, and openness to the world economy—is enormously productive of prosperity and hence of attack on poverty. Both Soviet Union and North Korea rejected the cocktail, foregoing markets, denying democracy and embracing autarky. In this regard, see also the discussion in my 1993 Rajiv Gandhi Memorial Lecture, *Democracy and Development*, reprinted in my essays, *A Stream of Windows* (Cambridge, MA: MIT Press, 2000).

8. In fact, I and other trade economists began writing about the rationale for, and design of, adjustment assistance in import-competing industries in the 1970s. I have often lectured also about the need to remedy the absence of such a safety net in the poor countries. They have now seen the benefits of trade liberalization and would like to profit from it, but are fearful to move on to the high wire when there is no safety net.

9. This is also the conclusion of Robert Feenstra and Gordon Hanson, reviewed in this book, in their study of outsourcing of components to Mexico from the United States and its effects on U.S. wages. While the wage differential between skilled and unskilled workers rises, the real wage of the unskilled rises as well.

10. The use of anecdotes and *bon mots* is a device for making abstruse economic arguments accessible and plausible to the public at large. Wit, irony, and even sarcasm are excellent aides in putting one's points across to the general public. I might also add that there is now a fetish, among even serious economists like Dani Rodrik, Jeffrey Sachs, and Robert Barro

(all associated with Harvard University, strangely enough), for mindless cross-country regressions, which serve as a substitute for analysis. The use of these regressions as "evidence," and the pretense that they are superior to, and a desirable substitute for conceptual and analytical arguments—Dani Rodrik once described conceptual analysis as "rhetoric" and his regressions as "evidence," committing two errors in one breath—are increasingly coming under fire.

11. Assar Lindbeck, in his recent writings on China, has also argued plausibly that even traditional trade, and not just trade in variety, can be confidently expected to grow between China and India, on the one hand, and the rich countries of today.

12. Culture, of course, is not immutable and changes over time, including in response to changing economic opportunities and challenges. But this does not mean that cultures are different at any point of time, yielding comparative advantage differences that imply that the world is not flat.

13. In fact, it was startling to see that the government of Karnataka, where India's Silicon Valley is located, passed legislation in September 2006 that threw out English from its public sector schools. Advertised as a measure aimed at helping the poor, it is, in fact, a dagger aimed at them: they want to learn English, but will not be able to, whereas the parents who can afford it will send their children to private schools or hire private tutors to teach English to their children.

14. I identified these reasons ten years ago in a review article in 1997 in *The New Republic*, titled "A New Epoch?" The review was actually written in 1994, but the Literary Editor, Leon Wieseltier, inexplicably sat on it for three years. Meanwhile, since I had given up hope of ever getting the review to see the light of day, it was circulated by me privately to many journalists and economists who then proceeded to reflect some of my views.

15. This implication of volatility of comparative advantage was noted by me in *The New Republic* article that I cited earlier.

16. Of course, the transition to new skills is a problem that can arise from domestic technical change and consumer demand shifts as well. But, as I argued in my 1988 book on *Protectionism* (Cambridge, MA: MIT Press), citizens do think that an extra element of assistance is necessary when the disturbance comes from abroad rather than from domestic policy and parametric shifts. This is not necessarily "xenophobia" but can be explained in other less condemnatory ways.

Index